HELPING CHILDREN OVERCOME LEARNING DIFFICULTIES

Helping Children
Overcome
Learning Difficulties

A Step-by-Step Guide for Parents and Teachers

SECOND EDITION

Jerome Rosner

WALKER AND COMPANY
NEW YORK

First edition published in the United States of America in
1975 by the Walker Publishing Company, Inc.

This edition published in 1984.

ISBN: 0-8027-7178-5

Library of Congress Catalog Card Number: 78-58599

Printed in the United States of America
10 9 8 7 6 5 4 3

CONTENTS

Acknowledgments

HOW CAN YOU thank everyone who has influenced your professional thinking over the course of thirty years? Obviously, you cannot. I know that I will omit some names that should not be omitted—not because I do not recognize their contribution to this book, but simply because of the fallibility of human memory and the practical limitations of space. I apologize to them in advance.

In addition, all of the thousands of children, and parents, and teachers I have worked with merit a "thank you" from me. I am grateful to them even though I do not list their names.

Specifically, major recognition must go to the staff at Pace School—to Emy Lou Lower, its co-founder and first Academic Director, now retired, and to Eugenia Donatelli, Pace's current head. Most of the suggested activities described in the last half of this book are standard procedures at Pace. In addition, special thanks is given to my various colleagues at the University of Pittsburgh—to Joanne Cass, Jim DiCostanzo, Terry Dombrowicki, Billie Slaughter, Larry Vaughan, and Phyllis Weaver, all of whom work with me daily on various aspects of my research; to John Bolvin, Bill Cooley, Bob Glaser, and Lauren Resnick, all of whom have helped me administratively as well as intellectually; to Dorothy Walsh and Ruth Stone at Oakleaf School, who provided both practical guidance and needed encouragement; to Karen Block and her research assistant, Dorothea Simon, whose ideas about spelling have had a mighty influence on mine; to Bernard Mallinger, my optometric associate, who provided many practical suggestions; and to countless others who should be mentioned but are not.

Finally, much more than tradition leads me to thank my wife, Florence, and my two daughters, Carolyn and Joyce, for their substantive contributions to this book, as well as for their support. Many of the ideas proposed in this book are the outcome of family discussions, and the shapes of those ideas reflect their thinking as well as my own.

Preface to the First Edition

A SURPRISINGLY LARGE number of children have difficulty in school. Some have trouble in one subject area only—reading or arithmetic, for example. Others have trouble in more than one subject area. Their learning problems are often hard to explain. They appear to be sufficiently intelligent and motivated, yet they do not seem to be able to catch on.

Many of these children have perceptual problems—a term I will define fully later on. In simple language, it means that they are not as capable as they should be in analyzing and organizing some of the details of what they see and what they hear in various instructional situations.

This book is concerned with ways to help those children. Although it is addressed to their parents, I hope that it will also be read by their teachers and all the other professionals who treat them because of their learning problems: psychologists, optometrists, physicians.

I started working with such children more than twenty-five years ago. Many were referred to me, a practicing optometrist, because they did such things as confuse *b* and *d*, and read *was* for *saw*. In some cases, my efforts seemed to help; in others, they did not, and for a long time I could not explain why. But I was not the only one who was stumped in those early days. Just about everyone was groping for answers.

In 1961, in search of those answers, I enrolled in an external studies program conducted at the Gesell Institute of Child Development, entitled "Vision—The School-Aged Child." The experience had significant impact on my professional development. Not that my questions were answered—they were not. But, it did help me start to formulate my questions a little better. And even more important, it helped me recognize the obvious: that a child is more than the sum of his parts; that it is not sufficient to examine one aspect of his make-up—vision, for example—and ignore the rest of him. This was made particularly apparent as I watched Dr. Frances Ilg evaluate children and discuss with us the outcomes of those evaluations from a frame of reference that reflected her broad knowledge of child development and her deep understanding of the child as a totality—a person.

Around that same time I met a teacher who was really worthy of the designation *teacher*—Emy Lou Lower. Mrs. Lower was teaching a Special Education Class—"educable mentally retarded," in school jargon—in the Oakmont, Pennsylvania, school system. I was conducting my practice in the same small community. We worked together on many children, and I started to get a real sense of what teaching is about when it is done as it should be. Emy Lou Lower is the kind of teacher all children should have. She is intelligent, motivated, and understanding. She accepts the responsibilities of being a teacher as a professional should. Her students do not fail; if they do not learn, she sees it as her failure for not being able to find a better way to teach them.

During the mid-1960s, I started more and more to shift my place of work to school buildings, working first with the Oakmont public schools and later with the Pittsburgh schools. In this latter situation, I worked in the Mental Health Services Division, focusing primarily on the learning problems of emotionally disturbed children.

All the while, I continued to maintain a private practice although a greatly reduced one. Working with the same type of child in both places—office and school—was enlightening. It takes a long time to help some children, and longer still when you have to coordinate your efforts closely with others who have daily contact with those children—particularly their teachers. It became apparent to me that much of what I was doing could and should be done at home and in school; that the solution lay in moving my work out of the doctor's office and into the domain of education—making it available and understandable to teachers and parents, so that direct and immediate impact on the children could be accomplished effectively and inexpensively.

In 1968, a group of us—Mrs. Lower, Dr. Harvey Lacey (a clinical psychologist then working at the University of Pittsburgh), and I, in conjunction with a few other professionals and some interested and committed parents—founded Pace School, a private school that was intended to provide for these children what the public schools seemed unable to provide at that time: effective instruction in how to read, write, spell, and calculate.

Our goal was to teach them, not cure them. The school has thrived, thanks to the dedication of its staff, board, and the community at large. It has helped many children and, perhaps even more important, its staff has helped some public schools initiate similar programs of their own. I do not work at Pace any longer, but I continue to be a member of its Board of Directors and an active participant in many of the research efforts that are conducted there.

About the same time that Pace was founded, the Learning Research and Development Center (LRDC) at the University of Pittsburgh started to develop a program for preschool children. The Center invited me to participate as a consultant. About a year later I accepted a full-time appointment as a Research Associate in LRDC and a faculty member in the School of Education.

I welcomed the opportunity. As a faculty member I could influence future teachers. As a researcher, I would be able to test out many of the clinical ideas

I had been using, determine which were truly important, which were superfluous, and why.

My research group called the Perceptual Skills Project, had four goals:

1. Identify the perceptual skills that are closely related to school achievement.
2. Determine whether these skills can be taught and, if so, how.
3. Determine whether learning these skills affects children's schoolwork—their ability to learn.
4. If the first three goals are achieved, design a curriculum to teach these skills; a curriculum that can be used by a typical teacher in a regular everyday classroom.

All four goals were accomplished. The Perceptual Skills Curriculum was published during the summer of 1973 and is now being used in more than 3,000 schools throughout the country.

But there are still unsolved problems. What about the child who is now in school and experiencing significant learning difficulties; the child who does not have adequate basic skills, either because he was not exposed to the Perceptual Skills Curriculum or because, for some reason, the Curriculum was not completely effective with him.

This child can be helped. Stated too simply, perhaps there must be a change in the way he is taught. We must find out his strengths and weaknesses—the skills he has and the skills he lacks—and then relate these to his daily learning activities so that he can start to succeed rather than flounder in school.

I have been working on this problem since my days of private practice. Despite its importance, I know of no adequate single written source on the topic—nothing that provides adequate direction for a teacher when he or she is confronted with a child who requires this kind of assistance.

Hence this book—but with one modification. I address it to parents rather than teachers. Not because I think parents are better suited to do the job, but rather because I know that in most instances, parents have more time to spend with their child than does his teacher, and a stronger reason for doing so.

I do not underestimate the importance of good teachers and what they can accomplish. On the contrary, I value them greatly. When there are enough of them, and when school administrators and school boards finally recognize that some children need not only good teachers but also small classes and individualized instruction, then there will be no need for parents to supplement teachers. Until that time, however, the parent's participation is essential.

This book is meant to be a practical resource. It tells, in some detail, what to do and when to do it. I have not tried to answer the question, "What's wrong with my child?". Rather, I have dealt with the question,

"What can I do to help my child do better in school?"

I have included some theory about *why* my suggestions are designed as they are. I have done this for two reasons. First, it will help parents use the procedures more effectively and adapt my ideas to their child's specific needs, rather than blindly following an inflexible formula. Second, I *do* hope to influence teachers; to show them how they can recognize and respond to the unique characteristics of all their students, and do so in their own classroom—with the help of their students' parents.

I do not have all the answers. But what I present is not based on speculation. Everything I suggest has been tried in Pace School and elsewhere and shown to be effective.

Too many parents and teachers have been convinced that children with severe learning difficulties cannot be helped; that they must accept their fate and learn to cope with it. That is not correct. These children can be helped —they can learn. *But they surely must be taught.*

Preface to the Second Edition

I wrote the first edition of this book a few years ago. My primary goal then was to help bring some reasonable order to the field of learning disabilities—especially in terms of what parents and teachers could do to help children who were so labeled.

In that volume I stressed the importance of certain basic abilities—visual and auditory perceptual skills. I described what they were, when children usually develop them, why they are important in the classroom, how to test them in order to determine whether a youngster has achieved the level of development necessary for success in the classroom, and how to teach them when they are found to be inadequate. I also suggested a number of tutoring procedures for helping children learn how to read, write, spell, and do arithmetic despite their persistent perceptual skills deficits. Finally I presented some methods for fostering the development of perceptual skills in preschool children.

I do not take a conflicting position in this volume. The information presented in that first edition is still valid and pertinent. But neither is this edition a rewrite of that earlier work. This edition differs in a number of ways:

The linkup between perceptual skills and school performance is brought into sharper focus with a fuller and more specific explanation of how a child's perceptual skills affect his ability to *remember* the information presented in his daily classroom lessons.

The section devoted to *teaching the child* has also been expanded significantly, based on research completed since writing the first edition. It now contains a larger assortment of activities for teaching perceptual skills and a much more complete battery of activities that have been shown to be effective in teaching reading, spelling, arithmetic, and writing to children with learning difficulties.

This edition also contains a section devoted to a topic that was not addressed in the first version: the questions of *what type of teacher* and *what kind of school environment* are best for the child with learning difficulties, as well as some suggestions for how to go about obtaining them for your child when they are not made available without your petitioning.

So although there are many similarities between this edition and the earlier one, this is a new book. Many teachers and parents have told me that the first edition of *Helping Children Overcome Learning Difficulties* was useful to them. My intention with this updated volume is to make the book even more useful.

INTRODUCTION:
TEACHING THE HARD TO TEACH

"YOUR CHILD is not keeping up with his class. He seems to be trying, but he is not making enough progress. He may have a learning disability." Many parents hear this crushing statement and go off in search of help. Anywhere. From anyone who appears to have something to offer.

All too often their efforts lead to nothing but frustration and anxiety. Their questions are answered in obscure, technical-sounding language—if they are answered at all. They talk to teachers, principals, psychologists, doctors; sit in countless waiting rooms; pay lots of bills for lots of tests; and end up knowing no more about their child's learning difficulties and how to help him than they knew when they started out. And their child continues to struggle with his problem!

Sometimes it is called something different—*dyslexia*. "What is that? It sounds so serious, so final. Is it worse than having a learning disability?" Sometimes they are told that a series of treatments are necessary: vitamin therapy; eye training; motor training. Costly. Time-consuming. "But what difference does that make if it will help?" And the treatments often do help —at least they help in terms of what they are designed to treat. The trouble is that the treatments are generally aimed at some supposed cause of the learning problem rather than at the learning problem itself. And somehow, even though the treatments seem to have a beneficial effect on the designated cause, the learning problem persists. Another case, figuratively, of "the operation was a success, but the patient died." Literally, of course, the patient does not die; he merely continues to fail in school.

Other times there are only opinions, no treatments. But even these differ widely, ranging from "Stop being an overanxious parent; there's nothing wrong with the child," to "Give him time; he's young; he'll grow out of it," to "You had better accept the fact that he's never going to be much of a learner; some children just aren't."

The result of all this? A pair of confused, unhappy parents who never expected their child to have trouble in school. "He always seemed bright and interested in everything around him. Oh, he may not have had the patience to sit in one place for very long and look at books, but there is no doubt that he is capable of learning. Just listen to the conversations he has with his friends and family. We didn't think he had a problem until he entered school. That is when this problem showed up."

This is the kind of child we will be talking about; the child who can and does learn many things. He* learns his way about his neighborhood, his town, and even larger territories. He masters the complicated controls of a color television set and, when he is older, of an automobile and other complex mechanical devices. He learns the rules and fine points of many games. He learns the batting averages of lots of baseball players, the repertoires of many popular musical groups, and much, much more.

But place him in a standard classroom where he is supposed to learn to read, write, spell, and do arithmetic, and what happens? He has serious difficulty. He tries—for a while—but is unable to catch on. He does not seem to be able to recognize any order or system in what is being taught, any connections among his daily lessons that weave the information into cohesive, memorable patterns. Hence, he has no alternative, if he is going to progress, but to try to memorize everything that is presented in his classroom by rote—as separate, unrelated pieces of information. This, of course, is impossible. In desperation he resorts to guessing. This does not work either. How can it? Ultimately he becomes so frustrated that he stops trying. He calls a halt to all personal involvement, and he is officially "failed."

If he has a certain temperament, somewhere along the way he becomes angry with everyone connected with his failure—his teachers, even his parents. He adopts an "I don't care" attitude. He misbehaves—something that is completely intolerable in a classroom. He is punished, psychologically if not physically. This, of course, aggravates the situation and inevitably leads to a confrontation between the child and the institution. The final outcome? An "incorrigible"—a youngster who "refuses" to follow the rules of society and therefore must be banished from that society. It is not difficult to see why so many of these young people end up as chronic offenders of society's rules.

If he has a more passive nature, he still fails, but he receives less punishment. He is tolerated, even given "social promotions"—that is, passed on from grade to grade despite his poor classroom performance—until he finally gains his freedom and, with it, the opportunity to find work that does not require academic skills.

In either instance he has a school learning problem, and unless something special is done to alter the situation very early in the child's school career, he is destined to be an incompetent reader and/or arithmetic achiever for the remainder of his life. Yet he continues to learn many things—outside the classroom.

---

*I *am* trying to overcome sexist tendencies. I will, however, constantly refer to the child as *he* and his teacher as *her*—simply for consistency and efficiency.

For whom is this book written?

My goal was to write a nontechnical, practical book for teachers and parents.

My interest in reaching teachers needs no explanation. After all, they *are* teachers; therefore, if what I have to say is valid, it will be immediately useful to them.

But why should this same information be of practical value to parents? That, perhaps, deserves some explaining. Ideally, I suppose, parents should not have to become directly involved in deciding how their children should be taught, but the idea is not all that farfetched either. Children with severe learning problems need advocates. School teachers and administrators are human, with limited time, energy, and professional knowledge. Their decisions about how best to teach special children are not always as objective and accurate as one would wish. It is, after all, simpler and easier to try to teach all children the same way. But, as a result, some children invariably have trouble in school.

Who is better motivated to provide the push needed to influence school decision makers, to convince them to do what is not all that simple and easy? The child's parents, obviously. To ignore a parent's potential value, to rule out their involvement arbitrarily because they are not professionals is senseless.

But if parents are to be involved in helping decide how their children should be taught, then they should know something about instruction—about teaching and learning; about who should do what, how, why, and under what conditions. That is one reason for my interest in having parents read this book.

There is a second reason. Most children with severe learning difficulties need more than the schools can provide, even when the proposed educational plan appears to be reasonable. The task is often just too great and too complex for the school to handle alone, either because there are insufficient resources —teachers, time, space, materials—to do the whole job or because the child may need the services of one or more health care professionals in addition to a special educational plan. In both of these situations parental involvement is called for. In the latter instance the parents' role is obvious. It is not so obvious in the first situation, but neither does it require very much imagination to recognize the potential value of having parents assume the obligation of supervising the specially designed drill and practice sessions their child needs in order to establish firmly in his memory the information his teacher is presenting in school.

I will describe what these drill and practice sessions should look like later on. At this time my goal is simply to establish the principle that parents' direct participation in an instructional program can be useful—but only if they know what to do and how to do it. Thus we arrive at a third reason for this book: to help parents acquire that knowledge.

Will teachers object to parental involvement?

No, they will not object. Teachers want to see "their children" learn. Generally they welcome any help they can get, so long as that help does not interfere with their day-to-day classroom teaching efforts.

Consider this: Approximately three hours of a child's school day in the primary grades is allocated to instruction in reading, writing, spelling, and arithmetic. If a child's class consists of twenty-five children, it means that, on the average, the teacher can give each student approximately seven minutes of individual attention per day, assuming no time at all is spent on group instruction. However, practically all teachers teach to groups; individualized instruction of any kind is still a rarity in our schools. As such, the teacher actually has *less* than seven minutes per day for each child. Of course, children are supposed to learn from group instruction—and they do. At least most do. Unfortunately the child we are talking about does not. He needs something different.

Now, how about the parents' time? Those parents are rare who cannot find at least thirty minutes a day to work with their child individually. By spending that thirty minutes each day with their child, they give him more than six or seven times the individual attention he can get from his teacher in a regular classroom.

This does not mean that I expect parents to take over the teacher's role. Rather they are to supplement the school program. If what they do complements what is being taught in school, it is bound to be helpful. The child will learn more. No teacher will object to that, nor will she perceive it as an intrusion into her professional territory. There is more than that to being a teacher. Teaching is complex; it is both a science and an art. It cannot be reduced to a collection of procedures in a book.

How much preparation do you need before you can use the information presented in this book?

If you have read this far and can understand what you have read, then you already have the skills you will need to take advantage of the information presented in this book. What I have to say will be said in nonprofessional terms; in language that does not require a degree in education to understand. In doing so, I may be criticized for oversimplifying a complicated subject. I would accept that criticism, but I would not agree that it is a fault. The information will be no less useful because it is described in everyday language.

Are learning difficulties a new phenomenon?

Learning difficulties have been with us for a long time. Only the labels have changed with the times. It is true that more persons have become aware of the problem during the last decade or two, probably because widespread educational testing that allows for close monitoring of student progress from kindergarten on has served to make us more aware of how our children are doing in the classroom. This, plus competition for college admission, has created a national issue out of what at one time did not cause much concern.

The label "learning disability" has emerged during the past fifteen years or so. It is now the label most often used to describe children with severe learning difficulties. It has more than one "official" definition, but in practice the term generally applies to any child who does not make normal progress in school, even though he appears to be sufficiently intelligent and properly motivated. He may have trouble in one subject or in more than one; his problem may be in reading or in arithmetic or in both. He is distinguished from the "slow" or retarded child by his apparent ability to learn outside the classroom, to learn in activities that do not involve reading, spelling, and arithmetic—that is, information that is represented by symbols. The slow child, in contrast, is slow outside the classroom as well as in.*

How about minimal brain dysfunction? Is that something different from a learning disability? For all practical purposes, no. In 1966 the United States Department of Health, Education and Welfare organized a task force to investigate this newly recognized and widespread problem. In their first report they listed well over twenty different labels that could be applied.** These included (along with *learning disability, minimal brain dysfunction,* and *dyslexia*) *educationally handicapped, educationally maladjusted, special learning disorder, emotionally handicapped, educationally maladjusted, special learning disorder, socially and emotionally maladjusted, neurologically handicapped, perceptually handicapped, extreme language disorder, specific language disability.* Formidable! Enough to strike terror into the heart of any parent.

Why so many different names? There are at least two reasons.

First, many different professionals from different disciplines seemed to recognize this pervasive problem at about the same time. If they were in education, they favored an educational label, such as *learning disability.* If they were in the health professions, their inclination was to use a medical-sounding term, such as *neurologically handicapped.*

Second (and this is not the case in every school, but it is certainly true in some), high-sounding labels are comforting to some educators because they provide an excuse to the educator for not succeeding at a primary responsibility: teaching children. I have heard more than one educator assert, "How can I teach this child? He's neurologically handicapped!" Once that attitude is

---

*As I write this, I feel uneasy about using such words as *retarded* and *slow.* There really are persons who are so limited in learning ability that they can accurately be labeled retarded. But there are also great numbers of persons who are called retarded simply because they scored below some arbitrarily determined level on an IQ test. I will discuss IQ tests later on. For now, I will settle for this: Many so-called retarded children would be called learning disabled if they had simply answered one or two more questions correctly on the IQ test that earned them the retarded designation. They can learn a great deal—*if they are taught properly!* To presume otherwise is wrong.

**S. D. Clements, *Minimal Brain Dysfunction in Children; Terminology and Identification,* NINDB Monograph No. 3 (Washington, D.C.: U.S. Department of Health, Education and Welfare, 1966).

taken, little teaching is likely to take place.

Along with the variety of official labels, a number of official definitions have been proposed over the past ten years. One states, "A child with learning disabilities is one with adequate mental ability, sensory processes, and emotional stability, who has specific deficits in perceptual, integrative, or expressive processes which severely impair learning efficiency. This includes children who have central nervous system dysfunction which is expressed primarily in impaired learning efficiency."*

Here is another one: "A learning disability refers to a specific retardation or disorder in one or more of the processes of speech, language, perception, behavior, reading, spelling, writing or arithmetic."** Try one more; this one from the United States task force itself: "Children with learning disabilities are those (1) who have educationally significant discrepancies among their sensory-motor, perceptual, cognitive, academic, or related developmental levels which interfere with the performance of educational tasks; (2) who may or may not show demonstrable deviation in central nervous system functioning; and (3) whose disabilities are not secondary to general mental retardation, sensory deprivation or serious emotional disturbance."†

Although these definitions differ, they all seem to agree on the basic point I mentioned earlier—that the term *"learning disability," or any of its counterparts, applies to those children whose poor achievement record in school cannot be explained in terms of impaired intelligence, emotional disturbance, or lack of motivation.* ‡ The key phrase in that sentence is "cannot be explained," an important thing to remember when we consider what tests should be given and how to interpret their results.

What are the signs of a learning difficulty?

How can you tell if your child has a learning disorder? A number of characteristics have been linked with the condition. These include inattentiveness, confused hand dominance, printing letters backward, reading certain words in reverse, poor handwriting, and general awkwardness. The list could be extended, but I question the value of doing that, since so many of these characteristics can also be found among children who are *not* failing in school. At the risk of seeming facetious, which is not my intent, the most reliable sign of a learning disability is the child's unsatisfactory, and unexpected, school

*R. Barsch, *Working Definition* (Council for Exceptional Children, Division for Children with Learning Disabilities).

**S. A. Kirk, "The ITPA: Its Origins and Applications," in *Learning Disorders,* vol. 3, ed. J. Hellmuthm (Seattle: Special Child Publications, 1967).

†N. G. Haring and B. D. Bateman, *Minimal Brain Dysfunction in Children, Phase II,* NESDCP Monograph (Washington, D.C.: U.S. Department of Health, Education and Welfare, 1969).

‡This is the working definition I will use in this book. In addition, I will use the terms *learning disability, learning difficulty, learning problem,* and *learning disorder* interchangeably. The same definition fits them all.

record—the learning problem itself. Why look for circumstantial evidence when the hard facts are so very apparent?*

A psychological problem, a medical problem, or an educational problem?

Should a learning disorder be seen as a psychological or medical problem that in turn causes an educational problem? Or should it be thought of as primarily an educational problem?

A little history would be helpful here. During the 1950s educators and parents started to place great emphasis on children's academic achievement, even in the very early grades. It soon became apparent that a significant percentage of students were not learning as well as would normally be expected.

Emotionally disturbed?

For a while most learning difficulties were attributed to "emotional blocks" and with good reason. Children with learning problems often do show signs of emotional disturbance. But then, how long would you remain calm if, no matter how hard you tried, you continued to fail daily in your job and, on top of that, had your failure widely advertised? You would be very upset! You would quit—if indeed you were not fired first! Children cannot quit elementary school—at least not literally. And they do not get fired. They merely get shamed in public as their failure is made known to their classmates and their parents. Then we urge them to try again and to try harder and to stop being so lazy. Only a fool would simulate the behavior of a squirrel in a wheel cage for very long. It should come as no surprise, therefore, when this child starts to act up during class. He is upset and angry! He is emotionally disturbed!

He is often referred to someone when this occurs. During the late 1950s and early 1960s this "someone" was most likely to be a psychologist or a counselor or a psychiatrist. Although there certainly are some successful psychotherapy cases around, the results of this approach were generally disappointing in terms of effects on the child's classroom performance. Worse yet, with each step of this referral process the child was removed further from the one place, and the one person, where he could be helped most directly—his classroom and his teacher.

Brain-injured?

In time the emphasis on emotional blocks started to diminish. Professionals began to talk more about the fact that many of these children showed characteristics very similar to those commonly found among individuals with

*Signs that can be seen *before* the child starts school are worth noting. These are discussed in the final section of this book, "Prevention."

some central nervous system problem. They were distractible, hyperactive, confused by symbols. Perhaps here was the real cause, the place to look for answers? *Brain-injured* became the popular term and with it more confusion.

Dyslexia?

The term *dyslexia* is a good case in point. At one time that term had a specific meaning. It described a condition in which a person literally could not read and in which the cause of the impairment could be traced directly to a damaged brain, the outcome of a penetrating wound, a blow to the head, or a stroke that affected a specific site in the brain. Today, however, the term has no precise meaning. It no longer refers to a specific condition with a clearly identifiable cause. Many people—professionals as well as lay people—now use the term *dyslexia* simply as a synonym for a reading problem, regardless of the cause or severity of the problem. There is nothing wrong with that; word meanings often change over time. The trouble arises when the two meanings are confused, when by using the term to describe a reading problem, the impression is given that the child is in fact brain-injured.

With this notion of brain injury in mind, the child's distractibility and hyperactivity were, for a while, seen as the possible causes of learning problems. "After all," it was reasoned, "how is the child going to learn when he can't sit still long enough to find out what his teacher is saying and doing?" The idea sounded reasonable. Many classrooms were converted into monochromatic cells—gray ceilings, gray walls, gray floors. In some places even the windows were painted over with gray paint. Children were placed in carrels —small enclosures, about the size of telephone booths. All this in an effort to get rid of extraneous stimuli, distractions that diverted the child from his learning tasks.

The approach seemed to help some children, but it certainly did not cure them. Their learning problems persisted. As this became apparent, investigators started once again to look for clues that might help solve the problem.

Minimally brain-injured?

During this same period educators began using a variety of tests that had been developed to identify "minimally brain-injured" children. (The word *minimal* is misleading in this phrase; it really means that the child *acts as though* he is brain-injured, even though no hard evidence of that damage can be found.) Screening examinations were conducted in schools all over the country. The results were astonishing and overwhelming. Conservative figures estimated that somewhere around 15 percent of all elementary school children would fail the screening tests. Sometimes these estimates rose to 25 percent, depending upon where the testing was done.*

---

*The percentages are even higher in the neighborhoods of certain minority groups and the poor. But these children are not ordinarily called learning disabilities. They are more often called culturally deprived. The fact of the matter, however, seems to be that many poor children

All over the country, children with learning problems were being identified as having something wrong with their brains—clearly not a matter for an educator to deal with! The children had to be referred. But to whom? Most physicians did not see where they fitted in. Brain injuries, if they really were that, are permanent. There is no known method for repairing damaged brain tissue.

Drug therapy?

At about this same time, however, some physicians observed that certain drugs helped at least some of these children control their behavior better, that under the influence of a particular drug, these children could sit still and be attentive for much longer periods of time, even without the assistance of a carrel. As the word spread, thousands of children started to take drugs prescribed for this purpose. And in many cases the drug did work—the child did quiet down—but he continued to display a learning problem, despite the fact that he was responding well, in medical terms, to the treatment.

Allergies?

There are a number of theories—and that number increases almost daily —that attribute learning difficulties to allergies of one sort or another. Some theories are specific, others general. Some fix blame on artificial food additives —certain food colorings, for example. Others condemn a broad array of things ranging from chocolate to fluorescent light. So far it is difficult to accept these claims. A few studies have been conducted. Results have been far from supportive of the claims. Yet there are parents who believe in them on the basis of what they seem to observe when their child is exposed to whatever it is that he is supposed to be sensitive to. In other words, it is too soon to tell whether some, if not all, learning difficulties stem from allergies of one kind or another. But for the present the theories must be treated as interesting prospects, nothing more.

Perceptually handicapped?

Perceptual skills became another topic of interest during the 1950s and 1960s.* These have been studied before, primarily by researchers investigating child development and psychologists interested in measuring intelligence.

Now, however, perceptual skills were seen as a way of explaining learning disabilities. Children's perceptual deficits—their disorganized ways of looking,

---

encounter the same confusion and frustration in the classroom as do their middle-class counterparts. Conceivably the cause for their school failure is different from what it is for the middle-class child; but not only is that a moot question, it is also irrelevant. There is every reason to believe, and several educational research projects support the idea, that the poor children of this country would benefit from the educational approach described in this book.

*Perceptual skills will be thoroughly discussed later on. For the present consider them simply as the capacity to analyze patterns of sensations—light (printed letters and numerals; geometric designs) and sound (spoken language)—in a detailed, organized way.

listening, writing, and speaking; their difficulty in using symbols in reading and arithmetic—were interpreted as indicators of a central nervous system problem. But they were not seen to be permanent conditions. Some clinicians—optometrists primarily—were convinced that children with substandard perceptual skills could be helped by putting them into training programs that taught them the skills they lacked.

Many children were entered into such programs, and in numerous cases they were in fact helped. The training programs varied extensively. Each clinician tended to do "his own thing," ranging from having children bounce up and down on trampolines, to having them creep about on hands and knees, to training them to trace geometric shapes with one eye covered.

A certain number of miracle cures were reported, but they could not be replicated with any degree of reliability. In other words, what seemed to work in one case did not work at all in the next, even though both cases seemed to be much the same. Sometimes the child's perceptual skills improved, sometimes they did not; sometimes his schoolwork improved, sometimes it did not —even when his perceptual skills did. It was the era of the bold innovator, who proclaimed new theories daily and discarded them when a more appealing one came along. He knew he was doing something right—sometimes. But precisely what that something was he could not say. He was a hero to some parents, a charlatan to others.

To the parents of a child with a learning disorder the situation presented a dilemma. What to believe and whom? Some experts urged that the children be referred to optometrists and psychologists who could give them perceptual training. Others, equally expert, said, "That's nonsense; training doesn't work. Send the child to a neurologist, who will give him a drug." To this, yet others responded, "I took my child off drugs. He walked around looking as though he had been doped. I didn't like it at all. It frightened me."

A learning problem is an educational problem.
Slowly the truth has become apparent. Learning problems should be treated in an educational setting, and by good teachers. Yes, these children often do display symptoms that are of clinical interest to neurologists, psychologists, optometrists, pediatricians, and heaven knows who else, but that is exactly what they are—symptoms, not causes, *just as the learning problem itself is a symptom of some basic, but as yet unspecified, condition.*

Many of the symptoms can be treated, often successfully; but the learning problem tends to persist unless it too is treated directly. It is the child's primary problem; all his other symptoms are of secondary importance.*

*Not all professionals have accepted this fact. There is still a fair amount of talk in some sections of the country about the "team" approach—about how the best way to help the child with a learning problem is by mounting a multidisciplinary attack on his problems, the team usually being heavily loaded with medically oriented specialists. There is emphasis placed on "staffing" the child; having the team convene around a large table to discuss the case and decide

Although we do not know what causes learning disorders (and it seems highly likely that there is more than one cause), it is obvious that in many cases the cause disappears as the child matures. He grows out of it. But the learning problem, originally a symptom of that cause, hangs on. It becomes firmly established, having gotten worse each year the child attended school and failed to make normal progress. Worse yet, the child often develops more than a learning problem. The trauma of failure takes its toll. Realizing the gap between where he is—what he knows, what he can do—and where his classmates are overwhelms him and destroys his motivation.

The child with a learning problem needs help. What should be done? Ideally, of course, the problem should be recognized long before the child begins his pattern of failure. But what about the child who was not identified early? All his symptoms should be treated. If he is hyperactive and drugs help him control it, then they should be used—under proper medical supervision, of course. If he has a perceptual problem, that too should be dealt with—preferably in school and at home, where understanding his perceptual skills will help his teacher and his parents better understand how to teach him. But most important, he should be taught in a way that recognizes his learning difficulty. Whatever benefit he derives from the other treatments is a bonus.

Said another way, the purpose of treating the other symptoms is to help the child achieve the ability to learn from regular teaching in regular classrooms. Treating the educational problem should involve a different approach: changing the instructional materials and conditions to accommodate the child the way he is. In the first instance, it is the child who is to change; in the second, it is the school. In the best of situations both approaches will be taken. In neither instance should lower academic goals be set for the child. These should remain the same as they are for all other children. Adapting means simply an acceptance of the fact that achieving those goals—learning to read, write, calculate, and spell—will necessitate certain teaching strategies and efforts that most children do not need.

Although this way of thinking may be relatively new when applied to children with learning disabilities, it is hardly new to the field of special education, to teachers of the blind, for example. The completely blind child cannot see, no matter how much his teacher urges him to try harder, no matter how large the print, no matter what medicine or eyeglasses are supplied. He cannot be cured of his blindness. Does that mean that we should not try to teach him to read, to write, to calculate? Of course not. We do teach him, but we take his blindness into consideration; we have him use his fingers in place of his eyes.

what to do. The fallacy in the approach becomes apparent when the maneuvering starts over who will sit at the head of the table; who will captain the team. Who do you think gets the worst seat and is generally ignored? Correct—the educator—the person who has the potential for doing the most for the child in question, the person who is able to treat the child's most important symptom, his learning problem.

The child with a learning disability also has a handicap. Obviously he is more fortunate than a blind child in many ways; his handicap is not so debilitating. Yet in another way he is worse off, because he looks normal. No one has to urge a teacher to provide special teaching conditions for a blind child. The same can hardly be said for the child we are concerned about here.

Teachability

All of this will be easier to translate into action if instead of thinking of children as having or not having a "learning disability," we shift our perspective and see them as varying in "teachability," that is, in how teachable they are, in how much information they can acquire from standard instructional programs taught in standard classrooms under the supervision of standard teachers.*

Some children are exceptionally easy to teach. Show them a pertinent situation, and they learn many things. They figure out the principles that are illustrated by the situation, ask pertinent questions, try out their intuitions, modify these in accord with what happens during the tryout, relate what they observe to information previously learned, and go on from there. Or give them a basic concept and they have no difficulty recognizing ways to apply it, adjusting their understanding of it as they go. In either set of conditions they learn a great deal—sometimes even more than what was anticipated—without special assistance.

Most children are not all that easy to teach, but they are not hard to teach either. They do not figure out everything on their own; they need *some* explicit instruction. But if you give them a fairly clear explanation of what it is they are to do, some appropriate examples, and some supervised drill and practice experiences, they learn—they make satisfactory progress in school.

Some children—the children who are the focus of this book—are hard to teach. They neither identify concepts intuitively nor recognize their applicability when the concepts are presented explicitly. They do not retain information very well, even after a reasonable number of repeated exposures. As a result standard instructional conditions do not meet their needs, and they fail. The underlying theme of this book is that it is not *their* failure, nor, for that matter, is failure inevitable. They can learn; they simply need help. The overall goal of this book is to define that "help" in practical language.

Develop a plan of action

You will have to deal with the situation in an organized way, step by step. A haphazard approach will at best add to your child's confusion, and yours

---

*Before I go any further, I had better state that the word *standard,* as used here, does not mean inadequate. By *standard,* I mean a situation in which a teacher with average training, skills, motivation, and energy is given commercially published materials and the task of teaching twenty-five or so children a certain amount of information and skills within the time constraints of the school schedule.

as well.

First, design a very simple plan of action. Write it down, and check off the steps as they are accomplished.

Start off by stating a final goal. This is a crucial point. It is easy to forget a long-term goal when you get caught up in worrying about day-to-day problems. What is that goal? It is for the child to be able to perform in school in a way that does not earn him the label "learning problem." Stated positively, your goal is: *My child will be able to read, write, spell, and do arithmetic as well as the other children in his class. His progress in school will be equal to the progress shown by the majority of his classmates, this despite the fact that he may continue to be hard to teach.*

Now that you have the goal identified, memorize it. Keep it in mind as you decide on the actions you will take to achieve it. Check every decision you make against that goal, and avoid decisions that divert you from it.

What next? Working backward from the goal, it is obvious that something will have to be done to help the child perform better in school. What is that something? Is it medical treatment, special tutoring, or what? You will not be able to answer that question until a certain amount of testing has been done. Thus, in broad terms, your plan of action should show two steps en route to the goal:

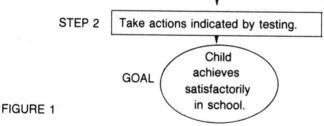

STEP 1 Administer tests to determine what actions should be taken to (a) help the child become less hard to teach; and (b) modify the child's instructional program in a way that takes his difficulties into account.

STEP 2 Take actions indicated by testing.

GOAL Child achieves satisfactorily in school.

FIGURE 1

Embedded in this diagram is a basic principle. Testing should be done *only* when it might provide information that will help you make decisions concerning actions you should take. Actions should be taken *only* if they appear to be justified, only when they are based on reason rather than wishful thinking.

Organization of this book

This book is organized around that plan of action. As such, it is divided into four major sections: "Testing the Child," "Teaching Perceptual Skills," "Helping the Child with School Subjects," and then a follow-up section, "Prevention," devoted to the prevention of learning problems through proper preschool activities.

In the section entitled "Testing the Child," we will consider:

What health-related and education-related tests are essential?

Who should administer these? A doctor, a teacher, or a parent?

What other tests might be called for and who should make that decision?

In what way do the tests relate to the child's learning problem? What can they tell you that will enable you to *help* him?

In the section entitled "Teaching Perceptual Skills" we will consider procedures for helping the child acquire better:

Visual perceptual skills

Auditory perceptual skills

General motor skills

In the section entitled "Helping the Child with School Subjects" we will discuss procedures for helping the child acquire better:

Reading skills

Arithmetic skills

Spelling skills

Handwriting skills

This section will also contain a discussion of the kind of teacher and the kind of school environment that best serve the hard-to-teach child.

In the final section, "Prevention," we will deal with early recognition of learning difficulties and what to do to spare children the trauma of school failure.

PART I

Testing the Child

HEALTH-RELATED TESTS

Remember, the reason the child is to be tested is because you are seeking information that will help you decide what actions to take to help you achieve your goal. It is essential that this be made clear to everyone who will be doing testing. Their goals may not be the same as yours.

The tests listed below are important. None should be omitted. Some of them can be administered only by highly trained professionals. Some can be given, and interpreted, by you.

The tests are organized into two categories: health-related and education-related. The health-related tests should be administered first. It would be foolish to search for better teaching methods without first making sure that the child's classroom difficulties do not stem from a health-related problem that could be successfully treated. Unfortunately, it is rarely that simple, but the possibility does exist and should be dealt with at the start.

GENERAL MEDICAL STATUS

"Is there some medical problem that is causing my child to be hard to teach?" You will need a physician to answer this one. Who? A specialist? If so, what kind? That depends. I think you will do well to call upon the physician who has been looking after the medical needs of the child up until this time. However, if your past experiences with this physician have convinced you that he will not look at the child with a fresh eye, that he does not recognize the seriousness of the situation and will tend to view it as inconsequential, then have someone else do it. In any case, the physician need not be a specialist; your family doctor is well suited to carry out this task.

State the purpose of your visit to his office at the very beginning: *"My child is having trouble learning in school. I am assured that he is smart enough; I know he is trying to succeed. I want to know whether you, in your examination, observe any medical problems that could be making him hard to teach?"* In

2

other words, "Can I rule out a medical factor as a potential cause of his school problem?"

Be careful not to state the question this way: "Why is my child having a learning problem?" That only sets the stage for speculation that could distract you from your mission. The doctor, after all, has had lots of schooling and may, therefore, consider himself knowledgeable in the field of education as well as medicine. He might be tempted to offer an opinion, even though that opinion is based solely on intuition. Obviously, if it is offered, even though you have not asked for it, listen to his opinion and assess its value. But remember that it is probably based on uninformed hunches rather than specific knowledge.

A decade or so ago very few physicians were aware of the possible relationship between certain medical conditions and learning problems. As I noted earlier, in those days the characteristic reaction was to assume that the child had an emotional disorder and to refer him to a psychiatrist. Today most physicians are more likely to be aware of the potential link between their field and education and will have informed opinions regarding the use of drugs that tend to lessen a child's hyperactivity, the use of certain vitamin therapies, and so forth.

Unless you are unfortunate enough to choose a physician who has not kept informed (and if you have, find another), accept his conclusions and recommendations at face value. If he says, "There is nothing wrong with your child," he means *medically* and is not arguing with the education diagnosis that caused you to go to him in the first place. As such, be grateful that the youngster is healthy, check that potential factor off your list, and move on. For your own mental (and economic) health, do not insist upon calling on a progression of physicians until you find one that tells you what you might want to hear—that he has an easy medical cure for your child's educational problem.

If, in contrast, your physician concludes that the child does have a medical condition that *could,* at least in part, be related to his school difficulties, follow whatever recommendations he makes, but do not stop there. The child will almost invariably also need educational help—special instructional assistance. Accept the physician's prescriptions and apply them, but continue with your plan of action. If your physician recommends that the child be seen by certain specialists, such as a neurologist or a psychiatrist, follow that recommendation if you can. If you cannot, because of the realities of economics, tell this to the physician and ask for his advice—"Is it essential to see this specialist? What should I do if I can't afford it?" Do not be ashamed to talk honestly regarding costs.

If you are referred to a specialist, approach him with the same set of questions. This is vital if you want to avoid a veritable merry-go-round of professional visits.

VISION

All right, you have received medical clearance. Your child is healthy. Now what? Are there others who should examine him? How about his eyes? Are they functioning properly? The answer to this last question is important. A child with a vision problem is apt to have trouble in school. Where can you find the answer? This one is sticky. Some will argue that the school nurse can supply it. "After all," you may be told, "she examines their eyes regularly, and if the child passes that test, it means his eyes are okay; he doesn't need to be examined by an eye doctor." That is not really accurate.

It is true that in many schools some sort of vision exam is conducted regularly and routinely. Unfortunately these so-called examinations are usually superficial and inadequate. Ordinarily the vision test is limited to checking how clearly the child can see a chart of letters from a distance of twenty feet. If he can see the "20/20" letters, or close to that, his eyes are judged to be normal and he is dismissed. The fact is, however, that 20/20 visual acuity (eyesight) is not sufficient evidence of adequate visual abilities in terms of the visual demands of a classroom. To do well in the classroom, the child must see clearly close up as well as at a distance. Clear eyesight at one distance does not necessarily guarantee clear eyesight at another. In addition, the child should be able to use his two eyes together efficiently, coordinating—aiming —them without undue strain. He should be able to shift his focus from a distance to close up and back again, with relative ease—from the chalkboard to his desk to the chalkboard.

Well, then, what if the school examination is more thorough? Is it still necessary to have a professional examination? Perhaps; perhaps not. Some school systems (too few, unfortunately) bring in a professional who, in conjunction with school nurses and volunteers, provides "vision screenings" that test much more than how clearly a child sees at twenty feet. Find out if your school does this. If so, fine. Accept the results of that screening, and if your child passes it, assume that his learning problem does not stem from an eye-related problem. If he fails that screening, then a visit to the eye doctor is essential. Screening examinations, even the better ones, never do more than "pass" or "fail." They do not, nor can they, take the place of a professional evaluation. They merely identify those who should have that professional evaluation.

Optometrist or ophthalmologist?

Whom do you call upon if you have to take your child to an eye doctor? Many parents continue to be confused by the available options and what they really are. There are two general categories of eye doctors. One group are medically oriented and, in the main, are currently identified as ophthalmologists, although there are still some who are called oculists and even eye-ear-nose-and-throat doctors. The others are called optometrists. Both groups are adequately trained to answer your questions *if* they will take the time to look for the answers. Both groups have their share of dedicated practitioners. Sometimes your child's teacher (or some other school person) will be able to help you make the choice, based upon the knowledge of the past experiences of other children with similar problems.

At any rate it is not so important which kind of eye doctor you take your child to so long as wherever you go, you make certain to ask the proper questions and not to settle for less than full answers. Do not allow yourself to be intimidated by the busy office, bustling office assistants, and elusive doctor. You have brought your child there to get answers to the following questions, and you should let the doctor know this and that you will not be satisfied with less: *"Does my child have a vision problem that could be causing or contributing to his school problem? Are his eyes healthy? Does he see well up close as well as at a distance? Can he shift focus easily? Do his eyes work together properly? Can he do all this without undue strain?"* Again, I caution you, do not get sidetracked by asking, "Why does my child have a learning problem?" Try to keep the issues clear.

Once you are satisfied that the eye doctor has taken your questions seriously, accept his conclusions and recommendations at face value. If he says, "There is nothing wrong with your child's eyes," be grateful. If he recommends glasses, procure them—after you have again asked the doctor if he thinks the need for glasses is relevant to the child's school problems. If he cannot support that relationship, then question why the glasses are called for. Glasses are often prescribed for extensive reading. That is fine if the child reads extensively. It is silly and wasteful for the child who can hardly read at all and never does so voluntarily. There is time for him to obtain glasses for extensive reading once he starts to overcome his reading problem.

If the eye doctor recommends a series of treatments to improve your child's perceptual skills, show him this book and ask him whether what he has in mind goes beyond what I am suggesting. And if it does, find out why he thinks this is warranted, what the extra benefits will be, and what the professional fees will amount to. Make your decision based upon that information. I do not argue against the relative value of a private practitioner over a book such as this one that is written for nonprofessionals. Obviously, the private practitioner's judgment should be better in individual cases. However, I do caution you to avoid committing yourself and your child to a series of treatments that may aim for skills he really does not need at the expense of neglecting skills that he needs desperately. This point will become clearer when we discuss perceptual skills in detail.

HEARING

Hearing is another important consideration, often overlooked. If the child has a reading problem, make certain that his hearing is unimpaired. Once again, the school nurse often investigates this ability, but you had better inquire as to whether it has been checked lately. If it has, and you are satisfied that the examination was adequate, leave it at that. If you are not convinced, then arrange for a professional evaluation.

Most reading problems are not caused by hearing problems. However, if the child does have a hearing problem, it will significantly affect his classroom performance, especially his ability to learn to read. Therefore it should be determined at the outset.

Assuming that you are not willing to accept the school nurse's opinion, who should do this? Ask your family doctor or pediatrician. His opinion will be helpful here. Obviously if a hearing problem is discovered, follow professional advice. If no problem is found, be grateful and proceed about the business of completing the first phase of your plan of action.

EDUCATION-RELATED TESTS

The tests discussed so far were all concerned with health-related matters: the child's general physical condition, his vision, and his hearing. Certainly all of these can affect how well a child will perform in the classroom, but other abilities should also be examined. Specifically the following:

Visual perceptual skills—his ability to analyze patterns of light (printed letters and numerals; geometric designs) in a detailed, organized way

Auditory perceptual skills—his ability to analyze patterns of sound (spoken language) in a detailed, organized way

General motor skills—his ability to analyze his own body movements in a detailed, organized way

I will discuss all of these thoroughly, but before I do, we should consider the question of who will conduct the examinations.

It is only in recent years that the close relationship between a child's perceptual skills and his ability to learn in school has been clearly recognized. When this occurred, many different disciplines became interested in perceptual skills at virtually the same time. These included, among others, optometry, psychology, education, and even occupational therapy. Each group developed its own tests. To some extent all of the tests are similar, but in other ways they do differ. Many of them are exceedingly complex; too much so, in terms of what we are concerned about—the child's school performance. In my judgment extensive testing is not called for. It is essential to test the three skills I listed above, nothing more.

Who should do the testing? A decade or so ago perceptual testing required a professional—an optometrist, psychologist, or occupational therapist who had become expert in the field of perceptual testing. And there were not too many who had. More recently some educators have begun testing perceptual skills, thus widening the range of professionals from whom to choose.

Today you need not be limited. You no longer have to search for a specially trained person. You can do it yourself. Further along in this section I will describe some perceptual tests that you can use. And I will tell you how to apply the information you acquire from them.

Well, then, given this choice, who *should* do the testing—a private practitioner, an educator, or you? That depends on your individual situation. Certainly, the private practitioner who understands this field should be able to do the most thorough job. The question, however, is whether such an in-depth investigation is warranted. If you have reason to think that it is—or if you feel too insecure to do the testing yourself—then by all means seek the services of a competent private practitioner. But if you have no reason to believe that you need professional involvement at this point, then do the testing yourself.

Before we turn our attention to the specific tests, how to administer them, and what they tell us, there should be some general discussion about perception, what perceptual skills are, and why they are important.

Perception

To *perceive,* according to my dictionary, is "to become aware of directly through the senses." To perceive is more than to see or hear or smell or feel or taste. To perceive is to interpret whatever information is being received, regardless of which senses are involved. To do this, the perceiver:

1. Pays particular attention to certain features of that information, features that he considers to be distinctive in that situation

2. Attaches to those distinctive features his own personal emotional, physical, and intellectual values

3. Comes to some conclusion, that is, interprets the information

For example, when I am shown a photograph of a person, I focus on certain features of that photograph, depending upon whatever is important to me at that time under those circumstances. If it is a photograph of a person I know, I will probably look at it differently than if I do not know the person. If it is a person I like, I will undoubtedly look at it differently than if it is a person I dislike. My perception is colored by past experiences that have shaped my personal values.

Suppose it is a photograph of someone I like and whom you, in contrast, dislike. Will we see the same thing? Literally, yes. But in terms of our examination of that photograph, no—we will *perceive* differently. I will pay particular attention to certain features and make my judgment primarily from those. You may perhaps look at the same details or, more likely, at other aspects of the photograph and come to a different judgment.

Perceptual Skills

Now, to get a little closer to the classroom, picture in your mind's eye two individuals walking in a forest. Imagine that one of these persons is a bird watcher. He has spent years looking at and listening to birds. He is very familiar with the characteristics of a great many species. Imagine that his companion is a lifelong city dweller who rarely gets out to the countryside. He can tell the difference between a pigeon and a canary, but beyond that he is lost. Suppose, further, that before this outing both men had had eye examinations and hearing examinations. It was established that both have equally excellent sight and hearing. Do you think they both hear and see the same in this forest? Literally, yes; but in terms of what they perceive, of course not. The bird watcher is aware of many distinctly different bird songs; his companion is aware of birdlike noises, but their songs all sound the same to him. The bird watcher is aware of many different birds all around him; his companion manages to notice a bird only when it flies across his path. The bird watcher can describe the birds verbally, that is, use words to define their distinctive visual and acoustical characteristics. His companion cannot, even though he knows all the words that the bird watcher uses. He knows the verbal code but is not sufficiently familiar with the bird's physical characteristics to use the code effectively.

Why the differences, since we know that both individuals have the same excellent visual and auditory abilities? The answer is obvious. The bird watcher knows *what to look for* and *what to listen for.* He is familiar with the acoustical features that distinguish the various bird songs and the visual features that distinguish the various bird forms. *He has acquired the perceptual skills needed to be a good bird watcher.* His companion is not at all familiar with those distinguishing features. To him, birds are simply birds; they all look and sound "alike" to him. He does not have the perceptual skills needed to be a good bird watcher.

Could this city dweller become a better bird watcher? Sure. He merely has to acquire the necessary visual and auditory perceptual skills, to be told—taught—what to look and listen for, and then to use what he has been taught. In fact he need not even be taught if he will devote the necessary time and effort to learning on his own, but this will take longer and demand more effort on his part. But what should we call him if, even after much effort, he continues to have trouble identifying, and keeping straight in his head, the distinctive acoustical and visual features of the various birds and the words that define these features? A learning problem—for that is what he would be in this situation.

Classrooms are not forests, and recognizing the distinctive physical features of birds and their songs is not the equivalent of recognizing the distinctive features of a reading, spelling, or arithmetic lesson. But there are some general principles that apply to both settings. Once understood, they will help us plan effectively for the hard-to-teach child.

To begin with, if we are going to help the hard-to-teach child, we have to understand how he differs from his more successful classmates in operational terms, that is, in what he can and cannot do. Once we have accomplished that, it will be easier for us to address the problem of what tests to use and how to teach him despite his being hard to teach.

What is it that easy-to-teach children can do, that hard-to-teach children cannot do, and that "counts" in the classroom? In other words, what characteristics do hard-to-teach children display that distinguish them from children who are not hard to teach and, when taken into account, provide information that is useful in designing effective instruction?

Hard-to-teach children display significantly less precise visual and auditory perceptual skills than do easy-to-teach children of the same age.

All normal children—children who have no nervous system impairments, whose "equipment" is in proper working order—acquire such skills naturally as they grow and develop. It is predestined by virtue of the fact that they are humans.

A very young child's perceptual skills are imprecise; he is not aware of many details. As he develops, his perceptual skills become sharper. Indeed, child development specialists frequently use these changes that occur over time as milestones for charting a child's maturation.

Three-year-olds, for example, are not expected to be as sensitive to the details of visual patterns as are six-year-olds. Three-year-olds ordinarily cannot draw geometric designs—even simple ones such as squares or triangles—the way six-year-olds can. They can identify them, even often name them, but they cannot single out the important features of the designs well enough to copy them accurately. The same is true regarding their sensitivity to what they hear. Three-year-olds ordinarily cannot identify the separate sounds of a spoken word the way six-year-olds can, even though they hear the words clearly, understand their meaning, and respond appropriately to such uniquely similar yet different words as *no* and *go* and *toe,* or *sick* and *sack* and *sock* and *suck.*

There are lots of other examples, but these will do for now, the key point being that young children do not have precise perceptual skills, but they can be expected to acquire them naturally as they mature, so long as they are free of central nervous system impairments.

How is it, then, that *hard-to-teach children with no apparent abnormalities typically display less adept perceptual skills than do easy-to-teach children of the same age?* A simplistic explanation is that children develop according to different timetables, and easy-to-teach children follow a significantly faster schedule than do hard-to-teach children. In other words, it is evidence of the normal variability of nature rather than the outcome of some specific underlying problem.

I doubt that explanation. Nature is not usually that capricious. Individual differences among children are common, of course, but not ordinarily to those extremes. We can reasonably speculate that there are two basic factors that affect a child's rate of development and that either, or both, might be influential in these instances.

One factor is that the child's neurological system may in fact not be in as good shape as it appears to be. This could have come from some minimal type of injury incurred prior to, during, or after birth; or it could be genetic in origin, where the child displays a "chip off the old block" syndrome, duplicating many of the traits that his father or mother showed when they were young.

The other factor is that the child's early life may have been too sterile, too devoid of the stimulating experiences needed to develop an awareness of details.* For example, perhaps he spent too many hours sitting passively in front of the TV set, looking and listening attentively but not coming into direct contact with what was being shown, that is, never manipulating it in a way that would sensitize him to its important distinctive attributes. And also, of course, the more time he spends in front of the TV, the less time he has available to examine the real world.

In essence, then, the factors may be either intrinsic—attributable to something within the child—or extrinsic—attributable to circumstances in the child's environment. In fact, of course, these two are so closely interrelated that it is almost impossible to consider them separately. The relationship between a child and his environment is interactive; the child reacts to his environment, and the environment reacts to the child. The child who has a physical impairment elicits certain responses from his parents, for example, which in turn shape his behavior, which—again in turn—causes his parents to treat him in a specific way, and so on.

As such, the question of underlying cause is moot. It is best we leave it, therefore, acknowledging that hard-to-teach children do lag significantly in their acquisition of pertinent perceptual skills and that this must be kept in mind when we set about deciding how to teach them to read and do arithmetic, despite this deficit.

There is another basic characteristic that distinguishes hard-to-teach from easy-to-teach children: *Hard-to-teach children know significantly fewer school-related facts than do easy-to-teach children of the same grade level.* Certain words in that sentence need to be defined: *school-related facts* and *know.*

School-related facts refers to information that is directly relevant to what is being taught in school and would not be known if it had not been learned —experienced—in one way or another, intentionally or otherwise; information that reflects the child's background. Vocabulary, for example. The nonreading child who never hears a particular word will not use that word, nor is he apt to know its meaning. A child who has never heard the word *six,* say, is not likely to know what it means, nor what the arabic numeral 6 represents, even though he may have seen sets comprising six things many times.

---

*I also have to acknowledge that too much stimulation can have a detrimental effect on the child's subsequent ability to recognize details. Excessive stimulation can cause frustration; whatever natural interest a child may have in examining his environment can be extinguished if there is too much thrust at him at too rapid a pace, the result being that he does not have the opportunity to deal with any one thing for more than an instant.

Know, in this context, means "securely stored in long-term memory,"* and readily recallable whenever conditions warrant. For example, you *know* your address, the multiplication tables, the name of the capital city of your state.

Now, what has been established so far? Hard-to-teach children differ from easy-to-teach children in two ways: *(a)* they lag behind in the natural development of perceptual skills—they are less aware of the pertinent details in what they look at and what they listen to than are easy-to-teach children; and *(b)* they lag behind in the acquisition of knowledge—they know appreciably less school-related information than they should, given their age.

The hookup between these two characteristics is apparent. The better the child's perceptual skills—that is, the better he identifies the distinctive similarities and differences in the things around him—the better he will be at classifying those things according to those distinctive features. For example, the more familiar he is with the fact that various objects in his home are the "same" as well as "different," such as food containers that are the same in color but differ in shape, the more readily will he understand the concept of classifying these containers according to their similarities and differences. The better his classification skills, the better—that is, the faster and more accurate—he will be at labeling information, associating it appropriately, and remembering it.

Thus he can acquire additional facts about food containers, identifying certain basic sets of characteristics instantaneously as he becomes totally familiar with them, which in turn improves perceptual skills even more in that he uses these larger units of analysis—categories—in his processing of information. That is, he learns to use what he already knows to acquire more knowledge; he learns to recognize that certain combinations of distinctive features occur often and can be identified as a unit—a "chunk," in the vocabulary of the psychologist—rather than as an assortment of separate, smaller units.

Being able to identify such chunks facilitates memory. Chunks are single things, even though they are relatively complex, and single things are generally easier to remember than collections of separate things.

Since he remembers more, the child learns more—acquires more factual knowledge—even during his preschool years. Hence, by the time he enters school, the child with sharper perceptual skills usually knows a good deal more about his world and therefore is easier to teach.

There is a third characteristic that differentiates hard-to-teach from easy-to-teach children, and it stems directly from the two we have already discussed: *Hard-to-teach children are less adept than easy-to-teach children at using or, when needed, inventing systems—rule-based strategies—for remembering things.*

Reading and arithmetic are representative of such systems. Knowing how

---

Long-term memory is the capacity to recall information acquired at some significantly earlier date, such as the day before, the week before, or whenever; *short-term memory* is the capacity to recall information encountered just minutes, or perhaps even seconds, earlier.

these systems work reduces the burden on memory significantly—for two reasons:

First, understanding that reading and arithmetic are based on systems where symbols represent sounds in the one case and quantities in the other allows the child to memorize facts gradually. The child who understands the basic system will use it to relate not-yet-memorized information to information that he has already learned securely, and he will then exploit that recognized relationship when he needs to recall the newer information. Unless the child can relate information—tie the new to what he already knows—he is in an "all-or-nothing, I-can-or-cannot-remember-it-as-a-separate-fact" situation. For example, the child who already knows what *fan, fat,* and *cat* say and who also understands the system that underlies reading will have relatively less difficulty remembering what *can* says. The child who fails to recognize the system is forced to memorize *can* as a separate entity; it is not any easier for him than remembering the other three, despite the fact that he has already securely learned those three. Or in regard to arithmetic, the child who already knows that $4 + 4 = 8$ and who also understands the system that underlies arithmetic will have relatively less difficulty remembering the answer to $4 + 5 = ?$.

The second reason is that when an exception to the system is encountered and rote memorization does become necessary—as in learning to read the words *ghost* and *yacht*—then understanding the system helps because it enables the child to identify the exceptions as well as the nonexceptions, the exceptions being those portions of the words that he must memorize specifically because they do not belong to a specific class of words.

All of this will be gone over again in the contexts of reading, arithmetic, spelling, and writing. For the present I can summarize these concepts in a single sentence: *Hard-to-teach children are hard to teach because they do not remember enough of what they are taught.*

I recognize that this last statement, taken literally and out of context, might be considered a gross oversimplification of a complex set of processes. You could logically insist—and there would be many who would agree with you—that no one should be expected to memorize very much; that it probably would not be desirable, even if it were possible. As a matter of fact in the past few decades more and more emphasis has been placed on *not memorizing* things in school. After all, the argument goes, the key to learning is knowing where to look up information and how to reason. Memorizing, from this point of view, is for those who do not know where to look things up and who cannot reason.

But think about the counterargument for a moment. You cannot reason effectively unless you can associate information, and you cannot associate information unless you can keep it in mind long enough to recognize where the associations are possible. You cannot profit fully from today's lesson unless you can remember yesterday's with relative ease. If you have to go through the process of figuring out, or looking up, yesterday's lesson again during today's lesson, then you will surely miss some of the information contained in today's lesson, simply because some of your attention will be directed elsewhere.

Why, then, does this notion of not memorizing appeal to so many? I suppose it stems from the fact that the easy-to-teach students—they are always the ones whose behaviors are applauded and chosen to serve as models—memorize things quickly and easily, almost without effort. They do not have to work at it, but neither do they spend time looking things up. As a result we have been deluded into thinking that no one has to devote effort to memorizing information, that it just happens.

In a sense, then, it is not inaccurate to identify the hard-to-teach child's basic problem as one of inadequate memory—so long as we realize that an adequate ability to remember information will not result from many separate and successive rote memorizing efforts but rather is the product of a capacity to analyze and organize different learning experiences in a way that links them on the basis of their common features.

Hence I suggest that adequate memory is the outcome of combining, on the one hand, the factual knowledge and the perceptual skills needed to reduce relatively large amounts of information down to a smaller, more manageable number of units with, on the other hand, an understanding of a system for organizing these units into cohesive groupings. The knowledge and perceptual skills in combination enable one to identify *what* is to be remembered. The *how* to remember it efficiently is accomplished by applying the rules of an existing system or, where called for, inventing a new strategy.

Some examples would probably help. Educators put a lot of stock in a child's visual and auditory memory—and with good reason, considering how often a child is required to remember what he looks at and listens to as he proceeds through a lesson. Let us take a look at how these memory abilities are tested.

WHAT DO VISUAL MEMORY TESTS TEST?

Consider the following visual memory task, a task that resembles many of the standard visual memory tests currently used in schools. Suppose you were asked to remember the array of designs shown here. Standard test procedures generally allow a controlled amount of time to study the designs; then—with the designs removed—the person being tested must either draw them or, in some tests, identify the correct patterns from a wider selection. Spend about ten seconds or so studying these patterns:

FIGURE 2

Okay? Now close the book and try to draw the row of patterns from memory. No simple task, to be sure.

Now, let us repeat the test, but this time I will try to help you a bit by applying some of the principles stated on the preceding pages.

This time I will highlight what you should pay special attention to—*what* you are to remember—and, in addition, I will make more evident *how* you should remember it; I will give you a system that should facilitate recall.

Once again, spend about ten seconds or so studying the patterns:

FIGURE 3

Now close the book and try to draw this second set of patterns. Easier? You bet! Why? Well, first of all there was a lot less of *what* you had to remember, and it was a lot easier to identify. You did not need such effective perceptual skills. The letters U, V, W, X, Y, and Z, in block form, were readily apparent, and remembering six letters, each embedded in a square, is a lot less demanding than identifying and remembering six different sets of line patterns, with their only common characteristic being the square.

But more than visual perceptual skills were needed to do this. You also had to know some facts. You had to know these letters and their names. If you were not familiar with the letters—collections of lines arranged in specific ways —the second memory test would be no easier than the first. In fact it might even be more difficult because of the varying pattern of dotted lines that appears in the outline of the squares.

Here, then, we see how factual knowledge interacts with perceptual skills to facilitate memory. Indeed, some of you may even have discovered these letter patterns in the first test, indicating that you had highly capable visual perceptual skills—but not necessarily that you had a greater store of factual knowledge. All of you know these letters. Those of you who perceived them before I made them very apparent are therefore simply demonstrating competent visual perceptual skills.

There was another helpful feature present in the second test—the *sequence* of the designs. The letters were arranged in alphabetical order, from U to Z.

That, too, was evident and useful *if* you had the prior knowledge about alphabetical order.

Another point. Go back to the first test, look at the patterns, and see how much easier the task is now. Does that mean that your visual memory has improved? Since I literally taught you how to do this specific task, it cannot be seen as a general improvement in visual memory. Correct? Probably, but let us check this out before we decide for sure.

Look at the set of designs below and see how well you can remember them after ten seconds of study, keeping in mind what you just experienced.

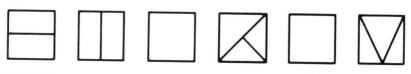

FIGURE 4

Was that as difficult as the first test? Perhaps yes, but possibly not—for some of you, at any rate. Why? Because I had just shown you a way to help you do the job—a *how.* I taught—alerted—you to search for block letters hidden in squares, and at least some of you were able to recognize in figure 4 the block letters H, I, J, K, L, and M.

Admittedly this one way will not always help your visual memory. In fact, it may never work again, because whatever you may be called upon to look at and remember in the future might not lend itself to this strategy of finding letter patterns arranged in alphabetical order. However, it was *a way*—a system—and more important, the way was made explicit. It should help you in future visual memory tasks, if only because you may be more apt to tell yourself to look for patterns that you can identify as units rather than attempting to memorize arrangements of separate lines that cannot be chunked readily. And, in addition, you will probably tell yourself to look for some system, some organized way of associating those patterns so that you can reduce even further the number of separate things you have to commit to memory.

One last point: Were the tasks you just engaged in really visual tasks, or were they simply memory tasks that presented visual stimuli? The latter, obviously. You certainly were not "taking pictures" of what you saw, without involving any of your other channels of communication and information processing. You looked, coded what you saw with language, and remembered. To consider it to be a task indicative of your "visual" abilities is ridiculous, yet that is how it is often conceived and interpreted by some persons who routinely use the test. Then, having done so, they compare it to the child's "auditory memory" skills and make suggestions regarding instruction on the basis of this comparison. The result? Improperly designed instruction. I will come back to this point later on, when we discuss how to teach reading to the hard-to-teach child. For the present, simply take note of the fact that a so-called visual memory test involves a lot more than vision.

WHAT DO AUDITORY MEMORY TESTS TEST?

Let us examine some typical auditory memory tasks. Most school-related auditory memory tests ask the child to listen to and then repeat a string of spoken numerals—but not because it is important to remember a string of numerals per se. This, in itself, is not that important—unless you are a switchboard operator working without a phonebook. Rather the test is thought to be useful because, supposedly, it helps us assess the child's general ability to remember what he hears. (Once again, it does not, but more about that later.)

Try this. (If you want, have someone read the numerals to you, although I think you will get the idea I am trying to illustrate just by imagining that someone is speaking the numerals to you.) Listen to, then repeat, this string of numerals:

1 . . . 2 . . . 3 . . . 4 . . . 5 . . . 6 . . . 7 . . . 8 . . . 9

That was easy! Why? The reason is obvious, of course. You did not have to remember nine separate numerals. All you needed were: *(a)* the analysis skills to identify *what* you were to remember, and that was exceptionally apparent—although it did require the factual knowledge that these were numerals being spoken, not gibberish—and this would not have been the case if you understood only Hebrew, say; and *(b)* recognition of the *"how"*—the system that would best facilitate your recall, that is, awareness of the fact that the numerals were arranged in sequence, from 1 to 9. As such, they could easily be identified as a single unit—a chunk—and therefore easily retained with remarkable accuracy. Under those conditions you could remember a virtually endless string of numerals.

Let us change the task a bit. Try to remember this sequence:

1 . . . 2 . . . 3 . . . 4 . . . 5 . . . 6 . . . 7 . . . 9 . . . 8

Not much harder, was it? Why? Because the only difference here was the reverse order of the 8 and the 9. That was the one thing you had to identify and remember as a separate unit, other than the basic operations required by the first task.

Another one. Listen and recall:

1 . . . 3 . . . 5 . . . 7 . . . 9 . . . 2 . . . 4 . . . 6 . . . 8

More difficult? Yes, somewhat. Again you had to identify numerals, but this time recognition of the system that determined the sequence was less obvious. It was not all that obscure, however, and most of you probably had enough time, even if you were listening to someone rather than reading it yourself.*

One more experiment. Try to recall these in correct sequence:

8 . . . 3 . . . 1 . . . 9 . . . 6 . . . 4 . . . 7 . . . 2 . . . 5

Now, that is really difficult. It demands the same fundamental analysis skills and the same fundamental knowledge as before—identifying the sounds as separate spoken numerals. But it presents a much more complex condition for inventing a system that will organize the sequence into a reasonable number of memorable chunks. Possible? Yes. Probable? No, not within the constraints imposed by the conditions of the task. Thus to remember the sequence, all nine numerals had to be hung onto separately, in correct order. A formidable challenge that very few can meet.

Has your capacity to remember strings of numerals been improved as a result of these experiences? I think so, at least to some degree. You probably have been sensitized to searching for some system that helps you tie together a chain of separate numerals, that enables you to reduce the information to a smaller number of units.

The system we used in all of these auditory tasks was based on principles of mathematics, and it has limitations. It is not the *only* system, but it is *a* system, and by using it and recognizing its value, you may be stimulated to search for other systems, and that would have some general positive value.

For example, try to remember this sequence:

1 . . . 2 . . . 6 . . . 4 . . . 5 . . . 9 . . . 3 . . . 7 . . . 8

Difficult? To be sure, but not quite as difficult, perhaps, as the preceding one. There are at least two systems that might work here.

One way: The chain of numerals could be analyzed—perceived—as three groups, three numerals in each. This, combined with the fact that each group is organized in an ascending order, may be sufficient.

Another way: Taking note, again, of the three groups, with three numerals in each group, organized in ascending order, recognize, in addition, that each numeral in the first group is spelled with three letters *(one, two, six)*, each in the second group with four letters *(four, five, nine)*, each in the third group with five letters *(three, seven, eight)*. A bit obscure for rapid identification? Certainly, but knowing some systems and working at finding additional ones does help one get better at doing it.

The major point to be made here is simply a repetition of what I said earlier. To learn means to remember. In order to remember, you must be able

*If you were reading it, then you surely got it—not because you are a "visual" learner but simply because you had more time. Visual information, by its nature, is more permanent than sound. Spoken information is gone immediately after it is uttered, and the only way to extend the time you have to examine it for patterns—if you did not catch it the first time—is to remember it well enough to repeat it to yourself. Hardly the same as a visual inspection task, unless the information is flashed on and off the screen.

to identify *what* is to be remembered and *how* to do it. You do this by combining what you *know* with whatever *perceptual skills* you may have in order to identify the salient components of the task at hand and, by employing a system that helps you organize those salient things into memorable patterns, thereby reducing even further the demands of the task.

All this improves your chances for recall. Human memory—especially short-term memory—has finite and rather marked limits, yet one cannot learn very much without it. Without the ability to identify *what* to remember and *how* best to remember it, school learning becomes virtually impossible.

By the way, were these so-called auditory memory tasks really testing your ability to remember what you heard or, rather, your ability to hear something and then "code" it spatially? The latter, obviously. So much for "auditory" memory tests.

The preceding pages were intended to illustrate the relationship between school learning and perceptual skills. Now it is time to focus more directly on these skills and how to test them.

VISUAL PERCEPTUAL SKILLS

To give you a clear idea of what we are testing when we give a visual perceptual skills test, try the following. Look at the upper pattern of the two shown in figure 5 and copy it on a separate piece of paper. Is it a difficult task? Hardly. If someone were to check the accuracy of your work, there would probably be total agreement that you had done what you were asked to do. Does your printing exactly match the printing shown in the book? No, but who cares?

FIGURE 5

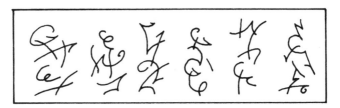

The task is a straightforward one of copying a word and, as such, so long as you spelled it correctly, it would be senseless to worry about whether your printing was an exact match. You were operating at a *symbolic level* of information processing. You were paying attention to a word—a meaningful unit made up of symbols—not the shape of the lines that form the letters that spell the word. You were not drawing shapes; you were reading and writing language. The skills you used to perform this task were high-level ones, but they were built on a base of adequate, lower-level perceptual skills.

Now copy the lower pattern. That is a very different task. Will one look be enough? That is, can you look at it, then reproduce it, as you did with the top pattern? Of course not.

Then what do you do in copying it if you are convinced that the task is an important one and really worth a try? You choose a place to start, a single line in the pattern. It is unimportant whether the line is at the left end, the right end, or, for that matter, somewhere in the middle. You study that line, figure out its shape, and attempt to draw it. You then focus on another line. Almost invariably this second line is one that is closely related to the first; probably one that intersects it. You then copy that second line and so on, working your way through the pattern. Each component part, each line, has to be dealt with separately; each one requires separate study and drawing. It is impossible for you to take one look, as you did with the upper pattern, and produce the copy.

This copying task calls for visual perceptual skills. You concentrate on the elements of the pattern—its parts—one at a time, figuring out as you proceed how those elements interrelate. This is not greatly different from the way many young children perform when they enter first grade and are asked to recognize and print letters and numerals. If they are not already familiar with these symbols, they will be looking at designs, and when they copy them, they will be drawing the parts, one at a time.

What are the chances that you will omit one or more elements in that lower pattern when you copy it, or misplace an element so that it ends up in a wrong position? It certainly is not unlikely, simply because of the many times you will have to look at the pattern, find your place, copy a line, look back at the pattern, and so on. It would not be surprising if you misplaced one of the lines, putting it on the left of another line when it really belonged on the right. What could cause this? Mirror vision? Is it possible that you literally saw the two lines in reverse? Of course not; you merely got lost in the detail. It would be silly to argue that this was evidence that you saw the world backward. No one does! Yet this is precisely what is often suggested when people examine and discuss the paperwork of a child with a learning problem. Many children do confuse *b*'s and *d*'s, but not because they literally see them backward. Rather, it is because either they do not accurately interpret the interrelationships of the parts that form the letters or they did not interpret these accurately when they were learning the letter names and, as a result, developed a faulty habit that persists.

Pretend that the lower pattern in figure 5, instead of being nonsense, is really a foreign language and that each separate cluster of lines represents a letter. If you were to enroll in a class that taught this language, your teacher would start to teach you to recognize these as *letters*—not as designs but as organized arrangements of lines that can be given letter names. The teacher would point out some of the distinctive features of each letter, you would observe others, and in time you would learn the letter names. No longer would you take notice of each squiggly line in each letter. You would have added to your store of school-related facts.

These individual lines could now vary quite a bit, yet the letters would still be recognizable—just as you can look at various English typefaces and never take notice of their differences. You would then be dealing with larger chunks of visual information; symbols, not designs that must be analyzed element by element. The difference, then, between perceptual and symbolic processing appears to be, at least in part, the nature of the features that are considered to be important. Perceptual processes focus on concrete sensory details—lines and the way they fit together. Symbolic processes focus on abstract information that is represented by those sensations. The latter is built on the former. Competent symbolic processes are based on competent perceptual skills.

One more step. Suppose you continue to study this foreign language. You learn to read it. You reach a point where you can read the pattern in figure 5 as a word. You learn that it says *perception.* You continue to study. You read that word in a variety of contexts. It becomes a familiar word. Once this happens, do you really look at each letter, let alone each element within each letter, as you read? No—nor should you. It would slow you down too much. Rather, you now read it as a *word;* even the precise spelling is not very important. Only when you come across a new word do you revert to paying attention to the individual letters. In fact, in time, finding misspelled words becomes a demanding job. To illustrate this, try proofreading something you have typed. Try to find errors. It is not easy to do; you have become too good a reader to focus on smaller units under normal circumstances.

The visual perceptual skills that you originally used in order to look at the pattern in some organized way have been replaced by symbolic processing skills. These enable you to function much more efficiently, to focus on—and remember—larger and more complex units of information that consist of a collection of less complex details, each of which once required your individual attention and in fact may do so again under conditions where a lower-level analysis—attention to less complex features—is called for. Your perceptual skills, though no longer employed, are still available. They can be called upon when necessary, that is, when your symbolic processing skills are inadequate to the task. Then the less efficient, lower-order perceptual skills will be put to use.

AUDITORY PERCEPTUAL SKILLS

These same concepts apply in auditory tasks. For example, say aloud the word *Massachusetts.* Difficult? Not for an average American adult who speaks the English language. You do not have to think very hard to produce the correct sounds in proper sequence. This, then, is like copying the printed word *perception.* You operate at a symbolic level in processing the information—listening to it being pronounced, recognizing it as a familiar word, and then saying it. You do not pay attention to the separate sounds. Surely, you would interpret the word correctly even if it was pronounced by someone with a southern drawl, a western twang, or a heavy French accent. Its perceptual characteristics—the separate sounds—would no longer be important.

Now think of a listening task that is analogous to copying the lower word shown in figure 5. Suppose I ask you to repeat accurately what a tobacco auctioneer says as he chants during an auction. Can you do it? Perhaps, but it is very difficult to do, even if you have excellent hearing. Why? Again, simply because the stream of sounds in that chant is too complicated, too full of details for the uninitiated. The only way you can begin to accomplish this task is by dealing with the chant one sound at a time, by analyzing the chant into its parts and figuring out how those parts—those separate sounds—are sequenced. In other words, by processing the information at a perceptual level, by using your auditory perceptual skills.

Once you have done this, repeating the auctioneer's chant will not be overly demanding, and, indeed, after some practice you will no longer be hearing or speaking his chant as segmented seminonsensical sounds. You will now be dealing with spoken language consisting of sounds that, in themselves, are not important and do not require close attention.

Some children have inadequate visual perceptual skills and adequate auditory skills, and some have the reverse problem. Some have trouble with both. It is important, therefore, to test both sets of skills. Then, based on the outcomes of these tests, you may or may not test certain general motor skills.

In addition to describing the tests you are to use with the child, I will discuss one standardized visual and one standardized auditory perceptual test frequently used by professionals. I have two reasons for doing this. First, to explain away some of the misconceptions—even mystery—that pervades this topic and add to your understanding of what perceptual skills are and why they are important. This will help you understand the child's classroom difficulties. Second, to help you see the similarity between the tests you will use and the ones that many professionals and schools use. This will help you understand the child's test scores.

TESTING VISUAL PERCEPTUAL SKILLS

Generally speaking, the best way to investigate a child's visual perceptual skills is with a copying test. There are other kinds of tests available—discrimination tests, for example—but they are not as useful to us.*

One of the better-known visual perceptual tests is the Gesell Copy Form Test. It was developed many years ago by Arnold Gesell and his coworkers at the Yale University Child Development Clinic. Gesell did not investigate school learning problems as such. He was interested in describing the various ways children change as they grow and develop from birth onward. With his Copy Form Test he showed that children are able to copy increasingly complex designs as they mature.

The test uses the seven designs shown in figure 6. Each one is presented to the child on a separate card that measures approximately 5" × 7".

The child is given an 8½" × 11" sheet of unlined paper and a pencil. He is then shown the first design, the circle, and asked to "make one like this on your paper." After he has done that, he is shown the second design, the plus sign, and asked to copy it. The designs are shown to the child one at a time until all seven have been copied.

I will not try to describe all of the things that a professional looks at in assessing the quality of the child's responses; this information is available elsewhere.**

It is sufficient, for our purposes, to know what Gesell found to be normal in terms of copying skills. His research showed that most children are able to copy a circle fairly accurately when they are about three years old. They are able to copy the plus sign somewhere between the ages of three-and-one-half to four, the square at about the age of four, the triangle somewhere around the fifth birthday, the divided rectangle at about age six, and the diamonds when they are about seven years old.

All these ages are approximate; a few months' variation is not significant. But the interesting fact is that most children do achieve these developmental milestones on schedule. As such, the test is a valid way of assessing a child's visual perceptual skills, of comparing what he can do with what is normal for

---

*Discrimination tests usually ask the child to match patterns, given an assortment from which to choose—"find the two that are the same" or "find the one that is different." In such tests, the child only needs to see differences in the patterns; he does not have to demonstrate that he understands how a specific pattern is constructed—how to break it down into its separate parts and figure out the interrelationships of those parts. Certainly you had no trouble recognizing that the two patterns in figure 5 were different. That does not mean, however, that you could copy the lower one accurately.

**A full description of this and other tests from the Gesell battery can be found in F. Ilg and L. B. Ames, *School Readiness* (New York: Harper & Row, 1964).

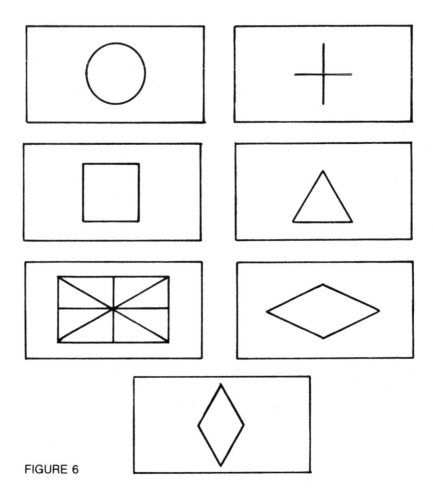

FIGURE 6

his age, that is, with what can be done by the majority of children of about the same age.

It will help to look at some examples. The four sets of drawings shown in figure 7 (reduced in size so that they all fit on the same page) were done by four different children, all about six years old. For discussion purposes we will identify them as Johnny, Jimmy, Mary, and Sue.

The drawings differ markedly. Johnny's drawings appear to be the poorest, then Jimmy's, then Mary's. Sue's are the best. What do these differences tell us? Let us study one design, the divided rectangle, and see how this varies among the four first-grade children. Figure 8 shows all four copies of the divided rectangle.

A logical first reaction could be that perhaps Johnny does not see the

Sue

Mary

Jimmy

Johnny

FIGURE 7

designs clearly enough and that Jimmy is not too much better off. Maybe this is so, but it is extremely unlikely that their very poor copying skills can be attributed to poor eyesight. However, as I pointed out earlier, this possibility should be investigated by an optometrist or ophthalmologist just to be safe.

Well, then, if it is not Johnny's eyesight, what is it? As noted, all four children are about six years old. All four have normal intelligence, which means that all four scored at least average or above on an IQ test. Maybe Johnny, despite his clear eyesight, literally sees the pattern in a distorted way? We can investigate that by showing Johnny all four patterns—his, Jimmy's, Mary's, and Sue's—along with the test pattern itself and asking him which one of the four drawings looks most like the test pattern. Almost invariably Johnny

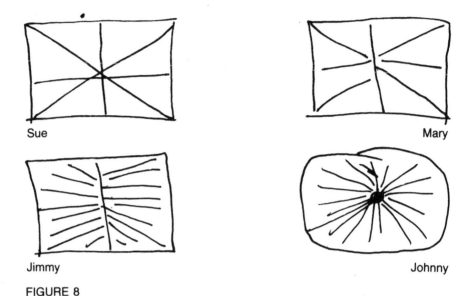

Sue

Mary

Jimmy

Johnny

FIGURE 8

will choose Sue's—the one that *is* the best copy—not his own. (That is why discrimination tests are so much less useful to us.) If this happens, then he really does not see a distorted pattern, even though the one he drew was quite distorted.

What else could be causing his trouble? Maybe it is because of his poor motor skills; maybe he cannot control a pencil adequately? We can reject that idea, since he satisfactorily drew the plus sign, which contains a vertical and a horizontal line, and he drew the diagonals of the triangle fairly accurately. Hence, he was able to draw all the lines of this design when they occurred in simpler designs. No, poor motor control does not explain his problem either.

In order to help you understand Johnny's inadequate responses, imagine the following task: Go into the park on a pleasant day in June and find a section of healthy lawn. Mark off one square foot of that thriving lawn and *copy* it, showing each blade of grass as it actually appears in its correct position and exact size.

Could you do it? No, there are just too many blades of grass. You are bound to omit some, misplace some, draw some too large or too small. The fact that you cannot accomplish this task is not surprising; no one could. And since no one can do it, no one else will design a lesson based on the assumption that you can deal with that much detail. Thus it is not a problem.

But most of Johnny's classmates, if they are in the first grade or higher, *can* copy the divided rectangle fairly accurately, which means that they can analyze it into its separate parts and recognize the interrelationships of those parts. That is, they can see it as a rectangle containing a vertical, a horizontal, and two diagonal lines; and they can also see how these parts fit together.

What can we say about the other three children? Jimmy's drawing shows that he is starting to analyze the pattern into its parts, but he is doing it rather poorly. He gets the rectangle and the vertical line, but that is about it for him. Mary is analyzing the parts accurately. That is, she draws the correct number of lines, but she is having trouble with the interrelationships. Sue is doing both tasks accurately—analyzing the parts and organizing them accurately. Hence hers is the best.

Skills for Learning Letters and Numerals

Since most of Johnny's classmates can manage that amount and type of detail and he cannot, he has a problem. They will be able to meet the demands of certain classroom tasks; he will not. For example, look at these letters:

m   n

How do they differ? Only in that the *m* has one more hump than the *n*. To recognize this difference, so obvious to anyone who is already familiar with the lowercase letters, you have to be able to analyze both letters into their separate parts. As you identify and compare the parts, the difference between the letters is apparent. If you were unable to isolate these individual parts—as is probably the case with Johnny—the differences would not be very evident. The humps would not be quantifiable. It is very difficult to count what you cannot sort out.

But breaking patterns down into their parts is only part of the picture. How about the additional task of recognizing the way those parts fit together? Consider these letters:

b   d   p   q

How do they differ? In each case, there are the same number of parts, and the parts are identical. It is only in how the parts are combined—their organization—that makes the difference. Again, then, visual perceptual skills of a certain level are required.

Look at yet another example:

a   d

Here, one of the two component parts of each of the letters differs, while the other one does not. Both letters contain a circle. However, the vertical line of the *a* is appreciably shorter than the vertical line of the *d*. Once more, it is the child's visual perceptual skills that enable him to identify this difference.

Recognizing the letters is important, but there are other reasons why visual perceptual skills are important to the elementary-school-aged child. After all, the letters of the alphabet are not that complex; they do not contain a great number of parts nor are the interrelationships of the parts that unique. True, there are certain pairs of letters that mirror each other, thus adding a confusing dimension. But there are not very many of these, and straightforward instruction and practice can usually get the child past this point of confusion.

Skills for Arithmetic

It is in sequential reasoning tasks, such as adding, subtracting, multiplying, and dividing, that visual perceptual skills are truly fundamental. I already made the point that if the child has trouble analyzing a visual pattern into its separate parts, he will also have trouble counting those parts accurately. To learn arithmetic, a child must be able to count objects accurately. Beginning counting skills are based on first being able to count aloud in correct sequence, starting with 1, and second, being able to coordinate that oral counting with whatever is being counted. Thus if the child is shown four objects and asked to count them, he characteristically touches each object in some order while reciting the sequence of numbers from 1 to 4. His understanding of the total quantity will be based on the last number he says aloud as he touches the final object. If his visual perceptual skills are poor—if he does not view the collection of objects as finite—he cannot view them as organized. Counting them, then, will be a random activity, where some objects may be counted more than once while others may be completely overlooked. That is one reason why visual perceptual skills are important in learning arithmetic.

There is yet one more way that visual perceptual skills relate to arithmetic. Numerals are used not only to represent quantity; they are also used to represent relationships. Not only must the child learn very early in his school career that the 1 stands for one object, the 2 for two objects, and so forth, he must also quickly catch on to the fact that certain quantities are both a *specific* and a *relative* amount larger or smaller than other quantities. Look at figure 9.

This is a typical first-grade arithmetic problem. What must the child do to complete this task? He must count the objects in the first box and record that amount (that is, print a number 2) on the line below the first box. He repeats this activity with the second box, recording a 4 on the appropriate line. Now he must draw the correct number of circles in the right-hand answer box and write the appropriate numeral, 6, below it. We have already discussed the importance of adequate visual perceptual skills for this task.

But there is something else he should see—namely, that there is a fixed *relationship* between the number of objects in each of the boxes. Thus if he is now asked to solve the problem $4+4=?$, he will not have to start counting from 1 again. He will be able to reason that since 4 is two more than 2, then $4+4$ must equal 8, two more than 6. In time he will see another relationship between these quantities, that 4 is *two* times $(2\times)$ 2, and 8 is two times $(2\times)$ 4. Then multiplication and division will start to make sense and remembering

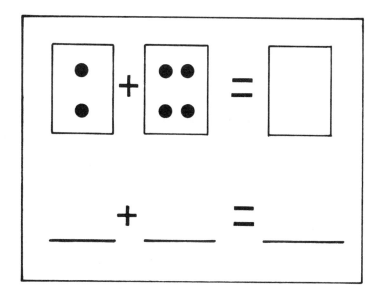

FIGURE 9

number facts will become easier.

Recognizing the dual function of numerals—that they may be used to represent both quantity and relationships—is very confusing to the child whose visual perceptual skills are less than satisfactory. In time he will learn to count accurately. But recognizing relationships? That is something else again. It is an elusive concept, yet one that is critical to understanding arithmetic as an orderly, systematic approach to describing absolute and relative quantity. Until the child acquires this ability, each arithmetic problem will be a new one. The fact that after much effort he has just solved $7 \times 7 = ?$ will not facilitate his solving $8 \times 7 = ?$. The only way he will be able to solve the second problem is by starting over again from the very beginning. He will not recognize its relationship to the first problem. You can imagine what a burden this gets to be by about the fourth grade, when most of his classmates have come to see these relationships among numbers and are able to apply the concepts in their daily arithmetic class.

Skills for Reading Comprehension

There is another reason why visual perceptual skills are important in school. This one is general, relating to all subject areas, although it probably is more closely linked to reading comprehension than to anything else. Reading for meaning requires the child to translate the letters on the printed page into language that has meaning, not just words. To gain meaning from that language, he has to organize the information he reads so that he can remember it long enough to associate it with other information. Remembering and associating information is exceptionally difficult unless it is properly organized. The child who reads words and tries to remember the text verbatim, so that he can repeat it upon request, is not likely to remember very much after a single reading, nor will he understand very much beyond the actual facts that are specifically stated in the text.

In other words, when the child reads a story that, say, involves people, animals, objects, and events, he is more likely to remember the central theme of that story if he classifies the information—sorts it out and organizes it—as he reads it. This classification strategy may simply be according to who or what in the story is a person, animal, object, event, and what they encounter. Or it may be according to a time sequence—what happened first, what happened next, and so on. Or it may be according to certain relationships—a boy and his pet, another boy and his pet, and so on. The point is that the strategy will vary from situation to situation, and the child, as he reads, must be able to classify the information in a variety of ways in order to meet those varying conditions.

One way of describing the child with inadequate visual perceptual skills is in terms of his substandard ability to classify information. Since he does not sort out and relate concrete information as readily as most of his classmates, he will not comprehend as well, even if he does know how to read all the words in the text.

The Test of Visual Analysis Skills (TVAS) —A Test You Can Administer

There are, as I mentioned, a number of visual perceptual tests on the market. Most of them are easy to administer. However, I am going to describe only one—the Test of Visual Analysis Skills (TVAS). This is a new test that will work well for you.

The TVAS is, in fact, more than a test. If you find that the child's visual perceptual skills are inadequate, it will also serve to define the goals for his instructional program. You will teach him to "pass the test."

That is a unique feature of the TVAS. Virtually every standardized test becomes invalid if you set about teaching the child to pass it. For example, if you intentionally set out to teach the child to copy a diamond, you will probably succeed. He will learn how to copy a diamond. But you certainly cannot infer from that accomplishment that he has also learned the underlying processes called for in copying all shapes of that complexity. Just because a child learns to copy a diamond, and copying a diamond is something expected of seven-year-olds, does not indicate that he has acquired the visual perceptual skills of the average seven-year-old.

The opposite is true with the TVAS. As you teach the child to pass the test, you will be teaching him underlying processes—perceptual skills. But more about that later on. Right now, let us look at how you can test your child's visual perceptual skills.

Preparing materials for the TVAS

First you must construct the test materials. Here is how:

1. Make *two copies* each of the 5-dot, the 9-dot, and the 25-dot maps shown below. Your maps should be the same size as the ones shown here. This is easily done by placing a sheet of unlined 8½" × 11" writing paper directly over a map and tracing it; or you may photocopy them.

2. Insert each of the six maps in a separate transparent plastic page protector, which you can purchase at most office supply stores. The page protectors will enable you to reuse the maps indefinitely.

3. Obtain two dark-colored wax crayons. You and the child will use these to draw on the plastic page protectors that are covering the maps. These lines are easily erased with facial tissue.

4. You are almost ready. You still need two more maps; a 17-dot one and a 0-dot one. Both are shown on page 33. Trace or photocopy

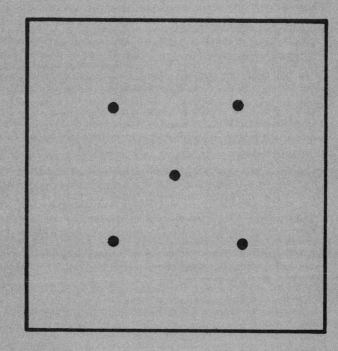

5-DOT MAP

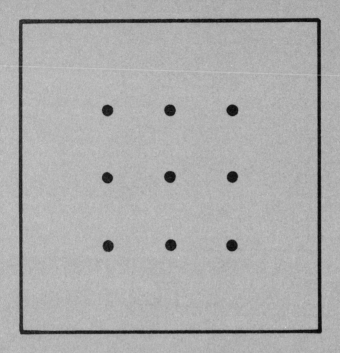

9-DOT MAP

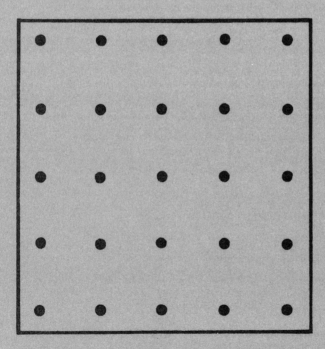

25-DOT MAP

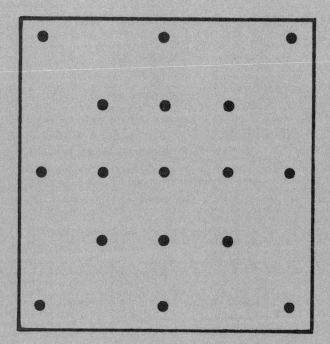

17-DOT MAP

0-DOT MAP

these just as you did the others, each one on a separate 8½" × 11" sheet of paper, and place both of these maps in plastic page protectors.

Giving the TVAS

Now you are ready to start testing. The test involves copying designs. You draw test patterns neatly on one map; the child must copy them on his map. Once a design is completed, erase the crayon lines with a facial tissue and proceed to the next pattern. The patterns are relatively easy at the start and become progressively more difficult. *Stop testing when the child makes errors on two successive patterns.*

The test items are shown in the pages that follow. Look at the first map. This test item shows a design drawn on one 5-dot map and another 5-dot map on which no lines have been drawn. You copy the test design neatly on one of your plastic-covered 5-dot maps—*out of the child's sight.* Then give the child the other plastic-covered 5-dot map and a crayon, and say to him, "Make your map look like mine. Draw the lines on your map so that it looks just like mine."

To be scored as correct, his drawing must have the right number of lines *and* they must be located on the proper dots. If he omits or adds a line, or if he locates a line on the wrong dots, score the item as incorrect. Although he should be encouraged to draw his lines neatly, that is not a critical factor. Accuracy is what counts. However, if one or more of his lines miss the dots, and you cannot tell whether he copied inaccurately or was merely being sloppy, have him do it over again, instructing him, "Make sure you connect your lines to the correct dots."

Do not coach him. This is a test, and although you want him to do well, it is essential that he be able to copy the designs without assistance. Remember, you are testing him to find out if he has learned the skills he needs in order to succeed in school. You will use this test information when you set about teaching him the skills he does not know. Hence, you want accurate information. You will not be doing him a favor if you help him or if you overlook his errors. You will be fooling yourself and denying him the important knowledge that he can acquire from being taught the skills he currently lacks.

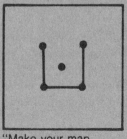

ITEM 1

"Make your map look like this"

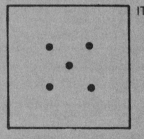

Child's map

Item 1 gives the first test design. Remember, you are to copy the test design on your map, out of the child's view. Then have him copy your drawing on his map.

Now check his work. Did he draw the correct number of lines? Are the lines positioned on the proper dots? Make a note of whether his copy was correct or incorrect, erase both your design and his, and go on to the test design in item 2. Be noncommittal with the child about his performance. Say words such as "okay" rather than "right" or "wrong."

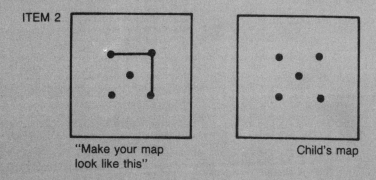

ITEM 2

"Make your map
look like this"

Child's map

Score this one as either correct or incorrect and go on to item 3.

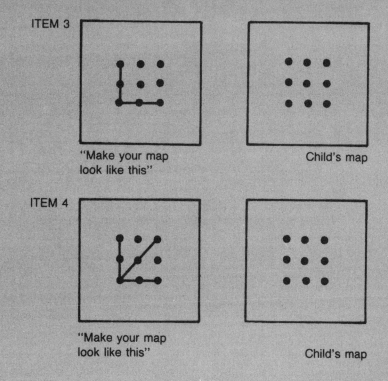

ITEM 3

"Make your map
look like this"

Child's map

ITEM 4

"Make your map
look like this"

Child's map

In the item 3 test you are to use a 9-dot map, but the instructions and scoring procedure are exactly the same as before. Once you have scored it, go on to the test designs in items 4 and 5. Remember, stop testing when the child is incorrect on *two successive* patterns. And when you end the testing, do it with some nonpunishing remark such as, "That's enough *for now.*" Do not fail him with your words or your actions.

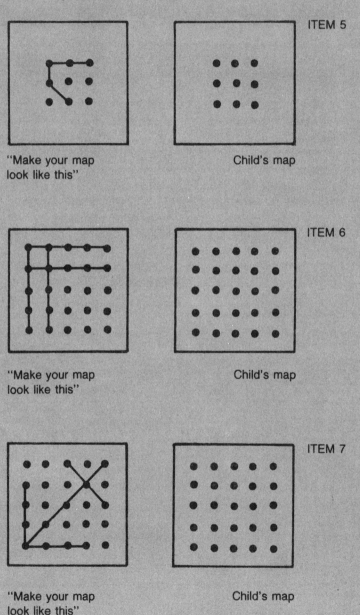

ITEM 5

"Make your map look like this"

Child's map

ITEM 6

"Make your map look like this"

Child's map

ITEM 7

"Make your map look like this"

Child's map

Now you are to start using the 25-dot maps (see items 6 through 9), unless the child has already committed two successive errors, in which case you are done testing. Again, the instructions to the child and the scoring procedure remain the same.

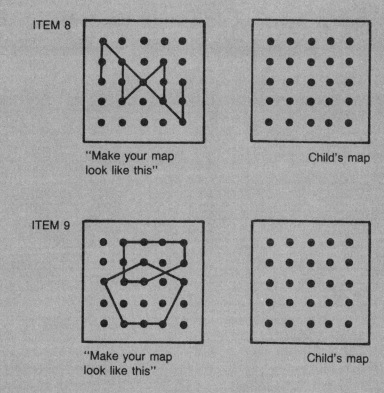

ITEM 8

"Make your map look like this"

Child's map

ITEM 9

"Make your map look like this"

Child's map

Now a small change is necessary in the instructions you give the child. Look at item 10.

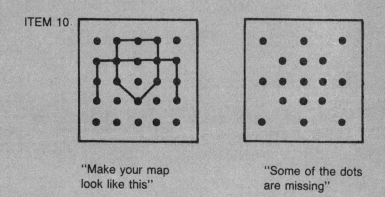

ITEM 10

"Make your map look like this"

"Some of the dots are missing"

With this item, say to the child, *"Some* of the dots are missing on your map. Don't draw in the dots. Just pretend they are there. Draw the lines on your map *as though* the dots were there." To score this, you too must pretend the dots are there and determine whether the child drew the correct number of lines and whether he positioned them in their proper places. If he did, fine. Give him credit for being correct. If he did not, note it as incorrect and move on to item 11—unless this is his second consecutive error, in which case, of course, you should stop testing.

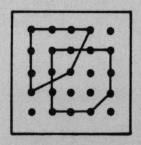

"Make your map
look like this"

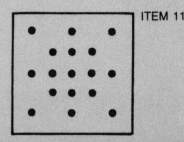

ITEM 11

"Some of the dots
are missing"

The instructions to the child for items 11 through 16 are the same as for item 10. Notice that more of the dots are missing. Score them as described in item 10.

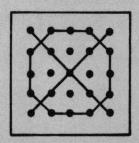

"Make your map
look like this"

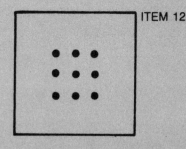

ITEM 12

"Some of the dots
are missing"

The instructions again change slightly for the last two items of the test, items 17 and 18. Now you say to the child, *"All* of the dots are missing on your map. Don't draw the dots. Just pretend they are there. Draw the lines *as though* the dots were there." Scoring is the same. If all the lines are copied

ITEM 13

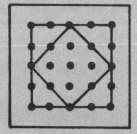

"Make your map
look like this"

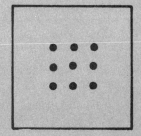

"Some of the dots
are missing"

ITEM 14

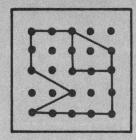

"Make your map
look like this"

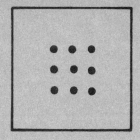

"Some of the dots
are missing"

ITEM 15

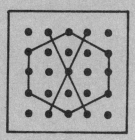

"Make your map
look like this"

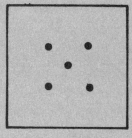

"Some of the dots
are missing"

ITEM 16

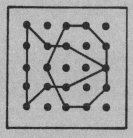

"Make your map
look like this"

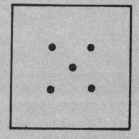

"Some of the dots
are missing"

and if they are positioned correctly (as though the dots were there), give him credit for a correct. If he leaves out one or more lines, or if he places any of the lines in the wrong position, score it as incorrect.

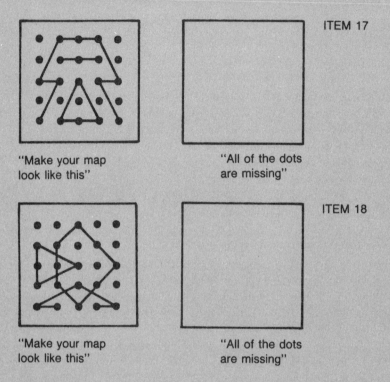

ITEM 17

"Make your map look like this"

"All of the dots are missing"

ITEM 18

"Make your map look like this"

"All of the dots are missing"

That is the end of the test if, indeed, he has lasted this long. Before I tell you how to interpret his performance, I will show you some examples of test responses and how they were scored. It might help prevent some confusion.

Shown on the pattern maps below are four responses, labeled A, B, C, and D.

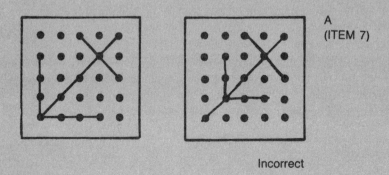

A
(ITEM 7)

Incorrect

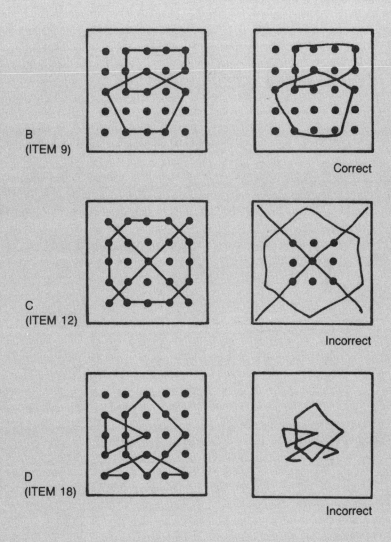

B
(ITEM 9)

Correct

C
(ITEM 12)

Incorrect

D
(ITEM 18)

Incorrect

"A" shows a child's incorrect response to test item 7. Can you see why it is incorrect? All of the lines are there, but some are positioned on the wrong dots. "B" is a correct response to item 9. All the lines are there, and even though they are not drawn precisely, it is obvious that the child was able to identify all the lines and their proper positions on the map. "C" is an incorrect response to item 12. Although all the lines are there, some are positioned incorrectly—you have to pretend the dots are there when you assess the child's performance. Finally look at "D". It is an incorrect response to item 18 because it, too, is not positioned properly—even though all the lines are there and the shape is drawn correctly.

Interpreting the test results

Scoring these items is not that confusing if you will keep in mind what is being tested—the child's ability to analyze a pattern into its separate parts, to read a map of dots, and to construct a map even after most of its landmarks (dots) are removed. The border is one of the landmarks, of course.

Now you have to determine whether the child's performance is adequate for his grade level. What is the last item he copied correctly before he produced two incorrects in succession? That is his score on the TVAS. For example, suppose he copied items 1, 2, 3, and 4 correctly, but was incorrect on items 5 and 6. His TVAS score would be 4. Try another; suppose he copied items 1, 2, and 3 correctly, was incorrect on 4, correct again on 5 and 6, and incorrect on items 7 and 8. The test ends here (2 incorrects in a row). His TVAS score would be 6.

Relate his TVAS score to this chart:

TVAS Score	Expected for Children In:
1	Preschool
2	Preschool
3	Kindergarten
4	Kindergarten
5	Kindergarten
6	Kindergarten
7	Kindergarten
8	Grade 1
9	Grade 1
10	Grade 1
11	Grade 2
12	Grade 2
13	Grade 2
14	Grade 2
15	Grade 2
16	Grade 2
17	Grade 3
18	Grade 3

To read the chart, find the child's score in the left-hand column. Opposite that number is the grade level of children who customarily earn this score on the TVAS. For example, if the child's score is 5, we would expect him to be in kindergarten. If, in fact, he is in kindergarten, you can assume that his visual perceptual skills are normal. If he is only in preschool, he is probably precocious. If, on the other hand, he is in first grade or beyond, you can assume that his visual perceptual skills are below the expected level and are contributing to his school learning problem.

A score of 10 would be satisfactory for a child in the first grade or below. If he is in a higher grade, his performance on the TVAS would be considered substandard.

As you can see from the chart, no item in the TVAS—not even the final two—should be too difficult for a child in the third grade or above. If it is, it again indicates inadequate visual perceptual skills.

Many people ask whether there should not be some more difficult items —items that would challenge sixth- and seventh-graders, for example. The answer is no, it is not called for. Once a child can respond accurately to the final items on this test, his visual perceptual skills are as good as they need be. That does not mean that a child who completed all the items of the TVAS could not be having difficulty in analyzing and organizing relatively complex spatial patterns. He could, indeed. But such a child will be better served if you deal with his problem in the subject areas themselves—reading, spelling, arithmetic, and writing—rather than by trying to teach him more elaborate perceptual skills. I will tell you how to do that later on.

What next? If the child's performance with the TVAS is not at an expected level, make a note of what he did score. We will discuss what to do about it in the next section. Right now move on to testing auditory skills.

TESTING AUDITORY PERCEPTUAL SKILLS

There are a variety of ways to test auditory perceptual skills, just as there are for testing visual perceptual skills. Most of these are auditory discrimination tests. In an auditory discrimination test the child is told to listen to a pair of spoken words that may or may not be identical, and he is then asked to say whether they are the same or different. For example, the pair *win-when* is stated by the examiner, and the child is expected to say, "Different." If the pair is *win-win,* the correct answer is, "Same."

Auditory discrimination tests have been used extensively with children from about five years of age and up, and some relationship has been shown between children's performance on this test and their reading achievement. I have two complaints about such tests. First, they require *only* a discrimination response; once the child recognizes that the two words differ, he need not analyze them further. He does not have to show that he knows how to analyze the whole spoken word down into its separate parts—individual sounds known as phonemes—and that he recognizes how those phonemes fit together, their sequence. Second, teaching a child to pass an auditory discrimination test does not appear to have any great value in helping him learn to read.

Skills for Reading

What does the child with inadequate auditory perceptual skills experience in the classroom? It is analogous, in a way, to a task I described earlier—copying a square foot of grass lawn. Consider the following (imagine that I am speaking to you orally, rather than through the medium of this printed page): "Please listen to this phrase and write it down *exactly* the way I say it. In other words, show me how you heard what I said, and do it in a way that represents my spoken message exactly. The phrase is *'I like you.'* I'll repeat it; *'I like you.'* Write that down exactly the way I said it."

Whenever I use this illustration, I invariably get the written answer "I like you." But what I literally said was *"ilikeyou,"* not pausing at all between the words. Was the conventional answer wrong? No. We all follow these rules when we put spoken language on paper. The rules say—and you were taught them so long ago that you no longer think about them—that when we represent speech with print, we must use certain organizational devices: small spaces to separate the individual letters within a word and larger spaces to separate the words; capital letters to indicate the start of a sentence, a period to signal its end, and a comma or some other punctuation device to separate clauses. A second line of print ordinarily parallels the first and is positioned a certain distance below; all lines of print start at the same place on the left side of the page—in other words, there is a margin. All these rules help the reader obtain information efficiently from the printed page. They are important rules. Imagine how difficult itwouldbetoreadfrompagesthatlookedlikethis.

We do not apply the same rules when we speak. Although we will pause between certain clusters of words (if only to breathe), we do not pause between each word. Indeed, who could tolerate us, let alone pay attention, if we did? It would be extremely dull, and, worse yet, the listener would be very likely to forget the first part of the sentence before the last part was spoken. This point is important. Visual information is relatively permanent. It stays visible as long as whoever is in charge allows it to remain in view. Acoustical information—spoken words—becomes inaudible immediately. There is no time to waste; if the listener cannot organize the information rapidly, he is bound to encounter difficulty.

To make matters worse, we all tend to use different speaking styles. Some of us talk fast, some drawl, some speak in long sentences, some in short sentences; all of which serves to place additional burdens on the listener. We assume that the listener will be able to deal with the job of organizing the sounds into proper clusters—a reasonable assumption if the listener not only knows all the words but knows them well enough to sort them out and keep them ordered as they are spoken in a continuous stream.

If you studied a foreign language for a few years while in school, try to imagine what this would be like: Say your foreign language was French and that you have a fair background in the language. Imagine that you are tuned to a French-language radio station and that you are trying to translate what the speaker is saying. It is challenging, to say the least, even though you may know every word that is being said. Being able to translate individual words is not equivalent to dealing with them in the context of oral language. When someone speaks rapidly, the task of translating becomes exceedingly demanding. Think, for example, of the old song "mareseatoatsanddoeseatoats, etc." —a long string of nonsense sounds until the sounds are sorted out and organized into meaningful words. Find someone who is unfamiliar with that song and ask him to memorize the first few lines. Difficult, to be sure. There are a lot of sounds to memorize. Now, speak the phrase, "mares-eat-oats, etc." so that each word is stated separately rather than run together. Memorizing would now be much easier. There are far fewer words than sounds, and to help matters, the words are meaningful.

Now back to the child with an auditory perceptual problem. Ordinarily he can hear as well as anyone else—although, by all means, have his hearing checked. Also in most instances he can identify the separate words in spoken language; if he has difficulty remembering what he is told, check his *visual* perceptual skills. His auditory perceptual skills deficit usually shows up in the fine-grained analysis of spoken words into phonemes, that is, sorting out the individual sounds within a spoken word. It is not difficult to see how this relates to reading. After all, what is involved in learning to read? Certainly the child must learn to discriminate the letters of the alphabet, to recognize them as distinctly different symbols, and to remember their individual identities. But he must do more. He must learn to relate sounds to these letters, that is, to attach certain specific spoken sounds to certain specific printed letters or combinations of letters.

It is true that some children learn to read by remembering whole words as "pictures" of a sort, rather than by "sounding them out." Such words are called sight words, and they are usually learned as units—memorized—since they cannot be sounded out very well. For example, the words *said* and *the*. But there is a limit to how many sight words a child can remember, and, even with sight words, certain key letters and their related sounds make remembering them a great deal easier. One cannot memorize the entire printed language.

This, of course, was the basis for the "Look—Say" method of teaching reading.* Indeed, a lot of children did learn to read with that method, but they certainly did not memorize all of the words as separate units. They had capable perceptual skills. They learned on their own and applied that system as they encountered more words.

Could the child have done this if he was not able to analyze spoken words into their individual sounds? Hardly! You have to recognize the elements that

*This and other methods of teaching reading are discussed thoroughly in the section of this book entitled "Teaching Reading."

are to be coded before you can use the code. This, then, is why capable auditory perceptual skills are vital to beginning readers. No teacher managing a classroom of twenty-five or more children can take the time to teach every letter-sound rule to every child, no matter how well trained and motivated the teacher might be. The children must discover some of the rules on their own or at least understand the concept—"get it"—the first or second time it is presented to them. If their auditory skills are such that they cannot readily isolate the individual sounds *within a spoken word,* the probability of their understanding the concept of letters standing for sounds is quite low.

Thus auditory perceptual skills are important because they make it possible for the child to be aware of the individual sounds that will be represented by letters when he starts to learn to read and spell. As such, he is more apt to recognize the system upon which reading and spelling are based. That is enough for now. We will examine all of this more thoroughly later on, in the sections devoted specifically to reading and spelling.

The Test of Auditory Analysis Skills (TAAS) —A Test You Can Administer

The Test of Auditory Analysis Skills (TAAS) is a mate to the TVAS. In fact, it was designed with the same general goals in mind—that is, not only to provide a way for testing a child's auditory perceptual skills but also to identify goals for teaching these skills. The child can be taught to pass the test, and the effects of the teaching will be apparent elsewhere—most important to us, in his reading and spelling.

First, I will give you a general description of what the test is about. Then I will describe the test itself. Later on I will tell you how you can teach the child the skills he needs to pass the test.

The TAAS starts at a relatively simple level; it can be used with kindergarten children. For example, the child is asked to analyze a two-syllable, compound word into syllables. He is told, "Say *baseball.*" Then, "Now say it again, but don't say *ball,*" or, "don't say *base.*" He is to say only what remains, once he has located and deleted the part of the word designated by the tester. Then three-syllable words are used. For example, the child is told, "Say *cucumber.*" Then, "Now say it again, but don't say *cue.*"

Once the child shows that he can deal with this task at the syllable level, he is confronted with a more refined unit of analysis—the phoneme—the single sound. For example, he may be told, "Say *meat;* now say it again, but don't say the /m/ sound."* To respond correctly, he must search for the /m/ sound

---

*When a letter is shown between slashes, /m/, for example, you are to say the letter *sound* "mmm," not the letter name "em"; for /s/, say "sss," not "ess"; for /r/, say "rrr," not "are."

in the word *meat,* delete it, and say what is left *(eat).* The position of the sound is controlled, starting with the easiest (the beginning sound as in the above example), then the final sound ("Say *wrote;* now say it again without the /t/ sound"), then part of a consonant blend ("Say *play;* now say it again, but don't say the /p/ sound"; or, "Say *stale;* now say it again, but don't say the /t/ sound").

Giving the TAAS

The test starts off with two demonstration items that are intended to show the child what he is expected to do. The first (item A) goes like this: "Say *cowboy.*" (Now pause and allow him to respond. This lets you know that he heard the word.) Then say: "Now say it again but don't say *boy.*" Give him time to respond. (The correct answer, of course, is *cow.*)

If he gets this one correct, move on to the second demonstration item. If he does not get item A correct, see if you can explain it to him. But if it requires more than a simple explanation, stop testing.

The second demonstration item (item B) is "Say *steamboat.*" (Pause—wait for his response.) "Now say it again, but don't say *steam.*"

If he answers both demonstration items correctly, start the test with item 1. If he does not answer both demonstration items correctly, do not administer any more items.

FIGURE 10

Item	Question	Correct Response
A Say **cowboy**	Now say it again, but don't say **boy**	cow
B Say **steamboat**	Now say it again, but don't say **steam**	boat
1 Say **sunshine**	Now say it again, but don't say **shine**	sun
2 Say **picnic**	Now say it again, but don't say **pic**	nic
3 Say **cucumber**	Now say it again, but don't say **cu (q)**	cumber
4 Say **coat**	Now say it again, but don't say /k/ (the **k** sound)	oat
5 Say **meat**	Now say it again, but don't say /m/ (the **m** sound)	eat
6 Say **take**	Now say it again, but don't say /t/ (the **t** sound)	ache
7 Say **game**	Now say it again, but don't say /m/	gay
8 Say **wrote**	Now say it again, but don't say /t/	row
9 Say **please**	Now say it again, but don't say /z/	plea
10 Say **clap**	Now say it again, but don't say /k/	lap
11 Say **play**	Now say it again, but don't say /p/	lay
12 Say **stale**	Now say it again, but don't say /t/	sale
13 Say **smack**	Now say it again, but don't say /m/	sack

NOTE:

Do not give him hints with your lips. Speak distinctly, but do not stress any particular sounds. In other words, do not give him any additional information that might make the task easier. Sure, you want him to do well, but not at the expense of looking better on the test than he really is. The results would be misleading and deprive him of the chance to learn the skills needed for reading and spelling. Just as with the TVAS, this test gives you a way to determine if the child's auditory skills are up to the demands of his classroom instructional program, what skills he already knows, and which ones he should learn next.

Remember, when you get to the items that ask the child to "Say the word, but don't say /. . ./ [a single sound]" you are to say the sound of the letter, *not the letter name.*

Stop testing after two successive errors—*two incorrects in a row*—and record the number of the last correct item before those two errors. That is his TAAS score. For example, if he was correct with items 1, 2, 3, 4, and 5, then incorrect on items 6 and 7, his TAAS score would be 5. If he was correct on 1, 2, and 3, incorrect on 4, correct on 5 and 6, then incorrect on 7 and 8, his TAAS score would be 6.

Interpreting the test results

That is the end of the test—if he has lasted this long.

Now you have to determine whether the child's performance was adequate for his grade level. Make note of his score—the last item he answered correctly before he produced two wrong answers in succession—and relate it to the following chart.

To read the chart, locate the child's score in the left-hand column. Opposite that number is the grade level of children who customarily earn this score. For example, if the child's score is 3, we would expect him to be in kindergarten. If he is in kindergarten, you can assume that his auditory perceptual skills are normal. If he is in preschool, he is probably precocious. If, on the other hand, he is in first grade or beyond, you can assume that his auditory perceptual skills are inadequate and, as such, are contributing to his school learning problem.

What if his score is 9? Then his auditory perceptual skills can be considered satisfactory if he is in the first grade or below. If he is in a higher grade, his performance on the TAAS is to be considered substandard.

As you can see from the chart, no item in the TAAS—not even the final ones—should be too difficult for a child in the third grade or above. If it is, it again indicates inadequate auditory perceptual skills.

TAAS Score	Expected for Children In:
1	Kindergarten
2	Kindergarten
3	Kindergarten
4	Grade 1
5	Grade 1
6	Grade 1
7	Grade 1
8	Grade 1
9	Grade 1
10	Grade 2
11	Grade 2
12	Grade 3
13	Grade 3

Just as with visual perceptual skills, many people are interested in finding auditory perceptual skills tests that are difficult enough to challenge older children—fifth- and sixth-graders, for example. In my judgment, this is not worthwhile. It would be possible to construct such a test, but there would be little practical value in it. Children who can pass all the items on the TAAS could perhaps still have some discrete auditory perceptual problem. But such children will be better served if you deal with their problem as it is revealed in the subject areas—reading and spelling—rather than by teaching elaborate auditory perceptual skills. After all, your goal is satisfactory classroom achievement, not superior perceptual skills.

Now what? If the child's performance with the TAAS is not at an expected level, make a note of what he scores. We will discuss what to do about it in the next section. Right now, move on to testing general motor skills.

GENERAL MOTOR SKILLS

So far very little mention has been made of general motor skills. What are they? Are they important? Should they be tested? By whom? How do they fit into what has already been discussed?

General motor skills have been associated with learning problems for some time. In fact, when professionals first became aware of the child with a learning disability, the major treatment methods emphasized motor training activities that helped the child become better coordinated. As time passed, it became clear that good motor skills, in themselves, were not the answer. We all know too many beautifully coordinated illiterates and too many clumsy geniuses to support that position.

It is true that many children with learning problems do display poor motor coordination, but there is little evidence that the one is the direct cause of the other. In a way, then, emphasizing motor skills is much the same as centering on such symptoms as distractibility and hyperactivity. Helping a child improve his motor skills and doing nothing else for him will not solve his learning problems.

Then, why test motor skills? Earlier in this book I observed that testing is justified only when it provides information that will help you make better decisions about how to help your child. We test general motor skills because although they are not *directly* linked to school achievement, they are related to the higher-level perceptual skills just discussed—visual and auditory analysis and organization abilities.

To explain that relationship appropriately, we will now look at how all these skills develop. This is of more than theoretical interest, for you will be identifying certain basic principles that can be applied in all of your subsequent work with the child. Then I will describe the general motor tests that he should take.

The Relationship of Perceptual Skills to Motor Development

No child is born with the skills that he will ultimately need in order to succeed in school. If he is lucky, he is born with the proper equipment—eyes, ears, hands, voice, and an intact nervous system that, in time, will be able to control that equipment efficiently. It is predictable that if these two conditions are met and nothing else occurs to interrupt normal development, he will acquire the skills necessary for school success. He is human and therefore genetically programmed to develop much the same as the rest of the members of the species. The big question, however, is, Will he acquire the skills on schedule, in accord with society's expectations? In other words, we know that he will enter the first grade sometime near his sixth birthday. Will his skills be ready for the task? How ready they will be is a function of his growth and development. It is an interaction between what he was endowed with at conception and the environment in which he spends his early years, the condition of his equipment at birth and how well he learns to use that equipment.

There are two general rules of development that apply throughout this discussion. The first is that all developed abilities are quite global—inseparable —when the child is very young, and after a period of time they become increasingly differentiated—sorted out. The second rule to bear in mind is that as children develop, they require less tangible confirmation of what they see and hear in order to analyze and organize it. That is, as they grow and accumulate experiences, it is not as important for them to touch what they see in order to be certain about the construction of what they are seeing nor to repeat what they hear in order to confirm the construction of the sounds they are hearing.

Gross-motor development

I will illustrate what is meant by the first rule—that all developed abilities are global at first and get more differentiated as the child matures. Think of the gross-motor actions of the newborn. He responds reflexively to stimuli in the environment; that is, he does not voluntarily control his actions. If you lay him on his back with his head turned to one side, he will assume a position called the tonic neck reflex. The arm and leg on the side toward which his head is turned will be extended; the opposite arm and leg will be flexed.

If the child's head turns or is turned to the other side, both arms and legs will shift position accordingly. The arm and leg that were extended will flex. The arm and leg on the opposite side will extend. It is evidence of the global nature of the infant's motor system; he does not move one part of himself without making some compensatory or balancing movements in the rest of his body. He has yet to learn that he is made up of a number of movable parts, many of which he will ultimately be able to control separately and precisely.

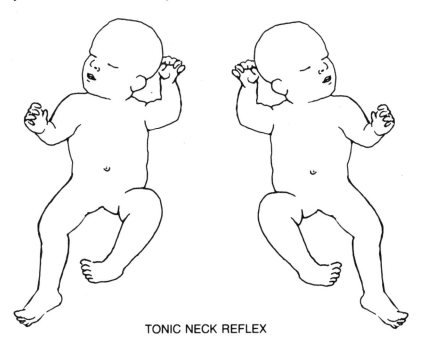

TONIC NECK REFLEX

Sometime around his sixteenth week of life this reflexive posture disappears, replaced by another that allows him a little more freedom of movement. Now he is able to move certain parts of himself—his arms, for instance—

without moving all of himself. As time passes, he continues to develop, learning to roll over at will, to sit up, creep, and stand with some support.

By the time of his first birthday he displays greater differentiation of his general motor skills. He is able to reorganize his body parts in a broader variety of ways. He is probably able to walk, with some support. In some cases he might even be able to walk without support, although this is not necessarily expected at this time in his life.

He has made obvious progress along the pathway of growth and development—learning differentiated control of his own body movements. But he has not yet reached the point where he can balance on one foot, hop on one foot, or skip. These will occur somewhere between his third and sixth birthday; he will learn to balance on one foot; awhile after that he will learn to hop on one foot; and ordinarily he will learn to skip during his kindergarten year.

What is so important about all this? First-grade teachers are concerned about teaching children to read, print, count; yet a knowledgeable first-grade teacher is not pleased when she observes that a child is poorly coordinated, that he cannot hop on each foot, for instance. The awkward child, the one who is poorly coordinated, is immature. Intuitively or otherwise, his teacher recognizes this and knows that it is not a good sign.

Most teachers know that if a child is immature in one aspect of his behavior, he is probably immature in others as well. Each of the behaviors I mentioned—early reflexive postures, sitting up, standing, walking, balancing on one foot, hopping on one foot, skipping, and others—show that the child is learning to understand his own body construction as a collection of separate parts that work together in a variety of ways. They are milestones in his development.

MOTOR DEVELOPMENT MILESTONES

Approximate Age	Motor Action
60 months	Skips
50 months	Hops on one foot
32 months	Balances on one foot
15 months	Walks unaided
14 months	Stands unaided
7 months	Sits up unaided
4 months	Rolls over unaided
0-4 months	Tonic neck reflex

There is an expected date when most children achieve these milestones, and although a certain amount of variance is acceptable, significant lags in reaching these stages signal immaturity and all that it implies. Each milestone is another sign of general maturation and a major factor in predicting classroom performance. Indeed, it is not by coincidence that most IQ tests for infants focus heavily on various motor skills.

Fine-motor development

How about the finer motor skills, especially those called upon in the classroom? These, too, progress along similar pathways. For example, the newborn does not use his hands in a very precise way. Yes, he will momentarily grasp a rattle when it is placed in his palm, but he will just as readily let it go. It is not a voluntary behavior. He has not yet gained any real control over his hands.

As he grows, he shows changes. At his first birthday he can intentionally pick up a block, although it is with his whole hand, in what is called a palmar grasp. He holds his spoon in his fist, a normal behavior. He manages to get food into his mouth, but not without a certain number of near misses that necessitate a general clean-up operation after each meal. Picking up small objects, such as raisins, is no small feat. He has not yet achieved the developmental stage where he can use one finger and the thumb together in a precise manner. But it will come.

By the time he enters the first grade, he should have gained precise control over the separate parts of his hand—his fingers—and learned how they can operate together in a variety of ways, depending on the task. If he still clutches a pencil with his whole fist, or if he still has to hold it with four or five fingers, it will signal something to his teacher. It will not necessarily be seen as a sign of low intelligence, but it will certainly be considered a sign of immaturity.

An experienced teacher will know that in many instances it predicts trouble. Why? Surely a child's ability to read, spell, and calculate should, to a large degree, be independent of the way he holds a pencil; and it is. But his pencil grip, his ability to tie his shoelaces into a bow, his ability to manipulate a scissors are all important indicators of his general development. Again, they are milestones that enable us to chart the child's maturation. As such, lags in the development of certain fine-motor skills may predict similar lags in other processes—processes that, when joined together, form the basis for the remarkably complex set of learning and thinking abilities that are called for in school.

Similar observations can be made of the infant's control over his speech production mechanism. He can make vocal noises at birth—undifferentiated cries that vary only in volume. As the infant grows, some mothers insist that their baby has more than one cry; that they can tell when he is crying from hunger in contrast to when he cries from pain—evidence of some sorting-out process but still quite gross. As he continues to develop, the baby starts to experiment with his vocal mechanism—cooing, babbling, and making all those marvelous sounds that babies make when they are content. Finally, he learns a word or two and is strongly applauded for the accomplishment. He learns more words, but his words are not clearly articulated. He talks baby talk— a totally acceptable behavior from a two- or three-year-old. But if he arrives in the first grade still talking baby talk—still unable to demonstrate that he has learned how the various components of his speech production mechanism work together—his teachers will be concerned. He will be showing that he is immature—not unintelligent but, rather, someone who has not achieved certain developmental milestones on schedule. Again, not a shameful state but one that tends to foretell less-than-satisfactory classroom learning performance.

We can discuss the child's ability to control his eye movements from this same aspect. It has been shown that the very young infant will, for very brief periods of time, look at and even follow a visual target that is unusually bright or otherwise interesting *if* the target is placed squarely before his eyes and then not moved too far away from the central zone of his vision. These are fairly elaborate abilities, but hardly up to the level called for in a first-grade classroom. By that time the child should be able to control his eye movements both accurately and easily. He should be able to shift his gaze from the blackboard to his desk to his teacher and wherever else with facility. He should be able to move his eyes across a line of print without losing his place and without devoting a great deal of mental energy to the task.

By the time the child enters the first grade, these should all be virtually automatic actions; he should not have to think about them, nor should they require a lot of physical effort. When he starts to learn to read, he should be moving his eyes, not his head, as he proceeds along a line of print. Is it bad to move the whole head rather than just the eyes? No, it is not bad, but it is inefficient. It is once again an indicator of immaturity, a sign that the child has not learned to use his oculomotor mechanism—the muscles that control his eye movements—in a precise way.

What does all this have to do with the visual and auditory analysis skills discussed earlier, skills that are so very important to school learning? This brings us to the second general rule relevant to developed functions. The first (the one we have been discussing for the past few pages) is that all these developed abilities are unsorted at first and get more differentiated over time. The second rule, you will recall, is that as children mature, they require less tangible contact with sensory information in order to understand it effectively.

What does that mean in practical terms? Simply, that young children tend to confirm what they see by touching or tasting or otherwise making physical contact. As they mature, this need diminishes. Most first-graders do not have to come into direct contact with everything they want to locate and examine. They can do it visually, from a distance.

For example, as a child develops, he is less likely to bump into doorways and furniture as he walks about. He reaches for his glass of milk with more precision. He places his feet more accurately as he goes up and down stairs. In part, of course, this can be attributed to the fact that his motor skills are becoming more differentiated. But it also is due to the fact that each physical contact with a visible object has helped teach the eyes to control the motor action a trifle more precisely. It is evidence that vision has slowly taken over the dominant role in guiding the child's actions, that he has learned to look, then act, and then learn from what happens.

In a sense it is as though the child has grown imaginary hands that extend from his eyes. He can grasp and explore with his eyes; certainly a more efficient process than literally needing to grasp and explore with his hands. His ability to investigate his visual world expands greatly and becomes more efficient. Said another way, by physically exploring the visual world and coming into contact with objects in that world with various parts of the body—particularly his hands—the child learns how the visual world is constructed, that it comprises many different elements that relate to each other in a variety of ways.

Eventually physical contact becomes relatively unimportant. Visual examination will do for most situations, that is, unless a sufficiently demanding or novel situation arises. Then the child, and indeed the adult, will behave in a less mature fashion and display the need for physical contact once again.

For example, suppose you found yourself perched on a narrow plank, high in the air. Which would you trust most, your eyes or your feet? What you saw or what you felt? Undoubtedly you would use both sources of information, but there is little question that you would explore that plank very carefully with your feet. Tangible information is highly important in such circumstances.

Here is another example, more familiar to many adults. Have you ever had the experience of getting new eyeglasses and noticing that despite the fact that you saw more clearly, things were not in their proper location? The floor looked too close, perhaps, or too far away, or distorted? What did you do about it? In the vast majority of cases you got used to the glasses. That does not mean you accepted the fact that the floor *should* look distorted. Not at all. You walked around with your new glasses on, you touched the floor with your feet, it *felt* level, and gradually the distortions disappeared. Your body actions and contacts taught your eyes. In a way this was a reliving of the kinds of experiences you had as a very young child, when the world around you was completely unfamiliar and had to be explored physically in order to be understood.

The need to touch, to explore physically, persists with some children. Some enter the first grade showing this very clearly. They seem unable to walk through a corridor or a classroom without touching walls, desks, other classmates. They have trouble discriminating between the *b* and *d* unless they go through the physical act of exploring, tracing over, the letter. In a primary arithmetic class their need to touch when counting objects continues far longer than it does for most of their classmates. Bad behaviors? No, merely inefficient

—and, once more, a signal that there is some lag in maturation.

A similar kind of relationship exists between the speech mechanism and the ears. Again, in a sense, one teaches the other. As the child learns to speak, he hears what he says, matches that with what he hears others say, speaks again—a trifle more distinctly—and so on. Gradually his auditory perceptual skills become more precise, which facilitates his acquisition of articulate speech, which, in turn, tends to make his auditory skills more differentiated. Again, it is a looplike hookup, with each function assisting the performance of the other.

Just as the hands enable the child to get tangible information about what he is seeing, so too does the speech production mechanism provide tangible information about sounds that are heard. It is the only way you can get your "hands" on vocal sounds. The /m/ sound and /n/ sound "feel" obviously different to the speaker—more different, actually, than how they sound to the ear.

But once the child enters first grade, it should no longer be necessary for him to repeat all that he hears in order to analyze and organize it. His ears should be able to function independently—and certainly more efficiently. Repeating words—making tangible contact with the sounds—should be unnecessary, except when a new and complex word is introduced. What if this behavior persists? Bad? No—just one more indicator of delayed maturation.

Now let us see if we can put all this information into some organized framework that will help us decide which of his general motor skills we want to test. The diagram shown in figure 11 illustrates the relationship between general motor skills, auditory and visual perceptual skills, and school learning —reading, spelling, arithmetic, and writing.

Note that the lower-level general motor skills are directly connected, as supports, to the auditory and visual perceptual skills. Also note that the general motor skills are shown as two clusters rather than as one general set of abilities.

On the left-hand side, shown as being more directly related to visual perceptual abilities, are those skills that indicate how refined a body concept the child has developed, how aware he is of his body parts and the way those parts can work together. These include such gross-motor actions as balancing and hopping on each foot and such fine-motor manual skills as cutting with a scissors, controlling a crayon or a pencil, and tying a bow. Oculomotor skills —the ability to control eye movements—also fall into this category. Certainly if the child is to learn by looking, then how well he can control where his eyes are aimed is pertinent.

On the right-hand side, more closely related to the auditory perceptual abilities, are those gross-motor skills that are essentially rhythmic in nature, involving a synchronized coordination of the two body sides. Skipping and

FIGURE 11

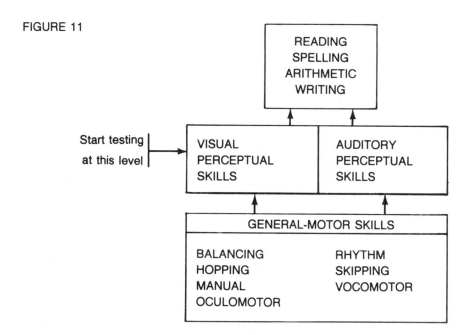

tapping rhythmically are representative. One fine-motor skill belongs in this cluster, the ability to control tongue, teeth, and lip movements—the vocomotor skills that are closely connected to speech production, which in turn is related to auditory perception.

As the diagram indicates, testing should start at the middle level—with the auditory and visual skills. If these appear to be adequate, there is no need to test the lower-level abilities, unless you have a separate interest in that information. If the middle level (visual and auditory) skills are not adequate, then you should test the general motor skills.

There is a second reason for testing general motor skills, namely, if you observe that the child's school performance is being directly affected by certain inadequate motor abilities, such as an inability to speak clearly or write legibly. Children are judged in schools not by what they know but by what they can demonstrate that they know. There are children who have trouble with the motor act of writing or, for that matter, speaking clearly—the two ways that are almost invariably called upon when the child is asked to show what he knows. It therefore makes sense to take a careful look at the child's fine-motor skills simply because of this efficiency factor. The harder the child has to work at writing legibly or speaking distinctly, the less opportunity he will have to devote attention to more abstract matters—the information he is trying to think about and communicate.

How to Test General Motor Skills

Manual skills are easy to assess; their investigation does not ordinarily require a trained professional. You are probably not as certain about your ability to test the child's speech production and eye movement skills. These two do warrant the involvement of trained professionals, if such persons are available and if you observe evidence that suggests the need for their participation. However, do not ignore these speech production and oculomotor skills if professionals are unavailable. You will not do the job as well as a professional, but some help for the child in these areas is far better than no help at all.

Actually, testing general motor skills is simple—that is, the general motor skills we are concerned about. Standardized tests are available, but in my opinion these are not necessary. Simply go through the following procedures.

If the child did not do as well as he should have on the TVAS (visual), see if he can:

Balance on one foot for about ten seconds; then on the other for ten seconds

Hop a distance of about fifteen feet on one foot, then on the other

Draw a pencil line connecting two dots situated four inches apart horizontally, then vertically, then diagonally

Cut along a line with scissors

Tie a shoe lace into a bow

Stretch his hands out in front of himself, thumbs held upright and about sixteen inches apart. Then, as you say "left," "right," and so forth, he is to *look at* his left thumb, his right thumb, and so forth, making five or six cycles. (This is not a test of his knowledge of left and right. Show him which is which.) Call out "left," "right," in a regular tempo, with the shifts occurring about every two seconds. (You do not need a stopwatch. The time is not that critical. Just do it at a moderate and regular pace.) Watch the child's eyes. Do they move together? Can he find the target quickly and stay on it until told to shift?

Follow a visual target with both eyes as it is brought toward his nose. He should be able to keep *both eyes* on that target, at least until it is within a couple of inches of his nose. His eyes should then appear to be crossed. Watch his eyes as you do this test.

If the child did not do as well as he should have on the TAAS (auditory), see if he can:

Skip, and maintain that pattern over a distance of about fifteen feet

Tap rhythmically, as follows (you, the examiner, demonstrate). Tap two times with your right hand, then two times with your left, then two times again with your right hand, and so forth, saying to the child as you tap, "Watch me, then tap this way . . . two times with this hand [R], then two times with this one [L], then two times with this [R]. Don't stop between any of the taps. Keep it up until I tell you to stop." The child is to tap at a steady, rhythmic pace. The taps should be spaced at about two per second. There should be no disruption in tempo when he shifts from one hand to the other, nor should he lose the right-left tapping sequence. Stop him at the end of five complete cycles if he gets that far. If he is eight years old, or older, introduce a more complex rhythm after you have tested him with the simpler one. This more complex one goes as follows (you, the examiner, demonstrate): Tap one time with your right hand, then two times with your left, then one time again with your right, and so forth, saying as you tap, "Watch me, then tap this way . . . one time with this hand [R], then two times with this [L], then one time with this [R], and so forth. Don't stop between any of the taps. Keep it up until I tell you to stop." The child is to tap at a steady, rhythmic pace, about two taps per second. There should be no break in tempo when he shifts from one hand to the other, nor should he lose the right-left tapping sequence. Stop him at the end of five complete cycles if he gets that far. Then repeat the test, this time with the right hand tapping twice and the left hand once.

Control his tongue movements to the extent that he can puff out his right cheek with his tongue, then his left cheek, then his right, and so forth, at a steady tempo. Show him what he is to do and set the pace by calling "right," "left," "right," "left," and so forth, at about a one-per-second pace. Stop at the end of six complete cycles if he has not lost the rhythm before that.

If the child is old enough to be in the first grade, he is old enough to be expected to perform all of the motor acts just described, with the exception of the 1-2-1-2 rhythmic tapping task (this is quite difficult for children younger than eight). Take note of the ones that he fails. We will discuss what to do about it in the next section.

This testing sequence could be extended further and made more elaborate, but what I have described is sufficient to get the basic information you need, namely, to find out whether you should have the child spend some time improving his motor skills, the justification being that the effort will pay off in the classroom. Once you have the answer to that question, additional tests are not necessary. There is no need to turn the affair into an exhibition, especially if the child is poorly coordinated. The repeated tests will merely ask him to display his inadequacies repeatedly.

OTHER KINDS OF TESTING—ARE THEY NEEDED?

IQ Testing

IQ testing is a well-established institution in our schools, yet rarely have I seen it used to the child's advantage.

What is an intelligence quotient (IQ)? It is easier to tell you what it is not. It is not a measure of a child's intellectual or learning potential. It is not a method for examining a person's brain. It does not predict the future; rather, it attempts to assess what has been learned up to the day of testing. It is not a stable index—it can vary a great deal with individual children. Hence it is *not* a foolproof predictor of how well a child will do in school.

A child's IQ is a number that tells you how well he did on an IQ test. That circular definition just about sums it up. If a child has the problem-solving skills (problems based primarily on tasks involving visual perceptual skills) and the general information necessary to answer the IQ test questions in the allotted time—and if he is motivated to perform well—he will earn a high score and have a better than average IQ. If, on the other hand, the child is not motivated, or if he does not have the skills and information necessary to answer the IQ test questions in the allotted time, he will do poorly on the test and have a lower than average IQ.

The rationale behind IQ testing is that if you measure what problem-solving skills and general (factual) information a child has learned up to some time in his life and compare it with that of other children of the same age, you can predict fairly accurately how well he will learn in the future. On the average, this rationale works quite well; but it is not infallible, particularly when applied to individual children. Nor does it take into account that the child may very well perform differently tomorrow than he did yesterday, particularly if he is treated differently or if he learns a set of problem-solving skills he never knew before or if he acquires some new factual information.

What does all this mean in practical terms? Should your child have an IQ test? I see no value in it, *unless* the information derived from the test is going to be used clinically for the child's benefit. If the psychologist who administers the test is going to interpret the child's performance in terms of how he can be helped, then fine, I have no reservations about having the child tested. If, however, the test is given to make certain the child has the potential to do better in school, then I strongly object to its use. What nonsense! To determine whether it is worth working with a child who is doing very poorly in school based on how well he has done in school in the past defeats the child before he begins. And, sure enough, once his teachers find out that he has a low IQ, he is not likely to evoke any inspired efforts from them. "After all, he is not too bright; he has a limited potential." So the prediction will come true. This process—a self-fulfilling prophecy—has had a devastating effect on many children. This does not mean that I deny the fact that some children can learn more and faster than others. Some children are indeed retarded. However, I have seen many retarded children learn to read because some dedicated person knew how to teach and took the time and the trouble to teach them. They were still retarded, in terms of their IQ score, but *they could read,* at least at a level where they could compete more effectively in the job market. Why predict? Why not try to help the child first? You will cause no harm, unless you treat him cruelly. And you might help a lot.

Academic testing

Should the child's reading, spelling, and arithmetic abilities be tested? I see no need for this. Such a general assessment offers nothing useful. Take his performance at face value without putting him through more tests that reveal his ineptness. Save testing his school-based knowledge and skills until there is something you specifically want to know. Then, by all means, test that. I will identify these in the sections that deal with specific subject areas.

All the testing you need to do before you can get to work helping your child acquire better skills has been outlined in the preceding pages. To review, I recommend the following tests:

Health-related
General medical status
Vision
Hearing

Education-related
Visual perceptual skills
Auditory perceptual skills
General motor skills (where indicated)

That is not a great deal of testing. In most cases one visit will suffice for each of the health-related tests. Unless you are extremely uncomfortable with the idea, test the child's perceptual skills yourself. The TVAS and the TAAS are simple to administer and easy to interpret—and in the next section I will tell you what to do with that information.

One final word about testing. All children are sensitive to being thought of as "different"; that includes your child. Avoid excessive testing. Not only is it expensive in terms of time and money, it may also be demoralizing for the child. Tell him why he is being tested: that it is not because you want to see if he is abnormal in some way but, rather, in order to find a way to help him do better in school. And assure him that he can be helped. It is essential that both he and you are convinced that this is really so. And it is.

PART II

Teaching Perceptual Skills

GENERAL PRINCIPLES FOR GOOD TEACHING

Now what? You have taken care of the activities described in the previous section; you have tested the child's perceptual skills and have had professionals check into the state of his health, vision, and hearing. You are following through on the various professional recommendations. What do you do next?

There are two approaches, and we will consider both of them in depth. Given a child with a learning problem and certain perceptual skills deficits,* you can:

1. Teach the child better perceptual skills wherever the testing shows a need
2. Help the child with his school subjects (reading, writing, arithmetic, and spelling) in a way that takes his perceptual skills deficits into account, thus making it easier for him to do what he cannot do well on his own: remember more of what he is taught by associating information on the basis of certain distinctive features.

Said another way, the first approach suggests that the child be helped to become easier to teach, that he be taught whatever basic perceptual skills he may lack so that he can learn to read, write, spell, and calculate as efficiently as his classmates do, using the same instructional materials they use. The second suggests that since his perceptual skills are substandard, he should be taught to read, spell, write, and calculate in special ways—ways that accommodate his inadequate perceptual skills and will help him catch up with his classmates. This means on-target teaching that is unambiguous, presented in

*This does not imply that every child who is having trouble in a school subject must also have some perceptual skills deficit. Some children have difficulty with some school subjects simply because they did not learn certain basic concepts *and would have had no trouble learning those concepts if someone had taught them in the standard way.* That is precisely how they differ from the child with inadequate perceptual skills. *He has unexpected trouble learning those basic concepts, even though someone has tried to teach them to him;* "unexpected" because he does not appear to have trouble learning in the real world outside the classroom, the world of real things rather than symbols. The procedures described in the school subjects section of this book will help both kinds of children, although there is little doubt that it will help the one—the child with adequate perceptual skills—much more rapidly than it will help the other.

easy-to-remember, appropriately sized, accurately sequenced portions; teaching that is provided by teachers who know what to do and have the temperament and administrative support to use what they know; teaching that takes place in environments that match the student's physical and psychological needs.

Which approach is best? Making him less hard to teach or teaching him in a way that takes into account his being hard to teach? Or should you combine them? In what proportions? It depends upon the child's age and the extent of his problem. The younger he is, the more I lean toward teaching him better perceptual skills. The older he is, the better it is to spend your time teaching him to read, spell, calculate, and write in ways that accommodate his needs. In any case, except for the very young, preschool child, you should not exclude one approach completely and concern yourself solely with the other. That would be foolish. Your central goal is to help the child succeed in school, and to achieve that goal it is important that you take advantage of all possibilities.*

Many of you, I suppose, are probably wondering, "Why even consider anything but the first option? Why not simply teach the perceptual skills that are lacking, thereby making the child less hard to teach, and leave it at that?" Logical question. But there is an equally logical answer to explain why this is not effective with children beyond the first or second grade.

There is limited value in trying to eliminate the learning difficulties of a child who is already behind in school—a child who is in the third grade or beyond, say—solely by teaching him the basic skills he should have had when he entered the first grade. It is not harmful, obviously; but neither is it "the answer," because by this time the child is behind in more than the development of perceptual skills. He is also lacking in what he knows, in the amount of factual information he should have learned during those earlier years but did not, because his skills were inadequate then also.

It is analogous to this: Suppose you blindfold me, then drive me from New York to Chicago, a trip I have never made before. Once in Chicago, you remove the blindfold and try to teach me a lesson that is based on—that

---

Note to parents: So far I have been assuming that you will be able to accept the role of "teacher-in-residence." I recognize, however, that some of you will be unable to do it, either because you literally do not have the time or because, in your particular case, the situation is so highly charged emotionally that the outcome might be catastrophic.

If you cannot take on the job, then by all means look for someone who can. Perhaps a friendly neighbor, a grandparent, a college student who is interested in education, or any other understanding adult who can spare the time and has the motivation and capacity to follow simple directions.

If you cannot find such a person, look beyond your personal sphere of relatives and friends to your child's school. Perhaps they have someone available. If so, lend them this book and offer them whatever support you can.

Or look to the community at large. In some areas parents have joined together for this express purpose. The Association for Children with Learning Disabilities (ACLD) is such a group. You can get information about them from their national offices at 5225 Grace Street, Pittsburgh, Pa. 15236.

assumes—certain factual knowledge I missed en route because I was blind-folded at the time. I would not profit fully from the lesson. I lacked the capacity —sight, in this example—to acquire the information that your lesson is based upon at the time when that information was being made available.

The fact that I can see now that I am in Chicago does not help fill in what I missed en route, when I could not see. I now have the ability to see—the aptitude to acquire visual information—but I still lack the background knowl-edge. If I am to profit from your lesson, you will have to accommodate that lack.

That is why teaching perceptual skills and doing nothing else will not produce completely satisfactory results with children already past the first or second grade, children who show a deficit in what they should know as well as in their perceptual skills. That is why special concern also has to be devoted to designing instruction specific to the needs of such children.

Before we get into specific procedures, I want to define the guidelines that underlie a good instructional program.

The goal of a teacher is to see to it that the student learns what he is supposed to learn. This can be accomplished in different ways.

First, the teacher can tell the student what it is he should know and then have the student memorize and restate the information to demonstrate that he has, in fact, learned it. This approach works well in situations where there is a specific and limited amount of information to be acquired, but in general it is not effective with the kind of child we are concerned about here.

A second way, also not suitable for the children under discussion, is to motivate the student to such a degree that he persists at whatever task is presented until he, himself, discovers what it is that he is supposed to know and devises a way for remembering it. This method works well with children who have competent skills but not with our child—he is not a good discoverer; he is not a good developer of methods for remembering information. He is not easy to teach.

A third way—the way that works best with the hard-to-teach child and the way that I will follow throughout this book—is to provide instructional conditions that you know are appropriate to the child's level of competence. It is a take-no-chances approach that is based on five basic principles, princi-ples that apply regardless of what is being taught.

Principle #1: Organize for success.
In practical terms this means limiting the amount of new information presented at any one time and presenting it in a simple, correctly sequenced way that highlights what is especially pertinent.

Principle #2: Make certain that the child really does have the factual knowledge he needs to profit from the lesson.

Assume nothing. Just because he seemed to know something at an earlier time does not guarantee that he retains it. Find out.

Principle #3: Make clear a system—a strategy—that will help the child retain information, that is, link up the information he is to learn with the information he already knows.

This system, if it is to work, must "make sense" to the child. It must serve to help him remember what he is supposed to remember, and to "figure it out" —recall it—when it slips his mind. Teach the system as explicitly and as basically as is necessary and, in instances where there are exceptions to the system, make sure that these exceptions are easily noted. Do not assume that the child will figure out the system simply by being given some pertinent examples or, even more unlikely, invent one on his own that serves well.

Principle #4: Encourage the child to use some of his other senses—not just his eyes and ears—to explore the concrete aspects of the task at hand.

This will force his attention to all of the pertinent details and further facilitate recall.

Principle #5: Provide enough repeated experiences to establish the information securely in the child's long-term memory.

Have him spend enough time at drill and practice so that he can perform virtually automatically, with a minimum of conscious effort; in other words, until he no longer needs to use the system you taught him to figure it out but simply knows it, that is, has the information at his fingertips when he needs it. This means regular sessions. The best rule of thumb is to schedule daily sessions and then make every effort to maintain that schedule. Keep the sessions short enough to be interesting and long enough to be effective. The first can be determined by observing the child's attitude; the second by looking at his progress. If progress is evident, if the child gets better at what he is working on, then the sessions are long enough. Generally speaking, daily twenty-minute sessions are effective at first. These can be extended when the child is able to see that he is making progress.*

Warning: Do not allow yourself to become impatient. That, of course, is easier to suggest than to live up to. But it is vital. One of the greatest problems that the child with a learning disability faces is the fact that he *learns slowly,* usually only after a substantial amount of drill and practice. To try to hasten that process unduly is to invite frustration, disappointment, and a marked lessening in the motivation that is so necessary both on the child's part and on yours. Take one step at a time and keep records so that you can compare where he once was with where he is.

But do not look at the records too often. He will not show daily progress on the charts. There will be days when he will seem to be bogged down completely or even a little bit worse than he

The foregoing five principles apply to all instructional situations, regardless of whether you are attempting to teach a simple fact or a complex concept. Consider this example of the former. You want to teach me that a red traffic light means stop and a green one means go. You start off by telling me: "A *red* light means *stop;* a *green* light means *go.* " Simple enough. You identified what I was to pay attention to, you kept it simple and limited in scope, and you did not say it in a complicated, wordy way. But you did assume certain prior knowledge of me. You assumed that I knew the meaning of the words *red, green, stop,* and *go.* In addition, you assumed that I would remember the association—which color meant which action—simply from having heard you say it.

Suppose you discover that I am hard to teach. What then? Suppose I am so hard to teach that I cannot retain the information in the above lesson, despite its simplicity and limited scope. How should you redesign the lesson to accommodate me, keeping the five basic principles in mind?

1. You should organize for success, limiting the amount of information even more than it already is if necessary. You could, for example, start off with "green means go," leaving "red" and "stop" for another time. That would help.

2. You should make certain that I do not need instruction on the meaning of the words in the lesson, and check me periodically to make sure that I remember them. If I need instruction then, obviously you should supply it.

3. There is still the problem of showing me a way to remember the information contaned in the lesson in the event that it starts to fade from my memory. What could you do about that? You could point out some rule-based strategy: that the words *green* and *go* both begin with the same sounds, for example. (This, of course, assumes that I understand what is meant by *beginning sounds.* You will have to find that out before you use the concept in your instruction. Otherwise you risk confusing rather than helping me.)

4. As an additional source of aid, you should probably encourage me to use more than my eyes and ears as I deal with the information contained in the lesson. For example, you could have me *color* a picture with red and green crayons, illustrate in action what the words *go* and *stop* mean, and have me demonstrate that I understand the basic associations between color and action by having me do all sorts of "stop" and "go" things that are controlled by red and green lights.

---

was the day before—as though he is never going to be any better. Nonsense! Delete the word *never* from your vocabulary when you work with him. He will progress if you and he stay with it. On those really bad days (yours or his), cut the session short and allow yourself to say, "I can't teach him *today.* But I will *tomorrow.* " And then begin tomorrow's session with fresh vigor.

5. Finally, you should have me engage in enough activities on enough different occasions until my responses to questions and other tasks that probe my recollection of what red and green indicate are given automatically, almost without any apparent "thinking," that is, without my having to resort to the system.

That is the general idea, applied on a very simple level. School instruction is rarely that simple. Learning to read and do arithmetic requires a much higher level of abstraction. They require the child not only to understand but also to *use* codes, complex systems where graphic and spoken symbols—numerals and letters—are combined in a variety of rule-governed ways to represent information. Even further, they require that all this be done with very little conscious effort so that primary attention can be devoted to the information represented by the symbols, not to the basic processes of reading and/or calculating.

TEACHING VISUAL PERCEPTUAL SKILLS

The central goal of a visual perceptual skills program should be to teach the child *how to* analyze relatively complex visual patterns into their separate parts and to recognize the way those parts fit together. Each lesson in the program should be based on the basic principles just defined.

Principle #1: Organize for success.
Avoid giving the child tasks that are too difficult for him. Start with relatively simple activities and move toward more complex ones only when the child shows that he is ready for them.

Principle #2: Make certain that the child really does have the factual knowledge he needs to profit from the lesson.
Ordinarily this is not a major factor in teaching visual perceptual skills, since the tasks do not usually require very much factual background. Your major concern, here, will simply be to avoid using words that are not well understood by the child, words such as *halfway, diagonal, middle,* and so on. (Or, better yet, if such words are not well understood, teach them rather than avoid them.)

Principle #3: Make clear a system—a strategy—that will help the child retain information, that is, link together the activities of the visual perceptual skills teaching program.
In this program the system is based on knowing how to interpret maps of dots, ultimately imagining that the dots are there even when they are not shown. For example, do you recall the illustration I used earlier, the one that asked you to imagine the difficulty you would have copying a square foot of grass lawn, blade by blade? Suppose this task was really important; that it was really worth the effort. How can I modify the task so that you have a better chance of succeeding? How about placing, over that mass of detail, a wire grid that divides the square foot of space into 144 square inches. The illustration in figure 12 shows a less complex visual pattern—a bouquet of flowers—handled that way.

FIGURE 12

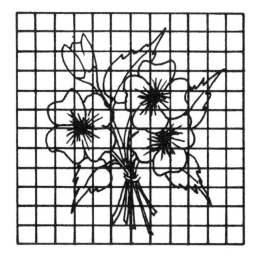

In addition to this, suppose I have you make your copy on graph paper on which the vertical and horizontal lines form one-inch squares. Now the task, still formidable, becomes a little more manageable. Given adequate time and proper encouragement, you can now choose any one of the one-inch spaces as a starting point and settle down to work. Once you have copied all the details in that square, you can move on to the next, and so on, until you are finished.

The grid provides additional information—a strategy that helped you deal with smaller portions of the task, one at a time, without getting lost. There is still the job of copying each detail, one at a time, but the total amount of detail that has to be dealt with in any given unit of work is greatly reduced—a 1/144th reduction, to be exact.

Let us apply this principle to a more reasonable task, one that is pertinent here, such as copying the diamond shown in figure 13. Your task is to copy it on a blank sheet of paper.

FIGURE 13

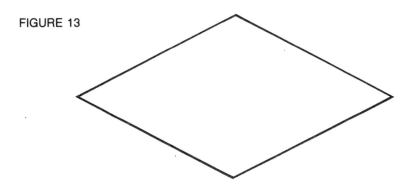

Now look at figure 14 for the same diamond—the same, that is, except that some lines have been drawn over it. Set below the diamond is a space containing similar lines; this is where your copy is to be drawn. Is copying the diamond now less difficult? Sure. There are now some reference points available, additional information that helps you accomplish the task.

FIGURE 14

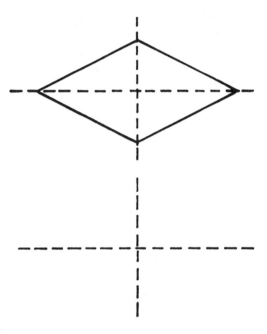

Now look at the next illustration, in figure 15. Again we see the diamond, but this time there are even more reference points. These have also been added to the space where your copy is to be drawn. The task is now relatively simple. All you have to do is to perceive the diamond as four separate lines, and position your four lines in the same relative position in your space. If you can read the map, there is very little challenge.

Look back at the original diamond in figure 13. Would copying that diamond be easier, now that you have seen the two that followed it? I think so. Even though there are no dotted lines over that original diamond, you now will tend to imagine the dotted lines; you will map the space in your mind's eye. You have learned how to do the task better and no longer need the full set of reference points. You have learned how to infer that information. It no longer has to be provided by someone else; it no longer has to be embedded in the task.*

*In truth, there is still a lot of helpful information embedded in the original "copy the diamond" task, even though there are no dotted lines. The edges of the page and the lines of print help you map the space. Is it any wonder that some children position all their arithmetic problems along one edge of a page? They get lost when they stray from that reference point.

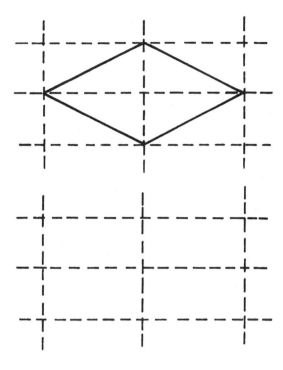

FIGURE 15

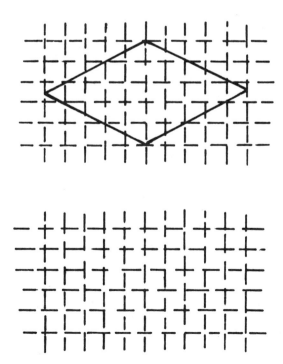

FIGURE 16

CAUTION: Do not supply too much additional information; do not make the system too complicated. It will confuse rather than help. There should be enough information to make the task understandable, and no more. Figure 16 illustrates this point.

The additional lines in the grid are no help, are they? In fact, they only make the job of copying the diamond more difficult.

Now we can move on to the next principle. Assume that the child is to be taught to copy fairly complex designs, as represented by the asterisk shown in figure 17.

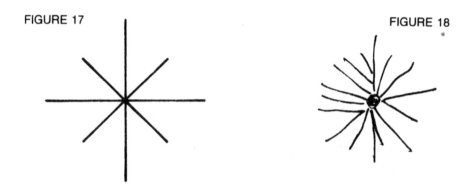

FIGURE 17

FIGURE 18

Suppose that when he was tested, his copy of the asterisk looked like the one shown in figure 18.

What can we infer from this? Simply that there are too many details in the design. What would help him respond more appropriately? Counting the lines, understanding that there are a finite number of elements in the design. But perhaps when he tries to count the elements, he gets lost in the details. How about having him touch each line while counting? Better yet, how about having him trace over a line, then copy it before proceeding to the next line, which he will again trace, then draw, and so on. As he does this, he is matching what he sees with what his hands feel. He is analyzing the design into its separate parts and succeeding at that analysis by coming into tangible contact with each part, one at a time. This brings us to the fourth principle.

Principle #4: Encourage the child to use all his senses to obtain full information about what he is seeing—by examining it manually as well as visually.

This does not mean that the child will always need this kind of support. In time he will learn to analyze with his eyes alone, using imaginary hands. He will learn to point with his eyes instead of his hand (unless, of course, the pattern gets too busy; then real hands will again be needed).

This last statement is important. Too often a child is prevented from using a crutch—a behavior or device that would help him—because "he has to learn to get along without a crutch and how will he so long as he uses one?" Well, we can also argue that to deny a crutch to a person with a broken leg does not hasten the healing process; it merely immobilizes him. What is the good of that? Allow the use of a crutch; indeed, encourage its use if it helps, because if it does help, the chances are excellent that in time it will not be needed— he will learn to imagine he is using it. And if he does continue to need it, so what? Is it not better to learn, albeit with a dependency on a crutch, than to not learn and to suffer all that that implies in this society?

Principle #5:

Now what? Practice, and lots of it, so that what at first required a great deal of concentration and step-by-step use of the system becomes efficient— automatic. This is crucial.

THE VISUAL PERCEPTUAL SKILLS PROGRAM*

Now we can turn our attention to instructional activities—what to do and when. Since you want to organize for success, you should avoid placing the child in situations that are much too difficult for him. You want to inspire motivation in him, not extinguish it with frustrating experiences. For this same reason you should avoid placing the child in situations that are much too easy for him. At best, this would be a waste of time. At worst, he will view it as "baby stuff" and lose interest in the whole enterprise.

To determine where the youngster should begin his learning activities, take a look now at his performance on the Test of Visual Analysis Skills (TVAS). You will recall that one of the test's features was that it could serve to define the instructional goals for your teaching program. Well, you are now ready to teach. The question is, Teach what? The answer to that, stated simply, is to teach the child the skills that are expected for his current grade placement, as measured by the TVAS.

Look back at the TVAS chart on page 42. The chart shows that if the child is currently in kindergarten, he is expected to score a 7 on the TVAS, that is, to complete the seventh item on the TVAS before being incorrect on two successive items. If he is in first grade, he will be expected to score a 10. If he is in second grade, 16; and third grade or beyond, 18.

*The activities described here resemble those that appear in a formal program of instruction now being used in many schools throughout the United States, Canada, and Australia—the Perceptual Skills Curriculum. Since I am its author, its similarity to the activities described in this book is not coincidence. As a parent, you do not need the curriculum. It was designed for classroom use. It is more extensive than is necessary for the purposes of one-to-one teaching. However, if your school is already using the curriculum in some of its preschool and primary-grade classes, the faculty may be willing to work with you. The curriculum is published by Walker Educational Book Corporation, 720 Fifth Avenue, New York, N.Y. 10019.

All right, now you know his instructional goal—what he is expected to be able to do, given his current grade placement. Where do you start? You start where he is. There is no justification for teaching him what he can already do, although a little overlap for review is not too bad a thing.

In appendix A you will find two hundred patterns that resemble those in the TVAS. You will teach the child how to copy these, because in learning how to copy them he will be acquiring critical visual perceptual skills; and he will display his learning by being able to pass TVAS items that he originally failed.* As you can see, the patterns range from simple to complex. He can probably do some of them already; some he cannot. Your next step, then, is to determine where he should begin and what he should do with each of the patterns.

Geoboards

First, you will need some simple equipment. I may as well tell you about that now, before getting started with teaching procedures. You will need a geoboard. The geoboard is an educational device that can be found in many mathematics classrooms. It usually consists of a panel of wood or plastic containing 25 pins (or posts) that are arranged in 5 rows, 5 pins in each row. Children stretch rubber bands between the pins to explore principles of arithmetic and geometry. Your child will use the geoboard for a similar purpose but in a much more organized way.

My visual perceptual skills program makes use of three different geoboard configurations—one with 5 pins, one with 9 pins, and one with 25 pins. These are shown in figure 19. (You may not need to use all three pin arrangements. It depends on where your child starts in the program. You will find this out when you get to the placement table on page 79.)

These three geoboards (5-pin, 9-pin, and 25-pin) may be purchased** or you can make them yourself easily and inexpensively. If you decide to make your own, obtain one square of perforated Masonite from your local lumberyard. The square should measure 9 inches on each side. The perforations should be spaced at 1-inch intervals. This will yield a board that contains 81 holes, arranged in 9 rows of 9 holes each. (One square is enough because you will be able to construct all three pin arrangements on the same square of perforated Masonite.) You will also need 25 bolts, each approximately 1 inch long, and 25 nuts to secure the bolts to the board.

Starting in the corner hole of a board, insert a bolt in every other hole and secure it with a nut. When completed, the board will contain 25 bolts, arranged

---

*And he will also display his learning by improved performance in other copying tasks, in neater paperwork, in improved arithmetic achievement (so long as he is also taught the relevant facts), and in general organizational skills. Research data to support these statements are available in my research publications (see bibliography).

**Available from Walker Educational Book Corporation, 720 Fifth Avenue, New York, N.Y. 10019.

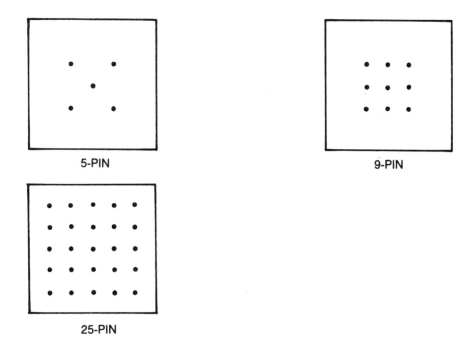

5-PIN

9-PIN

25-PIN

FIGURE 19 GEOBOARD ARRANGEMENTS

in a 5 × 5 pattern. This is shown in the sketch in figure 20.

If you need a 9-pin geoboard, simply do not insert the 16 bolts along the outside borders. This leaves only the 9 center bolts, arranged in a 3 × 3 pattern. Should you need a 5-pin geoboard, all you have to do is omit 4 more

FIGURE 20

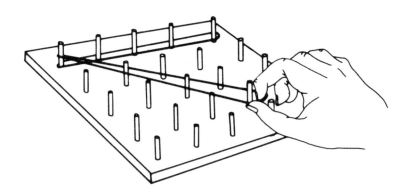

bolts—those positioned in the center of each of the remaining outside rows and lines. This will leave 5 bolts arranged as the corners of a 4-inch square with one additional peg in the center.

In addition you will need the acetate-covered maps you made when you were preparing to test the child's visual perceptual skills with the TVAS.

Getting started

Now you are ready to start teaching. The following table will tell you which pattern to begin with and which geoboard pin arrangement you will need.

To use the placement table:

1. In the left-hand column locate the child's TVAS score.
2. The second column then shows you which teaching pattern to start with (see appendix A).
3. The third column specifies the *map* onto which *you* are to copy that pattern. (Do not ask the child to copy the patterns directly from the book. They are too small, and there are too many on each page.)
4. The fourth column specifies the *geoboard* onto which *the child* will copy this pattern, using rubber bands.
5. The fifth column specifies the *map* onto which *the child* will then copy the geoboard pattern.

For example, if the child's TVAS score is 2, he will start his instructional program by learning to copy pattern 21 (which you have copied onto a 9-dot map) with rubber bands on a 9-pin geoboard, and then with crayon on a 9-dot map. (There is one additional thing that you are to do just before the child starts this last step of copying from the geoboard onto a map. I will describe it in a moment.) That means you will need a 9-pin geoboard and two 9-dot maps. (You have already prepared these maps for testing. Remember? Why *two* 9-dot maps? One onto which you will copy the pattern from this book, the other for the child to copy the pattern from his geoboard.)

To continue with examples from the placement table, if the child's TVAS score is 7, he will start with pattern 75, copying it with rubber bands onto a 25-pin geoboard, and then with crayon onto a 25-dot map. Hence you will need a 25-pin geoboard and two 25-dot maps.

What if his TVAS score is 9? Consulting the placement table, you will find that his first task is to start with teaching pattern 151. Notice that he bypasses the geoboard and moves directly to copying it with crayon onto a 17-dot map. Here he will have to "pretend the rest of the dots are there and draw the lines *as though* the dots were there." As such, you will need one 25-dot map and one 17-dot map.

Having gone through the above, you should now be able to identify the pattern the child will start with, the geoboard he may or may not need, and

VISUAL PROGRAM PLACEMENT TABLE

TVAS Score:	Begin with teaching pattern:	Parent copies teaching pattern from book onto a:	Child copies that teaching pattern onto the following	
			Geoboard map	
0	1	5-dot map	5-pin	5-dot
1	1	5-dot map	5-pin	5-dot
2	21	9-dot map	9-pin	9-dot
3	25	9-dot map	9-pin	9-dot
4	30	9-dot map	9-pin	9-dot
5	49	25-dot map	25-pin	25-dot
6	60	25-dot map	25-pin	25-dot
7	75	25-dot map	25-pin	25-dot
8	100	25-dot map	25-pin	25-dot
9	151	25-dot map	none	17-dot
10	160	25-dot map	none	17-dot
11	160	25-dot map	none	9-dot
12	165	25-dot map	none	9-dot
13	170	25-dot map	none	9-dot
14	175	25-dot map	none	5-dot
15	180	25-dot map	none	5-dot
16	180	25-dot map	none	0-dot
17	185	25-dot map	none	0-dot
18	190	25-dot map	no need to work in program	

the map onto which he will ultimately copy the pattern. There are still a few details to be covered. We will do that now so that you can get started with the job of teaching these skills to your child.

Find your child's TVAS score on the placement table and identify the number of the pattern he should start with. Find that pattern in appendix A and copy it neatly with crayon onto one of the maps. Make sure you use the correct map (one with the same number of dots). Place this before the child, alongside the appropriate geoboard or map, as indicated in the placement table. (As you can see from that table, if his TVAS score was 8 or below, he starts with a geoboard; if it was 9 or higher, he skips that step and starts directly with a map.)

Assume that his score was 8 or below. You would give the child the correct geoboard and some rubber bands and ask him to construct or "make" the pattern on his geoboard. He is to use one rubber band for each line in the pattern.

Do not help him except in the following ways: If he is unable to copy the pattern correctly, you have three options.

1. Have him place his rubber bands directly over yours, on your geoboard. (This way he is breaking the pattern down into its parts, but is avoiding completely the need to read the map.)
2. Make the task more concrete. You construct the pattern on a geoboard instead of on a map, place it next to another, matching geoboard, and ask him to copy the pattern on his geoboard. (You will need a second geoboard to do this, but do not prepare one now. Wait until you see if it is necessary; it does not happen very often.)
3. Move back to an easier teaching pattern, consult the table regarding what materials you will need, and start working with him at that level.

Only rarely, if ever, will you have to exercise any of the above options. Ordinarily, the child will be placed properly and will be able to construct the pattern on his geoboard without any assistance.

What next? After he has copied the pattern with rubber bands, rotate his geoboard 90° (¼ turn), remove your drawing of the pattern, give him another acetate-covered map (the one shown in last column of the placement table) and a crayon, and ask him to copy the pattern onto his map as it *now* appears on his geoboard. (It is a new pattern because the geoboard has been rotated 90°.)

When this is done and has been checked for accuracy, erase his drawing from his map, your drawing from your map, and remove the rubber bands from the geoboard. Then move on to the next teaching pattern and go through the same procedures. After the child has worked through ten teaching patterns in this fashion, go back to the one you originally started with and begin again, except that this time, once you have copied the teaching pattern from the book onto your map, you are to rotate your map 90° (¼ turn) *before* you give it to the child. It will then, in most cases, be a different pattern from what appears in the book. As before, he is to copy it onto his geoboard, after which you will remove your map, rotate his geoboard another 90°, hand him the proper map (as shown on the table), and have him copy that rubber band construction onto his map.

Repeat this entire procedure after the child has once more successfully completed these same ten teaching patterns, only this time you rotate your map 180° (½ turn) before you ask the child to copy it onto his geoboard. Finally, after the child has successfully completed the same ten patterns under these new conditions, repeat the entire procedure once again, this time rotating your map 270° (¾ turn) before giving it to him for copying onto the geoboard.

In this way each pattern will do the job of four—each can be used four times. Granted, some of them (a square, for instance) do not change when rotated, but most do. And there is something to be learned from those that do not change, by virtue of that fact alone.

Let us set up a hypothetical situation: The child's TVAS score was 6. The placement table indicates that he should start his program with teaching pattern 60. You find this pattern in appendix A, and since it appears on a 25-dot map, you copy it onto an acetate-covered 25-dot map. Give this to the child along with a 25-pin geoboard and ask him to make one just like it on his geoboard. He does. You then remove the drawn pattern that he just copied (the one you drew), turn his geoboard 90°, give him a blank 25-dot map and a crayon, and ask him to draw *that* (rotated) geoboard pattern onto his 25-dot map. If he is properly placed in the program, he will be able to do it.

Assume he is able to work through the nine subsequent teaching patterns (61–69) in the same way. When he completes pattern 69, you again copy teaching pattern 60 onto a 25-dot map, but this time you rotate the map 90° *before* giving it to him for reproducing on the geoboard. Then, when he has done this, the geoboard is rotated 90°, and that pattern is copied onto a 25-dot map. In this way he will work through teaching patterns 60–69 four times before he starts on teaching pattern 70.

Once the child has started to work through the sequence of teaching patterns, he need not stop unless he bogs down (remember, however, that each block of ten patterns is to be done four times—each time with the pattern oriented differently).

Continue this procedure until the child completes teaching pattern 150. Then two changes are introduced. First, he no longer uses a geoboard; he copies your pattern directly onto his map. Second, although you continue to use a 25-dot map, he now uses a 17-dot map and, thus, has to pretend the other dots are there.

He will follow this procedure through teaching pattern 160, at which time teaching pattern 151 is to be used again, this time rotated 90° *before* the child copies it onto his 17-dot map. Just as with the lower-numbered patterns, when he has worked his way through ten patterns (151–160), he again returns to pattern 151, which will now be rotated a half-turn (180°) before it is presented to him for copying, and so on. So you see, the major difference, once teaching pattern 151 is reached, is the elimination of the geoboard.

The child continues in this fashion until he completes all patterns through 200, copying each pattern four times (four different orientations) onto his

17-dot map. Then he once more returns to teaching pattern 151, and again copies each pattern (151–200) four times—but this time he copies them onto a 9-dot map (even though yours—the one he copies from—continues to be drawn on 25-dot maps). When these have all been accomplished, the cycle is repeated, except that he draws on a 5-dot map and, finally, on a 0-dot map.

The only exception to this routine occurs when a child initially places into the upper section of the teaching program—when his score on the TVAS is 11 or higher. For example, as the placement table shows, if the child's TVAS score is 11, he enters the instructional program with teaching pattern 160 and starts off copying your pattern on a 9-dot map. There is no need for him to engage in the simpler tasks, with the 17-dot map. Thus after he has copied patterns 160 to 200 onto a 9-dot map (each pattern oriented four different ways), he works his way through these same patterns again with a 5-dot map, and finally with a 0-dot map. If his TVAS score is 17, he starts off with pattern 185 on a 0-dot map and works through pattern 200. When that is accomplished, he is done with this program.

All this may sound very complicated, but once you get into it, the system will be apparent. It is designed to overteach; to help the child establish a skill that he then can use almost automatically.* But it is also designed to avoid starting the child off at too easy a level and thereby lowering his enthusiasm for the experience.

Even now, before you have had a chance really to use the program, I think you will see that as the child progresses through the teaching program, he is learning to do better in the TVAS. In reality, of course, that is of no great consequence. But inasmuch as we know that improved performance in the TVAS means improved visual perceptual skills in general, and therefore improved classroom performance, it is a worthwhile goal.

Although the program just described forms the core of the visual perceptual skills instructional program, it can be expanded. This is often advisable, both to add interest and to enhance the child's general abilities. For example:

Pegboards

Pegboards are readily available from any local school supply company and from many toy stores. Pegboards are devices that can be used in a variety of ways. Given a choice, purchase the kind that has 100 holes arranged in a 10 × 10 pattern. You will need two of these, along with 200 pegs—usually available in a variety of colors.

Start off by constructing patterns on your pegboard and having the child

---

*To help him acquire this automatic level, encourage him to take fewer looks at the pattern as he copies it. Initially, of course, he will probably look at the pattern frequently. As he gets better at it, he should be able to take larger "bites." But do not rush into this at the expense of accuracy. That comes first.

duplicate them on his pegboard. Recalling the general principles offered at the beginning of this section, you will, at the start, want to limit the complexity of the patterns you construct (use only a few pegs) and make available to the child whatever additional information he needs to meet the demands of the tasks. In this instance that means you should start off by placing pegs in the corners, where they are easiest to locate, and then in the outside rows.*

As the child catches on, make your patterns more complex and locate them more centrally—away from the edges. Eventually, eliminate your pegboard and draw patterns on graph paper. Outline an area the equivalent of the pegboard by drawing a black border around a square of 100 (10 × 10) spaces and insert the sheet of graph paper into an acetate page protector. This way you can draw your pegboard patterns without having to use a lot of paper. Finally, when the child is reproducing fairly complex patterns on his pegboard, reverse the situation and have him draw what you construct.

When he starts to acquire some ability here, switch roles with him. He constructs the model—you match it and have him check your work. Slip in an occasional error or two. It will sharpen his eye, and he will probably enjoy seeing that others can make errors too.

Parquetry Blocks

Parquetry blocks, also available at most toy counters, are another useful device. Purchase two sets. You construct patterns with your set; have the child duplicate them with his. Start with simple patterns and work toward more complex ones.**

To add another dimension, and interest, teach the child to see more at a single look by exposing your parquetry block construction for only a limited time (five or ten seconds). Then cover it and have the child construct his from memory. Needless to say, keep these patterns very simple when you introduce this activity, at least until you see what he can do.

Any number of other manipulatives—commercially prepared and home-made—can be used this way. For example, one-inch cubes arranged in patterns or wooden beads that can be strung on a shoelace are both appropriate here. Indeed, popsicle sticks and bottle caps are also suitable for constructing designs that the child can then copy. The important point to keep in mind is that you want to help the child learn how to view a pattern of things—whatever they may be—in an organized, analytical way. That is the essence of competent visual perceptual skills, regardless of the materials used.

---

*A sequence of pegboard patterns are shown in appendix B. These are organized in a sequence of relative difficulty. You can use these as a guide for designing additional patterns.
**A sequence of parquetry block patterns are shown in appendix C. These, like the pegboard patterns, are intended to be used as is, and to serve as a guide to help you design your own patterns in some reasonable order of difficulty.

Spatial Manipulation

This is a variation that can be used with any of the materials already discussed —the geoboard, pegboard, blocks, or what have you. I will describe how to use it with the geoboard materials. It should be immediately evident how to apply it to the other materials.

Start with a geoboard pattern that the child has already accomplished in the standard way. Draw that pattern onto an appropriate map of dots, place it in the center of the table, and supply the child with his own map.

Position the table so that it is away from the wall and can be approached from all four sides. Have the child view the pattern first from his own position, then have him move to the other three sides of the table, all the while looking at the pattern you drew, which is placed in the center of the table. Discuss with him the differences in the pattern when it is seen from the various positions.

The child then returns to his original position and is asked to draw the pattern as it would appear *if he were sitting* at one of the table edges other than the one where he actually is—in other words, rotated 90°, 180°, or 270°. At the beginning allow the child actually to rotate his own or your pattern in order to understand the demands of the task. Later on he is to do it without that help—to imagine how it would look.

Do this with a variety of patterns, working toward rapid and accurate performance.

Vocalizing Actions

This, too, applies to any of the activities already discussed—the geoboard, pegboards, and parquetry blocks. In essence your goal in this activity is to help the child acquire the ability to describe in words what he has learned to do with his hands—and to do it in a way that illustrates the versatility of verbal language as a medium for organizing information. I will explain.

For example, start off by showing the child a geoboard pattern that he already has accomplished in the standard way and have him *tell* you how to draw it onto an appropriate map of dots. No hands allowed, just words. You follow his instructions exactly, regardless of whether they are correct or not. It is his obligation to spot the errors and tell you how to correct them.

At first the child will probably use language that matches what he does with his hands, taking you through the patterns step by step, line by line. Once he shows this ability, urge him to provide clear instructions with fewer words. That is, encourage him—indeed, show him how—to identify subcomponents in the patterns that can be described with a word or two, despite the fact that they are made up of more than a single line. Words such as *square, cross, rectangle, triangle,* and *octagon* illustrate my point.

In effect this is merely an extension of what I suggested in the footnote on page 82 in regard to helping the child learn how to take larger visual "bites." Appropriate language can be very useful in defining those bites.

Games for Visual Skills

In addition to the activities already described, there are a number of less formal activities that can be used to advantage. I will describe some here. As you start to use them and as you gain insight into their value, I am sure you will think of others.

Card games. These are helpful, especially those that involve making sets (pairs, for example) and remembering and following rules. Rummy, Hearts, Casino, and Old Maid are all good. The many versions of Solitaire are also useful.

Memory games with cards. Concentration is a good activity. Do you recall it? All you do is arrange a full deck (less than that, if you think it advisable) facedown, in 13 rows—4 cards in each row. (This arrangement can be changed to suit your own taste.) The first player chooses two cards at random, looks at them, shows them to all players, and, unless they are a matched pair, returns them, again facedown, to their original positions. If they are a matched pair, he keeps them and chooses another pair. He keeps on choosing until he misses. The second player then chooses one card, turns it faceup, and tries to choose a second one that matches it. Obviously if the first card is a match to either of the two shown by the first player, it is helpful for him to remember where that card is. The game ends when all cards have been paired. The player with the most cards wins.

Memory games without cards. There are many of these, and they are adaptable. This one can be played at the dining room table after dinner. Everyone should participate. All players study the table, generally laden with dishes, utensils, and condiments. Then the first player closes his eyes while someone else removes one object from the table. The question to the first player then is, "What's missing?" As the game proceeds, the challenge lessens (and the table gets cleared!). *Note:* Start off with a limited assortment of objects. There is no need to make the game too difficult. "What's Missing?" can be played anywhere, with any assortment of objects: playing cards, household objects, candy, or whatever is handy. It can also be modified to "Which One Was Moved?" or "Which One Was Just Added?" and so forth.

"Robot." The goal here is the same as it was in the *Vocalizing Actions* activity described on page 84, except that in this instance it applies to any action, not just the ones pertaining to the analysis of patterns. For example, show him a single letter, an arrangement of sticks, or whatever else fits the situation, and have him tell you how to reproduce it, step by step. You in turn are to follow his directions precisely, doing just what he tells you to do, one step at a time. Start with easy tasks. This activity can be very difficult, even for adults. (Try telling someone how to draw a spiral. Remember, no hands.)

At the onset allow the child to use his hands, in addition to oral language, to describe what you are to do, but help him learn the words to replace those hand movements. For example, he may not know such words as *perpendicular, right angle,* and so forth, even though he can express them with his hands. Here, as always, the rule is "organize for success." Start with what the child can do and progress from there.

Board games. Checkers, chess, Monopoly, are all good. So are Tic-Tac-Toe, Cribbage, and the various dice games and map games sold at toy counters.

Construction activities. Tinkertoys, Erector sets, Lego, Lincoln Logs, and so on. Follow the general sequence described earlier. That is, if the child cannot follow the drawn patterns that come with the set, start off by having him superimpose pieces on top of other pieces that you have positioned. Then have him build easy constructions alongside your constructions. Then have him build from drawn plans.

Sorting. Use any materials that are available in different sizes, shapes, and colors. The child's job is to sort these according to one attribute. (For example, color: "Put all the *red* shapes in one pile and the *blue* shapes in another.") Then, if the materials are appropriate, have him sort them according to two attributes. (For example, color and shape: "Put all the *red squares* in one pile and the *blue circles* in another pile.") Coins are good for this. They can be sorted according to their value and their date. (For example, "Put all the pennies together," then, "Put all the 1972 pennies in one pile.") There are many other attributes you can focus on—weight, thickness, texture.

Time telling. This is difficult for most children who are not yet well into the second grade, so go easy. Obtain an old, large alarm clock that has an easily read dial and use it to teach the child the following things:

1. One hand is long—it is called the minute hand; one hand is short— it is called the hour hand.
2. The short hand (hour hand) points to the hour.
3. The long hand (minute hand) tells the number of minutes after or before the hour.
4. Start off by teaching the child how to read the clock when it is at the hour (e.g., one o'clock, two o'clock).
5. Have him move the minute hand (using the proper knob on the back of the clock) and observe how it makes one complete rotation for each hourly shift of the hour hand.
6. Then teach him how to read the half hour—"30 minutes after" and

"30 minutes before." (Teach him to read minutes as *after* until the minute hand reaches the half-past mark, and then, for the remainder of the hour, as *before.*)

7. Keep your language consistent. Do not use "quarter after" in place of "fifteen minutes after." There is time for all of this later.

8. Give him lots of practice and be patient with his confusion.

Chalkboard activities. The chalkboard is a remarkably useful device. It is large, can be erased easily, and is fun to use. (You can make one by painting a 4′ × 4′ section of smooth plywood with chalkboard paint.) Encourage the child to use it to draw pictures, print numerals and letters, play Tic-Tac-Toe, and other things.

One game children seem to enjoy is "Squiggles." One of you draws a single line or shape on the chalkboard. The other player then draws a picture that includes the initial line or shape (see example below). Change roles each time.

Predict a line. This, too, works well on the chalkboard. Start off by marking two X's on the board. Position the X's so that they are about 12 inches apart and at about the same height. Give the child a stick of chalk and ask him to "pretend there is a straight line on the board connecting the two X's." Then ask him to mark one or two X's *on that imaginary line.* In other words, he is to demonstrate the capacity to project an imaginary line between two points on a chalkboard.

Once he has drawn his X's, check his performance by drawing a straight line (use a straight edge) between the two X's and discuss with the child the accuracy of his performance.

When the child understands the concept, alter the task by varying the relative location of the X's, so that they are farther apart and at different heights.

Experiment with positions and keep him interested. This is a particularly useful activity for children who display persistent visual perceptual skills dysfunction.

As another variation, draw a short, straight, horizontal line at one edge of the chalkboard and have the child mark an X at the opposite edge of the board in the location where he thinks your line would terminate if it were extended. Once he has done this, extend the line in accord with its beginning segment and see how close the child was to being on target. Continue this, changing the line's orientation—vertical, oblique, from right to left, and so on —with the child's task remaining the same: to imagine where the line would end up once drawn to completion.

Matching sizes. Draw a line on the chalkboard. Then have the child draw a second line, making it the same length as yours. Check him for accuracy. At first his line may be positioned adjacent and parallel to yours. When he is ready—that is, when he can accomplish this initial task fairly well—have him draw his copy farther away from yours and not parallel. You may also replace the line with a geometrical shape such as a square, rectangle, triangle, and so on, but only after the child has displayed accomplishment at the basic level.

Teach him to use a calendar. Point out its organization—months and days of the week—and have him learn their names and their sequences. A good starting point is his birthday or Christmas or today. Each of these provides some focal point. Then, when he has established the basic facts, introduce the concepts of "day before," "day after," and so forth by playing such games as "What day comes after Thursday; before Tuesday?" "What is today's date?"

"How Do You Get There?" Have him tell you how to get from one place to another. For example, from the kitchen to the living room, from home to school, to grandmother's house, and so forth. Teach him to read simple road maps, tracing the route between two points. Then, when he can, have him tell

you how to get from *here* to *there* by consulting the map. As a variation, you describe a specific route but do not designate the destination; have him do that.

Analyze a story (or television show or movie or a real event). Get the child to tell you about one of his favorite stories or television shows and help him analyze and organize it by questioning him—*one question at a time.* For example, have him *(a)* identify the main and lesser characters; *(b)* identify their interrelationships; *(c)* describe the circumstances—place and time; *(d)* describe the events, emphasizing the pertinent points. Map out the story on a chalkboard, using simple symbols such as X's and O's for people, places, and events. Position them to reflect relationships. For example, if two people are closely connected, put their symbols closer together; if one person is larger than another, make his symbol larger.

This activity list could be extended, but I think you have the idea by now. The goal has been stated repeatedly—teach the child to analyze and organize spatial information (patterns) or, in these last suggestions, teach the child to analyze information that can then be organized spatially into patterns. Start with large units of information and very gross relationships. Work toward having him recognize refined units of information, and discrete and intricate interrelationships. (There will be more about this in the section devoted to teaching reading comprehension skills.)

One word of caution. Present all these activities as games—not as treatments. Let the child know that the formal program he is engaged in (the geoboard and map activities) is to be done on a scheduled basis; something he *must* do daily. These activities, in contrast, should be fun; they are not prescribed and formalized. These are the kinds of things you should do casually, while sitting around a fireplace, riding in a car, having dinner. If he begs off, allow him that privilege. He will play when he is ready or when the activity is sufficiently interesting or when he thinks he has a chance of succeeding. We all enjoy doing what we do well, so long as it is not too easy or too difficult. We all like to succeed. Give him plenty of opportunities to do so.

TEACHING AUDITORY
PERCEPTUAL SKILLS

The central goal of an auditory perceptual skills program should be to teach the child how to analyze spoken language into its separate sounds and recognize the sequence of those sounds. As the goal is achieved, the child will become increasingly familiar with the distinctive phonological features of spoken words, the sounds that are represented by letters in reading and spelling. The value of this will be evident not only in how capably the child discriminates sounds in spoken language but, more importantly, in how readily he learns to read and spell.*

There are a number of programs available for teaching auditory perceptual skills. Some devote a great deal of attention to teaching the child to discriminate—to hear the difference—between various nonverbal sounds; for example, between the sound of an airplane motor and the sound of a vacuum sweeper. The rationale, apparently, is that poor listeners tend to be as much confused by nonverbal as by verbal sounds. The fallacy, however, is that though this may be true, there is no practical value in devoting time to nonverbal sounds. It may be effective, and the child may become expert at noticing the difference between doorbells and telephone bells, but there is no evidence to suggest that the effect of instruction will be apparent when the child faces the task of analyzing verbal sounds—spoken language. It will not help him learn to read.

There are other programs, a little closer to the mark, that are designed to teach children to discriminate between similar spoken sounds; for example, between *bear* and *dare; mat, met,* and *mit; laugh* and *lath.* These, again, do not go far enough in that the child can answer correctly without doing a thorough analysis of the words.

The program I am going to suggest focuses on teaching the child to take words apart into their individual sounds. But first I want to give you a general idea of its design. Then we will take a closer look at the various procedures.

The auditory skills program is based on the same set of principles put forth in the visual skills section. I will not risk boring you by restating all of them here, but I do think that one of them—the fourth—does warrant some specific

*Research data to support these statements are available in my research publications (see bibliography).

discussion. As you will recall, that is the one that stresses the importance of encouraging the child to use some of his senses beyond his eyes and ears to obtain additional information about what he is trying to do: analytical listening, in this instance.

It is generally helpful to teach the child to examine sounds vocally; that is, to say them and simultaneously take note of what he hears and how his mouth feels. In a real sense the speech production mechanism is the counterpart of the hands in that it enables you to "touch" vocal sounds the way the hands can manipulate visual information. Even as adults, how else can we analyze fairly long words into parts, or syllables, words that are too long to visualize? For example, how many syllables are there in the word *hippopotamus?* You will not be able to answer accurately if you do not say the word either aloud or to yourself. Saying words aloud—even relatively short and simple words—helps the child identify the separate sounds, particularly if he speaks distinctly, pronouncing all of the sounds.

This last point is sensitive. The debate regarding whether or not to try to do something about a child's dialect continues to be heard around the country. One group argues that standard English and standard English pronunciation of words are desirable if only because they are the standard. The other group retorts that a dialect is the manifestation of the child's culture, and to try to eliminate it is tantamount to attacking that culture. I seek no quarrel with either group. But purely from a pragmatic basis, I must assert that a dialect can have a detrimental effect on a child's ability to identify all of the component parts—the individual sounds—of a spoken word. If he does not pronounce them, he will neither hear them nor feel them. How, then, can he identify them? Read them? Yes, he can read them—if he knows how to read. But that is not the kind of youngster we are worrying about here. The implications of a dialect, insofar as learning to read is concerned, are clear. This is especially so if the dialect is one wherein words are collapsed and word endings left off.

THE AUDITORY PERCEPTUAL SKILLS PROGRAM

Let us now look at specific instructional activities—what to do and when. Following the procedure we used earlier in the visual skills section, we will first look at how to place the child so that what he is asked to learn is neither too difficult nor too easy.

To determine where the youngster should begin his learning activities, take a look at how well he did on the Test of Auditory Analysis Skills (TAAS). What was his score?

Now look back at the chart on page 49. The chart shows that if the child is currently in kindergarten, he is expected to score a 3 on the TAAS—that is, pass the third item before getting two incorrects in a row. If he is in first grade, he is expected to score a 9; by the end of second he is expected to score an 11; and by the end of third grade he should be able to get through all the items and earn a score of 13.

You have now identified his instructional goal—the auditory perceptual skills level he should have achieved given his current grade placement. The rule, as you know, is to start where he is. In other words, what was the most difficult task he was able to complete on the TAAS? That is where he is. Now he should learn how to solve the next item on the TAAS.

Getting started

A reexamination of the TAAS (see page 48) will be helpful. As you will observe, the items are arranged in a specific sequence, going from easy to difficult. They fall into five categories. These are illustrated in figure 21.

The chart makes clear the five levels in the TAAS. You can see that placement is fairly simple. Items 1 and 2 fall into the lowest level (Level I) depicted on the chart. Item 3 belongs to the second category—Level II. Items 4–6 belong to Level III, items 7–9 to Level IV, and items 10–13 to the highest —Level V. Thus the child's TAAS score tells us where he should get started. This is shown in the Auditory Program Placement Table.

For example, suppose the child did very poorly in the TAAS; his score was 1. Consulting the Auditory Program Placement Table, you find that he

AUDITORY PROGRAM PLACEMENT TABLE

TAAS Score	Child should work in level:
1	I
2	II
3	III
4	III
5	III
6	IV
7	IV
8	IV
9	V
10	V
11	V
12	V
13	no need to work in program

LEVELS IN THE AUDITORY PROGRAM

LEVEL V
Identify and delete a final consonant
sound of a consonant blend.
Say **play**; now say it again,
but don't say /**p**/

LEVEL IV
Identify and delete a final consonant
sound in words where the consonant
is preceded by a vowel.
Say **meat**; now say it again,
but don't say /**t**/

LEVEL III
Identify and delete a beginning consonant
sound in words where that sound
is followed by a vowel.
Say **meat**; now say it again,
but don't say /**m**/

LEVEL II
Identify and delete one syllable
from a three-syllable word.
Say **cucumber**; now say it again,
but don't say /**cu**/

LEVEL I
Identify and delete one syllable
from a two-syllable compound word.
Say **cowboy**; now say it again,
but don't say **boy**

FIGURE 21

should work in Level I, going on to more difficult levels only when he can demonstrate that he has learned the skills of that lowest level. What if the child's TAAS score was 5? Again consulting the placement table, it is evident that the child should work in Level III, and remain there until he has learned the Level III skill. Then he will go on and work in Level IV.

All right, you now know how to place him in the program. What next? How do you teach him the auditory skills he needs to know?

The Auditory Skills Program is diagrammed in figure 22. In effect this is a map of the skills he should learn in order to progress from where he is to where he should be. For instance, if he should be in Level V and instead is in Level II, the best way of getting him up to Level V is by teaching him all the skills shown on that chart between Levels II and V. That, of course, is the purpose of the auditory program. Once you have placed the child, the program is easy to use. Simply follow the procedures described on the following pages.

If the child is in Level I, teach him to

1. Clap his hands in time to the syllables of a two-syllable compound word, saying them as he claps them. Say to the child, "Say *baseball*" (emphasizing the fact that there are two parts in that word). "Now say it again and clap your hands once for each part of the word; clap and say the parts at the same time." (Use Level I words, figure 24.*) When you see that he understands and can do this, move on. (His goal, here, is relatively simple—to show that he understands that words can be segmented into parts and that he can represent each part with a motor action—a clap.)

2. Draw a dash, from left to right, for each syllable in a two-syllable compound word, saying them as he draws the dashes. Say to the child, "Say *baseball.*" (Emphasize the fact that there are two parts in that word.) "Now say it again and draw a dash for each part while you say it." (Demonstrate to the child how the dashes are to be drawn; horizontally, from left to right; the first dash being drawn as the first syllable is said, the second dash being drawn as the second syllable is said.)

   Once he has grasped this, teach him to read the dashes in any order you designate. For example, if he drew two dashes for the word *baseball* and you then point to the first dash (the one to the left) and ask, "What does this one say?" his response should be "base." If you point to the right-hand dash, his response should be "ball."

   When the child has learned to write (with dashes) and read the

---

*You may add to this list of Level I words if you wish, but do *not* use words that are in the TAAS. Reserve those for testing to see whether he has learned what you set out to teach him.

THE AUDITORY SKILLS PROGRAM

LEVEL	Clap hands to:	Draw and read dashes for:	Find the hidden:	Say the missing:	Say the word without the:	Substitute:
V			part of a consonant blend	part of a consonant blend	part of a consonant blend	part of a consonant blend
IV			final consonant sound	final consonant sound	final consonant sound	beginning and/or final consonant sounds
III			beginning consonant sound	beginning consonant sound	beginning consonant sound	
II	syllables in a three-syllable word	syllables in a three-syllable word	syllable in a three-syllable word	syllable in a three-syllable word	syllable in a three-syllable word	
I	syllables in a two-syllable compound word	syllables in a two-syllable compound word	syllable in a two-syllable compound word	syllable in a two-syllable compound word	syllable in a two-syllable compound word	

FIGURE 22

two-syllable words from the Level I list, it is time to move on to the next task.

3. Find the hidden syllable. Tell him, "Say *baseball*"; then ask, "Did you say *ball?* Is the word *ball* hidden in the word *baseball?*" Or have him say *baseball,* then ask, "Is the word *doll* hidden in the word *baseball?*" The child's response in this activity is either yes or no. If he fails to grasp the concept, go back one step and have him draw dashes for the word before trying to decide whether a specific syllable is hidden in it. Figure 23 shows a list of word activities you can use for this step.

4. Say the part of the word that was missing. Say to the child, "Say *baseball;* now say *ball.* What did I leave out—what part is missing?" (The Level I list of words is suitable here. Vary the teaching pattern by omitting the first or second syllable in random fashion.)

5. Say the word without a specified syllable. Say to the child, "Say *baseball.* " (Pause while he repeats *baseball.*) "Now say it again, but don't say *ball.* " Or, "Don't say *base.* " (Use the Level I list of words.) If the child encounters confusion, back up a step or two.

When he shows that he understands what he is to do, retest him with items 1 and 2 of the TAAS. If he passes these—and he should if he has gone through the above five steps—move on to Level II.

If the child is in Level II, teach him to

1. Clap his hands in time to the syllables of a three-syllable word, saying them as he claps them. Say to the child, "Say *vacation*" (emphasizing the fact that there are three parts in the word). "Now say it again and clap your hands once for each part of the word;" then, "Clap and say the parts at the same time." (Use Level II words, figure 26.*) When you are able to see that he understands the concept that these words are constructed of parts, move on.

2. Draw a dash from left to right for each syllable in a three-or-more-syllable word, saying the syllables as he draws the dashes. Say to the child, "Say *va ca tion*" (emphasizing the fact that there are three parts in that word). "Now say it again and draw a dash for each part while you say it." (Show the child how the dashes are to be drawn; horizontally, from left to right; the first being drawn as the first syllable is said, the second being drawn as the second syllable is said, and so on.)

Once he has grasped the idea, teach him to read the dashes in any order you designate. (Use Level II words.) For example, if he drew

*You may add to this list of Level II words if you wish, but do *not* use words that are in the TAAS. Reserve those for testing to see whether he has learned what you set out to teach him.

FIGURE 23

Say **more**	Is the word **more** hidden in the word	**morning?** **farmer?** **mortgage?** **morbid?**
Say **ball**	Is the word **ball** hidden in the word	**ballgame?** **baseball?** **cowboy?** **bolt?**
Say **bun**	Is the word **bun** hidden in the word	**bunny?** **thunder?** **bundle?** **bunk?**
Say **pay**	Is the word **pay** hidden in the word	**repay?** **paper?** **daytime?** **pain?**
Say **see**	Is the word **see** hidden in the word	**seesaw?** **seaman?** **saddle?** **seed?**
Say **miss**	Is the word **miss** hidden in the word	**mistake?** **mister?** **master?** **mistletoe?**
Say **car**	Is the word **car** hidden in the word	**cargo?** **card?** **scar?** **star?**
Say **all**	Is the word **all** hidden in the word	**always?** **recall?** **illness?** **ball?**
Say **ant**	Is the word **ant** hidden in the word	**anthill?** **antelope?** **andy?** **cant?**
Say **pick**	Is the word **pick** hidden in the word	**picnic?** **pickle?** **packet?** **picket?**
Say **ray**	Is the word **ray** hidden in the word	**Raymond?** **radio?** **rain?** **write?**
Say **won**	Is the word **won** hidden in the word	**wonder?** **once?** **window?** **wedding?**
Say **ban**	Is the word **ban** hidden in the word	**bandit?** **bank?** **Benny?** **banquet?**

FIGURE 24: LEVEL 1 WORD LIST

sunshine	seesaw	motion
baseball	oatmeal	virture
someplace	window	morbid
steamship	recall	dispose
cowboy	paper	begin
mister	magic	defend
cupcake	after	bashful
into	dentist	cement
candy	monkey	muffler
person	sandwich	ocean
cartoon	shoeshine	murky
children	napkin	concert
sometime	daytime	vocal
bookcase	stingy	nasty
forget	upset	native
mountain	bargain	precise
doctor	surprise	measure
outside	himself	ordeal
daddy	mascot	selfish
doorbell	cardboard	vibrant
fancy	predict	indent
funny	airplane	famous
hunter	eyelash	protest
party	demon	except
business	hungry	obtain
garden	playmate	conceal
barber	ashtray	decay

three dashes for the word *vacation,* and you then point to the first dash (the one on the left) and ask, "What does this one say?" his response should be *va.* If you point to the middle dash, his response should be *ca,* and so on.

3. Find the hidden syllable. Ask him to say *"va ca tion."* Then ask, "Did I say/va/? Is the sound/va/ hidden in the word *vacation?"* Or "Is the sound /day/ in *vacation?"* The child's response will be either yes or no. If he fails to grasp the concept, go back one step and have him draw dashes for the word before trying to decide whether a specific syllable is hidden in it. Figure 25 shows a group of word activities you can use for this step.

FIGURE 25

Say **two** **toe** **row** **mar**	Is the word **two** **toe** **row** **mar**	hidden in the word **tomorrow?**
Say **car** **tar** **curb** **carp**	Is the word **car** **tar** **curb** **carp**	hidden in the word **carpenter?**
Say **man** **fish** **fast** **dish**	Is the word **man** **fish** **fast** **dish**	hidden in the word **fisherman?**
Say **knee** **noon** **moon** **honey**	Is the word **knee** **noon** **moon** **honey**	hidden in the word **honeymoon?**
Say **thunder** **stand** **under** **and**	Is the word **thunder** **stand** **under** **and**	hidden in the word **understand?**
Say **permit** **mint** **pep** **pop**	Is the word **permit** **mint** **pep** **pop**	hidden in the word **peppermint?**
Say **full** **once** **one** **fun**	Is the word **full** **once** **one** **fun**	hidden in the word **wonderful?**
Say **milk** **but** **bat** **tire**	Is the word **milk** **but** **bat** **tire**	hidden in the word **buttermilk?**
Say **ought** **melon** **water** **tear**	Is the word **ought** **melon** **water** **tear**	hidden in the word **watermelon?**

Say **pen**	Is the word **pen**	hidden in the word **independent?**
on	**on**	
dent	**dent**	
deeper	**deeper**	
Say **get**	Is the word **get**	hidden in the word **forgetful?**
full	**full**	
far	**far**	
for	**for**	
Say **cut**	Is the word **cut**	hidden in the word **caterpillar?**
pill	**pill**	
cat	**cat**	
pillow	**pillow**	
Say **fact**	Is the word **fact**	hidden in the word **manufacture?**
tear	**tear**	
man	**man**	
fit	**fit**	

4. Say the part of the word that is missing. Say to the child, "Say *va ca tion.*" (Pause.) "Now say *cation.*" Then, "What did we leave out—what part is missing?" (The Level II list of words is suitable here. See figure 26. Vary the teaching pattern by omitting the first or second or third syllable in random fashion.)

5. Say the word without a specific syllable (first or last). Say to the child, "Say *va ca tion.*" (Pause while he repeats the word.) "Now say it

FIGURE 26: LEVEL II WORD LIST

cantelope	peppermint	silverware	emptiness
basketball	classical	decently	departure
trampoline	valentine	naturally	extravagant
important	buffalo	resonant	institute
defenseless	babydoll	ridiculous	important
memorize	refreshment	superlative	substitute
mistaken	emergency	pantaloon	impersonate
gorilla	peanut butter	favorite	performance
carelessly	destiny	fanciful	dedication
yesterday	peninsula	hardiness	devotion
cornerstone	introduce	laboratory	undertake
limousine	independent	abdicate	advantage
September	classification	diplomat	represent
understand	occupation	workmanlike	vivacious
remember	upside down	clumsiness	atmosphere
microphone	newspaper	excitement	indignant
forgotten	friendliness	evasive	enormous
gasoline			

again, but don't say /va/. Or, "Don't say /tion/." (Avoid asking for omission of the middle syllable—work on the first or last only. Use the Level II word list.) If the child becomes confused, back up a step or two.

When he understands what he is to do, test him with item 3 of the TAAS. If he passes, as he should if he has worked through the five steps, move on to Level III.

If the child is in Level III, teach him to

1. Find the hidden beginning sound of a word. Tell him, "Say *mat.*" (Pause while he says it.) Then, "Does the word *mat* begin with an /m/ sound?" (Say the letter sound *mmm,* not the letter name.) Encourage the child to think about how his mouth feels as he repeats the word.

   The following words in figure 27 are suitable for this activity:

FIGURE 27

Does the word begin with an /**m**/ sound? (as in *mother*)

mix	Monday	money	fame
mate	time	make	time
neat	misty	came	monastery
comb	ram	many	name
fame	seam	melt	milkshake

Does the word begin with an /**a**/ sound? (as in *apron*)

aid	apple	ace	animal
ape	awful	August	afraid
open	acorn	ant	ate

Does the word begin with an /**e**/ sound? (as in *eel*)

Indian	evil	evict	team
eat	beef	ear	equal
even	every	sneeze	enemy

Does the word begin with an /**i**/ sound? (as in *idea*)

Indian	ice cream	find	grind
ant	item	icicle	ivy
ice	cry	plier	bike

Does the word begin with an /**o**/ sound? (as in *open*)

under	opera	omen	blow
over	know	bone	open
on	ocean	ox	boat

Does the word begin with a /u/ sound? (as in *useful*)

use	grew	union	unity
yeoman	usual	yule	ukulele
blue	umbrella	group	under

Does the word begin with a /b/ sound? (as in *big*)

dig	boy	brown	breakfast
bag	drag	hag	slab
peg	basket	bicycle	crib

Does the word begin with a /k/ sound? (as in *cup*)

cat	scare	kite	across
skin	castle	cartoon	smash
bake	color	lock	cash

Does the word begin with a /d/ sound? (as in *dog*)

day	done	muddy	devil
sad	toad	door	blood
trip	drag	sled	danger

Does the word begin with a /g/ sound? (as in *go*)

juggle	green	glow	ghost
dig	ragged	drag	glove
gold	gate	bag	grain

Does the word begin with a /h/ sound? (as in *hat*)

home	hair	shove	show
omen	ahoy	him	history
hop	hang	they	hill

Does the word begin with a /j/ sound? (as in *joke*)

Jane	rage	badge	Jim
jump	joy	chew	chase
goat	gyp	jar	cash

Does the word begin with a /l/ sound? (as in *lake*)

lane	love	lend	lead
flood	pickle	glare	land
hill	log	flag	click

Does the word begin with a /n/ sound? (as in *neck*)

snip	no	anthill	
kneel	fan	in	instruct
onto	needless	nothing	needle

Does the word begin with a /p/ sound? (as in *pick*)

spell	paint	stop	part
pray	drag	open	pill
plunge	blond	spill	clap

Does the word begin with a /r/ sound? (as in *ride*)

real	bring	ride	far
dart	rag	drip	wrinkle
river	grieve	rent	truck

Does the word begin with a /s/ sound? (as in *so*)

sand	smack	misty	wrist
score	miss	spell	scold
zip	silly	whistle	stick

Does the word begin with a /v/ sound? (as in *very*)

vote	victory	Viking	win
wish	reef	love	vicious
vocal	vanish	fat	fish

Does the word begin with a /w/ sound? (as in *win*)

swell	hole	wit	twine
twinkle	warm	vote	wedding
wag	wiggle	swim	wine

Does the word begin with a /y/ sound? (as in *yell*)

yes	youth	hit	yard
win	twin	joke	beyond
hang	girl	yank	young

Does the word begin with a /z/ sound? (as in *zip*)

zoo	zone	snip	tease
sow	zeal	zenith	zigzag
is	zoom	rose	toes

Does the word begin with a /ch/ sound? (as in *chew*)

champ	ship	charge	jump
shoe	camp	general	chip
chunk	chuckle	show	school

Does the word begin with a /sh/ sound? (as in *ship*)

shallow	see	chair	rash
soup	shave	jar	shun
chew	shine	shell	shrug

Does the word begin with an /ĕ/ sound? (as in *Eskimo*)

end	edit	ever	except
Esther	apple	into	up
eagle	empty	olive	elephant

Does the word begin with an /ĭ/ sound? (as in *igloo*)

into	end	iodine	at
pet	illegal	if	ice
important	impact	up	tin

Does the word begin with an /ŏ/ sound? (as in *octopus*)

opera	rod	under	pot
open	odd	old	object
apple	modern	on	officer

Does the word begin with an /ŭ/ sound? (as in *umbrella*)

under	undermine	sun	urge
use	offer	hunter	bulge
unable	up	usual	ugly

Does the word begin with an /ă/ sound? (as in *apple*)

ant	pen	add	ladder
cat	ask	attic	aide
ape	enter	ate	astronaut

Here is another activity related to this same skill. Ask the child to print the beginning sound (to be more exact, the letter that *stands* for the beginning sound) of this word. Use the Level III word list, figure 29.*

2. Say the sound that is missing. Tell the child to "Say *mat.*" "Now say *at.*" Then, "What sound is missing in *at* that you heard in *mat?*" (The answer, of course, is the /m/ sound.) Some suitable words may be found in figure 28. For more, see the Level III word list.

FIGURE 28

mat - at	meeting - eating	hand - and	wax - ax
mice - ice	tangle - angle	sigh - I	turn - earn
tan - an	small - mall	tape - ape	supper - upper
pat - at	merge - urge	table - able	sink - ink
date - ate	moat - oat	sash - ash	mare - air
mace - ace	mangle - angle	fall - all	mend - end
ball - all	mate - ate	told - old	tax - ax
my - eye	tin - in	tar - are	bait - ate
part - art	four - or	totter - otter	door - oar
deal - eel	call - all	sit - it	gate - ate
mall - all	Sam - am	soften - often	toe - oh
faint - ain't	race - ace	tin - in	win - in
sour - our	mask - ask	tote - oat	send - end
gone - on	pink - ink	meager - eager	march - arch
many - any	mad - add	meal - eel	sand - and
hate - ate	neat - eat	time - I'm	surge - urge
seat - eat	maim - aim	pin - in	mart - art
jar - are	limp - imp	fan - an	mold - old
lend - end	sad - add	tall - all	tone - own

*You may add to the list of Level III words if you wish, but do *not* use words that are in the TAAS. Reserve those for testing to see whether the child has learned what you set out to teach him.

till - ill	page - age	nice - ice	motto - Otto
nor - or	sold - old	tale - ail	slight - light
sew - oh	came - aim	sill - ill	rise - eyes
sought - ought	moan - own	socks - ox	mink - ink
tease - ease	fear - ear	sat - at	marrow - arrow
made - ade	tally - alley	will - ill	snip - nip
tie - eye	tile - I'll	teach - each	mow - owe
tear - air	soil - oil	make - ache	

3. Say the word without the beginning sound. Tell the child, "Say *mat.*" (Pause.) "Now say it again, but don't say the /m/ sound."

All the words on the Level III word list are suitable for this activity. They are printed with parentheses around the beginning sound. For example, the first word on that list is *(n)or.* The child is told the answer is *or.* Proceed through all the words in this fashion. "Say *nor*" (Pause.) "Now say it again, but don't say the /n/ sound."

FIGURE 29: LEVEL III WORD LIST

(n)or	(p)each	(w)oke	(p)itch	(m)ace
(b)urn	(b)ait	(p)ending	(n)ear	(m)ice
(h)eart	(h)arm	(r)ash	(f)ate	(s)our
(w)are	(d)oe	(w)onder	(b)eg	(l)ark
(p)ad	(j)oke	(d)are	(g)alley	(p)art
(r)oar	(g)ale	(h)ail	(b)all	(m)ake
(p)ink	(f)or	(r)each	(k)it	(f)all
(r)ant	(c)ash	(r)ally	(b)eat	(f)in
(c)all	(d)oubt	(w)ill	(h)aul	(m)at
(j)ar	(h)all	(h)ad	(l)ice	(f)an
(r)ail	(p)ouch	(p)air	(f)ern	(m)ill
(v)ery	(d)ate	(g)old	(h)am	(w)all
(p)ace	(b)oil	(d)ad	(h)and	(b)in
(b)at	(c)art	(b)ad	(h)eat	(r)an
(l)ake	(l)ark	(l)ace	(l)ad	(c)at
(l)it	(p)up	(g)oat	(k)eel	(p)ill
(f)ail	(d)art	(c)old	(n)ice	(s)in
(f)ace	(f)ox	(c)ame	(l)eave	(t)an
(f)oul	(c)an't	(h)as	(l)ax	(b)at
(l)ash	(j)am	(d)ear	(h)older	(s)ink
(g)ear	(l)ore	(d)ill	(w)age	(m)all
(l)earn	(b)and	(p)inch	(g)out	(s)eat
(v)an	(b)ake	(c)are	(w)itch	(t)each
(r)age	(r)amble	(b)ar	(v)owel	(b)each
(t)one	(w)eave	(w)ink	(p)arch	
(m)are	(t)ax	(s)old	(p)age	

When the child shows that he understands the process of deleting the beginning sound of a word, test him with items 4, 5, and 6 of the TAAS. If he passes, as he should if he has worked through the above three steps, start working at Level IV.

If the child is in Level IV, teach him to

1. Find the hidden final sound of a word. Tell him, "Say *make.*" (Pause while he says it.) Then, "Does the word *make* end with a /k/ sound?" (Say the letter sound, not the letter name.) Encourage the child to think about how his mouth feels as he repeats the word.

   The following words in figure 30 are suitable for this activity:

FIGURE 30

Does the word end with an /**m**/ sound? (as in *Sam*)

bend	trim	mush	roam
limp	land	beam	bump
rhyme	steam	green	chum
stem	mean	dimple	mix
bump	came	come	time

Does the word end with a /**t**/ sound? (as in *gate*)

write	slot	hot	boat
hat	goat	mouth	toast
tame	fighter	had	sled

Does the word end with a /**k**/ sound? (as in *make*)

back	bag	sick	rack
rocker	lock	fig	crib
score	wrinkle	clap	rag

Does the word end with a /**b**/ sound? (as in *gab*)

big	bone	slab	bent
crab	dabble	bait	dent
dig	best	ribbon	web

Does the word end with a /**d**/ sound? (as in *end*)

dog	raid	rode	ladder
food	ditch	mouth	mustard
meet	sweet	loud	decide

Does the word end with a /**f**/ sound? (as in *laugh*)

love	with	live	growth
graph	stuff	cliff	sunfish
fame	fish	fancy	bluff

Does the word end with a /**g**/ sound? (as in *pig*)

bike	sling	lock	ghost
rag	haggle	fog	plug
grain	wag	page	stick

Does the word end with a /j/ sound? (as in *edge*)

lodge	bed	which	badge
generous	justice	magic	batch
wag	wage	wash	wish

Does the word end with a /l/ sound? (as in *all*)

long	hello	pail	silk
boil	star	pillow	steel
sill	a	listen	stolen

Does the word end with a /n/ sound? (as in *in*)

pin	grain	bend	team
stone	bandit	grim	gown
sandy	shine	nudge	something

Does the word end with a /p/ sound? (as in *hop*)

puzzle	ripple	tide	hopped
paper	trip	defend	heap
rope	raft	crib	feet

Does the word end with a /r/ sound? (as in *or*)

ball	sorry	park	race
fur	sir	tear	squirt
strip	read	furry	fire

Does the word end with a /s/ sound? (as in *mess*)

race	mist	base	toast
rash	sock	least	loose
rise	fasten	please	lose

Does the word end with a /sh/ sound? (as in *push*)

bush	mushy	squash	match
witch	latch	dash	wishing
rush	show	rubbish	lash

Does the word end with a /z/ sound? (as in *eyes*)

rise	froze	puzzle	choose
hose	loose	shoes	chosen
zoo	lose	splash	size

2. Say the sound that is missing. Tell the child, "Say *make.*" (Pause.) "Now say *may.*" Then, "What sound is missing in *may* that you heard in *make?*" (The answer, of course, is the /k/ sound. The words in figure 31 are suitable here, as are the words on the Level IV word list, figure 32).*

---

*You may add to this list of Level IV words, but do *not* use words that are in the TAAS. Reserve those for testing, to see whether the child has learned what you set out to teach him.

FIGURE 31

make - may	loom - Lou	goat - go	grape - gray
beat - be	prime - pry	weight - way	bite - by
boil - boy	rhyme - rye	lime - lie	bait - bay
gate - gay	name - nay	like - lie	team - tea
made - may	same - say	mite - my	late - lay
rope - row	mean - me	base - bay	croak - crow
soap - so	safe - say	awake - away	freak - free
beam - be	rode - row	firm - fur	claim - clay
heat - he	soak - so	boat - bow	face - Fay
mate - may	toad - toe	loaf - low	feet - fee
home - hoe	ice - I	storm - store	grace - gray
lame - lay	pace - pay	time - tie	pike - pie
stake - stay	race - ray	type - tie	
boat - bow	dance - Dan	meat - me	

3. Say the word without the final sound. Tell the child, "Say *make.*"
(Pause.) "Now say it again, but don't say the /k/ sound." (Say the
letter sound, not the letter name.)

All the words on the Level IV list are suitable for this activity.
They are printed with parentheses around the final sound. For exam-

FIGURE 32: LEVEL IV WORD LIST

wa(ke)	rai(l)	wa(ge)	ra(ke)	wea(l)
tri(te)	plea(t)	du(ke)	lea(p)	coo(p)
mea(l)	shi(ne)	ha(ze)	ho(ne)	li(fe)
lo(be)	loa(m)	see(p)	ma(te)	ma(de)
ja(de)	sta(ge)	la(me)	bea(d)	coi(n)
di(re)	tea(k)	mi(ne)	ri(de)	goe(s)
kee(p)	ra(ce)	sa(ke)	grow(n)	ra(ge)
wai(t)	trai(n)	mi(ght)	coo(l)	ho(se)
no(te)	no(se)	how(l)	mea(t)	hi(de)
bi(de)	coi(l)	loa(n)	ru(de)	tee(n)
fee(l)	lo(pe)	see(n)	mi(le)	ba(se)
gra(ce)	plea(d)	mee(k)	pri(ze)	sie(ge)
fu(se)	boa(t)	lea(gue)	li(ke)	gra(pe)
ti(le)	ty(ke)	grou(p)	ga(ze)	loa(d)
lea(se)	hai(l)	ho(pe)	hee(l)	soa(p)
bi(ke)	pla(gue)	see(k)	stai(n)	pi(le)
sa(ne)	sea(t)	ti(re)	law(n)	bea(m)
boi(l)	mo(de)	gai(l)	pa(ge)	pla(te)
rai(n)	frea(k)	mi(re)	si(de)	lea(n)
kee(n)	la(ce)	joi(n)	hea(t)	
new(t)	sea(l)	goa(t)	pa(ce)	

ple, the first word on that list is *wa(ke)*. The child is told, "Say *wake.*" (Pause.) "Now say it again, but don't say the /k/ sound." The answer is *way*. Proceed through all the words in this fashion.

Although the child will probably be able to pass the appropriate items on the TAAS when he completes this exercise, I suggest you also use the following activity before leaving Level IV.

4. Substitute beginning or final sounds. Ask the child to "Say *make.*" (Pause.) "Now say it again, but instead of /m/, say /t/. Or (remember to say the letter sound, not the letter name) "Say *make;* now say it again, but instead of /k/ say /t/."

The word activities in figure 33 are appropriate for this step.

FIGURE 33

Say **sad**	Now say it again, but instead of /s/ say /m/	**mad**
Say **kale**	Now say it again, but instead of /k/ say /s/	**sale**
Say **tan**	Now say it again, but instead of /t/ say /m/	**man**
Say **sat**	Now say it again, but instead of /s/ say /k/	**cat**
Say **table**	Now say it again, but instead of /t/ say /k/	**cable**
Say **my**	Now say it again, but instead of /m/ say /s/	**sigh**
Say **make**	Now say it again, but instead of /m/ say /t/	**take**
Say **kill**	Now say it again, but instead of /k/ say /m/	**mill**
Say **mare**	Now say it again, but instead of /m/ say /k/	**care**
Say **milk**	Now say it again, but instead of /m/ say /s/	**silk**
Say **call**	Now say it again, but instead of /k/ say /t/	**tall**
Say **sit**	Now say it again, but instead of /s/ say /k/	**kit**
Say **task**	Now say it again, but instead of /t/ say /m/	**mask**
Say **cage**	Now say it again, but instead of /k/ say /s/	**sage**
Say **more**	Now say it again, but instead of /m/ say /t/	**tore**
Say **main**	Now say it again, but instead of /m/ say /k/	**cane**
Say **take**	Now say it again, but instead of /t/ say /s/	**sake**
Say **mend**	Now say it again, but instead of /m/ say /t/	**tend**
Say **tin**	Now say it again, but instead of /t/ say /k/	**kin**
Say **seal**	Now say it again, but instead of /s/ say /m/	**meal**
Say **cash**	Now say it again, but instead of /k/ say /s/	**sash**
Say **tangle**	Now say it again, but instead of /t/ say /m/	**mangle**
Say **sell**	Now say it again, but instead of /s/ say /t/	**tell**
Say **moat**	Now say it again, but instead of /m/ say /k/	**coat**
Say **tend**	Now say it again, but instead of /t/ say /s/	**send**
Say **fill**	Now say it again, but instead of /f/ say /h/	**hill**
Say **heart**	Now say it again, but instead of /h/ say /d/	**dart**
Say **lace**	Now say it again, but instead of /l/ say /p/	**pace**
Say **dart**	Now say it again, but instead of /d/ say /p/	**part**

Say **goat**	Now say it again, but instead of /g/ say /b/	**boat**
Say **fame**	Now say it again, but instead of /f/ say /g/	**game**
Say **hall**	Now say it again, but instead of /h/ say /w/	**wall**
Say **toss**	Now say it again, but instead of /s/ say /m/	**tom**
Say **boss**	Now say it again, but instead of /s/ say /t/	**bought**
Say **bait**	Now say it again, but instead of /t/ say /s/	**base**
Say **beam**	Now say it again, but instead of /m/ say /t/	**beat**
Say **lace**	Now say it again, but instead of /s/ say /t/	**late**
Say **lame**	Now say it again, but instead of /m/ say /s/	**lace**
Say **rack**	Now say it again, but instead of /k/ say /t/	**rat**
Say **rack**	Now say it again, but instead of /k/ say /m/	**ram**
Say **gate**	Now say it again, but instead of /t/ say /m/	**game**
Say **mate**	Now say it again, but instead of /t/ say /k/	**make**
Say **mite**	Now say it again, but instead of /t/ say /s/	**mice**
Say **bake**	Now say it again, but instead of /k/ say /s/	**base**
Say **seat**	Now say it again, but instead of /t/ say /k/	**seek**
Say **prime**	Now say it again, but instead of /m/ say /s/	**price**
Say **late**	Now say it again, but instead of /t/ say /m/	**lame**
Say **bite**	Now say it again, but instead of /t/ say /k/	**bike**
Say **fake**	Now say it again, but instead of /k/ say /s/	**face**
Say **base**	Now say it again, but instead of /s/ say /k/	**bake**
Say **leak**	Now say it again, but instead of /k/ say /s/	**lease**
Say **flame**	Now say it again, but instead of /m/ say /k/	**flake**
Say **face**	Now say it again, but instead of /s/ say /t/	**fate**
Say **well**	Now say it again, but instead of /l/ say /t/	**wet**
Say **steel**	Now say it again, but instead of /l/ say /p/	**steep**
Say **cash**	Now say it again, but instead of /sh/ say /n/	**can**
Say **cuff**	Now say it again, but instead of /f/ say /b/	**cub**
Say **drug**	Now say it again, but instead of /g/ say /m/	**drum**
Say **bead**	Now say it again, but instead of /d/ say /n/	**bean**
Say **safe**	Now say it again, but instead of /f/ say /j/	**sage**
Say **league**	Now say it again, but instead of /g/ say /n/	**lean**
Say **page**	Now say it again, but instead of /j/ say /l/	**pale**
Say **loaf**	Now say it again, but instead of /f/ say /d/	**load**
Say **stage**	Now say it again, but instead of /j/ say /t/	**state**
Say **grade**	Now say it again, but instead of /d/ say /n/	**grain**
Say **hope**	Now say it again, but instead of /p/ say /z/	**hose**
Say **gain**	Now say it again, but instead of /n/ say /z/	**gaze**
Say **hide**	Now say it again, but instead of /d/ say /r/	**hire**
Say **pan**	Now say it again, but instead of /n/ say /s/	**pass**
Say **win**	Now say it again, but instead of /n/ say /g/	**wig**
Say **plead**	Now say it again, but instead of /d/ say /z/	**please**
Say **fair**	Now say it again, but instead of /r/ say /l/	**fail**
Say **mail**	Now say it again, but instead of /l/ say /d/	**maid**

When the child has completed all these activities, he is ready to be tested.

Use the TAAS items 7, 8, and 9. If he passes, start working at Level V.

If the child is in Level V, teach him to

1. Find the hidden sound that, in this level, may be anywhere in the word. Ask him to "Say *camel.*" (Pause while he says it.) Then, "Is there a /m/ sound [say the letter sound, not the letter name] in camel?" Encourage the child to repeat the word to himself and to think about how his mouth feels as he says it.

The words in figure 34 are suitable for this activity.

FIGURE 34

Is there an /ă/ sound in this word? (as in *pat*)

wet	ladder	placid	shadow
racket	written	depend	dazzle
rake	sailboat	dancer	blade

Is there a /s/ sound in this word? (as in *lacy*)

beside	inside	wishes	placid
whistle	waste	luster	misty
brother	loses	mazes	muzzle

Is there a /t/ sound in this word? (as in *attic*)

brittle	handle	winter	paddle
waiter	weather	window	party
bother	model	alter	pathway

Is there a /b/ sound in this word? (as in *cabin*)

softball	super	sober	carpenter
soapy	laboratory	lipstick	mustard
gabby	grandpa	hamburger	applesauce

Is there a /d/ sound in this word? (as in *odor*)

midst	lately	muddy	comfortable
eighteen	stopwatch	pedigree	remainder
wonderful	codfish	weather	fracture

Is there an /ĕ/ sound in this word? (as in *leg*)

rest	feather	Wednesday	mint
wrist	window	defense	lend
meat	pin	domestic	handle

Is there a /f/ sound in this word? (as in *defend*)

baffle	wavy	defuse	prefer
weather	birthday	marvelous	wonderful
laughter	afterward	devise	pavement

Is there an /ĭ/ sound in this word? (as in *mist*)

listen	novel	mistletoe	master
western	whistle	lively	minister
lather	petal	wristwatch	messenger

Is there an /ŏ/ sound in this word? (as in *log*)

codfish	model	Boston	butterfly
shadow	bought	favor	poverty
showboat	protrude	strong	postpone

Is there an /ŭ/ sound in this word? (as in *but*)

nothing	mountain	insult	front
bought	blunt	subscribe	pendant
musty	instrument	design	horseman

2. Say the sound that is missing. Tell the child, "Say *slip*." (Pause.) "Now say *lip*." Then, "What sound is missing in *lip* that you heard in *slip*?" (The answer, of course, is the /s/ sound.) The words in figure 35 are suitable here.

FIGURE 35

spider - cider	stack - sack	hand - had	scale - sale
slip - lip	spin - sin	cast - cat	bent - bet
stack - tack	store - sore	sent - set	beast - beat
spin - pin	black - lack	start - star	boast - boat
stare - tear	fist - fit	slag - sag	fern - fur
best - bet	best - Bess	spank - sank	bank - back
ghost - goat	snap - sap	bright - bite	blow - low
trap - rap	spoon - soon	crow - row	pest - pet
best - bet	stick - sick	lint - lit	snip - sip
trim - rim	slam - lamb	cram - ram	hulk - hull
stop - top	swell - well	built - bill	lend - led
cork - core	flip - lip	fast - fat	drown - down
snap - sap	snip - nip	triple - ripple	string - sting
rust - rut	mask - mack	fend - fed	black - back
skill - sill	store - tore	bent - Ben	just - jut
fork - for	sunk - sun	snap - nap	mark - mar
try - rye	stir - sir	stick - tick	chart - char
felt - fell	scoop - soup	slam - Sam	west - wet
skein - sane	stake - sake	store - tore	roast - rote
milk - mill	swing - wing	black - back	skip - sip
land - lad	bark - bar	vest - vet	stick - sick
fluster - flutter	bend - bed	wilt - will	sting - sing
drip - dip	clasp - clap	bunt - but	
blow - bow	cart - car	scold - sold	
snap - sap	gland - glad	track - rack	

3. Say the word without the sound. Tell the child, "Say *stick*." (Pause.) Now say it again, but don't say the /t/ sound. (Remember, you say the letter sound, not the letter name.)

All the words on the Level V word list, figure 36, are suitable for this activity.* They are printed with parentheses around the sound that is to be deleted. For example, the first word in that list is *p(r)ay*. Tell the child, "Say *pray;* now say it again, but don't say the /r/ sound." Have him work through the entire list.

FIGURE 36: LEVEL V WORD LIST

p(r)ay	(g)rub	fil(m)	c(l)aim	(c)lock
g(l)ow	hal(t)	fin(d)	c(l)amp	c(l)ock
(s)lip	ha(n)d	(f)lair	(c)lamp	(c)olt
f(r)og	ha(s)te	f(l)air	f(l)eet	c(l)ot
ca(m)p	he(l)d	(f)lake	(f)lier	c(l)ub
clas(p)	he(l)m	f(l)ake	f(l)ier	c(l)utter
e(n)d	he(m)p	(f)lame	(f)light	(c)raft
ha(s)te	hem(p)	f(l)ame	f(l)ight	(c)ramp
be(l)t	hi(l)t	(f)lash	(f)lit	c(r)amp
bel(t)	hum(p)	f(l)at	f(l)it	cra(m)p
be(n)t	li(l)t	(f)law	f(l)oor	cram(p)
ben(t)	(p)laid	(f)lee	f(l)orist	(c)rank
ben(ch)	p(l)aid	f(l)ee	(f)low	cra(n)k
(b)lack	(p)lain	(f)leece	f(r)ame	(c)rash
b(l)ack	(p)ray	p(l)ain	f(r)og	c(r)ash
(b)lank	(f)lap	p(l)aint	f(r)izzle	(c)reep
b(l)ank	s(l)ip	(p)lank	(f)lume	c(r)eep
(b)lare	(f)lake	plan(t)	f(r)ee	(g)low
b(l)are	clam(p)	(p)late	f(r)yer	g(l)ow
(b)leed	fi(s)t	p(l)acque	ga(s)p	(g)lue
b(l)eed	fin(d)	(p)ly	(g)lad	(g)race
(b)lend	p(l)y	p(l)y	(g)land	(g)rade
b(l)end	b(l)ond	(p)rank	(g)lade	(g)raft
ble(n)d	b(l)ood	(p)ray	(g)lare	(g)rail
(b)less	(b)loom	p(r)ay	(g)lass	g(r)ail
b(l)ess	b(l)oom	(p)ry	g(l)ass	(g)rain
(b)lest	(b)lot	pu(m)p	g(l)aze	g(r)ain
b(l)est	(b)low	ra(m)p	g(l)ide	(g)rasp
(b)light	b(l)ow	(g)loss	ran(k)	g(r)asp
b(l)ight	(b)race	(s)lap	ra(n)t	gras(p)
b(l)ind	(b)rag	(s)tick	ri(n)d	(g)rate
b(l)oat	b(r)ag	f(l)ake	ski(m)p	g(r)ate
(b)lock	(b)rain	cla(m)p	skim(p)	(g)rave

*You may add to this list of Level V words if you wish, but do *not* use words that are in the TAAS. Reserve those for testing to see whether the child has learned what you set out to teach him.

(c)rest	b(r)ain	bes(t)	s(l)ed	g(r)ave
cres(t)	(b)rake	fil(m)	(s)lid	(g)reed
(c)rib	(b)ranch	s(t)y	s(l)id	(g)ray
c(r)ook	bran(ch)	(b)rig	(s)lit	g(r)ay
(c)ruise	(b)rat	b(r)ig	(s)lide	(g)rill
(c)rush	b(r)at	(b)right	s(m)ell	g(r)ill
cu(l)t	(b)ray	b(r)ight	s(p)un	(g)rip
(d)raft	b(r)ay	(b)rim	(s)wing	(g)round
d(r)aft	b(r)ay	(b)ring	s(w)ing	(g)row
(d)rag	(b)read	(b)room	(g)low	s(l)ide
(d)rain	b(r)ead	b(r)oom	s(l)ap	(t)rack
d(r)ain	(b)reed	(b)rought	s(t)ick	t(r)ack
(d)raw	b(r)eed	b(r)ought	buil(d)	(t)rap
(d)rank	(b)rick	(b)row	cla(s)p	t(r)ap
d(r)ank	(b)ride	b(r)ow	be(s)t	(t)rim
d(r)awn	d(r)ip	(b)rush	fa(s)t	t(r)im
(d)read	d(r)ive	bui(l)d	be(n)d	(t)ry
d(r)ead	(d)rove	buil(d)	c(l)aim	t(r)y
(d)ream	d(r)ove	bui(l)t	(c)lash	wi(l)t
d(r)eam	(d)rug	buil(t)	c(l)ash	wil(t)
d(r)eary	d(r)ug	ca(m)p	cla(s)p	s(l)it
(d)rill	(d)rum	cam(p)	(c)lass	(s)lim
d(r)ill	d(r)um	can(t)	(c)lean	(f)led
(d)rink	e(n)d	ca(n)t	c(l)ean	
(d)rip	fe(n)d	(c)laim	c(l)ing	

The child is now probably able to pass the last four items (10–13) of the TAAS. However, I suggest that you also use the following activity before ending the program.

4. Sound substitutions. Tell the child, "Say *pry.*" (Pause.) "Now say it again, but instead of /p/ [say the letter sound, not the letter name] say /k/." (The word thus becomes *cry.*) Or, "Say *cup.*" (Pause.) "Now say it again, but instead of /ŭ/ [the short ŭ sound, as in *cup*], say ă [the short ă sound, as in *at*]." (The word thus becomes *cap.*)

The activities in figure 37 are appropriate for this step.

FIGURE 37

Say **bleed**	Now say it again, but instead of /l/ say /r/	**breed**
Say **blight**	Now say it again, but instead of /l/ say /r/	**bright**
Say **broom**	Now say it again, but instead of /r/ say /l/	**bloom**
Say **brake**	Now say it again, but instead of /ā/ say /ō/	**broke**
Say **clamp**	Now say it again, but instead of /m/ say /s/	**clasp**

Say **clock**	Now say it again, but instead of /ŏ/ say /ĭ/	**click**
Say **crash**	Now say it again, but instead of /ŏ/ say /ŭ/	**crush**
Say **crest**	Now say it again, but instead of /s/ say /p/	**crept**
Say **crash**	Now say it again, but instead of /r/ say /l/	**clash**
Say **draft**	Now say it again, but instead of /ă/ say /ĭ/	**drift**
Say **drink**	Now say it again, but instead of /ĭ/ say /ă/	**drank**
Say **drip**	Now say it again, but instead of /ĭ/ say /ŏ/	**drop**
Say **drive**	Now say it again, but instead of /ī/ say /ō/	**drove**
Say **flame**	Now say it again, but instead of /l/ say /r/	**frame**
Say **flash**	Now say it again, but instead of /ă/ say /ĕ/	**flesh**
Say **free**	Now say it again, but instead of /r/ say /l/	**flee**
Say **fryer**	Now say it again, but instead of /r/ say /l/	**flyer**
Say **gland**	Now say it again, but instead of /l/ say /r/	**grand**
Say **glass**	Now say it again, but instead of /l/ say /r/	**grass**
Say **glow**	Now say it again, but instead of /l/ say /r/	**grow**
Say **grain**	Now say it again, but instead of /ā/ say /ō/	**groan**
Say **grate**	Now say it again, but instead of /t/ say /n/	**grain**
Say **grip**	Now say it again, but instead of /ĭ/ say /ō/	**grope**
Say **lint**	Now say it again, but instead of /n/ say /s/	**list**
Say **plank**	Now say it again, but instead of /l/ say /r/	**prank**
Say **pray**	Now say it again, but instead of /r/ say /l/	**play**
Say **ramp**	Now say it again, but instead of /m/ say /s/	**rasp**
Say **sled**	Now say it again, but instead of /ĕ/ say /ĭ/	**slid**
Say **swing**	Now say it again, but instead of /w/ say /t/	**sting**
Say **track**	Now say it again, but instead of /ă/ say /ĭ/	**trick**
Say **trip**	Now say it again, but instead of /ĭ/ say /ă/	**trap**

When the child has completed all the above activities, he should be ready to be tested. Use the TAAS items 10, 11, 12, and 13. If he passes, he will be demonstrating that he has acquired auditory perceptual skills adequate to any primary-grade reading program. He will be able to analyze spoken words into their separate sounds and recognize the sequence of those sounds. Reading will be less of a rote memorization task or a guessing game to him. Matching sounds to letters—the system that underlies reading and spelling—will seem more reasonable than it once did.

ADDITIONAL ACTIVITIES

The following activities are supplemental to the program of instruction just described. Use them casually, a few minutes at a time, in a car, at the dining table, whenever conditions are suitable. They all have one central goal: to teach the child to listen analytically to the sounds of spoken language.

Encourage him to talk and then listen to him. This is crucial. If he does not get much opportunity to speak, he will be deprived of the opportunity to manipulate the sounds in spoken language. If you do not listen to him, he will not speak very much. Explain the importance of this to his brothers and sisters. He is to have his turn to speak, and he should be listened to with the same attention given to everyone else.

Have him make up alliterative phrases. (An alliterative, as you know, is a string of words that begin with the same sound. "Peter Piper picked a peck of pickled peppers" is a good example.) Some may be silly, but see if they can be somewhat meaningful; at the start they need not be long. "Alice's aunt" is a good beginning. Play a game to see how long a phrase he can come up with. You state the sound; he constructs the phrase.

For example, you say, "Make up a phrase where all the words start with the /s/ sound." This is not difficult. For example, "Sam Smith sits sadly sewing Sarah's scarf." When he gets the idea, ask him to add words to a phrase you start, but do not tell him the sound. Let him figure it out. For example, you say, "My mother . . ." then have him say the next word.

"Who Said the Word That Starts With '?' Sound." This requires a few people; it is a good after-dinner, linger-at-the-table game. One person is "It" (not always the child) and closes his eyes. Each of the others says a word. Then someone asks It, "Who said the word that starts with the '?' sound?" For example, say there are five people at the table. Sam is It. Mary says *boat,* Jim says *cat,* Bill says *fish,* Ann says *plane.* Someone then asks Sam, "Who said the word that starts with the /f/ sound?" (Say the sound, not the letter name, to the child.) The child, of course, should answer, "Bill." You can also play this with ending sounds. That is, "Who said the word that *ends* with the '?' sound?"

Mix up the syllables of a word. Have the child figure out what word you have in mind. For example, "What word is this—*cuss-sir?*" The answer, of course, is *circus. Loaf-meat—meatloaf;* and so on. Use longer words also. For example, *zine-ga-ma—magazine.*

Rhyming words. State a familiar one-syllable word and see how many rhyming words the child can come up with. Do not insist that they all be meaningful words. It can be more fun if you allow the activity to be a little silly. For example, "What rhymes with *tip?*" The answer—*bip, cip, dip, fip, gip,* and others.

Lipreading. Ask the child to figure out what you are saying just by watching your lips. You, of course, will have to emphasize your vocal motions so that they are apparent. Start easy—one word at a time. Also, trade places with him so that he gets a chance to overemphasize the speech production motions.

Slow-motion speech. This one works well with a tape recorder that can be played at two different speeds. The goal is to speak slowly enough and in a deep enough voice so that when the tape is replayed at the faster speed, the taped message is still understandable. It takes practice and, most important, it requires the child to break the spoken message into parts and stretch those parts out so that they will be understandable when they are replayed at the faster speed.

Teach him to speak Pig-Latin. As you recall, this involves moving the beginning sounds of each word to the end of the word, and then adding *ay.* For example, *cat* becomes *atcay, boy* becomes *oybay,* and so forth. *Ildrenchay ovelay isthay.*

Imitate others' speech patterns. Everyone likes to mimic, but not everyone likes to be mimicked, so be careful not to insult someone who might be sensitive. The best approach is for you to assume some dialect (Spanish, British, Irish, French) and have the child converse with you—he, of course, using the same dialect. Do not worry about the authenticity of the dialect. The important thing is for the child to become sensitive to what he hears.

"What Word Is This?" First say only one portion of a word (for example, a syllable or a single sound). With this small clue, the child is to guess the word you have in mind. If he is correct, fine; if he is wrong, add another clue (syllable or sound) and keep at it until he gets it. Then trade roles with him. For example, "What word is this?—/tine/ [rhymes with *mine*]." Then, "Not enough? Okay. Here's another clue—/va/ [pause] /tine/." Then, "Still not enough? Okay /val/ [pause] /en/ [pause] /tine/—Get it? Right! *Valentine.*" Start with simple, well-known words, such as his name, and increase the complexity as he catches on.

Coding sounds. This activity, similar to spelling, involves representing sounds with letters. Provide the child with four cards, each of which displays a single letter:

t   a   p   s

Then make certain that he knows the sound of each letter (the *a* should be sounded /ă/ as in *cat*). Have him show you the card that says /t/. (He should show the *t* card.) Then ask him to add a card so that it says *at.* (Say the word, do not spell it for him. His job is to recognize what *sound* was added and where it belongs in relation to the *t* card.) Once this is accomplished, have him change it to *ta,* then to *sta,* then to *sat,* then to *ast,* then to *pat,* then to *taps,* and so on. Introduce additional sounds (cards) and more complex arrangements as he shows that he understands the concepts involved—that letters stand for sounds and that the left-to-right sequence of letters stands for the sequence of sounds.

Hidden-number words. How many spoken words can you think of that have a number hidden in them? For example *"won*der" (one), *"Tues*day" (two), "be*fore*" (four), "d*ate*" (eight).

Hidden-color words. How many spoken words can you think of that have a color hidden in them? For example, "b*read*" (red).

This activity list could be extended, but I think you have the idea by now. The goal is to teach children to analyze spoken language into component parts —first syllables and then individual sounds.

It is important that you treat these activities as games. Let the child know that the formal program, already described, is treatment; something he *must* do on a schedule. These activities, in contrast, are to be done when he feels like doing them. Engage in them casually. If he does not feel like playing, allow him that privilege. He will play when he thinks he can compete successfully.

TEACHING GENERAL MOTOR SKILLS

The central goal of a general motor skills instructional program should be to help the child recognize that his body is constructed of a number of movable parts that can be organized in a variety of ways. As the goal is achieved, the child will have better control over his movements—better not only in the precision of those movements but also in the ease with which he executes them. It is important to understand that the goal is not to teach a particular skill, such as hopping or skipping. Rather, the goal is to teach the child better coordination that he will then be able to display *by* hopping and skipping.

There are a variety of formal programs available for teaching general motor skills. Some are very elaborate—too elaborate, in my opinion, calling for such sophisticated paraphernalia as trampolines and the like. There is no need to go to this extent.

Ideally a variety of experiences should be provided in a variety of settings —ball fields, gymnasiums, swimming pools, and so on. YMCA and scouting programs can be exceptionally effective in helping the child achieve better motor abilities and, at the same time, help him grow socially and emotionally, as well as cognitively.

Therefore, even though I will limit my suggestions to a few basic activities, be assured that there are many alternative approaches. I should emphasize that you are not concerned with sponsoring the development of exceptional athletic abilities. The general motor skills that I identified as worthy of testing are, for the most part, those expected from an average six-year-old. Certainly it is desirable for the child to acquire good motor skills—they will serve him well in a variety of situations—but in the context of a discussion about perceptual skills as they relate to school learning, there is no justification for working toward motor skills that would make an Olympic participant proud.

The important question here, then, is when do you worry about the child's motor skills and just what do you do about them? It might be useful to refer back to figure 11, on page 38, which shows how general motor skills link up with visual and auditory perceptual skills that in turn link up with reading, spelling, arithmetic, and writing. You may recall that I suggested that you should not worry too much about testing the child's general motor skills until after you have tested his visual and auditory skills. If you found either of these to be inadequate, then you were to test those general motor skills that are directly related. If, on the other hand, the child's visual and auditory skills were satisfactory, you were advised that you need not worry about his general motor skills.

Now what? Suppose you found in your testing that the child's visual or auditory perceptual skills were substandard, then you tested his general motor skills and found these to be less than satisfactory. What should you do? You should help the child acquire the motor abilities he lacks, in accord with the test results. But remember, it is not enough that he learns to hop or balance or what have you by devoting full attention to the act. You want him to be able to do these things almost automatically, similar to the way an experienced driver controls an automobile.

That does not mean that the child should be able to show complete facility when he starts to acquire a skill. Obviously this will not be the case. For example, when he first starts to work on fine-motor finger skills such as cutting with scissors, he may very well have to devote as much attention to handling the scissors as the new driver does to handling his car. This level of operation is a start, of course, but not enough. He should be able to perform easily, and the only way this can ordinarily be brought about is through lots of practice. So in teaching general motor skills the five principles already defined apply once more.

Principle #1: Organize for success.

For example, if the child's goal is to learn to use a scissors effectively, it is not wise to have him start by trying to cut out intricate shapes. Start with a simple straight line and increase the complexity of the task as he acquires skill.

Principle #2: Make certain that the child really does have the factual knowledge he needs to profit from the lesson.

In this context that simply means making sure that he understands the instructions.

Principle #3: Make clear to him a system—a strategy—that ties together what he is to learn with what he already knows.

There is no real system here, other than the occasional mnemonic, or memory jogger, that he might need to recall just how to get started in a particular task.

Principle #4: Encourage the child to use all his senses to obtain additional information about what he is doing—by looking and listening as he acts.

Put simply, this suggests that the child will improve his motor skills more rapidly if he takes the time to look at and listen to what he is doing. This is true in all of the areas discussed here, but it is especially true in fine-motor abilities; watching the hands and what they are doing, listening as alliteratives are spoken, will increase the effectiveness of the activities.

Principle #5:
Practice! The importance of that is self-evident!

SUGGESTED ACTIVITIES

There are literally thousands of general motor activities. I will limit my suggestions to a representative sampling. Try to make the activities pleasurable. Give them a game format, a game that the child has a chance of winning, at least often enough to keep him interested.

The activities described here are organized according to the general categories of balance and movement skills, finger skills, oculomotor skills, vocomotor (speech) skills, and rhythm skills. As such, the first three relate more closely to visual perceptual skills, the last two to auditory perceptual skills.

Balance and Movement Skills

The activities in this category all present the child with the same general goal: movement that shows he understands that his body is made up of a number of movable parts and that he knows how these parts work together.

Walking games. Walk like a
Duck—squat on both feet and walk forward, backward, and sideways.
Rabbit—with hands and feet on floor, move both hands forward together, then both feet, and so on.
Kangaroo—take large hops, both feet together.
Crab—with chest up away from floor, hands and feet on floor, walk forward and backward without collapsing.
Elephant—walk on all fours, slowly and ponderously.

Roll across the room. Lie down on the floor, then roll over sideways, attempting to maintain the desired direction.

Hopscotch. This well-known game involves hopping, jumping, and balancing.

Jump rope. Start simply. It will be easier for the child to learn to jump rope if two others hold the rope. Start off by marking an X on the ground to show the spot where the child is to stand. Then the two persons holding the rope should swing it back and forth slowly and rhythmically while the child jumps over it. Do not swing it completely around him at first. Just keep it very close to the ground and swing at a pace that is manageable for the child, one that he is able to deal with effectively. When he is able to do this, extend the task by extending the swing of the rope. Do not try to impose difficult conditions on him until *he* knows that he can handle them.

Ball games. There is no need to describe any of these here. There are many and they are well known. One hint, however: It might be wise to start off using an inflated balloon rather than trying to teach the youngster to catch and hit a fast-moving object. A balloon is better than a ball because it moves much more slowly, is larger, and generally easier to manage. A good place to start is to have the child try to keep the ballon afloat by tapping it with his hand or head or foot while you keep track of the time. Perhaps the child will be interested in beating his record, especially if you reward that feat. Avoid organized and competitive sports until after he has acquired some basic skills. *Do not involve him in Little League* or the like until you are sure he has *some* chance of participating without embarrassment. He is experiencing enough failure in the classroom; do not seek it elsewhere as well.

Obstacle course. This may be any homemade activity—outdoors or in— that involves whatever objects are handy. Simply arrange a set of objects and instruct the child how he is to proceed through, over, under, or around them. For example, you might have him climb over a table and under a chair or slide down a rope. Timing him and keeping a chart of his progress might be motivating.

Balance rail. Procure from a lumberyard a ten- or twelve-foot length of a wooden two-by-four. Place it on the floor and have the child walk the length of it—forward, backward, sideways. His goal is to be able to walk it without stepping off. Once he can do this, complicate the task by having him walk the rail while he

    a. Places his hands on his hips, his head, his chest
    b. Walks heel to toe
    c. Holds a weight in one hand
    d. Balances a book on his head

e. Looks somewhere other than at the walking rail, straight ahead or at you for example

Again, remember the basic principles for teaching these skills. If a twelve-foot walking rail is too long, use a shorter one. If he cannot get across the rail without some support—a hand to hold—give him that support, then slowly withdraw it.

As you can see, this list of activities could be longer. You can take it from here, I am sure. Just keep the basic goals in mind. You want him to be able to pass the tests described on pages 58–59. These are not difficult tasks and should be accomplished fairly quickly. If you and he want to work for more elaborate skills, go ahead. It will do him no harm; but I do not think it will do much good, either, in terms of directly helping him to become a better reader, speller, calculator, or writer.

Finger Skills

The following suggested activities are again but a sampling of what could be a long list. They are designed for the same general purpose: to teach the child how to use his hands (fingers) in precise, controllable ways.

Moving a particular finger. Designate one finger (touch it or name it) and have the child extend it, keeping all of the others out of the way. (*Note:* He may want to use his thumb to restrain the other fingers; this is acceptable.) Then have him extend the same finger on the other hand. Start slowly; work on speed after he has learned the basic movements.

Folding paper. Origami activities are excellent. You should be able to find a book on origami in your library or local bookstore.

Crocheting, knitting, or weaving. These are valuable activities, particularly since a pattern is usually followed, thereby providing some instruction in visual perceptual skills as well.

Identifying objects with the hands. Place familiar objects in the child's hand(s) for him to identify without seeing them. Common household objects work well. So do coins of various denominations, cardboard or plastic geometric shapes, and buttons of various sizes.

Cutting, pasting, painting, or coloring. All are worthwhile activities that children tend to enjoy. Avoid activities that are too demanding. Do not give him tasks that depend upon facile fine-motor skills that you know, in advance, he cannot handle. Find uncluttered coloring pages.* There is time enough to give him intricate tasks after he learns the basic skills.

Buttoning buttons, zipping zippers, tying bows, and lacing laces. This implies that the child should dress himself, feed himself, and butter his own bread. And it is meant to. This is very important, even if it means that he will have to get out of bed a half hour earlier in the morning, or clean up a spilled glass of milk occasionally.

Toys and games. A walk through any toy store will provide countless ideas—construction toys, games that require drawing, and so forth. But you need not invest in a lot of commercial games. There are any number of materials around the house that will serve quite well. Anything that requires the child to use his individual fingers precisely rather than his whole fist will probably be useful—folding napkins and sorting buttons are good examples. And if, at the same time, he has to follow a pattern—thus employing his visual perceptual skills—all the better.

Oculomotor Skills

These activities are not in any way intended as a substitute for a visit to a vision specialist. As I suggested earlier, if your child's eyes do not appear to be normal, either in terms of how well he sees or in terms of how well he controls them, seek advice from a professional. (Remember, it is advisable to have a visual evaluation done when you first suspect a learning problem, even if his eyes seem to be free of problems.) The activities suggested here are a sampling of the kinds of general activities that can serve to foster better control of eye movements.

Following a smoothly moving target. Suspend a rubber ball from the ceiling on a string so that it is at about the level of the child's lower chest. Although size is not critical, something approximating baseball-size is fine. A variety of activities can be engaged in with this setup.

    a. Remove the strings from an old badminton racket (or fashion a similar loop from a coat hanger) and have the child keep the loop of the racket around—but not touching—the ball as the ball swings in a variety of motions. Also have him take the racket away, then return it to its position around the ball, without touching the ball.

---

*I recognize that many people believe that coloring books will have a detrimental effect on the child's creative abilities. I do not think so. Our most creative artists were well acquainted with their craft and media first. *Then* they were creative, that is, able to express their thoughts and feelings through some medium.

b. Have the child use his hands instead of the racket. He is to cup them near, but not touching, the ball as it swings.

c. Bunt the ball with a broomstick handle. The ball should be at the child's chest height. The child holds the broomstick handle at his chest with both hands and makes contact with (bunts) the ball. He maintains this bunting pattern as long as he can. The activity can be made more complicated and involve more complex eye movements by having the child lie down on the floor, faceup, and do his bunting from there. (Obviously the ball will have to be lowered.) As the child improves, encourage him to move his eyes, not his head, as he follows the ball.

Making the eyes hop. Contrary to popular belief, your eyes do not move smoothly across the page when you read. Rather, they hop across, stopping periodically to look at the words. You do not read when the eyes are in motion, only when they stop. So one way to improve reading ability is to make the eyes hop more accurately; if they land where they are not supposed to, you stand the chance of skipping a word or a line or, at best, wasting time finding your place.

The following activity can be conducted in any room containing furniture or other objects. Tell the child that as you name an object in that room he is to look directly at that object and keep looking at it until you name another object. When you do, he is then to move his eyes directly to that second object, then a third as it is named, and so on. If he takes his eyes from the object before he is told to, it is a miss. (Keeping score adds interest.) Do not make unreasonable demands on him. That is, do not call out a new object every second or two. That is too fast. Likewise, do not delay overly long between calls. Keep the pace somewhat irregular, but reasonable. If he needs additional support, have him point at the object with his finger as he looks at it. This will help him control his eye movements.

Vocomotor (Speech) Skills

These activities are not in any way intended to be a substitute for a relationship with a speech therapist. They are a sampling of the general activities that might foster more precise speech production skills. If your child shows any signs of a speech problem, seek professional advice.

As you will note, all the activities are designed to teach the child better control of his lips, tongue, and jaws.

Whistle through puckered lips.

Inflate balloons.

Play tabletop soccer. Use a Ping-Pong ball and straws, propelling the ball with air blown through the straws.

Click tongue. Click it against roof of mouth; click teeth; produce odd noises with vocal chords.

Say alliteratives rapidly. For example, "She sells seashells by the seashore."

Rhythm Skills

The rhythm skills we are concerned about here are those that require the child to coordinate his two body sides in a synchronized way. This is not the same as tapping out rhythms with one hand, although there is nothing wrong with doing that also.

Bongo drums. They are useful in generating interest, but they are not necessary. The child is to

   a. Tap one time with his right hand, then one time with his left, then his right, and so on (about one tap per second)
   b. Tap two times with his right hand, two times with his left, two times with his right, and so on (same tempo)
   c. Tap once with his right hand, twice with his left, once with his right, and so on (same tempo)
   d. Then do the reverse; twice with his right hand, once with his left, and so on (same tempo)

At first the child may have to count to himself as he engages in these various rhythms, saying "one-two, one-two," then "one, one-two, one, one-two." If he has to, fine, encourage him to do so. But his goal is to be able to tap these rhythms without losing the beat when he switches hands—while at the same time carrying on a conversation. This will take practice.

Ask questions. Once he has the rhythmic pattern established, start asking him simple questions, such as his age or his birthday. The questions can get more complex in time. The goal here is for him to be able to tap any of the rhythms upon request while simultaneously carrying on a conversation.

PART III

Helping the Child
with School Subjects

TEACHING SCHOOL SUBJECTS

Up to now I have focused on perceptual skills—the readiness abilities that are called for, in varying degrees, by all elementary-school reading, writing, spelling, and arithmetic instructional programs—skills that have a direct and significant influence on a child's teachability. I have traced their development and described how to test them and, when called for, how to teach them.

Most of you, however, are probably concerned about a particular youngster; and chances are that he is well beyond the readiness stage. As such, you are interested in finding out what can be done for a second-, third-, sixth-, or even tenth-grader who has a history of persistent school failure.

In other words, what about the fourth-grade child who is reading at a second-grade level or whose arithmetic achievement is far below what it should be? What do you do about him?

As already noted, improving his perceptual skills and doing nothing else is not the answer. True, accomplishing this will be helpful—it will make him less hard to teach. But it will not supply him with the information he should but does not have because he was also hard to teach when that information was originally presented. The only way to close those knowledge gaps is through effective instruction and plenty of it. In other words, the child who is behind in school needs more than a perceptual skills program. He needs to be taught what he does not know, in ways that take into account the skills and knowledge he has and the skills and knowledge he lacks.

The goal of this section is to suggest ways for teaching children who are in such circumstances. To achieve that goal, we must first determine what being able to read, write, spell, and do arithmetic require of the child—what he has to be able to *do* in order to make progress in those subjects. Then we can design ways to teach him how to do it. (Going back to the example of teaching the blind child to read, what he has to be able to do is to relate spoken language to symbols; Braille is the way that enables him to accomplish this.)

But first we must consider a general concept that distinguishes the teaching of perceptual skills from the teaching of such school subjects as reading and arithmetic. Improving a child's perceptual skills involves teaching him how to break down visual and acoustical patterns into their parts, as well as how to recognize the way those parts fit together. These are processes of analysis. Having acquired these skills, the child will have learned how to identify those features of spoken language and spatial patterns that letters and numerals represent in reading, spelling, writing, and arithmetic.

Learning to read, spell, calculate, and write is different. These involve *assembling processes.* Here the child has to learn to deal with as large a unit as possible, so that the assembling process is accomplished quickly and he has time to interpret—think about—the information represented by the symbols. You cannot very well think about how to solve a practical arithmetic problem if you have to work through the basic calculations of that problem step by step, counting on your fingers or in your head. And you cannot think about the meaning of a sentence if you have to work through its words, sound by sound, letter by letter.

Working through reading and arithmetic tasks in such small steps would rule out your chances of interpreting anything. It would consume too much time and mental energy. You would lose your train of thought. You would not be able to remember enough about the beginning of a reading paragraph or an arithmetic problem when you finally got to the end. The information would not be meaningful; it would have no unity; it would be a collection of separate segments.

The key words here are *larger units* and *remember.* As mentioned earlier, psychologists talk about two kinds of memory, long-term and short-term. Both are crucial to successful learning, and both are strongly influenced by our ability to assemble small units of information into readily identifiable larger units.

Both are what their names suggest. When you recall your telephone number, what you did last Christmas, or your mother's full name, you are using your long-term memory. It is information that you are not likely to forget, at least not for a while. It is information you have fully memorized. If you ignore it long enough—or if you get a new telephone number—it will be shoved aside for other, more pertinent information, but only then.

You use your short-term memory to store information for the moment. It is information that may or may not eventually be transferred to long-term memory, depending on what it is, how much you use it, and how unique it is. For example, when you look up someone's number in the telephone book, you remember it long enough to use it. Then you forget it, unless you use it frequently, memorize it intentionally, or (and this is most relevant to our concerns) associate it with something already memorized. (There are, of course, those isolated experiences, sufficiently unique, that seem to go directly into one's long-term memory; these are usually events that have strong emotional impact.)

There is a limit to the amount of information a person can hold in short-term memory at any one time. Psychologists suggest that seven units is about it; a seven-digit number, for example. Given that fact, how can we possibly hope to help a child learn to interpret sentences that contain more than seven words; for that matter, how are we able to do it ourselves?

We do it not by remembering *more* units of information but by remembering *larger* units—chunks—made up of familiar patterns of smaller units. (Recall the visual and auditory memory tasks I proposed earlier, pages 14–19.) Then when we encounter a set of new information that contains these chunks, we recognize them—remember them—with relative ease, thereby reducing the amount of new information that has to be remembered in that situation and thereby enhancing what we remember of that situation.

I presume, for example, that you can remember quite a bit of what you have read so far in this book. (At least, I hope so.) How have you managed it? Surely not by memorizing the words as you read them. You have done it by using at least two strategies:

1. You have not read every word—you chunked the words; you read fast enough to take your information in large, meaningful bites.
2. You attached the information contained in this book to knowledge you had already stored in your memory. Not all that I have said is new to you. What part do you remember least? That part that was most novel—probably the sections devoted to testing and teaching perceptual skills. There you most likely had to deal with the information in smaller bites and therefore can hardly be expected to recall very many of the details.

To achieve in school, the child has to learn to do these same things. If he approaches each learning situation with a clean slate and attempts to remember each piece of information separately, without attaching or relating it to something already remembered, he will fail. He will not remember enough; he will not learn enough.

The only way to profit from today's lesson is to see how it relates to previous lessons—how it differs, how it matches. Thus each new lesson, if it is properly designed, is not a big step beyond the previous ones. In fact, in terms of what the child is to *do* it should be remarkably similar; only the material he does it with should change—become more complex.

This is a general guideline that should underlie all the activities you use. By definition the child with a learning difficulty remembers too little of what he is taught because he does not have the ability to organize information effectively and see how separate segments fit together. He is slower to recognize patterns of pertinent similarities and differences. He therefore tries to memorize everything separately—as isolated segments—a task not unlike trying to memorize a long list of telephone numbers. An impossible goal. Thus your job will be to make certain that the child does recognize the important patterns and does have ways to remember them. If he remembers them, he will make progress in school. He will make progress at overcoming his learning difficulties.

TEACHING READING

To start, we have to define the word *reading*—what it is. Then we will identify some of the basic processes involved in learning how to read—what learning to read requires of the child. Then we will compare what is known about good learners of reading, poor learners of reading, and the various school programs for teaching reading. After this we will be able to think logically about how best to help the child who is having trouble learning to read, taking into consideration the demands made on him by the reading program used in his school.

First, then, a definition: *Reading,* in this context, refers to the act of reconverting symbols into a language with which the individual is already familiar.* That definition calls our attention to a couple of important facts. It identifies reading as a reconversion process, a restoring of the information back to its original oral form, thereby giving us the basis for making a distinction between a *reading problem* and a *language problem.* As such, it directs us to recognize that the two—the child's reading ability and his language ability—are separate, albeit closely related, concerns; and that if the child does have a language deficit—if he is not sufficiently adept with the spoken form of language—then we must do something about it if we hope to teach him to read. Trying to teach someone to read a language that he cannot understand in its spoken form is inevitably futile. True, they may very well memorize a handful of words, but they will not be readers.

Now, aside from being familiar with the spoken form of the language, what else must a child be able to do in order to become a competent reader?

Optimally when you read you are unaware of the separate words comprising the text. You do not try, literally, to memorize them. Instead you devote your attention to the information represented by those words. You sort and classify the information as you read it, mentally filing some away in memory,

*This definition does not limit reading to standard visual symbols and standard oral language. The same definition applies to the blind reader who converts tactile symbols to standard oral language; to the deaf reader who converts standard visual symbols to a nonstandard, nonoral language; to the telegraph operator who converts long and short tones to standard language; to the Chinese reader who converts pictographic symbols to standard language, and so on.

categorizing some as "I know that already," which then allows you to ignore it, and, once in a while, rereading something because it does not fit comfortably with the rest of the text or with what you already know about the topic. That is, it may conflict, or simply not match up well rather than actually conflicting. In any event, when you read, your energies are usually channeled into acquiring information, and the extent to which you can do this is evidence of what reading teachers call your reading-comprehension ability.

What must you be able to do in order to comprehend—think and understand—as you read? Of prime importance, of course, is your present knowledge about the subject. That is self-evident. The more you already know about what you are reading, the less *new* information there is for you to hang on to. Also, since what you already know about the topic provides the basis for the mental filing system for holding on to new information, coming to the task with a well-organized store of knowledge helps you to be a more efficient reader.

But there is another, equally critical, factor. You must also be totally familiar with the printed words that make up the text. That is, you have to be able to identify—decode—the printed words on sight, to recall, or figure out, what they "say" virtually automatically and instantaneously. Obviously the longer it takes you to recall the oral form of a printed word and/or the longer it takes for you to decipher a totally new word, the less efficient your comprehension will be.

True, it will not be all that important if you encounter unfamiliar words only infrequently and if you have some reasonably efficient strategy for figuring these out. But if such circumstances are frequent and if you do not have a reasonably efficient method for figuring out unfamiliar words, then the cumulative effect will be significant. Comprehension will be more difficult, simply because, like the rest of us, you have fixed limits on the amount of information you can handle within a specified period of time—you have a limited short-term memory capacity.

In short, then, efficient reading comprehension requires that you come to the task having already memorized a substantial number of the printed words you will be reading and that you have a pretty good method for figuring out those that you have not yet memorized completely. (*Memorized,* here, means that you are able to identify what the word "says" immediately upon looking at it.)

What would such a method look like? What do you do when you encounter a new word, one you have never seen before, or a word that is not totally new but neither is it yet well established in your memory? You search for useful clues, related information that might help you determine what the whole word "says."

Take, for example, such words as *astronaut* and *laser.* These were not in your reading vocabulary a couple of decades ago; they probably were not even recognized as words then. Yet when you encountered them for the first time —those of you who could read before these words were coined—you were able to read them because you were already somewhat familiar with their oral forms and their meanings and you could identify certain familiar letter sequences— letter strings—such as *astro,* which made the decoding possible.

That highlights another source of potentially useful clues that we all exploit when we encounter a new word. In addition to familiar letter strings and smaller phonic units of analysis, such as single letter-sound combinations, we also try to use contextual clues. All of us have experienced this: coming across a new word, tentatively sounding it out based on our familiarity with the individual letters and letter strings that comprise the word, and then coming to the final state that reading people call closure, when we realize what it probably says and means. Our ability to do this is based partly on the word's spelling, which helps us associate it with other words we do know; partly on the general theme of the text in which it appears that helps us guess at its meaning; partly, perhaps, on our having heard that word at one time or another; and partly on our familiarity with the grammar of the language— particularly the syntax—which guides us in expecting certain words to precede and certain words to follow others.

I started off this discussion by pointing out that competent readers do not ordinarily pay attention to every word in a text, at least not unless they are intent on memorizing the words, as might be the case in a situation where specific facts are important or where they are reading something in which the individual words are to be appreciated for qualities beyond their literal meaning, such as in poetry and in some prose. What it comes down to is that good readers are good—that is, "educated"—guessers. They anticipate a great deal of what the text will present, and they move their eyes across the lines of print faster than they could speak it. To do this, they make maximum use of clues: contextual, syntactical, grammatical, letter-sound associations, illustrations if they are provided, and whatever else is available and helpful, slowing down only when they have to because of encountering an unfamiliar and/or confusing word or thought.

In effect, then, competent readers display the following abilities:

They are familiar with the spoken form of the language they are expected to be able to read—its vocabulary, syntax, and grammar.

They already know enough about the subject matter to organize—sort out and classify—the pertinent information contained in the text.

They are completely familiar with the symbols—the printed letters—and the conventions that govern their use, such as the left-right spatial sequencing and so on.

They can recognize on sight most of the words they are to read. That is, they can connect, instantaneously, the correct oral form to the printed word.

They are familiar with the standard letter-sound associations, both letter strings and single letters. And they can apply this knowledge when they encounter an unfamiliar word.

Our next question, then—given that good readers can do all this—is: How do you teach these things to a hard-to-teach nonreader? Or, more to the point: What should the instruction program look like that will help you achieve this with children who deserve the hard-to-teach label? In other words, what specifically do you have to teach and how do you do it?

To address these questions, we will examine three types of reading-instruction programs, one of which is almost always present in a standard classroom. Then we will consider the problem of how to modify and supplement those standard programs so that they work better for the hard-to-teach child.

Generally speaking, schools use one of the following types of reading-instruction programs: *whole-word, linguistic,* or *phonics.* There are, of course, many reading programs around that attempt to incorporate features from more than one of these basic designs, but by and large they end up simply as variations on a theme rather than as something very new and different.

There are a variety of ways that these three types of reading programs can be characterized. Obviously they cannot be all that different from each other. How could they be when they are all designed, ultimately, to teach children the same basic ability—to read, to obtain information efficiently from printed text? For our purposes, at this point, it is enough to recognize that their main differences can be described in terms of the extent to which emphasis is devoted to teaching the child *the what*—to recognize words on sight—as compared with the extent to which emphasis is placed on teaching the child the standard letter-sound associations, which he can then use to recall partially memorized words and to figure out new ones—*the how.* This will become evident as we compare the three basic program designs.

Whole-Word Approach

When it comes to stressing the ultimate goal of reading instruction—*the what* —the whole-word method comes very close to being on target. Where it falls down is in teaching *the how.* Unfortunately this *does* have to be taught to some children because otherwise they will not learn it, even though other children seem to learn it intuitively.

In its prototypical form the whole-word, or sight, method was based on the observation that really good readers did virtually no apparent sounding out. Instead, they seemed to be able to read whole words from the onset, thereby allowing them to devote their energy to interpreting what they read. Given these insights, it seemed that the best way to teach this ability was to start off that way. Why not teach good habits from the beginning? was the reasoning. Why teach operations that will have to be eliminated later on? It was difficult to argue with that kind of logic.

The "look-say" methods of the 1940s and 1950s were representative of this. From the very beginning in these programs, children read "meaningful" sentences and—depending upon your understanding of the adjective—"meaningful" stories. At the onset they were taught—that is, shown and urged to memorize—a limited list of words. The list characteristically contained the "sight words": *look, oh, mother, jump, something, run, see,* and some common male and female names, such as *Dick* and *Jane* or *Jerry* and *Alice.*

The teacher was directed by the program manuals to make no mention of phonics principles—that certain letters represented certain sounds. All lessons were designed to focus the children on the task of memorizing the words as whole words. This took the form of giving the children many repeated exposures to these words, of providing illustrations that could be associated with the words, and of calling to their attention the fact that printed words tend to have specific configurations. For example, the word *look* was portrayed as

 , *jump* as , and so on.

From very early on, the children read simple "stories" constructed from these words, with the same words appearing frequently, usually more than once per page. Over time additional words were introduced, but the basic method remained the same, and the goal was clear: to foster memorization, or instantaneous "whole-word recognition" skills.

How well did this method work? The fact that I pose that question in the past tense hints at the answer. It did not work well enough. Yes, some children —a good many in fact—did learn to read with that approach, but not enough to defend continued use of the method when it was attacked as being the reason why so many children were encountering difficulty learning to read.

It will be useful for us to speculate as to why those who did learn to read with this method were able to do so and why the others attained their status of being unsuccessful.

Consider what is involved in learning to read with such a program. In order to make satisfactory progress with this method, children have to be very good memorizers. This is especially true once they are past the very beginning stages of the program and have to add about five to ten new words to their reading vocabulary each week while continuing to hold on to all those learned previously. Since no basic system of memorizing is provided other than repetition, illustrations, and the crude one of word configuration, all of which are insufficient once the vocabulary list gets beyond the primer level, this meant that the children had to be able to invent their own systems for facilitating memorization. This in turn meant that some children—the hard-to-teach— would have trouble, inasmuch as one of their distinguishing characteristics *is* an inadequate ability to invent systems that facilitate memorization.

For illustration let us reconstruct how two children—one hard to teach, the other not hard to teach—fared with the look-say method. Assume that both entered school with the same store of factual information. That is not always the case, of course, but for discussion purposes let us assume that it was the case in this instance. Hence both children were equally familiar with the spoken forms of the words they were supposed to learn to read, with the way these words were usually sequenced in sentences, and with the lowercase and uppercase printed letters and the conventions that govern the use of these letters when they are to represent spoken language.

It is likely that both children did fairly well in the initial stages of the reading program. Both were able to remember their beginning list of words, using whatever system for accomplishing this that they had stumbled upon or that the program provided. But in no instance were phonics principles taught as a method for helping them remember.* So far, so good. At the onset each child progressed; neither encountered difficulty.

But conditions soon changed. As the list of words to be remembered lengthened, the hard-to-teach child started to display difficulty. Why? Because he failed to discover the system that works best—the system based on the fact that there is a direct relationship between certain letters in a printed word and certain sounds in its spoken version. The other systems—the ones his teacher did reveal to him—were inadequate for his needs.

In the final analysis *the best system for remembering the spoken form of printed words is by using phonic clues.* ** It is one thing to remember the word *look* by its configuration but another to remember it by that characteristic when the list also includes such words as *took, book,* and *hook.* Another example: Take the word *something.* In the beginning reading stage, many youngsters remember this as "the long word"—not a bad idea. But not good enough once another, equally long word is introduced. Configuration, then, is not all that useful an assist.

Illustrations, too, are poor devices. They help at the beginning, when the list of words to be remembered is short. At that point in the instruction the illustrations do not have to be so precisely on target. But as the list grows, the value of the illustrations decreases. They tend to be too nonspecific, too ambiguous.

What about the other child, the one who is not hard to teach? What did he do under such an instructional program? Confronted with the realization that one system did not work adequately, he figured out other systems for helping him remember the words, and eventually he came upon—or someone

---

*This was not always the case. Many a clever, well-motivated teacher smuggled a little phonics into the classroom, despite what she read in the publisher's manual about "optimal instructional strategies."

**That does not necessarily mean that the best system for teaching reading is phonics; simply that, as a mnemonic system, phonics works better than anything else.

led him to—the one involving the use of phonics principles. I am not suggesting that he then started to sound out words. Rather, he started to identify certain key letters and letter strings in the words that could be used as "markers" for certain sounds that were distinctive to those words. This gave him a good system for remembering those words and figuring out new ones containing the same key letters and letter strings. It is the only reasonable way to explain his consistent progress in that kind of a whole-word reading program.

Why did the hard-to-teach child not come upon these same phonics principles of reading? What got in his way? It is highly likely that he entered school lacking adequate ability in at least one of the two aptitudes we discussed earlier. It is a safe bet that his auditory analysis skills were less than what he needed to discover these principles.

As you will recall, auditory analysis skills are those developed abilities that enable us to identify the separate sounds that make up a spoken word and the interrelationships among, or sequence of, those sounds. If these skills are deficient it is not very likely that the child will discover phonics principles on his own. One can hardly be expected to discover a system—in this instance, a connection between what is seen and what is heard—when only one-half of the code, the visual, is perceived.*

Going back to our hypothetical situation, then, all too often the hard-to-teach child's only option in reading class was to guess, but unfortunately not in a very "educated" way. True, he looked at the illustration on each page, at the configuration of the words and at the context, and they did help, especially in the early stages when he was expected to know only relatively few words. There his guesses were less risky; the chance of error was relatively small. But later on, as his word list lengthened, his guesses became less educated. They became more and more random—and wrong, something teachers do not applaud. This in turn heightened his problem, and, sure enough, in time we had another nonreader, a child who refused even to guess, refused to reveal that he "cared," refused—for fear of yet another failure—to try again.

"Look-say" failed and has been removed from the classroom,** but its direct successor, the current version of the whole-word approach, is not all that different. Yes, certain phonics principles are now taught in this method, but the original whole-word concepts continue to affect the appearance of the program. It is as though the phonics component was simply an "add-on." Words similar to those found in the original programs are still introduced first. Rote memorization of sight words is still stressed. But as an added component, children are also taught certain letter-sound connections. For example, they learn that such words as *mother, Mary,* and *man* all begin with the letter *m*

---

*Remember, this does not mean that the child cannot hear—simply that he is insensitive to the separate sounds in a spoken word and to the temporal sequence in which those sounds occur.
**It really did not fail. Rather, it failed to work with *all* children. We continue to seek *the* answer—the one way—and throw out everything else. Unfortunate but true.

and the /m/ sound. And this undoubtedly helps—but not enough to serve the needs of the hard-to-teach child. It introduces too many ambiguous situations where the letters do not match up with the sounds—not so much in the case of consonants as in that of vowels, where "irregular" spellings are commonplace.

The letter *a,* for example, has at least five sounds associated with it. Think of how the *a* sounds in: *man, mane, law, was,* and *many,* let alone the fact that it is silent—has no sound—in such words as *meat* and *bread.* So though learning certain letter-sound associations does help, it can also confuse, especially when the words the child is to memorize are not controlled so as to prevent exposure to irregularly spelled words until after some consistent patterns are established. It is not unreasonable to expect someone—even a hard-to-teach child—to learn exceptions to a rule. But it is unreasonable to expect this to occur before the rule and its basic application have been well established in the child's repertoire.

Thus from our base of comparison we can perceive the current whole-word method as presenting the child with a paradox. It attempts to teach him to read words as units—and, in order to ease the demand on the child's memory, to appreciate that these units contain certain letters that he can use to facilitate recall because they have semiconsistent sound representations. However, it fails to limit the introduction of words where letter-sound relationships are inconsistent, that is, exceptions to the letter-sound rules are introduced long before the hard-to-teach child has had a chance to learn the rules.

Hence, as noted before, the whole-word method can be scored high as a method that stresses the ultimate goals of a good reading program—the *what* —and low as a method for providing those children who need it with a *how,* that is, an effective system for achieving those goals, for remembering the words and figuring out new ones, especially as the list lengthens.

Hard-to-teach children need to be shown *how.* They need to have a system taught explicitly. They are not able to discover it on their own, certainly not with the obscure clues provided by the words of a whole-word program. As a result, their progress in such programs deteriorates at an increasing rate as time passes and the memorization burden grows. And in fairly short order they fall so far behind that, for all practical purposes, catching up on their own becomes an impossibility.

Despite all this, the whole-word method continues to be the one most commonly found in our primary-grade classrooms. Little wonder there are so many children with reading problems!

Linguistic Approach

If we apply the same criteria in assessing the typical linguistic program as we used with the whole-word approach, we note certain benefits and certain drawbacks. On the negative side, a linguistic approach—despite the fact that most of these stress a whole-word design—does not get as close to teaching the desired ultimate goal of a reading program as defined above: instant recognition of the words typically found in children's reading materials. On the other hand, it does come closer to doing what the whole-word system fails to do: make apparent to the child a phonics-based system that helps him remember a growing list of words.

For example, the typical linguistic program starts off like the whole-word method by presenting the child with a limited list of whole words that he is to memorize. It differs, however, in the kinds of words that make up that initial group. Whereas whole-word programs tend to group words that have little in common other than that they can be readily combined into something resembling a story, linguistic programs are designed to stress phonics principles.

The initial reading vocabulary in a linguistic program includes only words that have regular and related spellings. Irregular words are avoided, words such as *look, oh, say, boy,* and so on. Instead, words belonging to "families" are used: *cat, fat, can,* and *fan,* for example. To the child with "just-adequate" auditory analysis skills, these words often provide a reasonable basis for discovering the key principles of phonics. He can identify certain letter strings that recur and retain their sound value across words—the *an,* for example, or the *at.* And since the list of words is specifically controlled to do this, he is not confronted with inconsistencies that portray exceptions—rule breakers—until well along in the program.

However, even this type of instructional program is not always sufficiently explicit for the hard-to-teach child. Remember, if the child has difficulty learning to read, he probably lacks adequate auditory analysis skills and therefore often finds even the more clear-cut examples of a linguistic program too obscure for his deficient basic aptitude.

Combine this with the fact that the list of words that meet the demands of such a program is exceptionally limited—that, before long, irregular words have to be introduced because there is a limit to the number of different stories one can write about *Ed* and *Ted* who *met* and *led*—and it is not surprising that the linguistic program also falls short of what the hard-to-teach child needs. It does enable the child to make some limited headway at the onset—probably more than the whole-word approach does—but it, too, ultimately creates conditions that overtax the memory and the very limited systems-inventing skills of the hard-to-teach child.

Linguistic programs have value. To some extent they solve the problems of the whole-word programs by means of a compromise: From the start they stress the *what*—recognition of whole words, albeit short, regular words—and the *how*—the phonics principles of reading. But because of the nature of the program's design, neither the *what* nor the *how* is taught thoroughly enough for the hard-to-teach child. Linguistic programs work well with many children. But they do not meet the needs of the child with significantly substandard auditory analysis skills.

Phonics Approach

Given what has been covered so far, it would be logical for you to assume that a phonics program is the method of preference for hard-to-teach children. In some ways that is a correct assumption—but not totally.

Phonics programs vary, of course, as do all of those that fall within the other categories already discussed. However, the best of phonics programs—best insofar as meeting the needs of the hard-to-teach child is concerned—share certain characteristics.

First, they relieve the child of the responsibility for identifying the separate sounds in spoken language and, through this process, figuring out the phonics rules of our language from representative whole words. Instead, individual letters and their sounds are directly taught from the beginning, thereby making the concepts apparent to the child despite his inept auditory analysis skills.

Second, the letter-sound combinations are kept consistent, at least until after some basic learning has occurred. For example, the child is initially told that the letter *a* has a single sound, the short sound, as in *cat;* the letter *c* one sound, again as in *cat;* and so on. He is then given words to "read"—sound out—letter by letter, sound by sound, and finally short "stories" made up of these words.

The shortcomings of such a program? There are two. First, as with the other programs already discussed, the irregularities of English spelling get in the way fairly quickly. Exceptions to the rules have to be acknowledged, and to the child who memorizes information inefficiently, this causes confusion that disrupts the learning process. Second, it teaches reading in a way that is precisely opposite to what we identified as the ideal; it teaches reading in a sounding-out, segmented manner rather than through rapid recognition of whole words.

In essence, then, the phonics approach tends to solve the inadequacies of the whole-word method but then introduces other potential sources of difficulty. As you can see, it scores very low at teaching anything approximating *what* we recognize as the ultimate goal of a reading program—rapid and effortless whole-word decoding. Children are intentionally taught to read letter by letter, a far cry from the efficient, ignore-the-specific-words, read-for-information behavior of the competent reader.

On the other hand, the phonics approach scores high on teaching the *how,* in providing the child who has poor memorization skills with a useful system for figuring out and remembering what printed words say, letter by letter. This does help, so long as he has sufficient time to sound that word out and so long as the word is sufficiently regular in its spelling to allow the sounding-out process to work. But it is not enough. It may get him started, but it does little more than that.*

---

*To determine which of these approaches is being used in your child's classroom, examine his "reading words"—the words he is supposed to be learning to read. Pay special attention to

Alternative programs

There are a number of reading programs that seem to differ from the three already discussed. At least, they appear to be different when you read the promotional literature provided by their publishers.

Initial Teaching Alphabet (i.t.a.)

i.t.a.* attempts to solve the confusion caused by the irregular spellings of the English language. It uses an expanded alphabet—forty-four symbols in all —the twenty-six of our standard, lowercase manuscript alphabet (called "traditional orthography," or T.O., by i.t.a. people) plus eighteen new ones. These added symbols tend to be mainly variations and combinations of the T.O. lowercase manuscript letters. There is an i.t.a. graphic symbol for each sound. This makes it possible to spell each word just as it sounds, rather than sticking to the twenty-six T.O. letters and explaining away the exceptions. Not a bad idea. It has two drawbacks, however. One is that some of the letters that are unique to i.t.a. are very similar to each other or to the standard letters of our alphabet, differing only in their left-right orientation or in some other very subtle way. The child with less-than-competent visual analysis skills often has trouble keeping some of these straight, and many hard-to-teach children do have substandard visual analysis skills in addition to their substandard auditory analysis skills. Hence the system—the method that is intended to be helpful—often becomes a hindrance, aggravating rather than alleviating the reading problem.

The second drawback of this system is that there are very few books available in i.t.a., just those that have been produced specifically for use with the program in school. As a result the child does not have very much opportunity outside the classroom to practice what he is being taught. He does not see i.t.a. on TV, on billboards, in the supermarket, and all those other places where there are things to be read. That is not a trivial concern. Adequate beginning readers become good readers through practice. A lack of practice will have its effect.

---

the length and complexity of these words and the consistency of the letter-sound relationships they illustrate.

If the instructional program presents single letters and a single sound for each—such as the /ă/ sound, and *only* the /ă/ sound, for the letter *a*, the /k/ sound, and only the /k/ sound, for the letter *c*—then it is probably a phonics program.

If the program begins by presenting a single sound for each of the vowels—such as the /ă/ for the *a*, the /ĭ/ for the *i*, and so on—and places these in the context of short, three- and four-letter words—such as *cat, sat, fat*, and so on—then it is probably a linguistic program.

If, in contrast, words are used that show more than one sound to be associated with a single letter—such as the *a* in *apple, plate, law, above*, and *said*—then it is probably a whole-words program.

*There are no capital letters in the i.t.a. system, only large and small letters of the same form, hence the use of lowercase letters when the system is referred to in print.

Color coding

This, too, has been tried as a way to help children learn phonics principles. There are a number of these programs on the market, and though they do differ, they all tend to use specific colors to signal how certain multisound letters are to be pronounced in specific words. Then, after a while, the color clues are removed, or "faded," and the child is expected to do well without them. For example, the program may teach the child to produce a short vowel sound when the letter is printed with green ink and a long vowel sound when black ink is used.

Color coding, like i.t.a., has its problems. In some systems of this sort the color code is so complex that learning it becomes a greater problem than learning to read—hardly an advantage to a child already behind in school. The primary drawback, however, is that, again like i.t.a., color coding is confined to the classroom, and even there only a limited amount of printed material is available for practicing the skills taught by the program. And when the child goes into the supermarket with his parents, he is confronted with colored alphabets that are not in conformance with what he has been taught in school. This is another dilemma and not a good thing for a child who has basic difficulties in resolving dilemmas of lesser proportions.

Modality preference

This does not really refer to a different kind of program. Rather, it is an approach to reading instruction that is based on the erroneous notion that children will vary in how effectively they profit from "visual" versus "auditory" instruction. Some children, the hypothesis goes, are visual learners; others are auditory learners; and the way to teach each is to exploit this bias. Generally, modality preference is determined from the child's performance on visual and auditory analysis tests such as are described in the previous section of this book. Once a so-called modality preference has been determined, then the next step calls for teaching the child through his stronger or preferred channel. Hence, sight or whole-word methods are advocated for visual learners, children whose auditory analysis skills are significantly less adequate than their visual analysis skills. And an auditory or phonics program is recommended for the child with an opposite condition, one whose visual analysis skills appear to be less adept than his auditory analysis skills.

This is an unfortunate theory. True enough, it does seem to make sense. However, *the modality preference notion does not work.* It overlooks what reading really is: the converting of symbols into language. I suppose the concept gets some of its support from misinterpreting how blind children are taught to read. Blind children cannot see, so they are taught through a substitute and intact modality, their sense of touch. What is overlooked here is that the substitution does not alter the reading process. It merely replaces one type of symbol with another. It continues to be the relating of language to symbol.

Generalizing from this and arguing that when a child's auditory analysis skills are inadequate, he should be taught through his eyes is wrong. It ignores what reading is all about.

Modality preference is irrelevant to reading instruction. Ignore it and devote your attention to what is involved in teaching a child to read.

Multisensory instruction

This pertains to what the child *does* during instruction rather than to variations in what he is taught. In essence it is based on a rationale that proposes that the child learns better—remembers more—if he not only looks and listens during instruction but also says what he hears and traces or writes with his fingers what he sees.

Although I am inclined to disagree with some of the proponents of this method who try to explain its effectiveness with some vague, neurological handwaving, I have no quarrel with the activities themselves. As any good teacher will tell you, a child will remember more if he says it *and* writes it. This is reasonable. After all, saying and writing require more attention to details—a more thorough analysis—than does just listening and looking. So by all means use the so-called multisensory approach whenever you think it is helpful. But do not perceive it as a substitute for on-target instruction; view it, instead, as a systematic method for achieving such instruction.

CUSTOM-TAILORED
READING PROGRAM

To summarize, the hard-to-teach child faces a predicament with standard reading instruction programs. Learning to read requires the mastery of two abilities that seem to complement each other yet can also do just the opposite. One is the ability to become so familiar with printed words that they can be read virtually without conscious effort, thereby allowing primary attention to be devoted to the information conveyed by the words. The second is the ability to exploit the system of phonics *selectively,* not for sounding out words but, rather, for facilitating memory.

The predicament arises when the child is so lacking in auditory analysis skills—in his awareness of the separate sounds of spoken language—that he has to be taught to read with a full-scale "sounding-out" phonics system; when it and it alone gives him the information he needs to grasp the concept of letter-sound connections; when selective application of phonics principles falls short of what he needs.

This produces a paradox. Phonics, or sounding out, gets in the way of whole-word recognition, yet the hard-to-teach child seems to have no option. He has no other way of approximating what we call reading. The demands that the other methods impose on his memory are just too great.

Is there a solution to the dilemma? Yes, but it does not lie in any single alternative instructional program. The solution is in the hands of the teacher and those who can assist her on a day-to-day basis: the child's parents.

The solution is in designing programs of instruction that meet the child's unique needs by taking the good features from various standard instructional programs and blending them in a way that suits the child. It is neither cheap nor easy. But it is feasible and—if managed properly—affordable; more affordable, certainly, than what the nonlearners of today's programs cost us. Let us now turn our attention to what such a custom-tailored program should look like.

The program should be based on the same five principles identified earlier. I will repeat them here and suggest activities representative of these principles.

Principle #1: Organize for success

Limit the amount of new information presented at any one time and present it in a simple, correctly sequenced way that highlights what is especially pertinent. That statement requires no amplification other than to stress, once more, the need for patience. Hard-to-teach children can and will make progress, but they will make it in small steps and can get discouraged if those around them become impatient.

Principle #2: Make certain that the child really does have the factual knowledge he needs to profit from a lesson.

If he has gaps, identify them and help him fill them in—and do it thoroughly, so that this newly acquired knowledge is retained. This is a key concern. It will greatly influence the ultimate value of your efforts.

What factual information does a child have to know when he comes to a reading lesson? He has to have an adequate knowledge of the spoken language—both its words and its grammar. If this is lacking, if the child's vocabulary is limited, and/or if his way of putting words together into reasonable sentences is faulty, then take action to improve it. Remember, by definition he cannot read a text that is made up mainly of words that he is not familiar with, nor will he read adequately if he is unfamiliar with the standard form of sentence construction. There are lots of good language arts programs available in our schools. Use them. They help enormously. And do not hesitate to correct a child's nonstandard language. As we have already seen, he is not served well if he is not corrected and as a result grows up to be illiterate.

Activities that will help enhance a child's knowledge of the spoken language include the following:

Read aloud to him. Try to find material that he is interested in. In addition to what you can identify, ask your local librarian for assistance. If the child is interested primarily in comic books, then use those. The goal, here, is to improve his language skills—his knowledge of words and how to use them. Worry about quality of content later on.

Discuss things with him and give him ample time and opportunity to express himself. Try not to be overtly critical of his errors. Offer him constructive comments rather than negative ones; that is, suggest alternative statements rather than pointing out his errors.

Give him a dictionary that is appropriate to his abilities. You will find a variety in your local library.

Play word games with him. For example, develop a game where you say a word and he provides a synonym or an antonym. Start off with easy words

—for example, *hot;* synonym: *boiling;* antonym: *cold;* and go on from there.

Have him describe events that he has found to be interesting. It can be such things as ball games, TV shows, movies, or simply something that happened during his day.

Have him complete stories that you initiate. Do not fret about their literary value. Simply commence a tale—any set of events and conditions—and encourage him to complete it. Then reverse roles.

Initiate a "learn a new word every day" program. The child is given the task of adding a word to his speaking vocabulary each day. As part of the rules, have him use the word in conversation at least four times that day, and reuse it at least once each day for the remainder of the week. In other words, on Monday he learns word #1 and uses it four times that day. On Tuesday he learns word #2, uses it four times that day and also uses word #1 at least once. On Wednesday he learns word #3, uses it four times, and also uses words #1 and #2 at least once each; and so on.

You name an object. Then have the child see how many adjectives he can relate to that object. For example:

bread: crusty, chewy, warm, stale, dark, white
ice: cold, watery, smooth, chilly, hard

Similes. You supply the initial phrase and have the child complete it in as many ways as he can. For example:

as happy as: a child on Christmas; a puppy with a bone
as sad as   *as soft as*
as sleepy as   *as quiet as*
as bright as   *as hot as*
as loud as   *as cold as*
as slippery as   *as pointed as*
as fast as   *as slow as*

Keep your eye out for jokes, riddles, and puns that the child might enjoy. There are usually some on the comic pages of your newspaper. They may not be all that good, but keep in mind that the child's tastes are less sophisticated than yours.

The child must also bring to the reading lesson an adequate knowledge about the subject matter dealt with in the text, as well as a general understanding of how information may be classified and organized into categories. He must know enough about the subject matter to be able to organize, that is, sort out and classify, the pertinent information contained in that text. The subject matter in a primary-grade level text tends to be exceptionally concrete and well organized, if only because of its restricted vocabulary and themes. This is not the case, however, with material written for older children. Here the subject matter is likely to be much more abstract and complex. Hence you will have to fill the child in on whatever subject-specific background information he may need.

In any case, along with specific factual information you should devote some effort to teaching the child general classification skills—orderly systems for organizing information. This is crucial. Without such skills, acquiring and retaining factual information is an overwhelming—virtually impossible—undertaking.

Activities that will enhance the child's classification skills, thereby improving his ability to acquire and retain information include the following:

Show him how the information in a story can be organized under major headings and subheadings. Children differ markedly in this ability, and those who lack it will display that lack in their inadequate comprehension skills.

The poor comprehender generally lacks organizing skill. He tends to lump information together. For example, suppose the child has just read or had read to him a story about a boy named Jim who has a pet, a dog named Spot, and a girl named Ann who has a pet, a cat named Tiger. The story relates how Spot chased Tiger; Ann became frightened; Jim laughed; Ann became angry with Jim; Spot stopped chasing Tiger; Ann and Jim became friends.

The child with poor classification strategies, by definition, will remember assorted details in some random, nonassociated array. At best, he may be able to identify the children, the animals, and perhaps some events. But he will not be able to report how these separate details fit together. The diagram in figure 38 attempts to illustrate how he might organize the information in his memory.

FIGURE 38

The better performer is more likely to organize the important details of the story into a linear sequence that is similar to the way the story was written —what occurred first, second, and so on. This is depicted in figure 39.

The best performer will have a variety of ways to organize the story. He may very well do it as illustrated in figure 39, but he will also be able to reorganize the details and think of them as in figure 40.

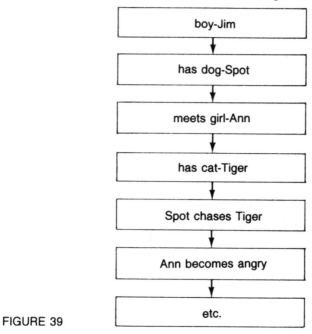

FIGURE 39

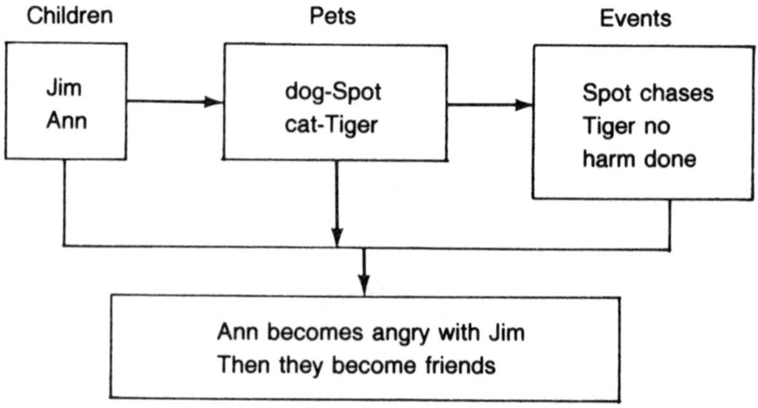

FIGURE 40

In other words, a good classifier is able to organize and reorganize information so that various aspects of the story can be related in a number of different ways. His ability to associate information effectively enables him to see abstract ideas.

Teach the child to sort out and organize information, then teach him to reorganize it. A good place to start is with the family. Show him a family tree, as in figure 41.

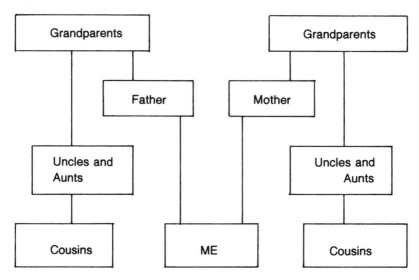

FIGURE 41

Then show him another organization, as in figure 42, and discuss with him how this same information can be arranged in different ways.

Do the same with other topics in which he has an interest. Animals perhaps. Animals can be classified in a variety of ways: size (large-small), habitat (air-land-water), color (light-dark or specific colors), relationship with humans (domestic-wild), and so on. Engage him in the task. Have him think of ways to classify information. That is the basic skill you are trying to teach.

Your primary goal in these activities is to teach the child that information can be organized after it has been sorted and that there is more than one way to classify the same set of information; that a classification scheme can range from simple to complex and that it can also be multidimensional. Animals can be sorted according to both their size and their habitat, for example. They can be large and live in water, or large and live on land, or small and live in water, and so on.

Charts. When he is ready, try to chart these on a two-dimensional map,

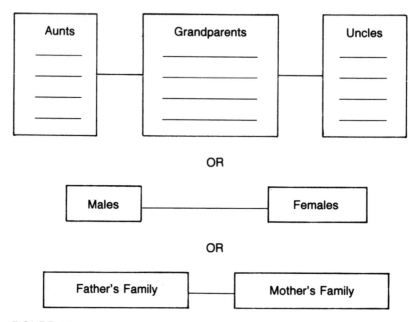

FIGURE 42

using either pictures of the animals or their names, in the cells of the map. Figure 43 illustrates this.

Have him practice doing this. It will be a worthwhile concept for him to learn. There are lots of things around that can be used in this kind of activity. For example, you can classify household objects according to location in the house, color, size, and usage; or clothing according to size, color, weight, specificity to one sex, and so on.

FIGURE 43

Habitat		Size	
		Large	Small
	Air	eagle	hummingbird
	Sea	whale	goldfish
	Land	elephant	mouse

When he has the idea, start using it with television stories, movies, and the material he has to read for school. Have him classify the main ideas, the people, and the events in ways that show he understands how it all fits together. Continue to lay out this information in charts until he is able to do it in his head without the charts.

The child must also bring to the reading lesson an adequate knowledge of the letters and the conventions that govern their use. If the child cannot demonstrate thorough familiarity with the capital and lowercase letters of the manuscript alphabet, teach them to him. If he is mature enough to be in the first grade and if his visual analysis skills are at the kindergarten level or above, then he is old enough to know letters—to be able to remember and print them accurately from dictation.

The easy-to-teach child can enter a reading program uncertain of his letters and still do well. It will not affect his progress very much because he will soon have the letters securely filed away in his memory. After all, he is easy to teach. The reason he did not know them at the onset was probably because he had not been exposed to them often enough. It does not work that way with the hard-to-teach child. Teach him the letters; do not trust to his learning them soon enough unless you do.

Activities that will teach the child the letters and the conventions that govern their use in reading include the following:

Determine which letters the child already knows, both capitals and lower-case. To be certain, have him print them from dictation. Teach him the ones he does not know; and teach him the letter names at the same time.*

Teach the capital letters first. They are less confusing and easier to print.

---

*There continues to be much debate among reading experts over the value of learning letter names. Some argue that this is a needless, perhaps even distracting step; that children do not need to learn letter names. Rather, they insist, children should be taught simply to connect the letter shapes with the sounds they make.

On the surface, this seems to be a valid argument. And it is, if the child displays the characteristics of a good learner that I described earlier. If, however, he does not belong to that group (and if he does, you probably would not be reading this), it will be easier for him to learn the sounds that the letters represent if he first learns the letter names.

Consider this analogous situation. Suppose you are introduced to three men, Jim, John, and Sam, and told that you are to remember the sounds of their voices and relate it to their faces and that you will shortly be asked to use this information to solve a problem. In a second situation, you are introduced to three other men, Tim, Tom, and Charles, and asked to do the same thing. Suppose that the only difference between these two situations is that you are given some time to study photographs of this latter trio before they are introduced, and told their names, learning which one is Tim, which is Tom, which is Charles. As a result, by the time they are introduced, you are completely familiar with each one's identity. You do nothing like that prior to meeting the first trio. With which group will you do a more accurate and rapid job of associating sound (of voice) with appearance (of man)? With the latter trio obviously. There you have only one new thing to learn about each of them. With the first trio, you have to sort out the three as well as relate face to sound. Teach the letter names as you teach the letter shapes—before you teach letter sounds.

Then teach the lowercase letters, in clusters, based on their construction, not their relative position in the alphabet.

Teachers have long known that it helps some children if you point out to them that the letter c is embedded (hidden) in certain other letters. These are:

a   d   e   g   o   q

There is a c hidden in each of these, and, in addition, if the letter does contain a vertical line, it is positioned to the *right* of the c—it comes *after* the c—just as the d comes after the c in the alphabet. This point should be stressed to the child. Two more letters can be added to this group, even though they do not contain the c. These are the j and the u. The former because it can be thought of as the g with the c removed; the latter because its vertical line is to the *right* of the body of the letter—the only other one, aside from those already identified, where this is so.

Once these have been learned fairly well, additional letters should be taught. *Learned,* however, means more than being able to discriminate one from another, although that is a good place to start. Discrimination skills can usually be taught by playing card games in which each card contains a letter (you can either purchase such cards or make your own). Play matching games —concentration (see page 85)—or variations of rummy. If the child has difficulty matching the letters, cut out pairs of cardboard letters and have him start off by placing his letters on top of your letters, and then alongside (as described in the visual skills program).

The next step in teaching the letters, once he can *match* them, is to teach him to identify—*point to*—the appropriate letter when it is named. You can use your deck of cards here too.

This again is insufficient evidence of mastery, as is the next step—having the child *name* the letters when they are shown to him. (Once more the deck is useful.)

As I said before, do not assume that the child knows the letters until he can print them accurately from dictation. Start him off at a chalkboard. Then work on lined paper. (For more about this, see the section entitled "Teaching Writing.")*

Another cluster of lowercase letters that appear to belong together are those that stem from the lowercase r, and if they contain a vertical line, it is located to the *left* of the main body of the letter. These are:

b   h   m   n   p   k   f

---

*I should acknowledge that the good learner does not need all this attention. He can be dealt with in a less structured way, skipping steps without too much risk. By definition, he sees the important details, recognizes how they relate to other details, and has a good memory; it is likely that he will continue to learn even after lessons are over for the day. He does not have to be taught as much. The poor learner will not do the same. Someone has to teach him in a way that recognizes his problem.

Once again, these should be taught to the point where the child can print them from dictation, built on a base of first matching shapes, then pointing to them when someone else states their names, and finally, naming them when someone else shows them.

The third cluster includes all those that remain. These are:

i l s t v w x y z

As with the others, these should also be taught to the point where the child knows them well enough to print them from dictation.

One additional point should be made here. Teach each group of letters separately, and be especially careful to avoid teaching the group that is related to the *r* until the group that is related to the *c* is well established. In fact, you really should teach the *r* group last.

Or, said another way, do not teach the *d* by pointing out to the child how it differs from the *b*. Yes, the differences are very obvious when the two mirror-image letters are shown in juxtaposition. But your goal is not to have the child be able to see differences; your goal is to have him be able to print and read the letters accurately, without confusion. There is less likelihood of the child becoming confused by *b*'s and *d*'s if he learns one of them thoroughly before the other is introduced. This way he has an established frame of reference, a standard to use for comparisons.

Consider this illustration. Suppose, in one situation, you already know Jim very well and are then introduced to someone who strongly resembles him, named Tim. Now, moving to a second situation, suppose you are introduced to both Jim and Tim at the same party. Where are you apt to get their identities confused, in the first situation or in the second? The inference should be clear. Teach one—I like to teach the *d* first—and make sure the child has learned it well before you teach the other.

Confusing b and d. For children who already know the letters but continue to confuse the *b* and the *d*, supply unambiguous hints where they appear to help.*

Underline with blue pencil every *b* in the child's reader. Point out to the child that the pencil is *blue*—stress the /b/ sound. Do not mark the *d* in any way. A single hint is fine. As soon as there are two—one for the *b* and one for the *d*—the child is faced with the problem of keeping the hints straight.

You may think it unreasonable to suggest that someone take the trouble

---

*There is no such thing as "mirror vision"; that is, no one literally "sees in reverse." Certainly there are children who display what is termed persistent reversal tendencies, writing *b*'s for *d*'s and reading *was* for *saw*. But these children *do not see backward*. As noted before, they are simply persisting in a bad habit that they acquired at an earlier time in their life and never overcame. This is the only sensible way to view reversal tendencies; surely it is the only way that leads you to sensible methods for remediating the situation—helping the child replace the "bad" habit with the "good" one.

to underline every *b* in the child's reader, but is it? If this is an effective way of helping to eliminate a major source of confusion, and if a simpler way cannot be invented, then it is not so unreasonable. In fact, the job can be given to the child himself and in that way turned into a learning experience rather than a tedious chore for some adult.

Simply provide the child with a model—a clearly printed *b*—and a sharpened blue pencil and instruct him to start on page one, line one, and track across each line, drawing a blue line under every *b* that he can find, saying *b* (the letter name) each time he does so. Monitor him, at least for a while, to make certain he understands the task, and do not assign too much work at any one sitting. It can even be turned into a game of sorts by imposing a time factor—seeing how many *b*'s he can find in a fixed amount of time—two minutes, say. Keep track of his daily performance by plotting it on a graph. Reward him appropriately when he surpasses his previous record.

Draw a blue vertical line down the left-hand side of every page the child is to read and every page on which he is to write. This provides a consistent and reliable reference point, in terms of direction. Explain its purpose—that he is always to begin reading and writing at the side of the page where the line is, and proceed across the page, away from it. (And stress the /b/ sound in *blue*—point out that the blue line is on the same side of the page as the straight line in the letter *b*.)

If the *b* and *d* confusion is firmly established (or any other letter, for that matter) provide the child with a large model of the letter you want him to learn and have him trace over it with his index finger (with the same hand that he uses for printing) as he says its name. Also point out the distinctive features of the letter. Do not wait for him to discover them on his own. In other words, if he is working on the *d,* call his attention to the position of the line in relation to the circle. Sandpaper letters may be used, but they are rarely necessary. Remember, do not include both letters in the same lesson. Teach one only, and stay with it until it is memorized.

Capital letters. If the child is unable to discriminate between the lowercase letters without a great deal of extra help but is familiar with the capital letters, use only capital letters until he learns the lowercase group. Again, this requires constructing lessons by hand—retyping or printing his reader in capital letters. But the effort will be worthwhile if it enables the child to start to learn. (This procedure is not needed very often. Most children will master the lowercase letters in a reasonable period of time.)

Teach the child that each new sentence starts with a capital letter and ends with a period. Do not assume he knows that until he demonstrates it for you. If you have any doubts, find a paragraph that he can read and have him read it aloud. Does he read in sentences? Does his voice show that he understands the concept of a sentence? If so, fine. If not, teach him—tell him—that sentences start with capitals, end with periods (or question marks or exclamation points), and have him identify some sentences in that paragraph and elsewhere. [Have him draw brackets around a few so that you can be sure he has the idea.]

This is a general suggestion. Take advantage of casual situations wherever they occur. For example, have him search for and count specific letters on license plates or on billboards while riding in the car. Turn it into a game. Assign a letter to him and a different letter to yourself, and see who can discover ten or more of "their" letter first. You can also do this with a newspaper page, a book, while shopping in a supermarket, or while watching TV commercials.

You can vary this activity by assigning two or three letters that must be found in sequence. For example, "Find a *C,* then a *J,* and then a *D.*" Or have him look for a newly learned and common word, such as *the.*

As you can see, there are lots of variations. My concern, here, is that you take advantage of those casual moments when they come along and give him the opportunity to practice newly learned abilities. Make it fun, of course, but also make it meaningful.

Highly important to the child's success in learning to read are adequate visual and auditory analysis skills. If these are lacking, take forceful action to improve them. Deficient visual analysis skills will get in the way of the child's general ability to organize information—to classify things according to distinctive characteristics, to recognize pertinent similarities and differences, to construct the mental filing systems he will need in order to retain information. They are worth improving, and ordinarily it is not all that difficult to do. Simply follow the directions shown on pages 70–89 of this book.

And as I have pointed out many times in this discussion, deficient auditory analysis skills interfere markedly with the child's ability to recognize the phonics principles that are so important in learning to read. The better the child's auditory analysis skills, the less he will have to be taught about pertinent letter-sound combinations; he will be much more likely to recognize them on his own. As a rule of thumb, if a six-year-old child enters a reading program with the auditory analysis skills typically expected from a child of that age, he will learn to read equally well with any reasonably designed program. If, however, his auditory analysis skills are deficient, special consideration will have to be given to the choice of the reading program, with the program of preference being one that supplies as much phonics instruction as he needs— but no more than that. Directions for teaching the child better auditory analysis skills are shown on pages 90–118 of this book.

Sight words. Finally, in order to begin the process of learning to read, the child must possess a beginning sight-word vocabulary. I have consistently stressed the importance of teaching the child how to use a rule-based, systematic approach to word recognition. Indeed, the section that follows this one is devoted to describing such an approach.

But we also have to recognize that *(a)* certain words in the English language are irregular; that is, they do not display consistent letter-sound relationships; yet *(b)* they should be learned early in a school program because they are so basic—they are words that children know and use, words that show up regularly in stories. In other words, the child should become familiar with them, that is, be able to recognize them on sight very early in his reading experiences. And since the list is limited, he is best off accomplishing the task on a rote memorization basis, more or less.

The following words are representative. They are what are known as sight words because they cannot be sounded out, at least not in their entirety, yet they are everyday words. Ask the child to read these and make note of how well he does.

SOME BASIC SIGHT WORDS

by	don't	eight	boy	could
the	laugh	does	shoe	would
said	I	warm	first	which
was	busy	every	where	move
their	one	there	these	because
they	does	goes	where	write
were	two	are	all	come
say	who	though	flew	once
know	right	bought	large	one
light	laugh	new	field	

To teach a sight word, first point out to the child those letters in the word that *do* represent their sounds in a predictable way. These, at least, will not have to be memorized. For example, if he knows the sound of the letter *s,* he knows the first sound of the words *said* and *saw.* All he has to do now is memorize the remainder of those words. If he knows the sound of the *d,* he also knows the last sound in the word *said.* Hence there is not very much left to memorize (and, in fact, he can now start to explore various vowel sounds systematically until he finds one that fits).

Once you have pointed out the consistent letter-sound combinations in the word, tell him what the word says and have him copy the entire word as he, himself, spells it aloud. He is to continue doing this until he can print the word correctly without looking at it. Then go one step further. Have him print it with his eyes closed, thinking about what his hand is doing as he spells the word. (Teach only a few sight words at a time. When these are learned, go on to others.)

If pointing out the important parts of a sight word is not enough, help him further by underlining them, thereby lessening even more the demands placed on the child's memory. For example, show him the word: "light" looking like this, and have him sound out the underlined letters: the l and the t—pausing where there is a space between the underlines.

I had better respond to critics who will now rush to remind me that a child should not learn to depend on such supports because, after all, they are not ordinarily available and "he does have to learn sometime!" I agree. He should not get dependent on the underlines. But, on the other hand, I see no harm in giving some hints that will facilitate his progress, so that he will stay on the job and ultimately learn to read without that help. I am not advocating that you tell him the sounds, merely that you call his attention to the letters in the word that can be translated directly into sounds; that you teach him a technique that you and I use all the time when we are faced with reading an unfamiliar word.

Obviously, underlining does not solve the problem completely. Even with the underlines, the child still has to memorize some portion of each word. But there is one immediate and beneficial effect derived from the technique. It forces the child to look at more than the first letter of the word. (If you have had any experience with a poor reader—and I recognize that you probably have—you are familiar with their tendency to say the beginning sound of the word correctly, and guess at the rest.)

The underlining procedure makes the child direct his attention to middle and final sounds as well as beginning sounds. As a result, his chances for reading the word correctly improve significantly.

Principle #3: Make clear a system—a strategy—that will help the child retain information, that is, link up the information he is to learn with the information he already knows.

The system, if it is to work, must make sense to the child, and it must be simple enough to be applicable in a variety of different situations.

If the system does not make sense—if it seems to him to be made up of unconnected, arbitrarily determined, ambiguous "rules"—then it will not help him. If the system is not simple—if, instead, it seems to him to be intricate, containing multiple branches—then once again it will not help him.

Keep in mind that he is hard to teach because he does not remember enough of what he is taught. The system should help him with this problem; it should help him remember more of what he is supposed to remember. If, instead, it becomes one more thing that he cannot learn, then surely it will not be a benefit. On the contrary, it will be another indicator of his learning difficulties —and he needs no more of those; he has enough already. The fewer clues he needs to recognize a word, the faster he will perform; hence the more fluent his performance. But, at the same time, this "best method for teaching a child to read" must also show him how and where to search for additional clues in the event that he needs them—in those instances where the minimum clues are insufficient for identifying a particular word.

Said another way, the best method for teaching someone how to put something together is to start with that something already in the "together" state and teach him how to take it apart systematically—first into appropriately selected larger segments, then these into appropriately selected smaller units. And while all this is going on, you continue to remind the student how and where these subcomponent parts, which have become apparent in the taking-apart process, fit into the total—"together"—unit.

What is such a system when it comes to learning to read? As we have already seen, reading is an act of synthesis—converting symbols into language. Reading is not efficient until it becomes fluent, until synthesis becomes something approximating an automatic process. This occurs when the reader has memorized most of the words he will encounter and can quickly figure out those other relatively few words that he has not yet memorized.

Thus the best method for teaching a child to be a reader is one that shows him how to apply the principles of phonics, in combination with a knowledge of the vocabulary and grammar of spoken language, to the recognition of printed words. And the best method for teaching him to be a *fluent* reader is to show him how to identify whole words accurately and rapidly on the basis of a minimum of phonic clues.

The system that we want to teach the child, then, is one that guides him in conducting that step-by-step analysis toward appropriately selected segments—from large decoding units (letter strings that help the child identify the whole word accurately and rapidly) to finer-grained ones (single letters) in an way that is orderly and applicable in a variety of conditions.

SPECIAL SECTION:
TESTING AND TEACHING
DECODING ACTIVITIES

The following section delineates an activity that will make apparent to the child a system for memorizing reading words, that is, for building word recognition skills.

Shown on pages 168–217 are 108 sets of word lists. Each set is based upon a designated "decoding unit," or letter string. Each decoding unit set is organized into four levels (A–D) of increasing difficulty.

Notice that each of the words within a decoding unit set, regardless of level, contains that decoding unit (for example, *ag* or *ad*). To this extent, the words at each level within a set are similar. They differ, of course, in their length—or, said another way, in the context in which the decoding units appear.

The words in each Level A list are short—one syllable. The decoding unit occupies a major portion of the word; it is joined with a single consonant only. As such, when the child identifies the decoding unit, he has most of the word figured out. At Level B the words continue to be single syllable, but the decoding unit is joined with more than one consonant. Thus though the words are longer at this level than they are at Level A, the only vowels in them are the ones in the decoding unit. The additional length derives from additional consonants. Level C words are two syllables long, with the decoding unit appearing in one of the two syllables, the other syllable varying according to the word itself. Level D words are three or more syllables long; the decoding unit occurs in one of the syllables, with the other syllables, once more, varying from word to word in random fashion.

I will not dwell on the purposes for this organization other than to state what probably is already obvious to you: *(a)* it provides an orderly method for teaching the child to identify whole words by focusing on key portions of those words that are already familiar to him; *(b)* it leads the child into drill exercises with a number of different words of varying length—thereby increasing the chances of his becoming adept at reading them with a minimum of "sounding out" activity; *(c)* as such, it teaches the child one of the basic skills of reading —automatic recognition of printed words, a skill that is crucial to competent comprehension of printed language. All of this is consistent with my earlier statement that, though we use a variety of clues to help us remember words, the best clues are the phonic-based ones.

You will use these word lists for two purposes: to *test* the child and to *teach* the child. *To test the child.* The purpose of your tests will be to place the child, that is, determine his ability to recognize specific decoding units that, in turn, will help him recall, or figure out, whole words.

1. Start off by asking the child to read the Level D list of words in the first decoding unit set, the one based on *an.* * Keep a record of the words he can and cannot read.**

2. If he cannot read all, or just about all, of the Level D list, then move down to the Level C words in this set.

3. If he cannot read all, or just about all, of the Level C words, then move down to Level B.

4. If he cannot read all of these properly, then scale down to Level A.

5. Stop the testing within a decoding unit set at the level where the child can read just about all of the words adequately, that is, accurately and rapidly. Make the assumption that if he passes a particular level, he can read the lower-level words in that set and therefore need not be tested at those lower levels.

6. If the child can read the Level C or Level D words in this first decoding unit set, then go through the same testing steps (#1–5) with Decoding Unit Set #2 *(ag)* and continue in this fashion until *(a)* you come to a set where the child cannot read the Level C words†; or *(b)* you have tested him with all of the sets.

7. Stop testing at this point.

What are you determining with this testing method? You are finding out: *(a)* whether the child can identify decoding units, made up of letter strings, when they occur in the context of meaningful words; and *(b)* the level of context complexity—word length—that he can deal with successfully.

8. Some children will not be able to read even the Level A list in a given decoding unit set. What are they showing? That they have not yet learned to perceive a part of a word—a letter string—as a decoding

---

*Chances are that the child you are concerned about will not be able to read the words in the Level D list. If he can read the words in the Level D list of this and the other decoding unit sets, then he probably does not have a word recognition problem. Hence, the remainder of this section will not be pertinent to whatever difficulties he does have. Leave it and go to some of the other sections in this book that appear to be more relevant to his learning difficulties.

**To be considered adequate, the child's responses must be both accurate and instantaneous. Do *not* score his performance as acceptable if he reads the words slowly, albeit correctly, more or less sounding them out.

†For children in the second grade change this to read *Level B;* that is, continue testing until you come to a set where the child cannot read Level B words. For children in the first grade change this to read *Level A.*

unit. In these instances you will have to find out if the child is able to read the decoding unit when it stands alone, out of word context.

9. That should be done now with those children who cannot read the Level A list adequately. To do this, show the child the decoding unit of that set and ask him to read it in this isolated, free-of-word-context state.

10. Suppose he cannot do even this very satisfactorily. What next? One final step will have to be taken eventually. You will have to determine if he knows that the separate letters of the decoding unit represent certain sounds. But there is no need to do this now. You will find that out when you start teaching him. Leave it until then.

11. You have completed the testing when you have done all that has been outlined in the preceding steps. You now have some idea of how well the child can identify decoding units, at least in the framework of this kind of test.

Once you have the test information, you can get started teaching the child how to do what the tests showed that he could not do.

To get started teaching the child to identify letter strings as decoding units:

1. Begin with the decoding unit set where the testing stopped.
2. Begin with the lowest level he failed.

The instructions that follow cover all possible test outcomes. They start with activities that are appropriate for the child who could not read even the decoding unit itself and go up from there.

Identify the entry level that is appropriate for your child and begin there. (But do not fret about the precise accuracy of your placement decision. If you find that he is overplaced or underplaced—and it will be immediately apparent —then simply move him up or down a level, as indicated. This will not be harmful, so long as you do not blame him for the misplacement.)

For the child who was not able to read the decoding unit of the set

1. Print on a chalkboard the decoding unit he was unable to read during testing. Let us assume, for illustration purposes, that this was the first decoding unit set. Hence the first decoding unit he should be taught is the an.(A chalkboard is best, but paper and soft pencil or felt-tip pen will do if a board is not available.)
2. Point to the an and say: "This says /ăn/."*
3. Now ask: "What does the a-n say?"**

*When one or more letters are shown within a pair of slashes—such as /an/, it means that you are to say the letter sound(s), not the letter name(s).

**When letters are shown underlined and separated by a hyphen—such as the a-n—it means that you are to name the letters one at a time, as though spelling a word.

4. Once he responds correctly—that is, states that the a-n says /ăn/— then ask: "Which of these letters says /n/?"

5. If he does not respond correctly, tell him the answer ("The n says /n/."), then repeat your query and continue with this until he can accurately state, "The n says /n/."

6. When he is able to respond correctly, show him the decoding unit *an* and say: "The a-n says /ăn/. Which of these letters says /ă/?"

7. If he displays confusion, go back to step #2 and repeat the activities from that point.

8. When he can connect the /n/ (sound) and the /ă/ (sound) to the proper letters, then show him the full unit again—the *an*—and tell him: "Make it say /ă/; cover up (or erase) the part of the word that does not belong."

9. If he responds correctly (covers up the *n*), ask him: "Tell me what the letter *a* says." That is, you want to hear him tell you the /ă/ (sound).

10. When he can do this, then again show him the full unit—the *an*— and tell him: "Make it say /n/"; cover up (or erase) that part of the word that does not belong."

11. When he has done this (covered up the *a*), then ask him: "Tell me what the letter *n* says." That is, you want to hear him tell you the /n/ (sound).

12. Once all of this has been accomplished correctly, show him the full decoding unit again—the *an*—and ask him: "Tell me what the a-n says."

13. When he shows that he knows the *an*, print this decoding unit on a 3″ × 5″ index card and store it in a file box, which you might want to call a Word Bank. These cards, as they accumulate, will be used for regular review.

14. It is now time to move up to a higher level (Level A) within this same decoding unit set.

For the child who was not able to read the Level A words accurately and rapidly but can read the decoding unit related to those words when it is shown in isolation

15. Print on a chalkboard one of the Level A words from the decoding unit set you are working on. If the child read any of the words correctly during the testing, use one of these for the initial activities. If he did not read any of them correctly, then choose any word from the Level A list. For illustration purposes, let us assume that you are going to work with Decoding Unit #1—the *an*—and have decided to start off with the Level A word *tan.*

16. Point to the word *tan* and say: "This says /tăn/."

17. Now ask: "What does the t-a-n say?"
18. Once he responds correctly—that is, repeats what you told him—then ask: "Which letters say /ăn/?"
19. If he does not respond correctly, tell him the answer ("The a-n says /ăn/."), then repeat your query. If difficulty persists, consider dropping back to the lower-level activities (steps #1–14) described previously, where the focus is on teaching the child to read the decoding units. The assumption when working on this level is that the child *can* read the decoding units.
20. When he is able to respond correctly, ask: "Which of these letters says /t/?"
21. If he displays confusion here, go back to step #16 and repeat the activities from there on.
22. When he can connect /an/ and /t/ to the proper letters, show him the full word again—*tan*—and tell him: "Make it say /ăn/; cover up (or erase) that part of the word that does not belong."
23. When he responds correctly (covers up the *t*), ask him: "Tell me what the a-n says."
24. When he can do this, then again show him the full word—*tan*—and tell him: "Make it say /t/; cover up (or erase) that part of the word that does not belong."
25. When he has done this (covered up the *an*), then ask him: "Tell me what the *t* says."
26. Once all of this has been accomplished correctly, show him the full word again—*tan*—and ask him: "Tell me what t-a-n says."
27. When he shows that he knows *tan*—can read it accurately and without delay—print it on a 3″ × 5″ index card and store it in his Word Bank.
28. Now choose another word from the Level A list (decoding unit *an*) —*ban*, for example—and go through these same steps (#15–27).
29. When you are satisfied that the child can correctly read these two words and, further, can relate the /ăn/ (sound) to the letter string a-n, the /t/ (sound) to the letter *t*, and the /b/ (sound) to the letter *b*, then print one of the two words on the chalkboard and ask him to read it to you.
30. Start with *tan*, for example. He should be able to respond correctly, of course. Once he does, ask him to: "Make it say /băn/; change it so that it says /băn/ instead of /tăn/."
31. Work your way through all of the Level A words in this decoding unit set (#1) this way—steps #15–30—stopping finally when the child can change any one of them to any other one on request, as illustrated in step #30. For example, when he can change /tăn/ to /făn/ to /păn/ and so on.

Where to next? You have two options. You might work up into the next level (Level B) within this same decoding unit set, or you might move on, at the same level (Level A) to the next decoding unit (Decoding Unit Set #2, for example). As a general rule, if the child is in the second grade or above, do the former—move up to Level B within the same decoding unit set. If he is in the first grade, move on to a new decoding unit set, remaining at the same level.

If you take this latter route, then your instructions remain the same as already covered here. Return to step #15 and start over with the Level A words from this new set. If, instead, you are now ready to move up to Level B within this same decoding unit´set, then proceed with the steps described in the following.

For the child who was not able to read the Level B words accurately and rapidly but can read the Level A words from the same decoding unit set

32. Print on a chalkboard one of the Level B words from the decoding unit set you are working on. If the child read any of the words correctly during the testing, use one of these for the initial activities. If he did not read any of them correctly, then choose any word from the Level B list. For illustration purposes, let us assume that you are working with the decoding unit *an* and have decided to start off with the word *ranch.*

33. Point to the word *ranch* and say: "This says /ranch/. The r̲ says /r/, the a̲-n̲ says /ăn/, and the c̲-h̲ says /ch/."

34. Now ask: "What does r̲-a̲-n̲-c̲-h̲ say?"

35. Once he responds correctly—that is, repeats what you told him—then ask: "Which letters say /ăn/?"

36. If he does not respond correctly, consider dropping back to a lower-level activity. The assumption, when working on this level, is that the child can read these decoding units out of context and is now ready to use them in context.

37. When he responds correctly, ask: "Which of these letters says /r/? Which say /ch/?"

38. If he displays confusion here, go back to step #33 and repeat the activities from there on.

39. When he can correctly connect the /r/ to r̲, the /ăn/ to a̲-n̲, and the /ch/ to the c̲-h̲, show him the full word again—*ranch*—and tell him: "Make it say /răn/; cover up (or erase) that part of the word that does not belong."

40. When he responds correctly (covers up the c̲-h̲), ask him: "Tell me what the r̲-a̲-n̲ says."

41. Once all of this has been accomplished correctly, show him the full word again—*ranch*—and tell him: "Make it say /ănch/; cover up (or erase) that part of the word that does not belong."

42. When he has done this (covered up the *r*), then ask him: "Tell me what the a-n-c-h says."

43. Once he has done this correctly, show him the full word again—*ranch* —and tell him: "Make it say /ăn/; cover up (or erase) those parts of the word that do not belong."

44. When he responds correctly (covers up the r and the c-h, then show him the full word again—*ranch*—and ask him: "Tell me what r-a-n-c-h says."

45. When he shows that he knows *ranch*—can read it accurately and without delay—print it on a 3" × 5" index card and store it in his Word Bank.

46. Now choose another word from the Level B list of this decoding unit set—*scan*, for example—and go through these same steps (#32–45) again.

47. When you are satisfied that the child can correctly read the first two words you worked on from this Level B list and, further, can relate the various single letters and decoding units to their appropriate sounds, then print one of the two words on the chalkboard and ask him to read it to you.

48. For example, let us assume that you started with *ranch*. He should be able to respond correctly, of course. Once he does, tell him: "Make it say /scăn/; change it so that it says /scăn/ instead of /rănch/."

49. Work your way through all of the Level B words in this decoding unit set this way—steps #32–48—stopping finally when the child can change any one of them to any other one on request, as illustrated in step #48. For example, when he can change /ranch/ to /scan/ to /bland/ to /pant/ and so on.

Where to next? You have two options. You might work up to the next level (Level C) within this same decoding unit set, or you might choose to move on to another decoding unit, beginning in that unit at the highest level possible for the child, as indicated by testing.

As a general rule, if the child is in the third grade or above, do the former —move on to Level C within the same decoding unit set. If he is in the first or second grade, move to a new decoding unit set, using the test procedures to determine his starting level.

If you take this latter route, then your instructions remain the same as already covered here. If, instead, you opt to move up to Level C within this same decoding unit set, then proceed with the steps described in the following.

For the child who was not able to read the Level C words accurately and rapidly but can read the Level B words from the same decoding unit set

50. Print on a chalkboard one of the Level C words from the decoding unit set you are working on. If the child read any of the words correctly during the testing, use one of these for the initial activities. If he did not read any of them correctly, then choose any word from the Level C list. For illustration purposes, let us assume that you are going to work with the decoding unit *an,* starting off with the Level C word *began.*

51. Point to the word *began* and say: "This says /began/. The b-e says /bē/, and the g-a-n says /găn/."

52. Now ask: "What does b-e-g-a-n say?"

53. Once he responds correctly—that is, repeats what you told him— then ask: "Which letters say /găn/?"

54. If he does not respond correctly, consider dropping back to a lower-level activity. The assumption, when working on this level, is that the child can read the syllables that contain the decoding unit and is now ready to learn to read the unit in the context of polysyllabic words.

55. When he responds correctly, ask: "Which of these letters say /bē/?"

56. If he displays confusion here, go back to step #51 and repeat the activities from there on.

57. When he can correctly connect the b-e to /bē/ and the g-a-n to /găn/, show him the full word again—*began*—and tell him: "Make it say /găn/; cover up (or erase) that part of the word that does not belong."

58. When he responds correctly (covers up the b-e), ask him: "Tell me what the g-a-n says."

59. Once all of this has been accomplished, show him the full word again —*began*—and ask him to "Make it say /bē/; cover up (or erase) that part of the word that does not belong."

60. When he has done this (covered up the g-a-n), then ask him: "Tell me what the b-e says."

61. When he shows that he knows *began*—can read it accurately and without delay—print it on a 3″ × 5″ index card and store it in his Word Bank.

62. Now choose another word from the Level C list of this decoding unit set—*manner,* for example—and go through these same steps (#50–61) again.

63. When you are satisfied that the child can correctly read the first two words you worked on from this Level C list and, further, can relate the various syllables to their appropriate sounds, then print one of the two words on the chalkboard and ask him to read it to you.

64. For example, let us assume that you started with the word *began*. He should be able to respond correctly, of course. Once he does, tell him: "Make it say /manner/; change it so that it says /manner/ instead of /began/."

65. Work your way through all of the Level C words in this decoding unit set this way—steps #50–64—stopping finally when the child can change any one of the words to any other in the list on request, as illustrated in step #64. For example, when he can change /began/ to /manner/ to /cannot/ to /candle/ and so on.

Where to next? You have two options. You might work up to the next level (Level D) within this same decoding unit set, or you might choose to move over to another decoding unit, beginning in that set at the highest level possible for the child, as indicated by the testing.

As a general rule, if the child is in the fourth grade or above, do the former —move up to Level D within the same decoding unit set. If he is in the third grade or below, move to a new decoding unit set, using the test procedures to determine his starting level.

If you take this latter route, then your instructions remain the same as already covered here. If, instead, you opt to move up to Level D within this same decoding unit set, then simply repeat the activities you carried out at the preceding level (steps #50–65), substituting the Level D words for those of Level C.

By now you have had a chance to go through the instructions, and you should have a fairly good idea of what is involved. It probably strikes you as a massive task. It is not. It requires some self-discipline and self-scheduling, but it can be worked through with a very reasonable amount of effort.

The following suggestions are pertinent to administering the activities and should serve as general guidelines for teaching the child to identify decoding units as aids in memorizing reading words:

1. Devote about ten to fifteen minutes *each day* to the activities spelled out on the previous pages. Start off each new day at approximately the place you stopped the day before. Ten to fifteen minutes each day may not sound like enough time to accomplish what has to be accomplished, but the cumulative effects will please you—and the child.

2. Spend about two to three additional minutes each day reviewing the words in his Word Bank. The goal here is instant recognition of the words. (It will also be helpful if you take time during this activity to define those words that the child is uncertain about.)

3. At the completion of each day's session write down a few sentences that contain the words that the child has been working on. Better yet, have him assist you in constructing these sentences. Then have him read the sentences at a pace that approximates fluent reading, no

sounding out permitted. If, the first time through them, he stumbles and/or reads too slowly, have him reread the sentences often enough to acquire a fluent pace.

4. One word of caution, particularly relevant to the words contained in the Level C and Level D lists. In one sense the activities are designed to help the child memorize these specific words. But, more important, the activities are designed to help the child learn to use a *system* for learning new words in general, not these words specifically.

With this in mind, I want to caution you that it is not critical for the child to learn every word on every list. I have used these activities often enough—and measured the effects on a child's reading abilities—to assure you that one more memorized word is not the key factor. What counts here is that the child catches on to the fact that there is a *system* available—a strategy that involves hunting out decoding units larger than single letters—that can help him remember his reading words. This, combined with a growing knowledge of the spoken language and the subject matter being addressed in the text, *plus steady reading practice,* * will change a stumbling reader, even someone who is almost a nonreader, into a fairly competent one who will continue to improve with continued exercising of proper reading habits.** And in essence that is what you are after with these activities: the establishment of proper reading habits.

List of 108 Common Decoding Units

Decoding Unit Set #	Decoding Unit	Decoding Unit Set #	Decoding Unit
1	*an*	14	*id*
2	*ag*	15	*ig*
3	*ad*	16	*im*
4	*at*	17	*ib*
5	*ap*	18	*ill*
6	*as*	19	*ick*
7	*ab*	20	*op*
8	*am*	21	*od*
9	*and*	22	*og*
10	*ack*	23	*ot*
11	*it*	24	*ong*
12	*ip*	25	*om*
13	*in*	26	*ob*

*See pages 218–219 for specific suggestions.

**Please do not interpret this phrase to mean that all that the child needs is motivation, that if he practiced, he would not have a reading problem. That is not the case. Sure, practice helps, but only if you practice the proper things. First you have to show him *what* to practice; then it will be helpful to motivate him to do so.

Decoding Unit Set #	Decoding Unit	Decoding Unit Set #	Decoding Unit
27	*en*	68	*old*
28	*ed*	69	*one*
29	*ess*	70	*oke*
30	*ell*	71	*eat*
31	*et*	72	*eam*
32	*em*	73	*ar*
33	*eck*	74	*all*
34	*eb*	75	*aw*
35	*est*	76	*ice*
36	*ent*	77	*ock*
37	*up*	78	*uff*
38	*ug*	79	*ush*
39	*un*	80	*able*
40	*ut*	81	*ight*
41	*ud*	82	*oll*
42	*ub*	83	*on*
43	*um*	84	*ook*
44	*uck*	85	*or*
45	*ash*	86	*ore*
46	*ast*	87	*(s)ow*
47	*act*	88	*(c)ow*
48	*ank*	89	*(b)ull*
49	*ang*	90	*(d)ull*
50	*iff*	91	*us*
51	*ing*	92	*ai*
52	*ink*	93	*are*
53	*ish*	94	*ee*
54	*ay*	95	*alk*
55	*ace*	96	*ev*
56	*ade*	97	*er*
57	*ape*	98	*ew*
58	*ate*	99	*ir*
59	*ane*	100	*ire*
60	*ake*	101	*oa*
61	*ame*	102	*oi*
62	*ale*	103	*(b)oo(t)*
63	*age*	104	*ou*
64	*are*	105	*eve*
65	*ide*	106	*ue*
66	*ind*	107	*ure*
67	*ite*	108	*tion*

SET #1

Decoding unit	A	B	C	D
an	ban	ranch	began	Santa Claus
	can	scan	manner	fantasy
	Dan	bland	demand	fantastic
	fan	pant	cannot	understand
	Jan	hand	handle	Canada
	man	chant	candle	outlandish
	Nan	stand	banner	ancestor
	pan	span	spaniel	animal
	ran	strand	Spanish	anniversary
	tan	land	standard	grandstand
	van	brand	dandy	antelope
		plant	landing	bandana
			lantern	advantage
			mantle	manufacture
			vanish	manager
			vandal	chimpanzee
			scandal	reprimand

SET #2

Decoding unit	A	B	C	D
ag	bag	drag	haggle	magazine
	hag	slag	swagger	aggravate
	jag	snag	braggart	magnify
	lag	stag	dragon	magnetize
	nag	shag	jagged	vagabond
	rag	brag	sagging	antagonize
	sag	crag	bagpipe	magnolia
	tag	flag	magnet	stagnation
	wag		stagger	agnostic
	gag		fragment	fragmentary
			flagship	
			flagstone	
			lagoon	
			saga	
			stagnant	
			straggle	
			wagon	

SET #3

Decoding unit	A	B	C	D
ad	bad	clad	bladder	readmit
	cad	glad	badger	radical
	dad	badge	daddy	advisor
	fad	add	paddle	admiral
	gad	shad	saddle	adventure
	had	brad	shadow	administer
	lad		admit	gladiator
	mad		caddy	admiration
	pad		padding	graduate
	sad		padlock	advertise
	tad		address	badminton
			adore	disadvantage
			adult	
			gladly	
			haddock	
			raddish	
			tadpole	

SET #4

Decoding unit	A	B	C	D
at	bat	chat	matter	satisfy
	cat	flat	chatter	attitude
	fat	hatch	clatter	habitat
	gat	slat	matching	latitude
	hat	spat	rattle	automatic
	mat	that	satin	smattering
	Nat	match	battle	tattered
	pat	scratch	splatter	gratitude
	rat	brat	batman	catapult
	sat	batch	attic	caterpillar
	vat	catch	attract	Saturday
			catcher	
			batter	

SET #5

Decoding unit	A	B	C	D
ap	cap	clap	happen	Japanese
	gap	slap	apple	apparatus
	lap	flap	happy	aptitude
	map	strap	napkin	appetite
	nap	wrap	wrapper	capitol
	sap	trap	rapid	happiness
	tap	scrap	napping	captivate
	zap	lapse	dapper	collapsible
	pap	chapped	captain	
	rap		captive	
	yap		trapper	
			mishap	
			madcap	

SET #6

Decoding unit	A	B	C	D
as(s)	bass	glass	passing	classification
	lass	brass	classy	exasperate
	mass	flask	cascade	fascinate
	pass	last	sassy	dastardly
	sass	blast	basket	gasoline
	gas	vast	nasty	
		crass	asset	
		grass	tassel	
		class	hassle	
		fast	morass	
		hasp	impass	
		task		
		clasp		

SET #7

Decoding unit	A	B	C	D
ab	cab	slab	shabby	fabulous
	dab	blab	blabber	habitual
	gab	drab	prefab	habitat
	jab	crab	cabin	laboratory
	lab	grab	Abner	tabulate
	nab	flab	habit	absolute
	tab	scab	rabbit	cabinet
		stab	rabid	metabolism
			absent	abdomen
			Sabbath	abdicate
			fabric	prefabricate
			abduct	
			absorb	
			baboon	
			cabbage	
			jabber	

SET #8

Decoding unit	A	B	C	D
am	cam	damp	camel	camera
	dam	champ	hamlet	lamplighter
	gam	lamp	lamplight	examination
	ham	ramp	stampede	ambition
	jam	tamp	sample	ambulance
	ram	stamp	pamper	family
	Sam	gram	rampant	enamel
	tam	lamb	exam	example
	yam	slam	ambush	stamina
		tramp	scamper	anagram
		vamp	bamboo	
		sham	gamble	
			campus	
			damage	
			glamour	
			vampire	
			Amtrak	

SET #9

Decoding unit	A	B	C	D
and	band	bland	handy	standardize
	land	grand	sandbox	candidate
	hand	brand	random	bandwagon
	sand	strand	candy	bandanna
		stand	expand	dandelion
		gland	command	understand
			standard	grandmother
			scandal	chandelier
			forehand	sandpaper
			handle	scandalous
			landscape	slanderous
			bandage	reprimand
			dandy	ampersand
			demand	incandescent
			grandstand	misunderstanding

SET #10

Decoding unit	A	B	C	D
ack	back	black	attack	mackerel
	hack	crack	blacken	packaging
	Jack	flack	hacksaw	racketeer
	lack	slack	cracker	lumberjack
	pack	stack	slacker	lackluster
	rack	shack	lacking	lackadaisical
	sack	track	tackle	
	tack	smack	racket	
		knack	package	
			blackboard	
			background	
			bracket	
			backpack	
			ack-ack	
			smokestack	

SET #11

Decoding unit	A	B	C	D
it	bit	mitt	armpit	visitor
	fit	knit	bitter	Italy
	hit	itch	rabbit	situation
	kit	twitch	pitcher	critical
	lit	switch	kitchen	literature
	pit	flit	visit	pitiful
	sit	spit	city	titillate
	wit	slit	little	handwritten
		grit	witness	
		quit	fitness	
			unfit	
			spitoon	

SET #12

Decoding unit	A	B	C	D
ip	dip	whip	catnip	hippopotamus
	hip	chip	chipmunk	Mississippi
	lip	trip	zipper	slippery
	nip	strip	slipper	equipment
	pip	flip	clipper	whippersnapper
	rip	drip	shipmate	stipulate
	sip	slip	zipcode	citizenship
	tip	blip	turnip	battleship
	zip	skip	parsnip	

SET #13

Decoding unit	A	B	C	D
in	bin	spin	inside	cabinet
	din	shin	winter	winterize
	fin	skin	ginger	independent
	pin	print	splinter	kindergarten
	sin	sprint	napkin	vicinity
	tin	grin	winsome	integrate
	win	inch	dinner	origin
	kin	wind	finish	cinema
		since	muffin	kinescope
			urchin	topspin
			muslin	
			kinfolk	

SET #14

Decoding unit	A	B	C	D
id	bid	slid	fiddle	midwestern
	did	ridge	middle	candidate
	hid	bridge	hidden	rapidly
	kid	skid	widow	vividly
	lid	quid	candid	consider
	mid	squid	kidney	kidnapper
	rid		midway	avidly
			midwest	forbidden
			rancid	humidity
			solid	videotape
			acid	
			arid	
			rapid	
			midnight	
			giddy	
			stupid	
			hybrid	

SET #15

Decoding unit	A	B	C	D
ig	big	twig	piglet	astigmatism
	dig	swig	bigger	ignorance
	fig	brig	jigsaw	dignity
	jig	prig	wiggle	dignify
	pig	sprig	spigot	thingamajig
	rig		wigwam	whirligig
	wig		trigger	iguana
	zig		ignore	significant
			igloo	
			bigot	
			giggle	
			zigzag	

SET #16

Decoding unit	A	B	C	D
im	dim	limb	limit	simplify
	him	trim	timid	immaterial
	rim	limp	himself	important
	vim	slim	chimney	immortal
	imp	brim	whimper	interim
		prim	improve	superimpose
		blimp	thimble	imposition
		whim	shimmer	
		skim	dimly	

SET #17

Decoding unit	A	B	C	D
ib	bib	crib	tribute	biblical
	fib	glib	quibble	bibliography
	jib	squib	ribbon	liberty
	nib		sibling	gibberish
	rib		scribble	attribute
			giblet	tributary
			dribble	contribute

SET #18

Decoding unit	A	B	C	D
ill	dill	chill	silly	illiterate
	fill	skill	pillow	silliness
	gill	spill	willow	willowy
	hill	still	until	illusion
	mill	drill	billboard	oscillate
	pill	thrill	sawmill	dillydally
	sill	trill	spillage	pillory
	till	frill	filly	pillowcase
	will	grill	shilling	
	kill	quill	pillar	
			instill	
			willful	
			fulfill	

SET #19

Decoding unit	A	B	C	D
ick	hick	stick	sticker	bricklayer
	lick	slick	wicked	hickory
	pick	trick	tricky	maverick
	sick	click	sickly	limerick
	tick	chick	sickness	rickety
	wick	quick	bicker	
	kick	brick	flicker	
		crick	picket	
			ticklish	
			stricken	
			icky	
			cowlick	
			sticky	
			cricket	
			wicket	
			sidekick	

SET #20

Decoding unit	A	B	C	D
op	cop	chop	sloppy	property
	hop	slop	stopper	opera
	mop	stop	chopping	lopsided
	pop	crop	popcorn	opportunity
	top	prop	hopscotch	operator
	fop	drop	copper	popular
	lop	flop	option	popover
	sop	shop	shopper	soporific
	opt	strop	atop	optical
			poplar	
			poplin	
			topple	
			shortstop	

SET #21

Decoding unit	A	B	C	D
od	cod	shod	shoddy	bodyguard
	hod	plod	codfish	godfather
	Tod	trod	body	somebody
	sod	clod	fodder	oddity
	rod	prod	sodden	moderate
	pod	dodge	modern	Ichabod
	nod	lodge	coddle	bodily
	mod		lodger	
	odd		tripod	
			slipshod	
			bodkin	
			peapod	

SET #22

Decoding unit	A	B	C	D
og	bog	smog	groggy	dogmatic
	cog	grog	dogged	togglebolt
	dog	flog	logger	logarithm
	fog	frog	jogging	loggerhead
	hog	togs	fogbound	epilogue
	log	clog	hogwash	toboggan
	jog		frogman	underdog
			soggy	
			boggle	
			prologue	
			eggnog	

SET #23

Decoding unit	A	B	C	D
ot	cot	scot	cannot	pottery
	dot	slot	blotter	lottery
	got	shot	plotting	Ottawa
	hot	plot	hotdog	cottonwood
	jot	trot	otter	botany
	lot	spot	cotton	tommyrot
	not	blotch	totter	polyglot
	pot	blot	robot	
	rot	clot		
	sot	botch		
	tot			

SET #24

Decoding unit	A	B	C	D
ong	bong	wrong	belong	belonging
	gong	prong	Ping-Pong	congregate
	long	strong	prolong	wrongfully
	pong	throng	Congo	Mongolia
	song	tongs	longterm	evensong
		thong	mongrel	
			stronghold	
			King Kong	
			headstrong	
			along	
			singsong	

SET #25

Decoding unit	A	B	C	D
om	Tom	stomp	bombard	combatant
	Dom	romp	Bombay	combination
	mom	pomp	common	commentator
		bomb	combat	communist
		clomp	combine	competent
			complex	dominate
			pompous	pomegranate
			somber	ominous
			pompon	

SET #26

Decoding unit	A	B	C	D
ob	Bob	slob	hobble	obstruction
	cob	blob	jobless	observatory
	fob	glob	lobster	lobbyist
	gob	knob	clobber	hobgoblin
	job	throb	obstruct	cobblestone
	lob		observe	obsolete
	mob		lobby	
	nob		hobby	
	rob		goblin	
	sob		goblet	
			cobbler	
			corncob	
			doorknob	

SET #27

Decoding unit	A	B	C	D
en	Ben	when	Jenny	opening
	den	wren	pencil	sensitive
	hen	send	open	sensational
	Jen	went	dentist	ventilate
	Ken	rent	mentor	tenderly
	men	sense	rental	enjoyment
	pen	blend	entrance	energy
	ten	trench	tender	seventeen
	fen	bench	encounter	entertain
	wen	then	penny	potential
	yen	bent	attend	gentlemen
	end	fence	amend	century
		mend	avenge	venison
		trend	seven	stupendous
			splendid	dimension
			central	encounter
			fender	
			vendor	

SET #28

Decoding unit	A	B	C	D
ed	bed	sled	meddle	federal
	led	sped	bedding	comedy
	Ned	fled	acted	editorial
	red	shred	wedding	meditate
	Ted	shed	pedal	sedative
	wed	bled	edit	sedition
	fed	bred	reddish	remedy
			redhead	medical
			cheddar	pedestal
			biped	quadruped
			worsted	pedigree
				underfed

SET #29

Decoding unit	A	B	C	D
ess	Bess	stress	confess	penniless
	less	press	homeless	messenger
	mess	chess	blackness	successful
	Tess	tress	message	possessive
	Jess	bless	lesson	merciless
		guess	unless	
			dresser	
			mistress	

SET #30

Decoding unit	A	B	C	D
ell	bell	swell	mellow	mellowing
	dell	smell	bellow	bellower
	fell	shell	fellow	rebellion
	hell	quell	befell	intelligent
	jell		Jello	excellence
	pell		yellow	cellular
	sell		hello	
	tell		belly	
	well			
	yell			
	cell			

SET #31

Decoding unit	A	B	C	D
et	bet	fret	forget	settlement
	get	etch	kettle	detonate
	jet	stretch	upset	lettering
	let	fetch	metal	letterhead
	met	ketch	network	metallic
	net	wretch	lettuce	petrify
	pet		letter	veteran
	set		metric	etcetera
	vet		petty	
	wet			
	yet			

SET #32

Decoding unit	A	B	C	D
em	gem	stem	temper	democratic
	hem	them	empty	feminine
	Lem	hemp	lemon	remedy
		tempt	member	memory
			embrace	membership
			temple	themselves
			hemlock	empathy
			remnant	demonstrate
			tremor	lemonade
			emblem	membrane
			blemish	seminar
			contempt	temporary
				eminent
				contemplate

SET #33

Decoding unit	A	B	C	D
eck	beck	fleck	beckon	reckoning
	deck	wreck	reckless	checkerboard
	heck	check	freckle	woodpecker
	neck	speck	feckless	
	peck		bedeck	
			heckler	
			checkers	
			necklace	
			shipwreck	

SET #34

Decoding unit	A	B	C	D
eb	deb	webs	Debbie	February
	reb		rebel	nebulous
	web		debris	Nebraska
	ebb		debut	debutante
	Jeb		pebble	nebula
			treble	rebellion
			debit	ebony

SET #35

Decoding unit	A	B	C	D
est	best	wrest	invest	yesterday
	jest	crest	hardest	interest
	lest	quest	bequest	restfulness
	nest	guest	biggest	destination
	pest	blest	restful	estimate
	test		festive	ancestor
	vest		arrest	estuary
	west		suggest	indigestion
	rest		question	easiest
			digest	protester
				restaurant
				crestfallen

SET #36

Decoding unit	A	B	C	D
ent	bent	spent	present	gentlemen
	dent	scent	convent	tentative
	gent		sentence	ventilation
	lent		entry	apartment
	pent		center	enterprise
	sent		repent	different
	tent		penthouse	centerpiece
	went		rental	centimeter
	vent		dentist	century
	cent		venture	entrance
	rent		event	portent
			enter	ventriloquist
			gentle	
			mentor	
			plenty	

SET #37

Decoding unit	A	B	C	D
up	cup		upset	buttercup
	pup		supper	supporting
	sup		uproot	abruptly
			support	corruption
			abrupt	interrupt
			erupt	upstanding
			pickup	upholster
			upper	
			upon	
			stirrup	
			puppy	
			rupture	

SET #38

Decoding unit	A	B	C	D
ug	bug	shrug	struggle	bugaboo
	dug	slug	ugly	ugliness
	hug	plug	buggy	pugnacious
	jug	smug	drugstore	ladybug
	lug	chug	humbug	repugnant
	mug	snug	dugout	
	pug	drug	nugget	
	rug	thug	luggage	
	tug		druggist	
			smuggler	

SET #39

Decoding unit	A	B	C	D
un	bun	bunt	bunting	understand
	fun	spun	bunches	bungalow
	gun	stun	under	undecided
	nun	bunk	funny	fundamental
	pun	munch	punish	punishment
	run	lunch	hunger	asunder
	sun	bunch	sunshine	unhappiness
		crunch	thunder	moribund
		trunk	rotund	
		runt	refund	
		grunt		
		shun		

SET #40

Decoding unit	A	B	C	D
ut	but	shut	butter	utterly
	cut	hutch	cutting	buttercup
	gut	crutch	cutlet	butterfly
	hut	strut	gutter	buttonhole
	nut	Dutch	nutmeg	shutterbug
	jut	smut	sputter	uppercut
	rut	glut	butler	guttersnipe
		putt	button	peanutbutter
			cutworm	
			stutter	
			utmost	
			haircut	
			peanut	

SET #41

Decoding unit	A	B	C	D
ud	bud	stud	budget	suddenly
	cud	thud	cuddle	suddenness
	dud	spud	sudden	ombudsman
	mud	fudge	huddle	
		suds	rudder	
		budge	buddy	
			udder	
			rosebud	
			shudder	
			puddle	
			muddy	

SET #42

Decoding unit	A	B	C	D
ub	cub	drub	rubber	publication
	dub	scrub	bubble	publicity
	hub	snub	blubber	submarine
	pub	stub	chubby	subtraction
	rub	club	hubbub	substitute
	sub	shrub	publish	subdivide
	tub		public	shrubbery
	nub		grubby	
			rubbish	
			subtract	
			subway	
			subdue	
			bathtub	

SET #43

Decoding unit	A	B	C	D
um	bum	dumb	slumber	umbrella
	gum	thumb	pumpkin	summertime
	hum	numb	album	summarize
	rum	slum	plumber	minimum
	sum	chum	umpire	modicum
	mum	dump	grumpy	cucumber
	yum	lump	thumbnail	
		stump	bumper	
		jump	dumpling	
		plum	summon	
		clump	summer	
		bump	umbrage	
		glum	mummy	
			talcum	
			rummage	

SET #44

Decoding unit	A	B	C	D
uck	buck	struck	bucket	chuckwagon
	duck	truck	duckling	puckering
	luck	shuck	woodchuck	buckeroo
	puck	chuck	buckskin	
	suck	stuck	huckster	
	tuck	cluck	buckle	
	muck		truckle	
			plucky	
			sawbuck	
			rucksack	

SET #45

Decoding unit	A	B	C	D
ash	bash	clash	fashion	bashfulness
	cash	crash	cashier	fashionable
	dash	brash	bashful	balderdash
	hash	flash	dashing	eyelashes
	gash	slash	flashes	
	lash	splash	ashtray	
	mash	thrash	flashlight	
	rash	trash	dashboard	
	sash	stash	ashen	
			rashness	
			thrasher	
			rehash	
			sashay	

SET #46

Decoding unit	A	B	C	D
ast	cast	blast	plaster	castaway
	fast	caste	master	fantastic
	last		chastise	asteroid
	mast		aster	castanet
	past		casting	masterful
	vast		vastly	astronomer
			drastic	astonish
			repast	gastronomic
			caster	masterpiece
			aghast	newscaster
			nasty	broadcasting
			miscast	pastoral
			forecast	astronaut
				pasteurized

SET #47

Decoding unit	A	B	C	D
act	fact	tract	actor	bacteria
	pact		fracture	factory
	tact		actress	tactfully
			active	practical
			tactic	practically
			tactful	factual
			protract	activate
			react	intractable
			action	counteract
			impact	cataract
			enact	attractive
				interaction

SET #48

Decoding unit	A	B	C	D
ank	bank	crank	hanker	thankfully
	dank	flank	thankful	bankruptcy
	rank	spank	lanky	frankfurter
	sank	stank	banker	mountebank
	tank	thank	blanket	lankiness
	yank	clank	anklet	cantankerous
		shank	ankle	
		plank	cranky	
			Yankee	
			plankton	

SET #49

Decoding unit	A	B	C	D
ang	bang	clang	mango	manganese
	fang	sprang	banging	angrily
	gang	swang	jangle	angular
	hang		strangle	triangle
	pang		angry	untangle
	rang		angle	stranglehold
	sang		bangle	boomerang
			angler	
			hangman	
			gangplank	
			hanger	
			mangle	
			tangle	
			gangster	
			mustang	
			tango	

SET #50

Decoding unit	A	B	C	D
if(f)	tiff	whiff	differ	difference
	miff	stiff	fifty	difficult
		shift	stiffen	stiffening
		cliff	nifty	whiffenpoof
		skiff	jiffy	chiffonier
		sniff	sheriff	terrific
		drift	bailiff	
		thrift	riffle	
			riffraff	
			chiffon	
			tariff	

SET #51

Decoding unit	A	B	C	D
ing	ding	bring	finger	opening
	ping	sling	jingle	dingaling
	ring	sting	nothing	atingle
	sing	fling	kingly	anything
	wing	cling	wringer	
	king	string	singer	
		swing	singing	
		thing	gringo	
			tingling	

SET #52

Decoding unit	A	B	C	D
ink	fink	clink	tinker	tinkerer
	kink	drink	slinky	brinkmanship
	link	slink	kinky	shrinkproof
	mink	blink	inkling	rinkydink
	pink	shrink	twinkling	unthinkable
	sink	stink	trinket	
	wink	brink	twinkle	
	rink	think	sprinkler	

SET #53

Decoding unit	A	B	C	D
ish	dish	swish	Spanish	fisherman
	fish	squish	dishes	accomplish
	wish		fishing	abolish
			vanquish	wishywashy
			publish	polisher
			mishmash	punishment
			selfish	publisher

SET #54

Decoding unit	A	B	C	D
ay	bay	tray	payment	repayment
	day	play	mayor	displaying
	gay	sway	rayon	bayonet
	hay	clay	replay	mayflower
	jay	slay	daytime	mayonnaise
	lay	stay	daylight	payable
	may	pray	repay	holiday
	nay	bray	dismay	popinjay
	pay	fray	playmate	stowaway
	say		saying	
	ray		essay	
	way		away	
			jaywalk	
			assay	

SET #55

Decoding unit	A	B	C	D
ace	face	space	misplace	replacement
	lace	trace	retrace	disgraceful
	mace	grace	spaceship	gracefully
	pace	place	deface	embraceable
	race	brace	pacer	populace
			placement	outerspace
			embrace	
			bracelet	
			apace	

SET #56

Decoding unit	A	B	C	D
ade	fade	apade	degrade	renegade
	jade	grade	faded	lemonade
	made	trade	parade	barricade
	wade	blade	invade	colonnade
	lade	spade	evade	invader
		shade	tirade	cavalcade
			cadence	motorcade
				balistrade

SET #57

Decoding unit	A	B	C	D
ape	cape	grape	escape	videotape
	nape	scrape	taper	drapery
	tape	shape	paper	jackinape
	aped	apes	scraper	
	gape	drape	grapefruit	
	jape		seascape	
			scapegoat	
			tapeworm	
			caper	
			landscape	

SET #58

Decoding unit	A	B	C	D
ate	date	grate	rebate	detonate
	fate	slate	inflate	invigorate
	gate	plate	relate	renovate
	hate	spate	debate	operator
	late	crate	grateful	arbitrate
	mate	state	statement	investigate
	rate	skate	berate	abdicate
	sate		crated	exterminate
			statement	celebrate
			create	communicate
				innovate
				caterer
				hatemonger
				refrigerator
				dislocate
				irrigate

SET #59

Decoding unit	A	B	C	D
ane	bane	crane	airplane	windowpane
	cane	plane	insane	cellophane
	dane	thane	inane	sugarcane
	lane		humane	weathervane
	mane		mundane	counterpane
	pane		arcane	hydroplane
	sane			
	vane			
	wane			

SET #60

Decoding unit	A	B	C	D
ake	bake	stake	baker	bakery
	cake	flake	maker	undertaker
	fake	shake	earthquake	mistaken
	lake	spake	mistake	foresaken
	make	brake	snowflake	fakery
	quake	drake	retake	johnnycake
	rake	slake	snakepit	
	sake	snake	milkshake	
	take	quake	rattlesnake	
	wake		makeshift	
	hake			

SET #61

Decoding unit	A	B	C	D
ame	dame	shame	nameless	shamefully
	fame	blame	rename	shamelessly
	game	flame	lamely	
	lame	frame	nickname	
	name		became	
	same		inflame	
	tame		selfsame	
	came		gamely	
			blameless	

SET #62

Decoding unit	A	B	C	D
ale	bale	stale	resale	balefully
	dale	scale	female	stalemated
	gale	shale	baleful	haybaler
	male	whale	alewife	nightingale
	pale		impaled	
	sale		inhale	
	tale		alehouse	
	vale			
	hale			
	kale			

SET #63

Decoding unit	A	B	C	D
age	cage	stage	engage	engagement
	gage	aged	enrage	outrageous
	page		sagebrush	
	rage		outrage	
	sage		ageless	
	wage		stagecoach	
			wager	
			teenage	
			agent	
			presage	
			cagey	

SET #64

Decoding unit	A	B	C	D
ave	cave	knave	pavement	slavery
	gave	brave	enslave	bravery
	pave	stave	concave	enslavement
	rave	shave	forgave	slavetrader
	save	slave	repave	misbehave
	wave	crave	enclave	
	nave	grave	behave	
	lave		deprave	
			engrave	
			navel	
			quaver	
			haven	

SET #65

Decoding unit	A	B	C	D
ide	bide	pride	bridegroom	tidewater
	hide	bride	aside	hideaway
	ride	slide	abide	homicide
	side	chide	glider	cyanide
	tide	stride	reside	idealism
	wide	glide	inside	countrywide
	ides		outside	override
			divide	
			provide	
			confide	
			astride	
			ideal	
			rider	
			strident	

SET #66

Decoding unit	A	B	C	D
ind	bind	grind	remind	reminder
	find	blind	kindness	unwinding
	hind		unwind	kindliness
	kind		blinders	womankind
	mind		mankind	mastermind
	rind		mindful	hindsight
	wind		behind	
			binder	
			grinder	

SET #67

Decoding unit	A	B	C	D
ite	bite	white	invite	dynamite
	mite	smite	polite	appetite
	site	spite	ignite	satellite
	kite	sprite	despite	stalagmite
	cite	write	item	recondite
		quite	campsite	incitement
		trite	recite	plebiscite
			lignite	exciting

SET #68

Decoding unit	A	B	C	D
old	bold	scold	resold	unfolding
	cold		soldier	goldenrod
	fold		golden	old fashioned
	gold		colder	refolded
	mold		molding	manifold
	hold		goldfish	smoldering
	sold		older	
	told		folder	
			stronghold	

SET #69

Decoding unit	A	B	C	D
one	bone	phone	postpone	telephone
	hone	stone	alone	saxophone
	lone	drone	ozone	tonelessly
	tone	shone	trombone	onerous
	zone	prone	toneless	cortisone
	cone	throne	condone	monotone
		crone	hailstone	baloney
		clone	lonely	microphone
			backbone	

SET #70

Decoding unit	A	B	C	D
oke	joke	bloke	joker	provoker
	poke	spoke	awoke	artichoke
	yoke	smoke	invoke	pokeberry
	woke	choke	provoke	pawnbroker
		broke	poker	
		stroke	hokey	
		stoke	token	
			yokel	
			broker	

SET #71

Decoding unit	A	B	C	D
eat	beat	cheat	repeat	eggbeater
	feat	eats	retreat	defeated
	heat	wheat	meatball	eatery
	meat	treat	treaty	repeater
	neat	cleat	neatness	
	seat	bleat	defeat	
	peat	pleat	meatloaf	
			heater	
			cheater	
			entreat	

SET #72

Decoding unit	A	B	C	D
eam	beam	scream	dreamer	streamliner
	ream	stream	dreaming	steam fitter
	seam	cream	steamboat	mainstreaming
	team	dream	daydream	
		steam	upstream	
		gleam	streamers	
			teamwork	
			moonbeam	
			squeamish	

SET #73

Decoding unit	A	B	C	D
ar	far	spar	afar	carpenter
	bar	star	darling	armory
	car	part	darkness	argument
	jar	scar	market	arbitrate
	par	dart	carpet	regardless
	tar	shark	farther	partnership
	gar	dark	ajar	motorcar
	mar	start	cigar	remarkable
	par	hard	startle	
		bard	army	
		card	harvest	
		smart	argue	
		lard	regard	
			partner	
			crowbar	

SET #74

Decoding unit	A	B	C	D
all	ball	stall	baseball	installer
	call	small	football	wallpaper
	fall	squall	nightfall	gallbladder
	hall		recall	waterfall
	tall		install	
	wall		taller	
	gall		appall	
	mall		enthrall	
			hallway	

SET #75

Decoding unit	A	B	C	D
aw	jaw	straw	outlaw	withdrawing
	haw	flaw	awful	strawberry
	law	claw	drawing	jawbreaker
	raw	thaw	lawyer	
	saw	gnaw	sawmill	
	caw	draw	mawkish	
	paw	bawl	southpaw	
	yaw	squaw		
		yawl		
		lawn		
		craw		
		crawl		

SET #76

Decoding unit	A	B	C	D
ice	dice	twice	device	sacrifice
	lice	splice	nicer	viceroy
	mice	slice	nicest	niceties
	nice	price	allspice	enticement
	rice	trice	iceberg	
	vice	spice	suffice	
		thrice		

SET #77

Decoding unit	A	B	C	D
ock	dock	clock	jockey	poppycock
	lock	knock	rocket	rockingchair
	mock	stock	pocket	pocketbook
	rock	flock	tick-tock	hammerlock
	sock	smock	hockey	landlocked
	cock	shock	unlock	crockery
	hock	block	peacock	mockery
	pock	crock	shocking	
		frock	stocking	
			blockhead	

SET #78

Decoding unit	A	B	C	D
uff	cuff	bluff	cufflink	suffering
	huff	fluff	puffy	ruffian
	muff	stuff	suffer	
	puff	gruff	handcuff	
	buff	snuff	puffing	
	luff	scuff	fluffy	
	ruff		buffer	
	guff		shuffle	
			scuffle	
			dandruff	
			muffin	
			creampuff	

SET #79

Decoding unit	A	B	C	D
ush	hush	flush	mushy	mushrooming
	lush	crush	brushing	hushabye
	mush	thrush	blushes	
	rush	brush	mushroom	
	gush	blush	gusher	
		slush	toothbrush	
		shush	usher	

SET #80

Decoding unit	A	B	C	D
able	cable	stable	unable	miserable
	fable	tabled	disable	
	gable		enable	
	sable		cablecar	
	table		unstable	

SET #81

Decoding unit	A	B	C	D
ight	fight	fright	fighter	frightening
	light	bright	frightful	oversight
	might	slight	uptight	nightingale
	night	knight	mighty	unsightly
	right	blight	rightful	fortnightly
	sight	height	upright	righteous
	tight	sleight	insight	foresighted
	bight		tightrope	lightning

SET #82

Decoding unit	A	B	C	D
oll	doll		holly	hollering
	moll		golly	jolliest
	loll		collar	collector
			dollar	collegiate
			trolley	volleyball
			volley	follicle
			jolly	follower
			folly	rollicking
			follow	
			college	

SET #83

Decoding unit	A	B	C	D
on	Don	fond	convict	vagabond
	con	font	convent	continent
	non	bond	bonfire	convention
	don	blonde	fondly	correspond
	Von	pond	nonsense	ponderous
	yon	frond	ponder	gondola
			tonsil	nonagenarian
			bonbon	
			icon	
			upon	
			ponder	
			sonnet	
			yonder	
			beyond	
			abscond	

SET #84

Decoding unit	A	B	C	D
ook	book	crook	foresook	bookkeeper
	cook	brook	bookshelf	
	hook	shook	rooky	
	look		cookie	
	nook		bookcase	
	rook		cookout	
	took		crooked	
			cookbook	
			mistook	
			lookout	
			outlook	

SET #85

Decoding unit	A	B	C	D
or	for	morn	dormant	forgetful
	nor	north	forget	organize
	tor	tore	morning	tornado
	ore	short	organ	toreador
		bore	resort	torpedo
		snort	shopworn	tormented
		sort	order	
		worn	border	
		lore	morbid	
		more	torpor	
		score	boring	
		yore	dormouse	
		fort		
		sport		

SET #86

Decoding unit	A	B	C	D
ore	bore	chore	restore	explorer
	core	store	deplore	furthermore
	fore	shore	storage	pinafore
	gore	swore	foreground	applecore
	lore	score	explore	
	more	snore	ignore	
	pore	spore	adore	
	tore		ashore	
	wore		scoreboard	
	ores		seashore	
			foreswore	
			folklore	
			boredom	
			furore	

SET #87

Decoding unit	A	B	C	D
ow	low	slow	bowstring	lawnmower
	bow	snow	mower	overflow
	mow	throw	towboat	overthrow
	row	stow	slowly	stowaway
	tow	glow	elbow	furbelow
		grow	window	wheelbarrow
		blow	shadow	
		crow	below	
		flow	rainbow	
		grown	scarecrow	
		show	bellow	
			bowtie	
			snowbound	
			borrow	

SET #88

Decoding unit	A	B	C	D
ow	cow	brow	towel	allowance
	bow	chow	trowel	cowardly
	how	brown	allow	anyhow
	now	plow	somehow	powderpuff
	vow	dhow	rowdy	allowance
	wow	scow	coward	dowager
	sow	frown	chowder	
		crown	reknown	
		town	downtown	
		crowd	countdown	
		down		

SET #89

Decoding unit	A	B	C	D
ul(l)	bull		pulley	beautiful
	full		spoonful	powerfully
	pull		bully	wonderfully
			bullet	plentiful
			awful	
			fully	

SET #90

Decoding unit	A	B	C	D
ul(l)	dull	skull	seagull	skulduggery
	cull	scull	insult	repulsive
	gull	mulch	duller	lullabye
	hull	gulf	mullet	scullery
	null	bulk	annull	nullify
	lull	cult	dullard	mulligatawny
	mull	hulk	impulse	difficult
			adult	
			result	
			consult	

SET #91

Decoding unit	A	B	C	D
us	bus	must	mustard	disgusted
	Gus	dust	mustang	discussion
	pus	fuss	musty	justify
		just	dusty	custody
		lust	gusty	sustenance
		rust	hustle	omnibus
		trust	discuss	justified
		plus	fluster	suspicion
		cuss	lustre	
		crust	cluster	
		thus	fussy	
		muss		

SET #92

Decoding unit	A	B	C	D
ai	air	bait	repaid	retainer
	aid	wait	waiter	faithfully
	ail	raid	failure	derailment
	aim	braid	sailboat	tailormade
		maid	tailor	curtailment
		paid	strainer	raillery
		waif	faithful	trailblazer
		bail	reclaim	
		fail	maiden	
		hail	detail	
		jail		
		mail		
		nail		
		pail		
		snail		
		rail		
		trail		
		rain		
		train		
		brain		
		strain		
		hair		
		claim		

SET #93

Decoding unit	A	B	C	D
are	bare	stare	prepare	unprepared
	care	scare	rarely	unaware
	dare	share	hardware	barefooted
	fare	snare	compare	faretheewell
	hare	flare	ensnare	daredevil
	mare	square	scarecrow	carefully
	rare	blare	nightmare	
	ware	spare	declare	
	pare		fanfare	
			farewell	

SET #94

Decoding unit	A	B	C	D
ee	bee	beef	sixteen	unforeseen
	see	feel	unseen	seventeen
	fee	knee	sweetheart	teenager
	tee	seen	meeting	greenery
	gee	seed	seeker	
	lee	seek	beseech	
	wee	reed	between	
		reef	seedling	
		reek	careen	
		steel		
		keen		
		feet		
		sheet		
		fleet		
		sleet		
		street		
		screech		
		creed		
		geese		

SET #95

Decoding unit	A	B	C	D
alk	talk	chalk	talking	talkative
	walk	stalk	walker	walkaway
	balk		chalkboard	
			chalkmark	
			sidewalk	

SET #96

Decoding unit	A	B	C	D
ev	rev		ever	everyone
			never	revolution
			seven	however
			clever	reverend
			devil	forever
			sever	inevitable
			lever	severance
			bevel	brevity
				several
				levity

SET #97

Decoding unit	A	B	C	D
er	her	herd	hermit	permanent
	per	perk	vermin	international
		germ	hunter	conference
		term	refer	concerted
		fern	permit	underrated
		pert	answer	concertina
		tern	lawyer	conservation
		jerk	barber	interview
		perch	burner	
		berth	termite	
		stern	kernel	
		serve	certain	
		terse		
		verse		

SET #98

Decoding unit	A	B	C	D
ew	dew	stew	jewel	jewelry
	few	flew	renew	renewable
	new	blew	dewdrops	brewery
	hew	chew	fewer	chewable
	yew	view	steward	newspaper
	mew	brew	mildew	
		crew		
		drew		
		slew		

SET #99

Decoding unit	A	B	C	D
ir	fir	first	circus	confirmation
	sir	stir	firmly	thirstily
		shirt	stirrup	infirmary
		bird	chirping	virtuous
		firm	thirsty	flirtation
		third	birthday	circumference
		chirp	circle	circular
		squirt	confirm	circumnavigation
		thirst	virtue	
		shirk	stirrup	
		birth	circuit	
		birch	dirty	
		girl		
		gird		
		flirt		
		dirge		

SET #100

Decoding unit	A	B	C	D
ire	dire	spire	admire	
	fire	squire	retire	
	hire		transpire	
	mire		expire	
	sire		require	
	tire		umpire	
	wire		aspire	
			direct	
			fireman	
			hireling	
			desire	
			wireless	
			tireless	

SET #101

Decoding unit	A	B	C	D
oa	oat	boat	toaster	overcoat
	oaf	foam	uproar	
	oar	loam	lifeboat	
	oak	roam	loafer	
		soap	seacoast	
		roar	steamboat	
		soar	uproar	
		hoax	oatmeal	
		toast		
		roast		
		loan		
		moan		
		groan		
		goat		
		throat		
		oath		
		loaf		
		toad		

SET #102

Decoding unit	A	B	C	D
oi	oil	foil	tinfoil	rejoicing
		soil	jointly	poisonous
		toil	poison	avoidance
		join	Detroit	joinery
		void	moisture	toiletries
		coil	pointy	
		roil	ointment	
		coin	avoid	
		choice	doily	
		moist	toiler	
		noise	toilet	
		joint	devoid	

SET #103

Decoding unit	A	B	C	D
oo	boo	boom	racoon	uprooted
	coo	boon	hootowl	paratrooper
	moo	boost	looter	proofreader
	too	boot	rooted	bandicoot
	goo	cool	trooper	
	woo	coon	booster	
	zoo	food	loosely	
		shoot	caboose	
		loot	moonstruck	
		root	papoose	
		proof	moonshot	
		roof	balloon	
		spoon	yoohoo	
		troop	reproof	
		boost		
		booth		
		choose		
		goose		
		spoof		
		school		
		spool		

SET #104

Decoding unit	A	B	C	D
ou	out	bout	around	boundary
	our	rout	bounty	bountiful
		loud	cloudy	cloudiness
		pout	proudly	roundabout
		oust	aground	tantamount
		tout	profound	
		bound	downspout	
		round	outright	
		clout	doubtful	
		shout		
		doubt		
		flour		
		hound		
		trout		
		stout		
		ground		
		drought		
		proud		
		found		
		pound		
		spouse		
		scout		

SET #105

Decoding unit	A	B	C	D
ove	dove	shove	shovel	governor
	love	glove	cover	recover
			grovel	discover
			hover	coveralls
			plover	
			oven	
			above	
			lover	
			hovel	

SET #106

Decoding unit	A	B	C	D
ue	cue	flue	Tuesday	discontinue
	due	glue	imbue	avenue
	rue	blue	pursue	residue
	hue	clue	subdue	ruefully
	sue	true	bluebird	misconstrue
		fuel	value	overdue
		gruel	duet	
		duel	argue	

SET #107

Decoding unit	A	B	C	D
ure	lure		endure	furniture
	pure		culture	reassure
	sure		obscure	manicure
	cure		vulture	immature
			impure	premature
			mature	literature
			unsure	expenditure
			inure	temperature
				surety

SET #108

Decoding unit	A	B	C	D
tion			nation	sensation
			ration	inflation
			station	devotion
			notion	commotion
			lotion	liberation
			potion	taxation
			caution	examination

Principle #4. Encourage the child to use sensory channels in addition to his eyes and ears to examine the concrete aspects of a task.

This will force his attention to more of the pertinent details and further facilitate his ability to recall what he has experienced.

This means, simply, that you should have the child write and say what he sees and hears. It acknowledges the fact that you have to look at and/or listen to more of the details in a pattern of sensations (visual or acoustical) in order to reproduce something than you do to merely identify it.

Representative activities

When you are conducting a lesson in identifying decoding units, stress to the child the importance of thinking about "how his mouth feels" when he repeats a decoding unit or a word and what his hand is doing when he writes these on the chalkboard.

If the child tends to lose his place on the page, and/or read certain words in reverse, such as *was* for *saw,* instruct him to use his index finger as a pointer. Insist that he always use the same hand—the one he prints with. Teach him to synchronize the movement of that finger with his eyes and his voice; in other words, the finger is to be pointing directly at the word he is looking at and reading, nowhere else. His finger is a source of support and will direct his eyes—show them where to look.

Principle #5: Provide enough repeated experiences to establish the information securely in the child's long-term memory.

The key concern here—once the *what* has been established and the system for helping him remember it, the *how,* has been taught—is that the child spend enough time in various drill activities so that he can perform virtually automatically, with a minimum of conscious effort.

In other words, the child should become so familiar with the *what* that he no longer has to use the system you taught him—the *how*—to figure it out: He simply knows it; he has the information at his fingertips. This does not come about without extended practice sessions—especially with children who are hard to teach.

In general these activities are task related. Hence I will not attempt to spell them out here. Just follow the basic rule of thumb that says it is not enough to know *how.* The child must practice to the point that he no longer has to resort to the *how* strategy.

For example, it is not enough to be able to sound out the words in a sentence. The child should practice reading those sentences over and over again, to the point where he reads them fluently, the way a reader should read. This is critical. Without fluency there is no comprehension; without comprehension there is no reason to read; without a reason the child will not read; and if he does not read, he can hardly be expected to become adept at it, fluent.

Stress practice, but do take care to make certain that what the child practices is worth the effort. Identifying that *what* is what this book is all about.

TEACHING ARITHMETIC

First, a definition. *Arithmetic,* as I shall soon explain, refers to the act of reconverting symbols into language with which the individual is already familiar. That definition brings into focus the fact that there is a language factor in arithmetic, along with the more traditionally identified one of calculation. As such, it directs us to recognize that if a child has an "arithmetic language" deficit, then we must do something about it if we hope to teach him to be competent in arithmetic.

Trying to teach someone to be competent in reconverting symbols into a language that he does not adequately understand is inevitably futile. True, he may very well memorize a handful of "words"—some of the basic number facts—but he will not master arithmetic.

Does this sound familiar? It should. I used these same words in my beginning remarks about reading.

How can that be? How can two so different processes as reading and arithmetic share a common definition? It is worth a moment or two to consider this question.

Why did man devise the processes of reading and arithmetic? It is not difficult to imagine the circumstances. Obviously man spoke before he wrote, and wrote before he read. In his early attempt at recording graphically what he spoke, he drew pictures. Not a bad idea, so long as he did not mind the limitations this imposed.

But he probably did mind, at least after a while—and reasonably so. There are too many drawbacks to a pictographic system, one of the most obvious being the significant restrictions it imposes on expressive vocabulary. Since there must be common agreement as to what the symbols represent—if the system is to be useful to more than one person—then a pictographic language has to be either quite circumscribed and simple or the writer and the reader have to risk the consequences of confusion created by ambiguity.

At any rate, in most places on the globe where graphic language systems developed, pictures were ultimately replaced by an alphabet—shapes that we call letters. We use these to represent the sounds of spoken language rather than the meaning. This simplified the coding system remarkably. There are far fewer different sounds in a spoken language than there are words. Hence there is less potential ambiguity with such a system, less confusion. In addition, since it takes far less effort and time to memorize a very limited set of code symbols (letters) than it does to memorize a wide variety of picture–spoken-word associations, the code becomes accessible to more people. New words can be added without the need for inventing a picture that is interpretable by all. All that is needed is a new *oral* label, a new sequence of verbal sounds that in turn can be represented—spelled out—with letters and subsequently read, or converted back into oral language, by the reader.

The idea worked. More and more of the world's population has become literate over the years. Is the system foolproof? Obviously not. If it were, would I be writing this or you reading it?

How about arithmetic? Its history is similar. Man calculated by applying mathematics principles—by recognizing the fundamental properties and inter-relationships of quantities and magnitudes—long before he was able to represent his calculations orally, let alone record them graphically. Certainly the caveman who tracked game, who anticipated the animal's path and moved diagonally to head him off or adjusted the aim and force of his weapon in keeping with the animal's speed and direction of movement, was making calculations based upon the recognition of certain properties and interrelation-ships of certain quantities and magnitudes.

Eventually there came a time when man felt a need to have a graphic record of his calculations—probably because his commerce required it. At first he used a crude, but logical, system of drawing a mark or using an object, such as a rock or a bone, for each unit he wanted to record. In time, as he commenced to comprehend even better the principles of efficient coding of infor-mation, he figured out how to represent groups of objects with single units—such as X for 10 and C for 100. He was forced to do this in the interest of time and space. Eventually he came to the idea of the numeral, as we know it, and its remarkable power to represent complex conditions with relative simplicity.

Just as with reading, there had to be agreement on the meanings of these symbols among the users of the system. But, once accomplished, numerical communications were possible, and one basic code came to be accepted by virtually all of us, regardless of the verbal language we use—testimony to the remarkable efficiency of this system and its power to express complex informa-tion simply. Thus when we come across the statement "Four dozen apples and twice as many pears," we can "read" it, that is, we can convert it not only into our verbal language but also into the language of mathematics, a language specific to the ordering and mapping out of information. And though our spoken words may vary across cultures, our interpretations of the quantitative information contained in such a statement—once we have interpreted it—do not.

The language of reading is a spoken language—sequences of sounds that have an accepted common meaning to a group of persons, words that are used to represent thoughts, actions, objects, what have you.

The language of arithmetic is nonverbal. True enough, it can be expressed verbally, but at its roots words are not required. It is the language of our spatial world—of *how many* and *where,* of the properties and relationships of quantities and magnitudes, to which verbal labels may be attached.

The language of arithmetic is a language of nonambiguous conditions. It is a universal language. It is not altered—influenced—by the code we use to represent it. We do, in fact, use a variety of codes, written and spoken, and though they may vary, the conditions they describe remain constant.

The language of reading is culture-linked and strongly influenced by the verbal code—the words we use to represent our thoughts and actions. Indeed, if we lack a specific word, we may very well not be able to conceptualize the thought.

If the child is exposed to spoken language—and if he is a "normal" child —he will learn that language. He will understand it; he will speak it. If the language he speaks at home is the same language he is asked to learn to read in school, and his knowledge of that language is age-appropriate, then he will enter school with sufficient information about the language to begin to learn to read it. This does not guarantee, of course, that he will master the concepts of letter-sound representation discussed in the section on reading, but at least it satisfies one of the prerequisites for understanding those coding concepts.

The same does not hold true for arithmetic. Learning the nonverbal language of arithmetic is not quite as dependent on direct social experiences. Although it is easy to see that marked environmental stimulation or deprivation probably does affect a child's acquisition of spatial concepts, it is also evident that *all* children, regardless of cultural background, tend to display an increased awareness of the concrete and relational attributes of their spatial world as they develop. Indeed, we use indicators of this increased awareness as milestones for charting development.

We know, of course, that a child's home life—experiences—will affect his ability to *communicate* certain spatial information verbally. Most children, for example, enter first grade able to count limited quantities of objects accurately (up to 10, say) or to recognize and name geometric shapes. This ability was not innate. Someone taught them, one way or another, how to do this.

But counting verbally and knowing the names of geometric shapes are only part of what the child needs to be able to do. If he is to profit from standard arithmetic instruction, the child must also have some basic knowledge of relationships, be able, to demonstrate an understanding of a 1:2 ratio, for example, not necessarily by using the correct numerical symbols but, rather, by carrying out various concrete operations that reveal his understanding.*

---

*I am not using the phrase *concrete operations* the way it is used in the Piagetian construct. On the other hand, it is not so far from correct to connect the child's ability to recognize relationships with his entry into the concrete operations stage, as defined by Piaget and his co-workers.

For example, the child who can copy a plus sign fairly accurately is demonstrating an ability to identify certain properties and relationships of certain quantities and magnitudes. After all, how is a plus sign constructed? Two lines that intersect at or near their respective midpoints. If he can also use such spoken words as *up, down, across, middle,* and *halfway* appropriately, so much the better; but his knowledge of the language of arithmetic is revealed by his construction—his drawing—not by his spoken words.

That, of course, is one of the fundamental differences between the language of reading and the language of arithmetic. The former is verbal but can often be expressed in actions. The latter can often be expressed verbally, but its essence is nonverbal. It is spatial, and it is possible to understand the language without knowing the spoken words. The reverse—knowing some of the spoken words of the spatial language—does not guarantee that the language itself has been adequately acquired. Rather, it is like learning by rote some phrases in a foreign tongue without knowing what they mean.

I want to go through these concepts again, with fewer and different words. The concepts may seem elusive at first, yet they are not all that complex, and they are central to the overall theme of this section: How do you teach arithmetic to the hard-to-teach child?

Knowing the spoken words of our verbal language is to reading what being able to identify the various pertinent features of a spatial array—such as quantity, size, shape, and location—is to arithmetic. Both may correctly be called vocabularies, in their respective contexts. Knowing the grammar of the spoken language you want to learn to read—the formal structure, the rules that predict the construction of the spoken words and how they all fit together— is analogous to knowing the "rules" that enable you to map out the relationships among the components of a spatial array—their *relative* quantity, position, size, shape, and so on.

In other words, there are a vocabulary and a grammar that represent our spatial world as well as those that represent our verbal world. The function of arithmetic is to enable us to perform calculations by representing that spatial world with a numerical code.

Now back to the original point. Arithmetic, like reading, is a reconversion act, a restoring of coded information to its concrete state. One main ability and four important subordinate abilities were identified in reading. The main ability: Instant—and virtually automatic—recognition of printed words, the ability to translate printed text into verbal representation at once, almost without conscious effort. The subordinate abilities, all four of which contribute to the acquisition of the main ability, are as follows:

1. Adequate familiarity with the spoken language—its vocabulary and grammar
2. Adequate familiarity with the phonological attributes of that spoken

language—the sounds of spoken words and the sequences in which those sounds occur

3. Adequate familiarity with the graphic symbol system of that spoken language—the letters and the conventions that govern their use

4. Familiarity with a system that links the graphic symbols with the phonological attributes in a way that makes it possible for the child to acquire an adequate sight-recognition vocabulary as well as figure out new words when they are encountered in text.

A similar set of remarks can be made about arithmetic. In order to be a competent calculator, the individual needs one main ability, which in turn derives from four subordinate abilities. The main one: The ability to perform instant computations, to translate a printed or spoken numerical statement into an accurate mathematical representation at once, almost without conscious effort. In other words, to have a large store of memorized number facts. The subordinate abilities are as follows:

1. Adequate familiarity with the spoken language of arithmetic—a capacity to count arrays of objects, identify sizes, shapes, positions, and so on

2. Adequate familiarity with the pertinent absolute and relational attributes of spatial patterns—the component parts and the way they interrelate

3. Adequate familiarity with the graphic symbol system of arithmetic—the numerals and other symbols and the conventions that govern their use

4. Familiarity with a system that links the graphic symbols with the absolute and relational attributes in a way that makes it possible for the individual to acquire an adequate number-fact vocabulary as well as solve unfamiliar calculation problems.

Just as with spoken language, it is possible for one to know a basic verbal arithmetic vocabulary yet lack the ability to make satisfactory progress in the classroom arithmetic program. Herein lies one of the major sources of frustration for some children and their teachers. A child may enter first grade with adequate verbal arithmetic vocabulary but inadequate knowledge in one of the other subordinate skills just mentioned. His teacher perceives him to be an apparently intelligent child—"Just listen to him talk"—whose intelligence seems to evaporate when he is confronted with tasks that require problem solving where a basic set of memorized number facts are to be combined with the recognition and exploitation of relationships.

And this does not refer solely to arithmetic tasks.* The child who does

---

*On the contrary, primary-grade arithmetic can be accomplished without recognizing relationships, simply by counting—but let us put that point aside for the moment.

not recognize spatial relationships as well as he should will display his deficit in many ways, over and beyond his inept arithmetic skills. He is also likely to lag behind other children his age in such activities as solving jigsaw puzzles, copying geometric designs, accomplishing pencil and paper tasks neatly and completely, and—unrelated as it may seem—in remembering and following a chain of verbal statements, such as this typical teacher request: "Do all the work of page seventeen, skip page eighteen, and then do the bottom section only on page nineteen."

It is as though a knowledge of the nonverbal language of space—an ability to order information according to its pertinent attributes—contributes to a general organizational ability that is used at many levels of information processing.

With that set of concepts serving as a base, let us now examine what it takes to do arithmetic and compare good arithmetic performers with not-so-good arithmetic performers. If we do this correctly, then we will be able to address the basic question: "How do you teach arithmetic to a hard-to-teach child?" and have hopes for coming up with some reasonable approximation of the correct answer.

What does someone with competent arithmetic abilities do when given a calculation problem that his less competent counterpart does not seem to be able to do? When we looked at this question as part of our discussion on reading, we observed that good readers are good—or "educated"—guessers; that is, they have already memorized most of the words they are to read and can figure out the few unfamiliar words they encounter by employing effective strategies such as taking advantage of context clues and illustrations and identifying key portions of the unfamiliar word—single letters and letter strings—that offer phonic clues and can therefore be used as the basis for figuring out and/or remembering the whole word.

It is not radically different in arithmetic. True enough, good calculators are not good guessers. That falls short of the mark in arithmetic, although there are many in the math education field who do argue that it is desirable to teach children to make good guesses—close approximations—at the solution to arithmetic problems. But that is another topic; best we put it aside.

There is little question that good calculators *are* good calculators because, like good readers, they enter the classroom with a fair knowledge base that they are then able to use effectively in figuring out answers to unfamiliar problems.

Consider this example. Children, confronted with an addition problem such as $56 + 75 = ?$ are taught to proceed through a series of operations. First they rewrite the problem in vertical orientation: $\begin{array}{r} 56 \\ +75 \\ \hline \end{array}$. Then they follow a sequence of steps—called an algorithm—that amounts to dealing with the problem as a collection of interconnected smaller problems.

Good arithmetic achievers differ from poor arithmetic achievers in their ability to do these smaller problems. They go through fewer steps; hence they take less time. Whereas the good calculator usually arrives at the answer to the first step in the above problem (6 + 5 = ?) in seconds, the poor calculator is apt to need substantially more time. Why the difference? What does the latter do with all that time? He literally counts. To him 6 + 5 means counting six "things" (1, 2, 3, 4, 5, 6); then five more "things" (7, 8, 9, 10, 11), maybe on his fingers, maybe just in his head, but one way or another he counts in units of one. And he almost invariably starts his counting at 1, despite the fact that he may already know—have securely memorized—that 5 + 5 = 10. He does not seem to be able to do what his better-performing classmate can do: perceive the value of starting the counting operation at 10—if, indeed, counting is even necessary—using appropriate knowledge, acquired earlier, in the solution of this related problem.

You can see how similar this is to reading situations, where one child will identify an unfamiliar word based primarily on some of its subcomponent decoding units, combined with context clues, while another youngster will see no alternative but to memorize or sound out the whole word as a separate, new unit of information; to sound out *sand*, for example, despite the fact that he has just sounded out *and.*

Thus not only is the poor calculator slower, he is also more apt to make errors because of the increased number of steps he goes through; and the two, in combination, create significant difficulties for him. This is particularly true when he moves into the intermediate grades (4, 5, and 6), where the arithmetic problems are more complex and involve greater quantities and where the time allowed to do the calculations is dramatically reduced.

It comes down to this: To be a good arithmetic achiever, the child has to know more than *how* to do a calculation—more than the algorithms—and more than the fact that numerals signify quantities and therefore all calculations can be solved by counting with units of one. Being able to solve a problem through counting is valid, obviously, but it is not enough. It creates situations similar to those described in the previous section on reading. Counting by one in arithmetic is analogous to sounding out, letter by letter, in reading. It works in reading, to a limited extent, so long as the words are spelled regularly and comprehension demands are minimal. It always works in arithmetic, but it does not work adequately. It is a slow, inefficient process that gets in the way of our ultimate goal for arithmetic instruction.

What is that goal? In reading, you will recall, it is to prepare the student to be a fluent reader so that he can *think* about what he is reading *while* he is reading, rather than having to devote his energy to the decoding portion of the reading process. This in turn was shown to depend upon his sight-recognition vocabulary, which derives from his knowledge of the vocabulary and grammar of spoken language as well as his ability to employ effective strategies for figuring out unfamiliar and partially memorized words.

In arithmetic the goal is the same: to prepare the student to be a competent calculator so that he can *think* about what he is calculating *while* he is doing it rather than having to devote his energy to the decoding portion—counting by ones—of the calculation process. This obviously depends upon the size of his store of memorized number facts—in effect, his sight-recognition vocabulary—which in turn derives from his knowledge of the vocabulary and grammar of spatial language and his ability to employ effective strategies for figuring out unfamiliar problems.

An ample store of memorized, or "sight," *number facts* is crucial in arithmetic. But, as in reading, knowing the goal—the *what*—does not tell us *how* to achieve it. We know that it is fruitless to expect the hard-to-teach child to memorize a lengthy list of reading words without also showing him a system for accomplishing the task and then giving him enough practice to make the system unnecessary. It is equally nonproductive to expect the hard-to-teach child to memorize a long list of answers to calculation problems—number facts —until you provide him with an efficient system for facilitating memorization of those facts and then sufficient practice to make that system less and less necessary.

Time for some illustrations. Let us first address the question, what kinds of programs are typically used to teach arithmetic? Then, how do you teach a child to be a good calculator when that child is hard to teach?

There are not as many different kinds of programs in arithmetic as there are in reading. For all practical purposes we can limit discussion to two types, and even these do not differ all that much. Typically they tend to be labeled basic, or traditional, math and modern math. I am going to use different labels. I will call basic, traditional math a *number facts* program and modern math a *math concepts* program, and I will continue to draw upon the preceding section on reading for contrasting illustrations.

A *number facts* program tends to stress the ultimate goal—the *what*— without devoting very much attention to the underlying concepts—the *how*. It is analogous to the whole-word reading program. A *math concepts* approach is comparable to a phonics reading program in that it tends to put more importance on explicating the principles of the calculation process, in showing the child *how* all calculation problems can be solved through counting, that counting can be done efficiently if certain mathematic principles are applied, and that, having learned these, the rest will come automatically.

Unfortunately neither approach works very well, at least not with the hard-to-teach child.

MATH CONCEPTS

The math concepts type of program emphasizes precisely what its name implies—the concepts that enable the child to carry out the basic calculations of addition, subtraction, multiplication, and division of whole numbers and fractions through application of a counting procedure—the proper algorithm—and certain mathematical principles. In other words, it focuses on preparing the child to *understand* arithmetic. As such, it reflects the same kind of self-deception that trapped the reading-program planners: "Show them how, and the rest comes easy." This is not always the case obviously, but they used easy-to-teach children as their test cases. You see, easy-to-teach children, by definition, memorize their basic number facts without very much effort. All they seem to need is to learn how to count accurately. This, combined with an intuitive understanding of the concepts of "more than," "less than," and "the same as," enables them to catch on to the fact that there are certain shortcuts in calculations that make the processes clear and easy: that $1 + 2$ is the same as $2 + 1$, and 1 less than $1 + 3$; that $9 + 7$ can be restated, and thus made easier to solve, as $10 + 6$; that—in a base-10 system—$17 + 4$ is exactly 10 more than $7 + 4$; that $5 + 3$ can be reversed to read $3 + 5$ without changing the answer, and that $8 - 3 = 5$; that $4 \times 6 = 24$ can be reversed to read $6 \times 4 = 24$ and $24 \div 6 = 4$; and so on. With these insights comes the practical advantage of markedly reducing the amount of raw information to be memorized. The child who recognizes the fact that $2 + 3 = 3 + 2 = 2 + 2 + 1$ has far fewer separate facts to memorize than the child who perceives these as three unrelated units of information, each requiring its own space in long-term memory.

All of these operations have been identified by mathematicians as basic concepts. They all have verbal labels—names—and these, too, are taught in a concepts program. Hence we hear small children talking about the commutative properties of numbers, and so on. But it is obvious that children who do grasp these concepts do not do so by first memorizing their names and their definitions. In fact, trying to understand the concepts in advance of being able to perform the operations is like trying to memorize the grammatical rules of your first spoken language before beginning to learn to speak it. It simply does not work. The concepts make sense after the fact only, and indeed, those of us who were successfully taught in the premodern math era grasped and could use these concepts even though they were not specifically identified and we did not know their names. This of course is what caused all the confusion among parents and teachers when modern math was introduced into the schools. They could do the operations; they just did not know the associated vocabulary.

At any rate the reasoning behind the math concepts approach appears to be: Teach the children how to calculate by counting by one, teach them the algorithms, and then teach them key concepts that provide for shortcuts in those calculations—for weaving separate calculations into a network of interrelated facts—and they will learn the basics of arithmetic. Then, having learned these basics, they will go on to acquire a large store of number facts without really trying; and this in turn will further their progress in arithmetic.

It is much like the promoters of phonics in reading, who propose that once the child knows the letters and their sounds, he will take it from there. Indeed, he might—but only if he really did not need phonics in the first place.

Children who are hard to teach in arithmetic do poorly with the math concepts approach. First of all, if they are hard to teach, then they are likely to be lacking in visual analysis skills. That is, they probably are not as adept as they should be in identifying the key attributes of spatial patterns—the properties and relationships of quantities and magnitudes. As such, they are lacking in a knowledge of spatial language—its (nonverbal) vocabulary and grammar. Trying to teach them how to "read" and "spell" a language with which they are so unfamiliar will not be productive. True, they will probably learn to count, but lacking the ability to recognize relationships, they will face the insurmountable task of trying to memorize a vast array of number facts that, from their viewpoint, are unrelated, each to be memorized independent of the others and none supplying any helpful hints for recalling any of the others. Formidable!

NUMBER FACTS

The number facts approach is hardly any better. It compares to the whole-word method of teaching reading. That is, its promoters argue, given enough good examples, certain fundamental principles should become apparent to the child, and he should then be able to apply these generally. And in the meantime he will be learning his basic number facts.

For example, if the child memorizes the facts $3 + 3 = 6$ and $4 + 4 = 8$, then surely he will soon "know" that $3 + 4$ "must" equal 7, just as in reading, if *cat* says /cat/, *fat* says /fat/, and *can* says /can/, then surely *fan* "must" say /fan/.

Well, it is not all that obvious to the hard-to-teach child. Once again, his inept visual analysis skills—his unfamiliarity with spatial language—obscures the "obvious." So here too he is stuck with the task of memorizing a long list of facts without a system for helping him remember them.

His alternatives are *(a)* to persist at the rote memorization task, the drill exercises, an unlikely choice, since no one stays with anything that he does so poorly, unless he has no other options; or *(b)* to guess at the answers, hardly an acceptable method in any case.

What happens then? Generally the child finally does memorize *some* facts, guesses at the rest, avoids arithmetic whenever possible, and fails.

There are some alternative arithmetic programs available, but again, as in reading, they are not all that different nor that effective. By and large they tend to be programs that emphasize counting, typically using blocks as "counters." Many of them also illustrate relationships—by using materials, where this can be done—but the illustrations are usually relatively obscure visual hints instead of overt, direct instruction. As such, the information to be communicated tends to remain unavailable to those who most need it. This is not meant to imply that programs that use manipulatives are not useful. On the contrary, they can be exceptionally useful. But the teacher should realize that the power of the method is not in the devices themselves but, rather, what can be taught with them.

The field of arithmetic instruction faces a dilemma that is in some ways the same as and in some ways different from the one we noted in the discussion on reading. It differs in that in arithmetic the dilemma stems from the fact that all arithmetic *can* be solved by counting, at least in theory. Knowledge of the language does not, on the surface, appear to be so crucial as it actually is. As a result, many children make some progress in arithmetic, memorizing a small assortment of basic number facts as the outcome of extended drill, yet go no further, because they lack adequate understanding of the language of mathematics. They learn what arithmetic they can in a way that resembles how we usually commence to learn a foreign language—by memorization and translation. They do not think in the language.

On the other hand, teaching children the language of mathematics is usually neither well understood nor well done. It is not the same as helping the child increase his speaking vocabulary or improve his grammar. There, at least, what is to be learned can, by definition, be verbalized. Increasing a child's understanding of the language of mathematics cannot be accomplished verbally—at least not without resorting to the abstraction of using numerals and other symbols to represent what is to be comprehended. And that, clearly, is well beyond the capabilities of the children we are discussing here.

Learning arithmetic requires two central abilities. One is the ability to identify certain key properties and relationships among quantities and magnitudes. The other is an understanding of how numerals can be used to represent these attributes and in a virtually limitless set of alternative arrangements—for example, that we can express the number fact $5 + 5 = 10$ as $4 + 1 + 5 = 10$ or as $3 + 5 + 2 = 10$ or as $(10 - 2) + (10 - 8) = 10$ and so on and on and on.

From these two abilities come two other central abilities: *(a)* the ability to memorize a store of basic number facts; and *(b)* the ability to restructure computation problems so as to exploit that knowledge *selectively* for recalling facts not yet securely memorized and for solving unfamiliar problems.

For example, most children encounter little difficulty memorizing the number fact $2 + 2 = 4$. Indeed, they generally have the spoken phrase memorized, by rote even, before they can perform the calculation itself, before they comprehend its meaning. Not too much later on they tend to memorize the fact $3 + 3 = 6$. If they perceive the relationships between these two facts —that is, if they are not hard to teach—then they will be able to solve the problem $2 + 3 = ?$ fairly easily, by applying what they already know to the solution of the new problem. They will reason that "2 + 3 is 1 more than 2 + 2" or "1 less than 3 + 3" and, in either event, come up with the correct answer. What they will not do—but what their hard-to-teach classmate, who does not perceive relationships, will do—is solve the problem by counting "two 1's, then three more"; this despite the fact that they, too, have memorized the facts 2 + 2 = 4 and 3 + 3 = 6. The hard-to-teach child stores his number facts as separate, independent items, whereas the child who perceives relationships stores them as links in an ever-expanding network of interconnected units of knowledge; as such, he grows in his ability to solve problems of greater complexity, involving higher numbers without always having to go back to the beginning.

This, then, brings us to a restatement of the dilemma in a way that resembles what we observed in our discussion of reading instruction. There I identified substandard auditory analysis skills as the factor that necessitated the use of a program that explicates the principles of phonics. In mathematics the key factor is, again, perceptual skills; but in this instance it is the visual analysis skills that count.

The child to whom it is hard to teach arithmetic almost invariably displays deficient visual analysis skills. Therefore, if the instructional system is to be effective, it must be one that makes explicit the relationships among quantities. Unless that is accomplished, or unless something is done to make the child more intuitively aware of relationships, instruction will not be effective. There is just too much to memorize independent of a system, and the *best system for memorizing new number facts is one that is based on an understanding of the interrelationships that exist between all number facts.*

CUSTOM-TAILORED
ARITHMETIC PROGRAM

Children differ, and so do arithmetic programs. Your goal is to design the program to fit the child rather than simply trusting to luck and the child's motivation. To accomplish this fit, you will have to take the good features from various instructional approaches and blend them in a way that meets the child's unique needs.

What would such a program look like? It should be based on the same five principles that I have presented previously.

Principle 1: Organize for success.

Nothing new to say here, other than that it does not hurt to be reminded that the child *can* learn. He has learned many things up to this point in his life, and he will learn many more things—even if you do nothing to help him. But since schools follow schedules and will therefore fail a child who cannot keep up with their schedule, it is advisable that you try to do something to help the child satisfy that schedule. And if what you do is what the child needs, he will make progress.

So although it is essential that you keep your long-term goals in mind, make certain that they do not distract you from setting up reasonable, short-term, day-to-day goals and working hard to achieve them.

Principle #2: Make certain that the child really does have the factual knowledge he needs to profit from a lesson.

If he has gaps, identify them and help him fill them in—and do it thoroughly, so that this newly acquired knowledge is retained. This is critical. It will greatly influence the ultimate value of your efforts.

What factual information does a child have to know when he comes to an arithmetic lesson? As discussed earlier—and the sequence in which they are listed here does not imply any order of relative importance—he has to have an adequate:

a. Knowledge of spatial language. If this is lacking, if the child's visual perceptual skills are deficient, then take action to improve them. Unless they are improved, it will place the child in the situation where he is asked to try to learn how to read a language that he cannot understand. It simply will not work.

A thorough description of how to go about improving a child's knowledge of spatial language is available on pages 75–91. Take a look at those instructions now and make plans to implement them.

b. The child must also bring to an arithmetic lesson an adequate knowledge of the graphic numerals and the conventions that govern their use. If the child cannot demonstrate thorough familiarity with the printed symbol system of arithmetic, then teach it to him. As stated in the section on reading, if his visual analysis skills are at least at the kindergarten level, then he is old enough to be taught—and to learn—the numerals, that is, to be able to print them from dictation. And, as with the letters, if he displays reversal tendencies, treat these as bad habits that should be eliminated by practicing alternative, good habits. (See pages 234–235.)

Activities that will enhance a child's knowledge of the graphic numerals and the conventions that govern their use include the following:

Determine which numerals the child already knows and which ones remain to be learned. To determine this, have him print them from dictation. Do not assume that he knows them—at least not to the point that he must know them if he is to deal with them virtually automatically in the context of an arithmetic lesson—unless he can print them from dictation with no errors.

Start off by finding out whether the child is completely familiar with the numerals, 0 to 9. Completely familiar, in this instance, means that he can do all of the following:

(a) match numeral shapes;
(b) point to the proper numeral upon request;
(c) name the numerals correctly when they are shown to him in some random order; and
(d) print the numerals from dictation.

If he cannot do this last, find out what he can do in that sequence of abilities and teach him from that point on. In other words, if he cannot print them accurately but can name them when they are shown to him, then set about teaching him to print them. If, on the other hand, he can do no better than match up printed numerals, then do not start teaching him to print them. Rather, teach him first to identify them—then move on.

How do you teach him? Drill and practice. Fortunately there are only ten symbols to start with, so the task is fairly well defined.

Teaching matching skills. Play card games, concentration, board games that use a spinner, and other games involving printed numerals.

Teaching the names of the numerals. This usually comes about quite readily by playing the games, but if extra help is needed, provide it. Although drill and practice will work, a game format makes it more interesting for the child. Using a small electronic hand calculator, call out a single number and have the child punch it out on the keyboard. To add interest and some extra value to the activity, call out two, three, or even four numbers in succession and see if he can also keep the sequence straight while finding the proper buttons. If you do not have a calculator, use a typewriter, and if there is not one of these available, simply use homemade cards (playing-card size) on which numerals have been printed.

Teaching him how to print the numerals. There is only one good way— Give him a pencil, a crayon, or a piece of chalk and set him to work. To facilitate the process, have him first trace over numerals that you print. Then have him copy numerals alongside ones that you print. Finally have him print them while his eyes are closed, thinking about what his hand is doing.

Where a reversal tendency is observed, take actions to teach the correct pattern. For example, if the child tends to reverse a particular numeral, then try to identify a mnemonic, or memory aid, that will help him resolve the difficulty. And, by all means, avoid giving him more than one mnemonic at a time—otherwise you will find that the child has to spend too much time memorizing, and confusing, the mnemonic. As such, the treatment becomes worse than the disease.

One effective mnemonic for remembering the directional orientation of numerals is:

1. Determine if the child is completely familiar with the (capital) *B*. If he is, it will be the child's "home base," his point of reference. (The instructions that follow assume that he is familiar with the *B*.)
2. Ask the child to print the *B*.
3. Have him print the *B* again, but this time have him separate the vertical line from the remainder of the letter, thereby producing a 1 and a 3.
4. Point out to the child how the *B* transforms—breaks apart—into these two numerals.
5. Now introduce other numerals that share certain key features with the 3. For example, the 2.
6. In printing the 2, you start off just as you do with the 3—from top left, moving toward the right. Hence there is a link between the 1, the 2, and the 3. They all stem, in a way, from the *B*.
7. Now introduce the 7. This, too, is printed in a way that resembles the 2, in that you start at the top, move to the right, and so on.
8. Make certain that, as you introduce new numerals, you review the

older one, constantly stressing the central mnemonic—that from the *B* come the 1, the 2, the 3, the 7.

9. Now introduce the 9. Its connection with the ones already discussed is clear. It follows nicely from the 7, in that it differs from the 7 only in one small part of its construction.

10. Now introduce the 4. The 4 links up with this group of numerals, particularly the 9. In a way, it is very similar to the 9, differing only in one aspect of its shape. The 4 and the 9, when printed, both have their vertical lines to the right of the rest of the numeral. (This is also true, obviously, of certain of the other numerals introduced thus far.)

11. Only a few numerals remain: the 5, 6, and 8. The 8 is easy; it has no directional component of consequence. Once the 8 is learned, point out to the child that when these numerals are printed in sequence from 1 to 10, they are all represented except for the 5 and the 6, the middle ones. Hence the only two that remain that are potential sources of directional confusion are the 5 and the 6.

12. Start with the 6, by introducing a second reference point—mnemonic: the capital *C.*

13. If the child can print the *C* accurately, he has the basis for keeping straight in his memory the orientation of the 6. Point this out to him —but, by the way, do not move to these last two numerals until after the child has demonstrated a fairly well-established familiarity with the numerals just discussed. Once ready, however, the child should have little difficulty in recognizing how the *C* can serve as a memory clue for the 6.

14. Now all that remains is the 5. Teach it on the basis of its resemblance to the 6 and its proximity to that numeral when counting.

Teach him to print the numerals from 0 to 100. Show him that when he gets past the 9, two digits are used, and that the first one written is a 1 from 10 to 19, then the first one becomes a 2 from 20 to 29, and so on. This is best done by aligning them vertically on graph paper, rather than horizontally. It is easier to see the system that way. For example,

1	11	21
2	12	etc.
3	13	
4	14	
5	15	
6	16	
7	17	
8	18	
9	19	
10	20	

is better than this:

1, 2, 3, 4, 5, 6, 7, 8, 9, 10, 11, etc.

Point out to him that once he is past the teens, the first number in the sequence is the one said first. For example, *twenty*-three, *sixty*-seven, and so on.

c. Finally, in order to begin the process of learning to calculate, the child must bring to the lesson an adequate *knowledge about relevant subject matter.* This refers to the verbal language of arithmetic, for example, the ability to match up the graphic numeral 6 with the spoken word /six/, as well as with a collection of six objects. It also refers to an operational understanding of the terms *more than, less than, the same as,* and *so forth.* If confusion exists here, strive to eliminate it rapidly.

Activities that will enhance a child's knowledge of the verbal language of arithmetic include the following:

Eliminate whatever confusion may exist around the terms just mentioned through the use of explicit instruction accompanied by illustrations that employ concrete materials. For example, use collections of objects to illustrate *more than, the same as,* and so on, teaching synonyms at the same time, that is, *equal, greater than, fewer,* and so forth.

Where needed, teach the child to count accurately and to record those quantities with the correct numerals, by the use of interesting, gamelike activities. There are many sources for these. Children's magazines, the comic pages of newspapers, and other periodicals of that sort should be looked at first. Then, too, your local librarian will be able to recommend a number of children's books that incorporate pertinent counting instruction into the story line. Beyond this, your own imagination can be very productive.

Card games, such as War and various others that involve matching cards and/or competitions where the higher numbers win can be very useful.

Teach him to count up to 100.

a. Take walks and count steps. See how far 100 steps will take you. (Compare the outcome of taking long steps with taking short steps —in this way, you will be teaching relationships at the same time.)
b. Have him count out 100 pennies or poker chips, or what have you.
c. Have him bounce a ball 100 times or more if he can, and keep score. Have him establish a record and then try to beat it. Once he has pretty well learned how to count to 100, start questioning him about what number comes just after—? or what number comes just before—?

Teach him to record quantities—to count objects and write down the amount—ranging from 0 to 100.

    a. Have him develop a set of directions—a map—for moving from one point in the house or the backyard to another. For example, ask him to measure the perimeter of your yard in footsteps, record it, and compare that with the neighbor's yard. (This can be added to the "take a walk and count the steps" activity just described.) Measuring things and comparing them is excellent training for a variety of arithmetic skills.

    b. Have him write down the number that comes just before or just after___.

    c. Obtain 100 white poker chips and a marking crayon. Number each of the chips from 1 to 100. Mix them up, then have the child arrange them in numerical sequence, stacked in piles of 10 chips each, with the lowest number in each pile on the top. He should end up, then, with 10 piles, where the chips on top of each pile look like that shown in figure 44. Time him, and keep track of his improvement.

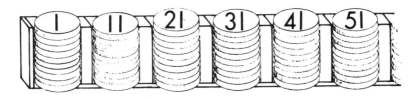

FIGURE 44

(*Note:* Draw a bar under each potentially ambiguous number, so that there is no difficulty distinguishing the 6 from the 9, the 61 from the 19, 81 from 18, and so on.)

Principle #3: Make clear to the child a system—a strategy—that will help him retain information, that is, link up what he is to learn with what he already knows.

I have stressed the importance of system throughout this book. I have also stressed that the system must make sense to the child and be simple enough —sufficiently free of complications and exceptions—to be applicable without modification in a variety of different situations. If the system does not have these qualities, it will not be very helpful. If the system seems, to the child, to be made up of unconnected, arbitrarily determined, ambiguous rules, or if it seems to have so many exceptions that using it requires a thick rule book, then again it will not be very helpful. Remember, he is hard to teach because he does not remember enough of what he is taught. The system must either help him with this problem, or it should be avoided altogether.

What does this mean in practical terms? What is the approach I propose? It entails two parts. First, it focuses on helping the child memorize a basic store of number facts by presenting them to him with the easiest to remember facts first. Second, it illustrates to the child the precise and fixed relationships among specific quantities. For example, that 6 is always 1 more than 5, 1 less than 7, twice as much as 3, and so forth. These two, in combination—memorizing a set of basic facts and recognizing how other facts link up with that basic set —are extremely pertinent to making progress in elementary arithmetic.

But keep in mind that your goal is not to make the child dependent upon a system. If a system is to be truly helpful, its ultimate effect is that it becomes superfluous. Its main purpose and benefit, in this instance, is to identify for the child *what* facts are easiest to learn at the start and *how* best to learn them. Then, once he has learned them, how to use this basic knowledge in learning even more complex facts.

If the child does become dependent upon the system—using factual knowledge as the starting point for counting—he will never do as well as he should in arithmetic. The system will not produce a fluent calculator. If he learns to depend on it, the child will become a solve-the-problem-in-fewer-steps-than-he-used-to-need kind of calculator, which is a step in the right direction, of course, but it is not fluency.

The fact is that the child cannot be fluent in arithmetic until he has memorized a sizable store of number facts—until he can respond with the correct answer to all addition, subtraction, multiplication, and division calculations involving quantities of, say, 100 or less, almost automatically—independent of system. This, in conjunction with the ability to restructure arithmetic problems in a way that enables the child to use what he already knows for solving problems involving even larger quantities, is essential to fluency. It is like the adequate reader who, upon encountering a novel word, uses the strategy of searching for some clues in that word—one or more familiar letter strings—that might help him read the full word. Ultimately he becomes familiar with that once-novel word if he continues to encounter it. It does not remain unfamiliar and needful of all those extra decoding steps. In fact, it will eventually serve as a reference point in decoding other unfamiliar words.

SPECIAL SECTION: ACTIVITIES FOR MEMORIZING NUMBER FACTS

The following pages present a program that will help the child to memorize number facts; to recognize the precise, fixed relationships among specific quantities; and to gain fluency in calculating. The activities will help the child memorize number facts that, in turn, he will be able to use to solve ever more complex calculations. The material is organized in a sequence that follows the simple logic of learning how to take the first step before taking the second.

I have to admit, however, that defining a step-by-step sequence for teaching arithmetic facts and concepts is not as orderly a process as it is for reading. There is something quite different—and unique—about arithmetic.

Reading is a linear process. You consistently read in a single direction—in English, from left to right. Our letter coding system reflects that consistency, even though the letter-sound connections are somewhat inconsistent.

The same is not true of arithmetic. The numeral-quantity connection is fully consistent, but the calculation process is multidirectional. The elegance of the coding system we use in arithmetic often allows us to rearrange the sequence of the numerals without altering the essence of the problem. Hence $2 + 3$ is the same as $3 + 2$, is the same as $2 + 2 + 1$, is the same as $3 - 2 + 4$, and so on. Indeed, even the reasoning in arithmetic calculations is multidirectional. We often redefine a problem conceptually to facilitate our solving it.

At any rate, despite all of these insights, the objectives defined here are best dealt with in sequence, starting with the first one and working through the others in the order of their appearance, one at a time. They represent facts that are to be learned—absorbed to the place where the child can state the answers to the problems automatically—without needing to "figure them out." This is essential. Unless this state is achieved, the child's arithmetic skills will be inadequate—laborious, inefficient, always requiring him to begin his calculations at a level far below what is optimal for competent performance.

Accompanying the directions for each objective is the suggestion that you first pretest the child in order to determine whether, in fact, he has not already mastered that objective. Obviously there is no value in having the child learn what he already knows. To avoid this, test the child in his knowledge of the calculation facts listed for the objective you are preparing to work with.

Present them to him as arithmetic problems and assess his responses. Use both oral and written formats. If he shows that he has already memorized the answers to these problems, make note of it and move on to the next objective.

As in reading, he is to show this by responding accurately *and* rapidly. If he is inaccurate, then obviously he is to work on the material. If he is accurate but slow—if, for example, he appears to solve calculation problems by counting, aloud or to himself—then do not consider it to be adequate. Engage him in the activities and credit him with having achieved the designated objectives only when his responses become virtually automatic.

You will need a teaching aid for these activities—a homemade calculator. To construct it, you will need the poker chips described on page 237, each one bearing a number from 1 to 100. In addition you will need a map containing 100 squares, arranged in 10 rows of 10 squares each. This can be made with a piece of poster board, available from any art supply house, or for that matter any piece of cardboard.

Draw the map so that each square is just large enough to contain one poker chip. The map should look like that shown in figure 45.

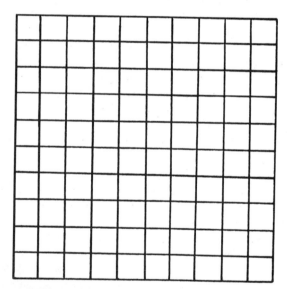

FIGURE 45

That is all the equipment you will need to get started.

Once you have constructed the calculator—obtained and numbered the chips and completed the 100-cell map—then it is time to begin the instructional activities. Start with Objective #1. If the child shows mastery of this objective, go on to Objective #2, then to #3, and so on.

Note: All of these objectives and the activities for teaching them are based on the assumption that the child can count objects accurately—at least up to about 20—and is completely familiar with the written symbol system of arithmetic. If he is lacking in any of these, that is, if he cannot count collections of twenty or so objects accurately, or if he is insufficiently familiar with the printed numerals, the various operations signs (=, −, ×, ÷, =, etc.), and the conventions that govern their use, then go back to pages 233–237 and review this material with him.

Objective #1: The child is able to state the following number facts rapidly and accurately:

$$1 + 1 = 2$$
$$1 + 2 = 3 \qquad 2 + 1 = 3$$
$$1 + 3 = 4 \qquad 3 + 1 = 4$$
$$1 + 4 = 5 \qquad 4 + 1 = 5$$
$$1 + 5 = 6 \qquad 5 + 1 = 6$$
$$1 + 6 = 7 \qquad 6 + 1 = 7$$
$$1 + 7 = 8 \qquad 7 + 1 = 8$$
$$1 + 8 = 9 \qquad 8 + 1 = 9$$
$$1 + 9 = 10 \qquad 9 + 1 = 10$$

1. Pretest and proceed accordingly. If he has not yet fully mastered this objective, then:
2. Write the first statement on a chalkboard, show it to him, and say: "This says $1 + 1 = 2$."
3. Have the child repeat that statement to you. "Tell me what this says."
4. Now ask him to "solve the problem" with the poker chip calculator. To do this, he should remove the first chip from the storage rack (the chip numbered 1) and place it on the first (left-most) cell of the top line of the map, as shown in figure 46.
5. Next he is to remove the second chip from the storage rack (the chip numbered 2) and place it in the first cell of the second line on the map, again as shown in figure 47 (page 243).
6. When these two are in place—the first one representing the first quantity of the problem and the second one representing the second quantity of the problem—he is to restate the fact ("$1 + 1 = 2$"), reading the answer from the highest-numbered chip on the map—the 2, in this case.
7. As a final step he is to regroup the chips, moving chip 2 up to the top line and positioning it in the cell just adjacent to chip 1. The value of this will be more evident when sums greater than 10 are introduced, but it is a habit that should be established early on.
8. When you are satisfied that the child understands what to do with the calculator, and when he is able to respond appropriately to the

question "What is the sum of 1 + 1?" then have him write this statement of fact (1 + 1 = 2) on a 3" × 5" index card and place it in a file box as the first entry in his Number Facts Bank.

9. Now work your way through the other facts that have been assigned to this objective using the calculator as described for the first item and making entries into the Number Facts Bank as they are earned.

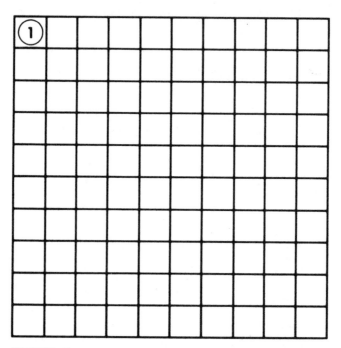

FIGURE 46

10. When you complete all the items, take time to explain and demonstrate the reversibility of the components of an addition problem—that it does not matter which of the two numerals is entered first in a problem of this type, that (1 + 2) = (2 + 1). Show this to the child with the calculator as well as in words.

11. When he has memorized all of the items of this objective and made entries into his Number Facts Bank, move on to #2.

Objective #2: The child is able to state the following number facts accurately and rapidly:

$$1 + 1 = 2 \qquad 4 + 4 = 8$$
$$2 + 2 = 4 \qquad 5 + 5 = 10$$
$$3 + 3 = 6$$

1. Pretest and proceed accordingly. If he has not yet fully mastered this objective, then:

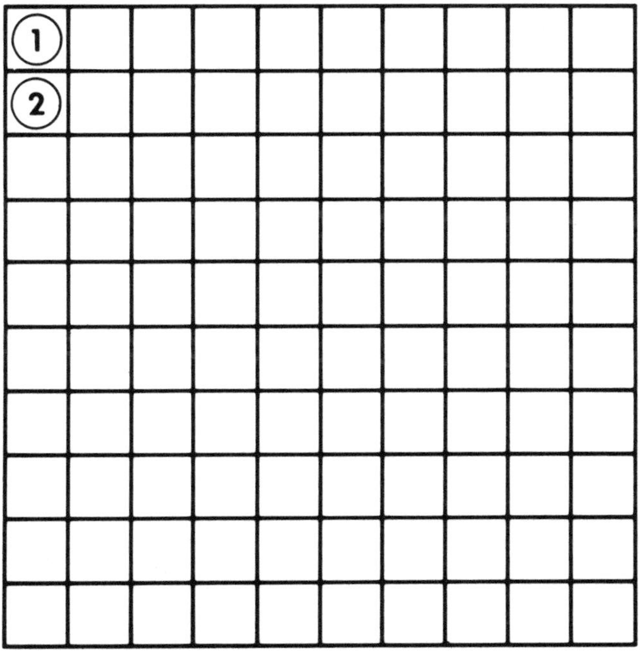

FIGURE 47

2. Teach the above number facts, following the procedures described under Objective #1. As you teach these, emphasize that the components of the facts of this objective are always paired. This makes them easier to remember.
3. When he has memorized all of the items of this objective and made entries into his Number Facts Bank, move on to #3.

Objective #3: The child is able to state the following number facts accurately and rapidly:

$$1 + 2 = 3 \qquad 2 + 1 = 3$$
$$2 + 3 = 5 \qquad 3 + 2 = 5$$
$$3 + 4 = 7 \qquad 4 + 3 = 7$$
$$4 + 5 = 9 \qquad 5 + 4 = 9$$

1. Pretest and proceed accordingly. If he has not yet fully mastered this objective, then:
2. Teach the above number facts, following the procedures described under Objective #1. As you do this, incorporate into the procedure the following activities:
3. Say to the child: "Is 1 + 2 more or less than 1 + 1?" (If the child displays uncertainty, review the concepts of "more" and "less," using the chip calculator.) If he responds appropriately, then ask:
4. "How much more?" (If the child indicates uncertainty, review the concepts of "how much more" with the calculator.) If the child responds appropriately, then say:
5. "Correct." "1 + 2 is 1 more than 1 + 1. What is the sum of 1 + 1?" (He should already have that fact well established in his memory and filed in his Number Facts Bank. If he does not recall it, review it with him accordingly.) When he responds correctly, ask: "Well, then, what is the sum of 1 + 2, since 1 + 2 is one more than 1 + 1?"
6. Now ask: "Is 1 + 2 more or less than 2 + 2?" Proceed from here as already described, by probing "How much more?" etc. (You recognize, of course, that in each instance the point of reference—the number fact used as the basis for calculating "how much more" or "how much less"—is a fact that has already been covered in an earlier objective.)
7. Repeat this for all of the other items listed, constantly seeking to link the items with closely associated, already learned facts. In other words, 2 + 3 links up with 2 + 2 (1 more than) and with 3 + 3 (1 less than); 3 + 4 links up with 3 + 3 and with 4 + 4; and 4 + 5 links up with 4 + 4 and with 5 + 5.
8. When he has memorized all of the items of this objective and made entries into his Number Facts Bank, move on to #4.

Objective #4: The child is able to state the following number facts accurately and rapidly:

9 + 1 = 10	4 + 6 = 10
8 + 2 = 10	3 + 7 = 10
7 + 3 = 10	2 + 8 = 10
6 + 4 = 10	1 + 9 = 10
5 + 5 = 10	0 + 10 = 10

1. Pretest and proceed accordingly. If he has not yet fully mastered this objective, then:
2. Teach the above number facts, following the procedures described under Objective #1. As you do this, make sure to point out repeatedly that each of these items yields a sum of 10 and that the difference between the items stems from how the quantities are distributed. And be sure to use the calculator to illustrate this.
3. When he has memorized all of the items of this objective and made entries into his Number Facts Bank, move on to #5.

Objective #5: The child is able to state the following number facts rapidly and accurately:

10 − 1 = 9	5 − 1 = 4
9 − 1 = 8	4 − 1 = 3
8 − 1 = 7	3 − 1 = 2
7 − 1 = 6	2 − 1 = 1
6 − 1 = 5	1 − 1 = 0

1. Pretest and proceed accordingly. If he has not yet fully mastered this objective, then:
2. Teach him the above number facts as follows: Write the full statement on a chalkboard, show it to him and say: "This says 10 − 1 = 9."
3. Have the child repeat that statement to you. "Tell me what it says."
4. Now ask him to solve the problem on the calculator. To do this, he should take the first 10 chips from the storage rack and place them on the first line of the map.
5. Then remove the last chip (chip #10) from its original position on the map, and locate it in the first cell of the third line, thereby indicating that it is being removed, or *subtracted,* from the original set. The map will then look like that shown in figure 48.

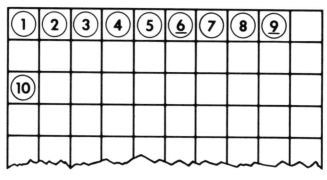

FIGURE 48

6. Now record the answer—that is, the number of chips remaining in the original group. Point out to the child that subtraction is really the direct opposite of addition, since the map is now almost set up to add: 9 + 1. All he has to do is move the tenth chip from the third line up to the second line.
7. Work your way through the remainder of the items this way.
8. When he has memorized all of the items of this objective and made entries into his Number Facts Bank, move on to #6.

Objective #6: The child is able to state the following number facts rapidly and accurately:

$$2 - 1 = 1 \qquad 8 - 4 = 4$$
$$4 - 2 = 2 \qquad 10 - 5 = 5$$
$$6 - 3 = 3$$

1. Pretest and proceed accordingly. If he has not yet fully mastered this objective, then:
2. Teach the above number facts, following the procedures described under Objective #5.
3. Notice that these subtraction statements are directly analogous to the addition statements that appear under Objective #2; that is, they involve matched pairs of numerals. Review that objective and incorporate into your instructions whatever might appear to be useful. (I am assuming that the child has already completed Objective #2; otherwise he should not be working at this level.)
4. When he has memorized all of the items of this objective and made entries into his Number Facts Bank, move on to #7.

Objective #7: The child is able to state the following number facts rapidly and accurately:

$$3 - 1 = 2 \qquad 3 - 2 = 1$$
$$5 - 2 = 3 \qquad 5 - 3 = 2$$
$$7 - 3 = 4 \qquad 7 - 4 = 3$$
$$9 - 4 = 5 \qquad 9 - 5 = 4$$

1. Pretest and proceed accordingly. If he has not yet fully mastered this objective, then:
2. Teach the above number facts, following the procedures described under Objective #5.
3. Notice that these subtraction statements are directly analogous to the addition statements that appear under Objective #3; that is, they link up with the number facts addressed in the preceding objective (Objective #6). Review Objective #3 and incorporate into your instructions whatever might appear to be useful.
4. When he has memorized all of the items of this objective and made entries into his Number Facts Bank, move on to #8.

Objective #8: The child is able to state the following number facts rapidly and accurately:

10 − 1 = 9	10 − 6 = 4
10 − 2 = 8	10 − 7 = 3
10 − 3 = 7	10 − 8 = 2
10 − 4 = 6	10 − 9 = 1
10 − 5 = 5	10 − 10 = 0

1. Pretest and proceed accordingly. If he has not yet mastered this objective, then:
2. Teach the above number facts, following the procedures described under Objective #5.
3. Notice that these subtraction statements are directly analogous to the addition statements that appear under Objective #4. That is, they pertain to combinations that add up to 10. Review Objective #4 and incorporate into your instructions what might appear to be useful.
4. When he has memorized all of the items of this objective and made entries into his Number Facts Bank, move on to #9.

Objective #9: The child is able to state the following number facts accurately and rapidly:

1 + 2 = 3	2 + 1 = 3
2 + 2 = 4	
3 + 2 = 5	2 + 3 = 5
4 + 2 = 6	2 + 4 = 6
5 + 2 = 7	2 + 5 = 7
6 + 2 = 8	2 + 6 = 8
7 + 2 = 9	2 + 7 = 9
8 + 2 = 10	2 + 8 = 10

1. Pretest and proceed accordingly. If he has not yet fully mastered this objective, then:
2. Teach the above number facts, following the procedures described under Objective #1.
3. Notice that these are, once again, addition statements. Also notice that some of the facts included under this objective are repeats. They are included for two reasons: *(a)* for thoroughness, in that they also belong to this set; and *(b)* as established reference points for facilitating retention of the information introduced here.
4. When the child has memorized all of the items of this objective and made entries into his Number Facts Bank, move on to #10.

Objective #10: The child is able to state the following number facts accurately and rapidly:

1 + 3 = 4	3 + 1 = 4
2 + 3 = 5	3 + 2 = 5
3 + 3 = 6	
4 + 3 = 7	4 + 3 = 7
5 + 3 = 8	5 + 3 = 8
6 + 3 = 9	6 + 3 = 9
7 + 3 = 10	7 + 3 = 10

1. Pretest and proceed accordingly. If he has not yet mastered this objective, then:
2. Teach the above number facts, following the procedures described for Objective #1. Here again some of the facts are repeats. As explained under Objective #9, they are to be exploited as established reference points for facilitating the retention of the new facts introduced here.
3. When he has memorized all of the items of this objective and made entries into his Number Facts Bank, move on to #11.

Objective #11: The child is able to state the following number facts accurately and rapidly:

1 + 4 = 5	4 + 1 = 5
2 + 4 = 6	4 + 2 = 6
3 + 4 = 7	4 + 3 = 7
4 + 4 = 8	4 + 4 = 8
5 + 4 = 9	4 + 5 = 9
6 + 4 = 10	4 + 6 = 10

1. Pretest and proceed accordingly. If he has not yet mastered this objective, then:
2. Teach the above number facts, following the procedures described for Objective #1.
3. When he has memorized all of the items of this objective and made entries into his Number Facts Bank, move on to #12.

Objective #12: The child is able to state the following number facts accurately and rapidly:

1 + 5 = 6	5 + 1 = 6
2 + 5 = 7	5 + 2 = 7
3 + 5 = 8	5 + 3 = 8
4 + 5 = 9	5 + 4 = 9
5 + 5 = 10	

1. Pretest and proceed accordingly. If he has not yet mastered this objective, then:
2. Teach the above number facts, following the procedures described for Objective #1.
3. When he has memorized all of the items of this objective and made entries into his Number Facts Bank, move on to #13.

Objective #13: The child is able to state the following number facts accurately and rapidly:

1 + 6 = 7	6 + 1 = 7
2 + 6 = 8	6 + 2 = 8
3 + 6 = 9	6 + 3 = 9
4 + 6 = 10	6 + 4 = 10

1. Pretest and proceed accordingly. If he has not yet mastered this objective, then:
2. Teach the above number facts, following the procedures described for Objective #1.
3. When he has memorized all of the items of this objective and made entries into his Number Facts Bank, move on to #14.

Objective #14: The child is able to state the following number facts accurately and rapidly:

1 + 7 = 8	7 + 1 = 8
2 + 7 = 9	7 + 2 = 9
3 + 7 = 10	7 + 3 = 10

1. Pretest and proceed accordingly. If he has not yet mastered this objective, then:
2. Teach the above number facts, following the procedures described for Objective #1.
3. When he has memorized all of the items of this objective and made entries into his Number Facts Bank, move on to #15.

Objective #15: The child is able to state the following number facts accurately and rapidly:

$$1 + 8 = 9 \qquad 8 + 1 = 9$$
$$2 + 8 = 10 \qquad 8 + 2 = 10$$

1. Pretest and proceed accordingly. If he has not yet mastered this objective, then:
2. Teach the above number facts, following the procedures described for Objective #1.
3. When he has memorized all of the items of this objective and made entries into his Number Facts Bank, move on to #16.

Objective #16: The child is able to state the following number facts accurately and rapidly:

$$1 + 9 = 10 \qquad 9 + 1 = 10$$

1. Pretest and proceed accordingly. If he has not yet mastered this objective, then:
2. Teach the above number facts, following the procedures described for Objective #1.
3. When he has memorized all of the items of this objective and made entries into his Number Facts Bank, move on to #17.

Objective #17: The child is able to state the following number facts accurately and rapidly:

$$10 - 2 = 8 \qquad 5 - 2 = 3$$
$$9 - 2 = 7 \qquad 4 - 2 = 2$$
$$8 - 2 = 6 \qquad 3 - 2 = 1$$
$$7 - 2 = 5 \qquad 2 - 2 = 0$$
$$6 - 2 = 4$$

1. Pretest and proceed accordingly. If he has not yet mastered this objective, then:
2. Teach the above number facts, following the procedures described for Objective #5.
3. Notice that these are subtraction statements. Also notice that some of the facts included here are repeats; they are included here for two reasons: *(a)* for thoroughness, in that they also belong to this set of facts; and *(b)* as established reference points for facilitating retention of the information introduced here.
4. When the child has memorized all of the items of this objective and made entries into his Number Facts Bank, move on to #18.

Objective #18: The child is able to state the following number facts accurately and rapidly:

10 − 3 = 7	6 − 3 = 3
9 − 3 = 6	5 − 3 = 2
8 − 3 = 5	4 − 3 = 1
7 − 3 = 4	3 − 3 = 0

1. Pretest and proceed accordingly. If he has not yet mastered this objective, then:
2. Teach the above number facts, following the procedures described for Objective #5.
3. When the child has memorized all of the items of this objective and made entries into his Number Facts Bank, move on to #19.

Objective #19: The child is able to state the following number facts accurately and rapidly:

10 − 4 = 6	6 − 4 = 2
9 − 4 = 5	5 − 4 = 1
8 − 4 = 4	4 − 4 = 0
7 − 4 = 3	

1. Pretest and proceed accordingly. If he has not yet mastered this objective, then:
2. Teach the above number facts, following the procedures described for Objective #5.
3. When the child has memorized all of the items of this objective and made entries into his Number Facts Bank, move on to #20.

Objective #20: The child is able to state the following number facts accurately and rapidly:

$$10 - 5 = 5 \qquad 7 - 5 = 2$$
$$9 - 5 = 4 \qquad 6 - 5 = 1$$
$$8 - 5 = 3 \qquad 5 - 5 = 0$$

1. Pretest and proceed accordingly. If he has not yet mastered this objective, then:
2. Teach the above number facts, following the procedures described for Objective #5.
3. When the child has memorized all of the items of this objective and made entries into his Number Facts Bank, move on to #21.

Objective #21: The child is able to state the following number facts accurately and rapidly:

$$10 - 6 = 4 \qquad 7 - 6 = 1$$
$$9 - 6 = 3 \qquad 6 - 6 = 0$$
$$8 - 6 = 2$$

1. Pretest and proceed accordingly. If he has not yet mastered this objective, then:
2. Teach the above number facts, following the procedures described for Objective #5.
3. When the child has memorized all of the items of this objective and made entries into his Number Facts Bank, move on to #22.

Objective #22: The child is able to state the following number facts accurately and rapidly:

$$10 - 7 = 3 \qquad 8 - 7 = 1$$
$$9 - 7 = 2 \qquad 7 - 7 = 0$$

1. Pretest and proceed accordingly. If he has not yet mastered this objective, then:
2. Teach the above number facts, following the procedures described for Objective #5.
3. When the child has memorized all of the items of this objective and made entries into his Number Facts Bank, move on to #23.

Objective #23: The child is able to state the following number facts accurately and rapidly:

$$10 - 8 = 2 \qquad 8 - 8 = 0$$
$$9 - 8 = 1$$

1. Pretest and proceed accordingly. If he has not yet mastered this objective, then:
2. Teach the above number facts, following the procedures described for Objective #5.
3. When the child has memorized all of the items of this objective and made entries into his Number Facts Bank, move on to #24.

Objective #24: The child is able to state the following number facts accurately and rapidly:

$$10 - 9 = 1 \qquad 9 - 9 = 0$$

1. Pretest and proceed accordingly. If he has not yet mastered this objective, then:
2. Teach the above number facts, following the procedures described for Objective #5.
3. When the child has memorized all of the items of this objective and made entries into his Number Facts Bank, move on to #25.

Objective #25: The child is able to state the following number facts accurately and rapidly:

$$6 + 6 = 12 \qquad 9 + 9 = 18$$
$$7 + 7 = 14 \qquad 10 + 10 = 20$$
$$8 + 8 = 16$$

1. Pretest and proceed accordingly. If he has not yet mastered this objective, then:
2. Teach the above number facts, following the procedures described under Objectives #1 and #2.
3. Once the problem has been worked through on the calculator, remember to relocate the chips so that the top line is fully occupied, thereby highlighting the fact that the number statement just calculated could also be written to read "10 + __ = sum" (for example, that 6 + 6 is the same as 10 + 2).
4. When the child has memorized all of the items of this objective and made entries into his Number Facts Bank, move on to #26.

Objective #26: The child is able to state the following number facts accurately and rapidly:

$$6 + 5 = 11 \qquad 8 + 7 = 15$$
$$6 + 7 = 13 \qquad 8 + 9 = 17$$
$$7 + 6 = 13 \qquad 9 + 8 = 17$$
$$7 + 8 = 15 \qquad 9 + 10 = 19$$

1. Pretest and proceed accordingly. If he has not yet mastered this objective, then:
2. Teach the above number facts, following the procedure described under Objective #3. (*Note:* This involves exploiting the concepts of "more than" and "less than." Make certain that you review the directions under Objective #3 for full information.)
3. When the child has memorized all of the items of this objective and made entries into his Number Facts Bank, move on to #27.

Objective #27: The child is able to state the following number facts accurately and rapidly:

$$12 + 10 = 22 \qquad 10 + 34 = 44$$
$$23 + 10 = 33 \qquad 10 + 19 = 29$$
$$27 + 10 = 37 \qquad 13 + 10 = 23$$

1. Pretest and proceed accordingly. If he has not yet mastered this objective, then:
2. Teach the above number facts, following the procedures described under Objective #1. (*Note:* Since these facts involve sums that exceed 10, use the calculator to emphasize how quantities may be regrouped—and perceived—as being so many sets of 10, plus a given quantity of less than 10. Hence $43 = 4$ tens plus 3, or $40 + 3$.)
3. When the child has memorized all of the items of this objective and made entries into his Number Facts Bank, move on to #28.

Objective #28: The child is able to state the following number facts accurately and rapidly:

$$1 \times 1 = 2 \qquad 4 \times 4 = 16$$
$$2 \times 2 = 4 \qquad 5 \times 5 = 25$$
$$3 \times 3 = 9$$

1. Pretest and proceed accordingly. If he has not yet mastered this objective, then:
2. Teach the above number facts using the following procedures:
3. Make sure, first, that the child knows the multiplication sign and differentiates it from the plus sign.
4. Then, using the calculator, explain—and illustrate—that, for example, the number statement 3 × 3 means three groups, each containing three things. With this information, he should place the first set of three chips on the top line of the calculator, the next set of three chips on the second line of the calculator, and the third set of three chips on the third line. How the map should appear is shown in figure 49.

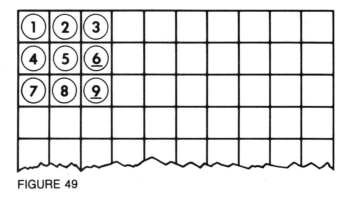

FIGURE 49

5. He can read the answer directly from the last chip, but while he is at it, you should point out that he can also find the answer to 1 × 3 and to 2 × 3 by reading down the right-most column of chips.
6. Work through the other multiplication statements of this objective with the calculator. As you do so, point out to the child that each of these statements involves a pair of identical numerals, for example, 2 × 2, 3 × 3, etc. This feature makes them easier to remember.
7. When the child has memorized all of the items of this objective and made entries into his Number Facts Bank, move on to #29.

Objective #29: The child is able to state the following number facts accurately and rapidly:

2 × 1 = 2	1 × 2 = 2
2 × 2 = 4	
2 × 3 = 6	3 × 2 = 6
2 × 4 = 8	4 × 2 = 8
2 × 5 = 10	5 × 2 = 10
2 × 6 = 12	6 × 2 = 12
2 × 7 = 14	7 × 2 = 14
2 × 8 = 16	8 × 2 = 16
2 × 9 = 18	9 × 2 = 18
2 × 10 = 20	10 × 2 = 20

1. Pretest and proceed accordingly. If he has not yet mastered this objective, then:
2. Teach the above number facts, following the procedures described under Objective #28.
3. When he shows that he can do these operations on the calculator without assistance, introduce the concept that 2 × 1 is the same as 1 × 2, by rotating the map 90° (¼ turn) counterclockwise. Of course, the chips will not be in a proper arrangement, but without rearranging them, you can still point out how two groups (lines), each with one chip, is really the same as one group (line) with two chips.
4. Once the child has learned to display these number statements on the calculator and has begun to be familiar with the above number facts, then introduce the concept of counting by 2's, from a starting point of 2; in other words: 2 . . . 4 . . . 6 . . . 8 . . . 10 . . . . 20.
5. When the child has memorized all of the items of this objective and made entries into his Number Facts Bank, move on to #30.

Objective #30: The child is able to state the following number facts accurately and rapidly:

5 × 1 = 5	1 × 5 = 5
5 × 2 = 10	2 × 5 = 10
5 × 3 = 15	3 × 5 = 15
5 × 4 = 20	4 × 5 = 20
5 × 5 = 25	
5 × 6 = 30	6 × 5 = 30
5 × 7 = 35	7 × 5 = 35
5 × 8 = 40	8 × 5 = 40
5 × 9 = 45	9 × 5 = 45
5 × 10 = 50	10 × 5 = 50

1. Pretest and proceed accordingly. If he has not yet mastered this objective, then:
2. Teach the above number facts, following the procedures described under Objective #28.
3. Once the child has learned to display these number statements on the calculator and has begun to be familiar with the number facts of the objective, then introduce the concept of counting by 5's, starting from 5; in other words: 5 . . . 10 . . . 15 . . . 20 . . . . 50.
4. When the child has memorized all of the items of this objective and made entries into his Number Facts Bank, move on to #31.

Objective #31: The child is able to state the following number facts accurately and rapidly:

$$1 \times 1 = 1$$
$$1 \times 2 = 2 \qquad 2 \times 1 = 2$$
$$1 \times 3 = 3 \qquad 3 \times 1 = 3$$
$$1 \times 4 = 4 \qquad 4 \times 1 = 4$$
$$1 \times 5 = 5 \qquad 5 \times 1 = 5$$
$$1 \times 6 = 6 \qquad 6 \times 1 = 6$$
$$1 \times 7 = 7 \qquad 7 \times 1 = 7$$
$$1 \times 8 = 8 \qquad 8 \times 1 = 8$$
$$1 \times 9 = 9 \qquad 9 \times 1 = 9$$
$$1 \times 10 = 10 \qquad 10 \times 1 = 10$$

1. Pretest and proceed accordingly. If he has not yet mastered this objective, then:
2. Teach the above number facts, following the procedures described under Objective #28.
3. *Note:* Do not assume that the child understands the concept of multiplying by 1. In many ways it is an elusive abstraction. Have him work these out on the calculator, despite the apparent simplicity of the task.
4. When the child has memorized all of the items of this objective and made entries into his Number Facts Bank, move on to #32.

Objective #32: The child is able to state the following number facts accurately and rapidly:

3 × 1 = 3	1 × 3 = 3
3 × 2 = 6	2 × 3 = 6
3 × 3 = 9	
3 × 4 = 12	4 × 3 = 12
3 × 5 = 15	5 × 3 = 15
3 × 6 = 18	6 × 3 = 18
3 × 7 = 21	7 × 3 = 21
3 × 8 = 24	8 × 3 = 24
3 × 9 = 27	9 × 3 = 27
3 × 10 = 30	10 × 3 = 30

1. Pretest and proceed accordingly. If he has not yet mastered this objective, then:
2. Teach the above number facts, following the procedures described under Objective #28.
3. Once the child has learned to display these number statements on the calculator and has begun to be familiar with the number facts of this objective, then introduce the concept of counting by 3's, from a starting point of 3; in other words: 3 . . . 6 . . . 9 . . . . 30.
4. When the child has memorized all of the items of this objective and made entries into his Number Facts Bank, move on to #33.

Objective #33: The child is able to state the following number facts accurately and rapidly:

4 × 1 = 4	1 × 4 = 4
4 × 2 = 8	2 × 4 = 8
4 × 3 = 12	3 × 4 = 12
4 × 4 = 16	4 × 4 = 16
4 × 5 = 20	5 × 4 = 20
4 × 6 = 24	6 × 4 = 24
4 × 7 = 28	7 × 4 = 28
4 × 8 = 32	8 × 4 = 32
4 × 9 = 36	9 × 4 = 36
4 × 10 = 40	10 × 4 = 40

1. Pretest and proceed accordingly. If he has not yet mastered this objective, then:
2. Teach the above number facts, following the procedures described under Objective #28.
3. Once the child has learned to display these number statements on the calculator and has begun to be familiar with the number facts of this objective, then introduce the concept of counting by 4's, from a starting point of 4; in other words: 4 . . . 8 . . . 12 . . . . 40.
4. When the child has memorized all of the items of this objective and made entries into his Number Facts Bank, move on to #34.

Objective #34: The child is able to state the following number facts accurately and rapidly:

$$1 \div 1 = 1 \qquad 16 \div 4 = 4$$
$$4 \div 2 = 2 \qquad 25 \div 5 = 5$$
$$9 \div 3 = 3$$

1. Pretest and proceed accordingly. If he has not yet mastered this objective, then:
2. Teach the above number facts, using the following procedures:
3. First, make certain that the child knows the division sign and differentiates it from the minus sign.
4. Then, using the calculator, explain—and illustrate—that the number statement $9 \div 3 = 3$, for example, means: "You start off with a group of nine chips. You want to break this up—*divide it*—into smaller bunches, each one containing three chips. *How many groups of 3 chips each will that make?*"
5. Do not state the problem thus: "Divide this group by 3." I agree that the two wordings are essentially the same, but it is much more difficult for the child to deal with this second wording.
6. In using the calculator the child starts off by taking the first nine chips from the storage rack and constructs groups of chips, three in each group; that is, he places three chips on the first line of the map, three chips on the second line, and the last group of three chips on the third line. He will then have used all his chips, and the map should look like the one shown in figure 50.
7. By counting the number of groups, he derives the answer. But also point out to him that $9 \div 3$ is very closely related but opposite to $3 \times 3 = 9$, and also to $3 + 3 + 3$. Do not make too much of it at the start, but by all means point it out.
8. When the child has memorized all of the items of this objective and made entries into his Number Facts Bank, move on to #35.

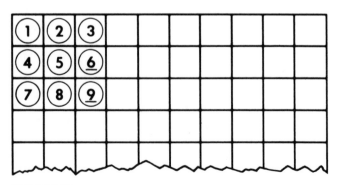

FIGURE 50

Objective #35: The child is able to state the following number facts accurately and rapidly:

$5 \div 5 = 1$	$30 \div 5 = 6$
$10 \div 5 = 2$	$35 \div 5 = 7$
$15 \div 5 = 3$	$40 \div 5 = 8$
$20 \div 5 = 4$	$45 \div 5 = 9$
$25 \div 5 = 5$	$50 \div 5 = 10$

1. Pretest and proceed accordingly. If he has not yet mastered this objective, then:
2. Teach the above number facts, using the procedures described under Objective #34.
3. Once the child has worked through all the division statements on his calculator, show him the close relationships, in words as well as fact, between such facts as $10 \div 2 = 5$ and $10 \div 5 = 2$, etc.
4. When the child has memorized all of the items of this objective and made entries into his Number Facts Bank, move on to #36.

Objective #36: The child is able to state the following number facts accurately and rapidly:

$2 \div 2 = 1$	$12 \div 2 = 6$
$4 \div 2 = 2$	$14 \div 2 = 7$
$6 \div 2 = 3$	$16 \div 2 = 8$
$8 \div 2 = 4$	$18 \div 2 = 9$
$10 \div 2 = 5$	$20 \div 2 = 10$

1. Pretest and proceed accordingly. If he has not yet mastered this objective, then:
2. Teach the above number facts, using the procedures described under Objective #34.
3. When the child has memorized all of the items of this objective and made entries into his Number Facts Bank, move on to #37.

Objective #37: The child is able to state the following number facts accurately and rapidly:

$1 \div 1 = 1$	$6 \div 1 = 6$
$2 \div 1 = 2$	$7 \div 1 = 7$
$3 \div 1 = 3$	$8 \div 1 = 8$
$4 \div 1 = 4$	$9 \div 1 = 9$
$5 \div 1 = 5$	$10 \div 1 = 10$

1. Pretest and proceed accordingly. If he has not yet mastered this objective, then:
2. Teach the above number facts, using the procedures described under Objective #34.
3. When the child has memorized all of the items of this objective and made entries into his Number Facts Bank, move on to #38.

Objective #38: The child is able to state the following number facts accurately and rapidly:

$3 \div 3 = 1$	$18 \div 3 = 6$
$6 \div 3 = 2$	$21 \div 3 = 7$
$9 \div 3 = 3$	$24 \div 3 = 8$
$12 \div 3 = 4$	$27 \div 3 = 9$
$15 \div 3 = 5$	$30 \div 3 = 10$

1. Pretest and proceed accordingly. If he has not yet mastered this objective, then:
2. Teach the above number facts, using the procedures described under Objective #34.
3. When the child has memorized all of the items of this objective and made entries into his Number Facts Bank, move on to #39.

Objective #39: The child is able to state the following number facts accurately and rapidly:

$$
\begin{array}{ll}
4 \div 4 = 1 & 24 \div 4 = 6 \\
8 \div 4 = 2 & 28 \div 4 = 7 \\
12 \div 4 = 3 & 32 \div 4 = 8 \\
16 \div 4 = 4 & 36 \div 4 = 9 \\
20 \div 4 = 5 & 40 \div 4 = 10
\end{array}
$$

1. Pretest and proceed accordingly. If he has not yet mastered this objective, then:
2. Teach the above number facts, using the procedures described under Objective #34.
3. When the child has memorized all of the items of this objective and made entries into his Number Facts Bank, move on to #40.

Objective #40: The child is able to state the following number facts accurately and rapidly:

$$
\begin{array}{ll}
6 \times 6 = 36 & 36 \div 6 = 6 \\
7 \times 7 = 49 & 49 \div 7 = 7 \\
8 \times 8 = 64 & 64 \div 8 = 8 \\
9 \times 9 = 81 & 81 \div 9 = 9 \\
10 \times 10 = 100 & 100 \div 10 = 10
\end{array}
$$

1. Pretest and proceed accordingly. If he has not yet mastered this objective, then:
2. Teach the above number facts, using the procedures described under Objectives #28 and #34.
3. Once the child has learned to display these multiplication and division statements on the calculator, point out to him the fact that each of the statements involves a pair of matched numerals, for example, 6×6, 7×7, etc.
4. When the child has memorized all of the items of this objective and made entries into his Number Facts Bank, move on to #41.

Objective #41: The child is able to state the following number facts accurately and rapidly:

10 × 1 = 10	1 × 10 = 10
10 × 2 = 20	2 × 10 = 20
10 × 3 = 30	3 × 10 = 30
10 × 4 = 40	4 × 10 = 40
10 × 5 = 50	5 × 10 = 50
10 × 6 = 60	6 × 10 = 60
10 × 7 = 70	7 × 10 = 70
10 × 8 = 80	8 × 10 = 80
10 × 9 = 90	9 × 10 = 90
10 × 10 = 100	10 × 10 = 100

1. Pretest and proceed accordingly. If he has not yet mastered this objective, then:
2. Teach the above number facts, following the procedures described under Objective #28.
3. Once the child has become relatively familiar with the number facts of this objective, then introduce the concept of counting by 10's, starting from 10; in other words: 10 . . . 20 . . . 30 . . . 40 . . . 50 . . . . 100.
4. When the child has memorized all of the items of this objective and made entries into his Number Facts Bank, move on to #42.

Objective #42: The child is able to state the following number facts accurately and rapidly:

6 × 1 = 6	1 × 6 = 6
6 × 2 = 12	2 × 6 = 12
6 × 3 = 18	3 × 6 = 18
6 × 4 = 24	4 × 6 = 24
6 × 5 = 30	5 × 6 = 30
6 × 6 = 36	6 × 6 = 36
6 × 7 = 42	7 × 6 = 42
6 × 8 = 48	8 × 6 = 48
6 × 9 = 54	9 × 6 = 54
6 × 10 = 60	10 × 6 = 60

1. Pretest and proceed accordingly. If he has not yet mastered this objective, then:
2. Teach the above number facts, following the procedures described under Objective #28.
3. Once the child has become relatively familiar with the number facts of this objective, then introduce the concept of counting by 6's, starting from 6; in other words: 6 . . . 12 . . . 18 . . . 24 . . . 36 . . . . 60.
4. When the child has memorized all of the items of this objective and made entries into his Number Facts Bank, move on to #43.

Objective #43: The child is able to state the following number facts accurately and rapidly:

$7 \times 1 = 7$	$1 \times 7 = 7$
$7 \times 2 = 14$	$2 \times 7 = 14$
$7 \times 3 = 21$	$3 \times 7 = 21$
$7 \times 4 = 28$	$4 \times 7 = 28$
$7 \times 5 = 35$	$5 \times 7 = 35$
$7 \times 6 = 42$	$6 \times 7 = 42$
$7 \times 7 = 49$	$7 \times 7 = 49$
$7 \times 8 = 56$	$8 \times 7 = 56$
$7 \times 9 = 63$	$9 \times 7 = 63$
$7 \times 10 = 70$	$10 \times 7 = 70$

1. Pretest and proceed accordingly. If he has not yet mastered this objective, then:
2. Teach the above number facts, following the procedures described under Objective #28.
3. Once the child has become relatively familiar with the number facts of this objective, then introduce the concept of counting by 7's, starting from 7; in other words: 7 . . . 14 . . . 21 . . . 28 . . . 35 . . . . 70.
4. When the child has memorized all of the items of this objective and made entries into his Number Facts Bank, move on to #44.

Objective #44: The child is able to state the following number facts accurately and rapidly:

8 × 1 = 8	1 × 8 = 8
8 × 2 = 16	2 × 8 = 16
8 × 3 = 24	3 × 8 = 24
8 × 4 = 32	4 × 8 = 32
8 × 5 = 40	5 × 8 = 40
8 × 6 = 48	6 × 8 = 48
8 × 7 = 56	7 × 8 = 56
8 × 8 = 64	8 × 8 = 64
8 × 9 = 72	9 × 8 = 72
8 × 10 = 80	10 × 8 = 80

1. Pretest and proceed accordingly. If he has not yet mastered this objective, then:
2. Teach the above number facts, following the procedures described under Objective #28.
3. Once the child has become relatively familiar with the number facts of this objective, then introduce the concept of counting by 8's, starting from 8; in other words: 8 . . . 16 . . . 24 . . . 32 . . . 40 . . . . 80.
4. When the child has memorized all of the items of this objective and made entries into his Number Facts Bank, move on to #45.

Objective #45: The child is able to state the following number facts accurately and rapidly:

9 × 1 = 9	1 × 9 = 9
9 × 2 = 18	2 × 9 = 18
9 × 3 = 27	3 × 9 = 27
9 × 4 = 36	4 × 9 = 36
9 × 5 = 45	5 × 9 = 45
9 × 6 = 54	6 × 9 = 54
9 × 7 = 63	7 × 9 = 63
9 × 8 = 72	8 × 9 = 72
9 × 9 = 81	9 × 9 = 81
9 × 10 = 90	10 × 9 = 90

1. Pretest and proceed accordingly. If he has not yet mastered this objective, then:
2. Teach the above number facts, following the procedures described under Objective #28.
3. Once the child has become relatively familiar with the number facts of this objective, then introduce the concept of counting by 9's, starting from 9; in other words: 9 . . . 18 . . . 27 . . . 36 . . . 45 . . . . 90.
4. When the child has memorized all of the items of this objective and made entries into his Number Facts Bank, move on to #46.

Objective #46: The child is able to state the following number facts accurately and rapidly:

$10 \div 10 = 1$	$60 \div 10 = 6$
$20 \div 10 = 2$	$70 \div 10 = 7$
$30 \div 10 = 3$	$80 \div 10 = 8$
$40 \div 10 = 4$	$90 \div 10 = 9$
$50 \div 10 = 5$	$100 \div 10 = 10$

1. Pretest and proceed accordingly. If he has not yet mastered this objective, then:
2. Teach the above number facts, using the procedures described under Objective #34.
3. When the child has memorized all of the items of this objective and made entries into his Number Facts Bank, move on to #47.

Objective #47: The child is able to state the following number facts accurately and rapidly:

$6 \div 6 = 1$	$36 \div 6 = 6$
$12 \div 6 = 2$	$42 \div 6 = 7$
$18 \div 6 = 3$	$48 \div 6 = 8$
$24 \div 6 = 4$	$54 \div 6 = 9$
$30 \div 6 = 5$	$60 \div 6 = 10$

1. Pretest and proceed accordingly. If he has not yet mastered this objective, then:
2. Teach the above number facts, using the procedures described under Objective #34.
3. When the child has memorized all of the items of this objective and made entries into his Number Fact Bank, move on to #48.

Objective #48: The child is able to state the following number facts accurately and rapidly:

7 ÷ 7 = 1	42 ÷ 7 = 6
14 ÷ 7 = 2	48 ÷ 7 = 7
24 ÷ 7 = 3	56 ÷ 7 = 8
28 ÷ 7 = 4	63 ÷ 7 = 9
35 ÷ 7 = 5	70 ÷ 7 = 10

1. Pretest and proceed accordingly. If he has not yet mastered this objective, then:
2. Teach the above number facts, using the procedures described under Objective #34.
3. When the child has memorized all of the items of this objective and made entries into his Number Facts Bank, move on to #49.

Objective #49: The child is able to state the following number facts accurately and rapidly:

8 ÷ 8 = 1	48 ÷ 8 = 6
16 ÷ 8 = 2	56 ÷ 8 = 7
24 ÷ 8 = 3	64 ÷ 8 = 8
32 ÷ 8 = 4	72 ÷ 8 = 9
40 ÷ 8 = 5	80 ÷ 8 = 10

1. Pretest and proceed accordingly. If he has not yet mastered this objective, then:
2. Teach the above number facts, using the procedures described under Objective #34.
3. When the child has memorized all of the items of this objective and made entries into his Number Facts Bank, move on to #50.

Objective #50: The child is able to state the following number facts accurately and rapidly:

$9 \div 9 = 1$	$54 \div 9 = 6$
$18 \div 9 = 2$	$63 \div 9 = 7$
$27 \div 9 = 3$	$72 \div 9 = 8$
$36 \div 9 = 4$	$81 \div 9 = 9$
$45 \div 9 = 5$	$90 \div 9 = 10$

1. Pretest and proceed accordingly. If he has not yet mastered this objective, then:
2. Teach the above number facts, using the procedures described under Objective #34.
3. When the child has memorized all of the items of this objective and made entries into his Number Facts Bank, he will have completed this program. He will have learned enough number facts to perform satisfactorily in an elementary-grade arithmetic program.

By now you have had a chance to go through the instructions, and you should have a fairly good idea of what is involved. Here, as in the reading section, you probably perceive the task as massive. It is not—although by no means is it trivial. It requires self-discipline and strict scheduling, but it can be worked through with reasonable effort, and the results will make it worthwhile.

The suggestions offered in the reading section (pages 167–168) pertain here as well and should serve as general guidelines for teaching the child number facts. They are in brief:

1. Devote about ten to fifteen minutes *each day* to teaching the various objectives.
2. Spend a few additional minutes *each day* reviewing the cards in the child's Number Facts Bank.
3. To the extent possible, engage the child in problem-solving activities, preferably practical ones. And as you do this, urge rapid—and accurate—responses.
4. Encourage the child to discover—and appreciate—the interconnections among these number facts. In essence, they are linked together in a network. The clearer this is to the child, the faster he will benefit from your efforts.

The following activities may be considered supplemental, to be engaged in on a less formal, less regularly scheduled basis. I do not mean to imply by this that the activities are not as potentially helpful as the number facts activities that appear in the preceding pages. Rather, I am merely acknowledging that there are only so many hours in a day, so much motivation and energy in a person, and lots of other things to do during the course of a day. So as you have time—and as the child has energy, interest, and time—engage him in one or more of these additional activities.

Activities using cubes. The following activities call for a set of cubes, the one-inch cubes commonly found in primary-grade classes, for example, although size is irrelevant, so long as all the cubes are the same size.

 a. Point to a single cube and say to the child, "This stands for 1." Then show him two cubes and ask, "How many does this stand for?" The answer, of course, is 2.

 b. Again show the child one cube but now say, "This now stands for 2." (If he is confused, give it more concrete meaning by saying, "Pretend this weighs two pounds.") Then show him two cubes and ask, "How many does this stand for now?" (Or, "How much does this weigh?") The answer should now be 4, since there are twice as many cubes.

 c. Continue in this way, assigning different values to one cube and then asking how many some multiple of that cube would stand for. (For example, if one cube stands for 3, then three cubes stand for 9.)

 d. Now alter conditions a bit and start off with more than one cube. For example, show him three cubes and say, "These stand for 3." (Or, "Altogether these weigh three pounds.") Then show two cubes (or one cube) and ask what they (or it) stand for. Now show him the same two cubes and tell him that, together, they stand for 1 (or weigh one pound). Then ask, "What does one cube represent?" (They represent ½, of course.)

The goal you are after with these activities is for the child to recognize the interrelationships between numbers, that if something or some collection of things is 1, then twice that amount is 2, three times that amount is 3; one-half that amount is ½, and so on. These are not difficult abilities to acquire, but they do take some time and effort, particularly for children with poor visual analysis skills. Work on it—it will pay off.

Carry out this activity with a variety of materials. For example, use time as an illustration. Sixty seconds constitute one minute. Hence 60=1. Following this concept, 120 would equal 2, and so on. Also use the concept of 1 coin —the nickel—representing 5 coins—pennies—yet that same nickel representing only ½ the dime. Our environment is full of quantifiable items; our culture is a measuring and quantifying culture. Exploit that in your teaching.

Have him search for patterns in numbers; for example, that the 9 table is interesting in that the first number goes up 1 each time while the second number goes down 1 each time: 09—18—27—36, etc.

Have him solve puzzles involving number patterns. For example:

1, 2, 3 . . . what number comes next? (4).
2, 4, 6 . . . what number comes next? (8).
1, 2, 4, 8 . . . what number comes next? (16).
1, 11, 21, 31 . . . what number comes next? (41).
5, 4, 10, 9 . . . what number comes next? (15).
2, 5, 4, 7, 6, 9 . . . what number comes next? (8).

As you can see, there is no limit to the number of puzzles you can develop. Your goal here is to teach him to use all available information when solving a problem and to find organized patterns.

Any activity that is based on seeing patterns will be useful. These include

a. Construction toys and all the other materials already mentioned in the visual perceptual skills section of this book (pages 75–89).
b. Playing a musical instrument, particularly a percussion instrument in a rhythm band. (This involves counting time, keeping his place, recognizing where he fits in.)
c. Keeping score at athletic events.

Principle #4: Encourage the child to use some of his other senses—not just his eyes and ears—to explore the concrete aspects of a task.

It is not difficult to see the potential benefit of *touching* and *saying* in conjunction with *looking* and *hearing* when it comes to learning arithmetic facts. Just watch a preschool child count a set of objects. What does he do? He touches—or perhaps points to—each object as he counts it aloud. In fact, it is when he reaches the state where hand is synchronized with voice that accurate counting skills first begin to emerge. Prior to that time most children *do* point and *do* count aloud, but the two are not necessarily linked up. That kind of mismatch, obviously, does not result in accurate tallies.

As the child matures, he depends less on the support that direct contact —touching, manipulating—offers him in performing calculations. In fact you can more or less chart a child's development—in the context of arithmetic— by his ability to do calculations without such concrete supports as fingers, wooden cubes, or other counters, real or pretend. This, along with a reduction in overt vocalizations—saying aloud or to himself what he is calculating—are clear indicators of the child's development.

None of this is difficult to explain. Such changes occur when the child's store of memorized number facts has increased to the point where he no longer has to recalculate each problem from scratch.

Consider, also, the value of concrete experiences—touching, in particular —when it comes to comprehending the verbal abstractions of arithmetic: "equal to," "more than," "less than," and so on. Manipulatives portray these abstractions visually. But they do more than that. They also provide the child with the opportunity to *experience* concretely—directly—what he sees, and the value of that should not be underestimated.

Each time you have the child work through a number facts statement on the poker chip calculator, you are creating a condition that requires involvement of sensory channels in addition to vision and hearing. In order to promote these activities further, simply apply this principle to other situations.

Principle #5: Provide enough repeated experiences to establish the information securely in the child's long-term memory.

I hesitate to put you through this same set of words again. From the very beginning of this book I have stressed—some might say harped on—the necessity for sufficient on-target drill. Indeed, a significant portion of the activities described here are for that purpose: so that you will drill the correct things. Drilling the wrong things—practicing improper behaviors—fosters the better establishment of those improper behaviors, not a very desirable goal.

Anyway, for the sake of thoroughness, and an unwillingness on my part to paraphrase solely for the purpose of offering up different words to express the same information, I am going to repeat here exactly what I said in the preceding section on reading in regard to the principle of drill.

The key concern—once the *what* has been established and the system for helping the child remember it, the *how*, has been taught—is that the child spend enough time in various drill activities so that he can perform virtually automatically, with a minimum of conscious effort.

In other words, the child should become so familiar with the *what* that he no longer has to use the system you taught him—the *how*—to figure it out. He simply knows it; he has the information at his fingertips. This does not come about without extended practice sessions—especially with children who are hard to teach.

TEACHING SPELLING

There are many poor spellers. And not all of them have a learning disorder. Indeed, some of the world's most competent scholars are poor spellers. Well, then, is it worth worrying about, especially when the child we are discussing has so many other problems in school? Yes, it is worth worrying about—especially because he has so many other problems in school.

If the child's only problem were his spelling—if he were competent in reading and arithmetic—you would probably shrug, smile, and acknowledge that no one is perfect. But if the youngster is a poor reader and a poor arithmetic problem solver in addition to being a poor speller, no one will smile. They may shrug, but its meaning will be different—"What's the use!"—and no one will even try to do anything about it.

Should they try? Yes. Good spelling instruction will probably help the child with his reading, and that makes it worthwhile.

What is it that makes a good speller? What does the good speller do that the poor speller does not do? It appears to be connected, to some extent, with reading skills but certainly not completely. Not all good readers are good spellers; but, on the other hand, poor readers are never good spellers. So good reading ability is part of the difference, but there is more to it than that.

If we analyze the processes that underlie spelling, it appears that the good speller—the child who learns how to spell a vast assortment of words—is able to do certain key things.

First, he is able to read the words, decode them. (He need not understand the words, but obviously that is not undesirable.) If he cannot decode the words, then he has an additional mental task to contend with, one that is probably insurmountable if he is to learn to spell more than a very few words.

Along with being able to read the words he is to learn to spell, he can also analyze them into their pertinent sounds and match those with the letters in the word. If there is a perfect match—if there is a sound for each letter in the word and the sounds are specific to those letters and those letters alone—and if the child already knows those letter-sound combinations, then the task is accomplished. The child will be able to spell the word. He will not have to memorize a thing. Words such as *mat, fit, run,* and *hot* belong in this category. If the match is not perfect—if there are inconsistencies or irregularities, such as there not being a sound for each letter, or if the letter used to code a sound is one that is not customarily associated with that sound—then a potential problem arises. The child will have to memorize the spelling of at least a part of the word. He will not spell it correctly if he simply sounds it out and then writes the letters that go with those sounds. There are plenty of words in this category; for example, *their, bought, blew, rough,* and *slice.* To learn these, he will have to be able to employ effective strategies for remembering the inconsistencies and irregularities.

Suppose we try to imagine how this sequence of abilities works. How does a child who learns to spell very easily deal with a new word? Take the word *consistent;* many adults have trouble with that one, often spelling it *consistant.* The very good speller reads the word, pronouncing it clearly. Then he analyzes the word into its sounds, matching those individual sounds with individual letters.

Consistent turns out to be a fairly easy word for this part of the task; there is a sound for each letter. If he is careful to pronounce the word correctly, he notices that only the *o* and *e* stand for ambiguous sounds, sounds that could be coded by certain other letters. Both of these, in the word *consistent,* are schwa sounds.* The child (remember, he is a very good learner of spelling), having recognized these two potential trouble spots as the only parts of the word that he will not be able to sound out and then spell with complete confidence, devises a strategy to help him remember that the first schwa sound is coded by an *o* and the second by an *e.*

What is his strategy? It can vary, but with this word he probably pronounces the word to himself incorrectly, giving the *o* a short ŏ sound, and the *e* a short ĕ sound. That helps him remember. (We will examine various other strategies later in this section.)

We should try another word; one that has some different kinds of trouble spots. Take the word *receipt*—a sixth-grade spelling word in most schools. The very good speller reads the word, breaks it down into its separate sounds, and recognizes that two of the letters in that word do not get sounded—the *i* and the *p.* Having noticed these inconsistencies, he devises a strategy to help him remember to include these letters when he writes the word. He does not worry about the rest of the word. He can spell that part just by writing the sounds down in correct sequence.

There is one more step in learning to spell a word—this one, again, something that the easy-to-teach child does with virtually no outside assistance. He reads and he spells the word frequently, using whatever strategies he

---

*The schwa is a very common sound in our language; it can be represented by virtually every printed vowel in the alphabet. For example: *the; above; nation.*

originally devised to help him spell it accurately. In time he no longer has to think about the strategy. The word becomes a unit rather than a string of separate letters. He memorizes it. What originally required his special attention no longer does. He has chunked the letters into a word or a subcomponent of a word—a spelling unit*—and spells the word almost automatically.

In fact the only time he stops to think about the separate letters is when someone asks him for assistance in spelling that word. Then he has to stop and think for a moment. Indeed, he may even have to write it down.**

What about the child who is neither very easy to teach nor hard to teach but, rather, falls somewhere in the middle, the child who does not have too much trouble with spelling but is not as good a speller as the one we just described? Suppose he has to learn to spell *receipt.* Chances are he will be able to read it. He is, after all, a fair student. He will also probably be able to break it down into its separate sounds, and he may even notice that the *i* and the *p* do not have sounds in the spoken word. However, what happens if he does not notice it? If his spelling program is a good one, it will be designed to make those inconsistencies apparent to him. In other words, *receipt* will not be taught as an isolated word but rather as part of a group, all of which will share the same characteristics—the *ei* sequence. His teacher will call his attention to the similarity of the words in that group, thereby emphasizing it (for example, *receive, deceive*). And, in addition, she will devise a way to help him remember—perhaps "*i* before *e* except after *c.*" She will also devise one for the silent *p;* perhaps she will have him pronounce the word with the *p* sound included, just to emphasize the fact that it is there—*recei-p-t.* Then, to top it off, she will have him practice spelling the word and writing it a number of times to help him remember it.

Now, what about the hard-to-teach child who has a spelling problem? What does he do when faced with the task of learning how to spell *receipt?*

First of all, he probably cannot read the word; his teacher has to read it to him. Thus he is in trouble from the start. Since he is a poor reader, it is predictable that he will be a poor sound analyzer; he will probably have difficulty breaking down the word into its individual sounds. He will also have real difficulty matching sounds to letters, even when the match is a regular one. The fact that this word is being taught as part of a group of words, all of which share the same characteristic, will not help him be aware of those characteristics. He will have trouble with all the words in the group, so no one of them

---

*The four letters *tion* is an example of a spelling unit. Once the child learns that these letters constitute a chunk that consistently represents the same sound, he no longer has to deal separately with the four letters.

**This is not dissimilar to many other skills we acquire. Take this question: "Is the vertical line positioned to the right or the left in the lowercase *d?*" Most of us would have to stop for a moment and mentally reconstruct the letter or look at one already in view, even though we are very familiar with the letter. We are so familiar with it, in fact, that it has become something we do without thinking.

helps him with the others. There is too much to be aware of, let alone to memorize.

Finally, when his teacher shows him some strategies for keeping the irregularities straight in his mind, they are promptly forgotten. He is coping with a major and basic problem; he does not know how to match the regular sounds very well. Thus, talking to him about irregularities is useless; it is superfluous information—he has no way of understanding it, let alone using it. (It is a little like talking to a beginning swimmer about how to cup his hands in a particular way to get a little extra speed. He is devoting all his attention to staying afloat; there is little energy available for thinking about small sub-components of the act.)

At any rate, suppose he has been through the lesson, and it is now time to practice writing the newly learned word. He practices and may even manage to write it accurately a few times. But he is depending completely upon rote memorization of the *entire* word, not just certain strategic parts of it. It is just too much to remember. By tomorrow the word will be gone, and the youngster will fail again.

HELPING THE POOR SPELLER

This section contains a number of suggested activities that will help the poor speller. They do not constitute a complete spelling program that can replace his school program. Rather they focus on skills that are vital to satisfactory spelling in general, skills that will help the child become a better speller.

As always, coordinate your efforts with your child's teacher. Ask her for spelling words that are appropriate for him. And show her what you are doing, so that she can add suggestions.

Once more the activities are based on the same instructional principles that have been cited repeatedly in this book.

Principle #1: Organize for success.
As always, avoid overplacing him.

Principle #2: Make certain that the child really does have the factual knowledge he needs to profit from a lesson.
What factual information does a child have to know when he enters a spelling lesson? I have already mentioned some points, but I will restate and expand on them here. Do not infer anything from the order in which I discuss them. They are all critical and, in fact, interrelated. To address one of them, you will probably have to be concerned about the others as well.

For one thing the child has to have adequate *reading skills*. He has to be able to read the words he is expected to learn how to spell. That is a major order obviously, one that may force you to put aside spelling concerns for a long while. But you have no alternative. If the child cannot read a word, you can bet that he is not going to be able to identify its pertinent sounds and their relative positions in the sequence of sounds that comprise the spoken word. From this you can conclude that learning to spell that word will require rote memorization of the most difficult kind. On the other hand, if you address the child's reading problem effectively—if you teach him to do what I outlined in the previous section on reading—not only will he acquire better reading skills but he will also become a better speller.

The basis for that statement should become obvious to you if you will now review the activities described in the reading section (pages 145–158). Certainly many of these could be labeled "activities for improving a child's spelling." They are that. The fact that they are catalogued under the heading of reading simply indicates the very close relationship between the two processes.

The child must also have adequate *auditory analysis skills.* This hardly requires an explanation. Clearly if one of the basic abilities of a speller is to memorize the mismatches between the sounds of a word and its spelling, then the matches first have to be identified. The necessity for competent auditory analysis skills is therefore obvious.

So if you have not already done so, proceed now to test the child with the TAAS (see pages 46–49) and begin teaching him those skills that appear to be lacking. You may continue to work with the other suggested activities at the same time.

And finally the child must bring to the spelling lesson *visual analysis skills.* These skills are perhaps not quite as critical in learning how to spell as are the auditory analysis skills, but they do count. Therefore if you have not yet done so, test the child with the TVAS (see pages 30–43) and begin teaching him whatever skills he appears to be lacking. You may continue to work with the other suggested activities at the same time.

> *Principle #3: Make clear a system—a strategy—that will help the child retain information, that is, link up the facts he is to learn with what he already knows.*

What is this system? As in reading, there can be more than one. But, also as in reading, there tends to be a *best one.* In spelling it is the system that sensitizes the child to identifying and remembering the letter-sound mismatches in words, the "irregularities" in a word's spelling.

There are certain letter-sound spelling mismatches that recur in groups of words, for example, the *-ight* in *fight, light, sight,* and so on. Becoming familiar with those types of mismatches is most useful to the speller, since they have a certain general applicability rather than pertaining to a single word or two.

Some activities for helping the child learn the system that will aid him in spelling more accurately include the following:

Teach the child to recognize mismatches between letters and sounds.

a. Dictate a word from his classroom spelling list and have him write it down the way he thinks it should be spelled. Have him say the word aloud, distinctly, and instruct him to put every sound down on paper. (If the child already knows how to spell the word correctly, do not insist that he spell it phonetically. You do not want him to practice incorrect spellings if they are not necessary.)

b. Now show him the correct spelling and have him write it and compare his spelling with that. Do they agree? If not, do they differ only in those portions of the word where the letter-sound combination is irregular? (If there are other errors—if the child coded some regular sounds inaccurately—then he needs work on that part of the task. Have him underline every letter in the correctly spelled word *except* those letters that caused him trouble: *(a)* letters for which there were no sounds (for example, the *e* in ca<u>me</u>, the *t* in <u>listen</u>, the first *d* and second *e* in <u>Wednesday</u>, the *a* and the final *e* in lea<u>ve</u>, the *b* in <u>doubt</u>); *(b)* letters that are not ordinarily used to code the sounds they are coding in this particular word (for example, the *gh* in <u>rough</u>, the *c* in <u>ocean</u>, the *o* and the *e* in <u>one</u>).

c. You can make a game out of having him hunt—in whatever material he can read—for words that present mismatches. There are lots of these.

Help the child memorize these mismatches. In the activities just described you had the child discover mismatches and mark them by underlining all of the word except for those problem areas. Now you want to teach him to remember these potential trouble spots, because unless he memorizes them, he will continue to make errors—errors that are not the result of poor auditory analysis and coding skills but that are rather due to the idiosyncrasies of the English language. Try any of the following techniques and, if necessary, use more than one of them:

a. Find a word the child knows how to spell correctly that has the same characteristic as the word you are working on. For example, if he misspelled *motion* (moshun) and yet knows how to spell *station,* then use that latter word as a model to teach him that the syllable *tion* is almost always spelled *t-i-o-n*.

b. Have him pronounce *all* the letters in the word, even though they are not all sounded out when the word is read in customary fashion. For example, the word *knife*. If he reads it and says it aloud as /k/nife/ (pronouncing the *k* sound) when he learns to spell it, he is more apt to spell it correctly. He no longer has to memorize the *k* visually, so long as he pronounces it to himself when he writes it. As another example, consider the word *teach*. Have him read it as /t/e/ā/ch/

—*tea-atch*. Sure, it is sort of silly, but that in itself will probably help him remember it and therefore spell it correctly.

c. If the problem area he has identified can be explained by a rule, teach him the rule. The one I mentioned before, *i* before *e* except after *c*, is a good one, but even it is not foolproof (for example, *protein*). There are others, such as doubling a consonant when adding *ed* to the end of a word if the accent falls on the final syllable (as in *occur-occurred; hop-hopped*).

d. Have him practice rote memorization—not of the entire word, but rather of that portion of the word that cannot be sounded out accurately. For example, there is no reasonable explanation for the spelling of the word *once,* but that does not mean that the entire word has to be memorized. The *n* and the *c* fit—that is, match the sounds of the word. Only the first and the last letters are difficult to explain through the principles of letter-sound relationships. They will have to be memorized, although in keeping with the second suggestion on this list, if the child can spell *one,* then it would be wise to show him the similarity between *one* and *once.*

Decoding activities. In addition to the foregoing, it will be useful to engage the child in the activities of the decoding units section (see pages 168–217).

Principle #4: Encourage the child to use some of his other senses—not just his eyes and ears—to examine the concrete aspects of a task.

This notion is particularly useful in improving spelling skills. Writing out a word really does require you to pay attention to its spelling, and more importantly, it leaves you with a visual trace that is available for careful inspection. Spelling a word aloud is not as satisfactory, in that the signals are fleeting; they disappear immediately upon being uttered.

Try this procedure:

a. Show the child the word he is to learn to spell and have him read it. (If he cannot read it, he is placed way beyond where he should be.) Have him say it aloud, first in the correct way, then pronouncing every letter.

b. Now have him copy it, saying the letters aloud as he does. Repeat five times. When he can do this accurately, go to the next step.

c. Have him write it without copying, that is, from memory, spelling it aloud as he does. Repeat this five times. When this can be done accurately, go to the next step.

d. Have him write it five times with his eyes closed, spelling it aloud as he does and thinking about what his hand is doing.

e. Finally, have him write a sentence using the word appropriately. If he can make up the sentence himself, all the better.

Principle #5: Provide enough repeated experiences to establish the information securely in the child's long-term memory.

This is essential, as it is in all other subject areas. I have probably already stressed this to the limits of your ability to tolerate redundant information, so I will leave it at this: Provide drill sessions to the extent that they are necessary, that is, to the point where the child begins to spell his words automatically.

The following activities may be useful in adding some variation to those drill sessions. It is not essential that you use them. Rather, introduce them when you think they may help.

Games. Scrabble, Spell-It, and Anagrams—all sold in book, variety, and department stores—are excellent activities. They do not teach spelling, but they do make learning how to spell a little more fun.

Make small words out of larger words. For example, show the child the word *alligator* and ask him to construct as many words as he can, using the letters in that word. For example:

all	gill	tail	rat	lit
goat	lot	grill	tall	till

TEACHING HANDWRITING

Almost every first-grade child is taught to print (manuscript) rather than to write (cursive). In some schools cursive is introduced in the second grade, in others in the third grade.

This was not always so. Years ago only cursive was taught, and good penmanship was an important goal. Around thirty or so years ago the emphasis started to shift to manuscript printing. After all, the argument went, the child has to learn to read manuscript. His books are printed, not written in longhand, and besides, manuscript can readily be converted to cursive writing by connecting the letters.

The reasoning seemed sensible, the switch occurred, and with it additional sources of confusion for the children we are concerned about here.

First of all, teachers devoted less time to penmanship, to teaching and having the children practice how to write or print neatly. In a very real way they started to neglect precisely those factors that the hard-to-teach child needs: being made directly aware of *what* to learn, *how* to learn it, and then being given enough repeated experiences to establish it firmly in his repertoire.

Second, directional confusions were experienced. It is not very difficult to remember the difference between a *b* and a *d*, but you certainly cannot say the same for their manuscript counterparts—the *b* and the *d*.

Third, and not to be ignored, cursive writing is more efficient, that is, less time-consuming. You do not have to start and stop continuously. It is not a series of separate acts; it has a continuity and a rhythm that appear to make it a better system for some children.

Does that mean you should teach cursive writing to first-graders and ignore manuscript? If you can do so without complicating his school life, yes, by all means. However, if doing so will only serve to get him into even deeper difficulty in his classroom, then, of course, the answer is no. Teach him better manuscript skills.

Is cursive writing harder to learn? And will he still be able to read his books? After all, they are printed. No, cursive writing is not more difficult to learn. It is a manual skill, as is manuscript, and if he is taught what he has to be taught and if he practices, he will learn it. As for being able to read printed books, that too is not much of an additional burden for the child who learns cursive writing instead of manuscript. To read, he only has to recognize the letters. He does not have to know how to print them. And actually printing them is appreciably more difficult than recognizing them. (If you do not remember the distinction, go back to the section on visual perceptual skills.)

Enough, now, of the argument between manuscript and cursive. If you have a choice, fine, teach him cursive; if not—if his class is learning manuscript —teach him that.

I will list some teaching suggestions in a moment, but first I want to lay out the skills you should focus on and what they mean in practical terms.

When a child first starts to learn to write, he *draws* patterns. He is not printing letters until he thinks of them as symbols. Then, as he learns the individual letter names and their patterns—as he chunks individual elements into a larger unit—he *writes* or *prints* letters, but he has to think about them and how to make his hand perform the necessary movements. As he practices, he acquires facility. Just as the new driver becomes the experienced driver and is able to stop thinking about what separate actions he is to perform, so too does the new writer become the experienced writer and stops thinking about how to control his hand. Surely you do not devote any significant amount of thought to executing the letters when you write. Rather, you think about what you want to say, the thoughts you want to express. The mechanical aspects of the task have become automatic. What if they had not? Try to write backward and assess the effects. How does it affect your speed, your facility, your ability to think as you write? The effects will be apparent at once.

As always, it is an error to expect facility at a particular stage if the child has not established some degree of competency at the lower stages. As the child acquires basic skills—as he learns to copy the letters accurately—more complex tasks will require less conscious thought. As he becomes able to organize the letters he prints and the space in which he is printing them so that what he produces is recognized as legible language, he will be better able to think about the meaning of what he is writing rather than its physical appearance.

The stages will merge and the only time he will regress to a lower level of performance is when some disrupting factor is introduced into the activity —writing backward, for example or, more realistically, writing neatly when that is not the normal pattern. When this occurs, performance deteriorates. The child's writing will become less neat, and he will have to think more about the physical act of writing. He will have less time available to think about what he is writing.

My point? Spend enough time practicing the lower-level skills so that they start to approximate automatic performance. If you ignore these basic stages, the outcome of your efforts—and the child's—will not be as satisfying.

I should also say something here about handedness. The child should

always use the same hand, and it should be whatever hand he writes best with.*
If you are uncertain about which one that is, test him. You do not need a
formal test. Have him write or print with one hand, then the other, and
compare the two. Almost invariably one will be better than the other. That
is the hand he should write with. If he tends to forget and continues to switch
hands from time to time, put a wristband of some kind (a leather strap, a
ribbon) on the side he is supposed to use and be firm in your directions to him.
He is to use that hand for writing, and only that hand.**

HELPING THE CHILD WITH POOR HANDWRITING

Once more I will make suggestions that are based on the five principles that
I have referred to throughout this book. The activities that appear here do not
constitute a complete writing program that could substitute for the one used
in school. These activities simply focus on certain skills that will help the child
become a better writer.

Make certain that what you do is compatible with what is being taught
in the school program. There is more than one printing program used in our
schools. For example, some schools teach this † , and others teach this
† . Although it does not appear to be a crucial consideration in the long run,
it is best if you teach the child to make the letter look the way it does in school.
Ask his teacher to print or write the alphabet in the style she favors and use
that as your guide.

Principle #1: Organize for success.

*Principle #2: Make certain that the child really does have the factual
knowledge he needs to profit from a lesson.*
What factual information does a child have to know when he comes to
a printing/writing lesson? Obviously he has to have adequate familiarity with
the letters themselves—their construction and their names. If there are gaps
here, refer back to pages 151–154 and teach him whatever is necessary.
Furthermore, the child should have adequate visual analysis skills. Once

*This refers to school-aged children, children past their sixth birthday. Preschool children
often alternate hands for various activities, and so far as is known, this is not bad—it is normal.
However, by the time the child enters first grade and is expected to learn to read, calculate, spell,
and write, he should have developed a dominant hand. Otherwise he will experience much
confusion in remembering the directional conventions of the language, that is, reading and writing
from left to right, distinguishing a *b* from a *d*, and so forth.
**I have intentionally avoided discussing a so-called dominant eye and its relationship to a
dominant hand. I stated very early in this book that the question I wanted to address was "How
can I help the child do better in school?" not "What is the cause of his problem?" Even if I believed
that a consistent hand-eye dominance was an important consideration—and at this date there is
no substantive evidence to think so—it would still be irrelevant to this book.

more, use the TVAS to determine whether the child is lacking in his ability to analyze a spatial pattern into its salient component parts and to map out the interrelationships among those parts. Follow the instructions on pages 31–43 to teach him whatever skills he may be lacking.

Principle #3: Make clear a system—a strategy—that will help the child remember information, that is, link up information he is to learn with information he already knows.

This principle is not nearly as pivotal in teaching a child better printing/-writing skills as it is in teaching reading, arithmetic, and spelling. In those latter three the key concern is accumulation of vast amounts of information, secure memorization of a great number of facts.

In teaching writing, the same target exists—memorization to a level of automatic performance—but the body of information to be memorized is greatly reduced. There are not that many letters.

To the extent that one is needed, a system for aiding the child in remembering the letters was described earlier, on pages 151–154.

Principle #4: Encourage the child to use some of his other senses—not just his eyes and ears—to examine the concrete aspects of a task.

In regard to teaching a child to print, this principle is superfluous. Although it is true that there have been writing programs developed that attempt to teach the child how to write by making visual judgments—simply distinguishing correct from incorrect letter patterns—it is so obvious that such programs cannot work that there is no need to dwell on them here. Writing is, by definition, a manual activity. It stands to reason, therefore, that most of the learning will involve use of the hand.

Principle #5: Provide enough repeated experiences to establish the information securely in the child's long-term memory.

You might find the following activities useful for providing some diversity in the practice sessions that are so essential to developing better writing skills. To the extent that they are helpful, use them, but do not view them as any more important than that.

A chalkboard is a necessity for the following. Paper and pencil will inhibit the motor facility you want the child to acquire.

Rhythmic writing. The goal of this activity is to have the child be able to draw repetitive patterns across the chalkboard in a fluent, rhythmic fashion. The fact that some of the patterns are letters is not relevant. But at the same time it is not accidental. Where letters make up the pattern, point them out to the child, but do not stress the fact. Pay attention to smooth production of the patterns. Figure 51 shows the patterns you should use (although there is nothing wrong with modifying and adding to these).

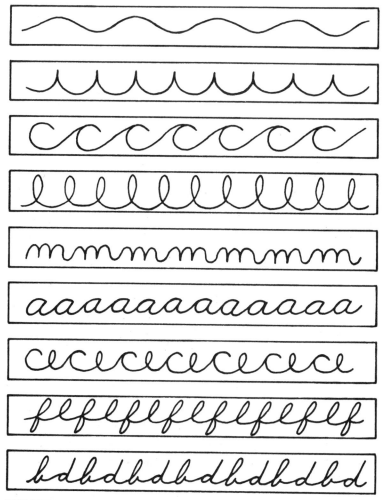

FIGURE 51

Draw the first pattern high on the chalkboard, repeating it across the entire board. Then ask the child to draw one like it lower on the chalkboard (at about his chin level). Show him how to hold the chalk (resting across the four fingers and secured by the thumb). Urge him to move his whole arm freely. You want neatness but not at the expense of fluid movement. First work on ease of movement then on the neatness. Some children move more freely to music. Try it if you wish, but it is not critical.

Have him erase his drawing and try again. Caution him to think about what his hand is doing, but again not at the expense of the rhythmic movement.

After about five or ten tries, his pattern should start to approximate yours. When it does, have him repeat the exercise with his eyes closed. Then move on to the second pattern. There is no need to remain on one pattern until it is perfect, although you should go back and review patterns from time to time. Be sure to comment on his improvement if it is observable.

After he starts to show some facility at the chalkboard, introduce some pencil and paper activities.

    a. Show him how to hold the pencil—with his thumb and index finger. And do not allow him to pinch the pencil at its point. His index finger should not extend beyond the painted portion of the pencil.

    b. Show him how to position the paper—slanted so that it aligns with the writing hand. That is, this way for a right-hander:

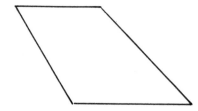

The opposite for a lefty:

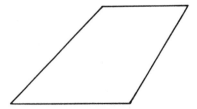

    c. Show him how to hold the paper in position by placing his nonwriting hand at the top edge of the paper. If he cannot do this adequately, secure the paper to the desk in its correct position with masking tape.

    d. Make certain that he is seated comfortably and properly. The desk top should be below chest level. He should be able to place his feet flat on the floor. A slant-top desk is desirable, but it is not essential.

    e. Supply him with primary-grade paper—the kind that has a middle line in addition to a top and bottom line.

    f. Have him draw letter elements: circles; single vertical lines that extend from the bottom line to the top line, as in *d* or *b*, and from the middle line to below the bottom line as in *p;* and diagonal lines, as in the *w, m,* and *n.*

The following activities are designed to help the child acquire more acceptable penmanship skills. This goes beyond a concern for motor control. True, if the child lacks fine-motor control, he is not apt to be a good printer. But he will need more than fine-motor control. He will also have to be sufficiently familiar with forming the letters and arranging them appropriately on a page so that the process requires very little conscious thinking from him.

There is only one way to achieve this level: practice. But practice without direction is foolish, at best. As always, a good teacher shows her skill by making certain that the student pays attention to what is important for him to see and hear. It is not enough to send the child to a chalkboard, show him a letter, and request that he copy it over and over again until he reaches some satisfactory level. That technique might very well work—if the child is both motivated and able to identify the important features. But we know too well that the child we are discussing usually lacks both of these attributes.

These activities, by the way, can be combined with teaching the child the letters themselves, as described in the section devoted to helping the child become a better reader (see pages 144–158).

Blackboard activities. Have the child stand at the chalkboard with his eyes closed, or—if you want to and if he enjoys it—blindfold him. Place a piece of chalk in his writing hand and guide his hand to produce a single letter. Make the letters large—about six to ten inches high—and move his hand at a rate that approximates the speed at which you yourself print or write. The child's task is to answer the question "What letter did we make?"

If necessary, describe what your hands (yours and his) are doing as the letter is being printed. In other words, if you are printing an *a,* say as you print, "We are starting at the top and drawing a circle—like this. Then we are adding a short straight line to the right side of the circle—like this." Your goal is to point out whatever it is he should pay attention to when he prints an *a.*

Include all the letters—lowercase and capitals—in your activities. Work on one at a time, in random order, and review periodically. When the child is able to recognize the letters easily, start working with two in succession. In other words, you guide his hand in printing *at,* then ask, "What letters did we print?"

This procedure can also be used in conjunction with helping the child improve his spelling. Guide his hand in printing his spelling words. He then reads the word to you while still blindfolded.

You may extend this to include any number of sequenced letters (or, for that matter, numerals). Do not make the task unreasonably difficult. Remember, your foremost goal is to help the child reach the stage where he can execute the letters without having to think very much about what his hand is doing.

When the child is able to print or write both legibly and relatively rapidly at the chalkboard, then switch to paper and pencil. But do not try to direct his hand under these conditions. Modify the procedure so that he, alone, prints or writes while his eyes are closed. He is to strive for accuracy, neatness, and facility.

When he starts to approximate these goals, move on to helping the child print or write without conscious thought about what his hand is doing.

For some children, this final stage is difficult to achieve, but it is important if he is to progress satisfactorily in school. How can it be achieved? Once more —practice.

Have the child print or write while talking about something else. Start off simply. Show him a single letter—the *a,* for example—and have him print *a*'s on the chalkboard as he sings a very familiar song. Then engage him in a simple conversation as he prints a row of a particular letter. Do not make the conversation abstract. Keep it on simple topics—but topics that do require some thinking, such as his favorite baseball team, a pet, a TV show.

As he demonstrates the ability to do both of these activities at the same time, increase the complexity of the copying task. Have him print or write a series of letters repeatedly as he converses. Three or four letters in repeated sequence is sufficiently complex (for example, *beta*).

Have him copy printed text from an appropriate book, a book that he can read and understand. His goal here is to copy the text both accurately and in a reasonable amount of time. This activity is identical to one described in the section devoted to helping the child improve his reading skills.

Save and date samples of his paperwork. He will improve as you work with him, and comparing before-and-after samples can often be inspiring.

ON TEACHERS AND SCHOOLS

To this point I have focused on the child—both *(a)* how to change him, that is, how to help him acquire more effective visual and auditory analysis (perceptual) skills and the factual background he will need when he enters into a specific program of instruction; and *(b)* how to design instruction for him, that is, what to teach and how to present it so that he is likely to learn it.

I assure you that if you do either of these, the child will be helped and will demonstrate it in the way he performs in the classroom. If you do both of these, he will be helped significantly—he will make marked headway in overcoming his learning difficulties. And unless I have been more obscure than I intended to be, I do not think you are surprised at these assurances. Why should he not make progress? He can, after all, learn—there is plenty of evidence of that. The reason he has learned what he has is because he was aware of what he was to learn and was not confused by how it was presented. There is no reason to think that the outcomes will be different with arithmetic or reading just because the *what* and the *how* are subject-specific.

Now I want to discuss something apart from the theme we have followed so far, which was how to change the child and how to change the instructional program to accommodate the child the way he is. Schools contain more than children and books. Schools also contain teachers, school administrators, and classrooms that are designed, furnished, and used in various ways. All of these have a major impact on how well a child learns—particularly the hard-to-teach child. Yet too often decisions are made about these factors without any regard to how they affect the children who attend that school.

Strange as it may seem, we tend to forget that *schools are constructed, furnished, staffed, and supported to TEACH our children*—not to give school teachers and administrators employment; not to provide clients and customers for architects, builders, and the manufacturers of school equipment and books; not to give tax collectors a fiscal challenge.

Surely, then, our first concern when we consider how those schools are constructed, furnished, staffed, and supported, should be the children.

Here are some guidelines we can use when we determine how well a school system performs its teaching mission.

THE TEACHER

Teachers vary in many ways; some of the obvious ones are age, sex, knowledge, temperament, commitment, and experience. All of these have some effect on what happens in the classroom when a teacher interacts with her students.

It follows, then, that some teachers are much better suited than others to work with hard-to-teach children. Yet, as apparent as this is, it never seems to be much of a consideration when teaching assignments are determined. Whatever criteria are used to decide those assignments, they clearly are not based on the teacher characteristics just noted.

What characteristics should the teacher of hard-to-teach children show? I shall discuss them in what I consider to be their order of relative importance.

Knowledge

The teacher of hard-to-teach children has to know her business. By definition, these are children who do not do well at teaching themselves, at gaining relevant information out of nonexplicit situations. Children who are not hard to teach often learn much more than the lesson of the day appears to teach, and sometimes it seems as though they learn despite their classroom experiences. In contrast, hard-to-teach children will learn only what they are taught directly, and even this has to be offered up in small portions, repeated a fair number of times, and specifically linked with other information so that the child has a way of remembering it and of understanding how and where it fits into a larger context.

The knowledgeable teacher is one who knows *what* to teach and has some idea about *how* to do it. She knows, further, that once the child learns a basic *what*—some basic fact—this can be incorporated into a future lesson—into the *how*—for teaching some subsequent fact. She is firm in her pursuit of specific instructional goals and steers as direct a course as possible toward them, understanding that they will only be reached slowly, after hard and sustained effort. To change goals—to skip about, hoping for some magic cure—is seen as neither sensible nor productive. That does not mean that she will never try new procedures. On the contrary, the knowledgeable teacher is constantly looking for better, more effective methods. But new procedures and new techniques are not introduced into the classroom on a helter-skelter basis. When something new is announced somewhere and, at least on the surface, looks worthy of trying out, she does this in a reasonable way, not on the basis of wishful thinking. She uses the new procedure and assesses its effects; and when a new technique is tried and the child does not learn, it is the technique that is failed and rejected, not the child.

Where do you find such teachers? How will you know them? What credentials do they usually hold? You can find them everywhere, but they are not that common nor that easy to identify on the basis of their age, sex, or educational credentials. They may or may not hold a special degree, other than a degree of wisdom and a sense of security that derives from the combination of knowledge and self-assurance. They are usually experienced, but not jaded. They know they can succeed; they also know that they can fail. They work to accomplish the former and use their failure experiences as a means of growing professionally—of learning what not to do the next time.

You identify them by watching them teach—not a single lesson but over time—and by looking at what they have accomplished. If you see a hard-to-teach child who displays a systematic approach to reading or arithmetic that seems to be sensible and effective, then you are probably observing the fruits of good teaching. If, in contrast, you see a child who has no system—who, though he may look happy, has no methodical way of approaching a reading or arithmetic task—then you are probably observing the barren harvest of inappropriate teaching.

As in all fields, in education there are good talkers and good doers. Sometimes you find both qualities in the same person. When you do, all well and good. But if you can find only one of these qualities in a teacher, make sure it is the latter.

Temperament

The teacher of hard-to-teach children is often faced with the situation where her students forget their lesson immediately after it has been presented; where the lesson has to be repeated, maybe many times; where vague instructions are simply not grasped; where each step the child is to take must be defined precisely. The teacher of the hard-to-teach child should have a temperament compatible with those conditions: even-tempered and willing to present information slowly, even pedantically; organized and willing to help others organize themselves; secure in the understanding that a good teacher, in terms of the needs of the hard-to-teach child, is a teacher who literally teaches every step of the way.

I realize that the kind of person I am describing is not all that easy to find, particularly when, along with the characteristics just listed, we want her to be knowledgeable too. This brings us to another consideration: Teachers, even the very best of teachers, are human and therefore display human flaws. We have to know in advance that all teachers, even the ones we perceive as ideal, will have days when all those marvelous qualities we once observed in them will not be very apparent. Those are the days when the good school administrator provides the kind of moral support that, in effect, says to the teacher: "Look, I know these are very hard-to-teach children and that this is not one of their days, nor perhaps one of yours. So do not take it all that hard. Try your best, and be secure in the fact that you do know your business and that although they do not appear to be making very much progress today, they will tomorrow, or the next day. Giving up helps no one." That brings us to the next characteristic we hope to find in the teacher of the hard-to-teach child.

Commitment

The teacher of hard-to-teach children has to be dedicated to her task. But so, too, does every other teacher. It is incorrect to think that one teacher needs to be more committed than another. Teachers are professionals. Professionals are committed. It is as simple as that. But their commitment has to be rational. They know that their best efforts will not always work, but they continue to try nonetheless.

Sex and Age

These two characteristics are also important, but less so than the ones already discussed. Although I have consistently referred to the teacher as a female, I do recognize that there are many male teachers and that some children do, in fact, appear to respond differently to males than to females.

However, I maintain that the sex of a teacher is relatively less important than the teacher's knowledge and temperament. If the person knows what to teach, knows how to teach it, and has a temperament that keeps flare-ups— incidents of frustration and anger—at a minimum, then that person's sex is irrelevant. If, on the other hand, not much teaching is going on in the class-room and social interactions are the primary events that take place there, if the teacher is more concerned about how the child "feels about himself" independent of school learning, then of course sex differences will have a major impact.

I am going on the assumption that the business of the classroom is instruction and will leave it at that. I have no argument with persons who say that we must also consider the child's emotional state—how he feels about himself and his interrelationships with others—but when the educator tries to deal with these emotions and ignores the one area where they are supposed to be the experts—teaching—then there is no reason to think that they will be very successful. *The best way to help a child feel good about himself in school is to make it possible for him to learn*—that is, to make real progress in reading and arithmetic. Teachers should leave psychotherapy to psychotherapists.

The preceding comments pertain also to the teacher's age. Neither it nor the teacher's sex, are critical factors, all else being equal. There are young and old teachers who are either not sufficiently knowledgeable or whose tempera-ment makes them unsuitable for teaching hard-to-teach children. Likewise, there are young and old teachers whose qualities make them highly suitable for such situations. Those are the ones we want for our hard-to-teach children.

It comes down to this: All of our teachers should be excellent. All of our teachers should be knowledgeable and blessed with temperaments that make it possible for them to adjust to the needs of the children they face in their classrooms. But given that the situation is not ideal, that our teachers vary in any number of different ways, my argument is simple and pragmatic: We should be *especially* careful when choosing the teachers of hard-to-teach children. There is less room for mismatch in those instances; the teacher is important in every classroom and with every child. But she is especially important with hard-to-teach children.

THE INSTRUCTIONAL ENVIRONMENT

Schools used to all look more or less the same—not on the outside, of course, but in terms of what you saw when you toured the building during a day when classes were in session. A couple of decades ago, when you entered a school, you typically saw a collection of fairly equal-sized classrooms, each one set up to accommodate about twenty-five to thirty children, each containing a chalkboard, a few bookshelves, a pencil sharpener, a bulletin board, a desk for each student—these arranged in some orderly fashion and generally bolted to the floor—and a larger desk and chair for the teacher.

The teacher customarily taught—presented information—from the front of the classroom. All of the children worked on the same lesson at the same time, sometimes from a textbook, sometimes from workbooks or teacher-prepared work pages, sometimes from the chalkboard.

When a child wanted to speak or leave his desk for some reason, he raised his hand to get his teacher's attention and request her permission to do what he wanted to do. When the children moved around the school building, they remained clustered together, sometimes in lines, and noise was kept to a minimum. There were rules of behavior, and the children knew them well.

Report cards were issued every nine weeks or so. These contained letter grades that reflected the teacher's view of the child's performance in various subjects.

Homework was a standard. A moderate amount was assigned almost daily, to be handed in the following day. The teacher checked over the assignments fairly speedily and usually returned them to her students—with her judgments on the quality and/or accuracy of the work—that day or the next.

The school principal paid a couple of visits to the classroom each semester, ostensibly to observe the teacher's classroom technique. Beyond that the children saw very little of their principal—unless they committed some offense that required "discipline." For that matter the children rarely saw anyone but their regular teachers and classmates, except in very unusual situations. Learning specialists, resource room teachers, psychologists, and counselors were not in evidence.

Was all this good? Am I yearning for the "good old days?" No, I am not. They were not good old days for the hard-to-teach child; at least, not unless the hard-to-teach child was a true "late bloomer" and never got too far behind his class. If, however, he was like the children I have described throughout this book, then he was not served well in such a school setting, for he was not taught despite his poor teachability. He failed, and that was that.

But those days were not all bad either. At least the hard-to-teach child did not have to figure out the rules of behavior he was expected to follow nor what he was to learn in the classroom. These were made apparent to him. Hence even if he "failed" in his academic endeavors, he had a chance of "passing" in the "expected behavior" portion of his day, because there he was advised of what to do, and he usually did it.

In recent years, as we are all aware, education has adopted a lot of so-called modern ideas. These have changed our schools radically—for the better for some children, for the worse for other children.

It is time that educators took an objective look at what these modern ideas have produced, but they must do this sensibly, methodically, in a way that takes the individual differences of the students into account when the judgments are made. It is time to recognize that some children not only do better with certain types of programs and teachers, they also do better with certain specific sets of school conditions, while others seem to thrive under a different set of conditions. It is time to start constructing school environments that accommodate these differences among children, rather than simply introducing change for the sake of change itself; or because it is different and appears to work well with easy-to-teach children. (Here again is that same old trap: If a certain school arrangement works well with easy-to-teach children, then it is reasoned that the thing to do is to provide that arrangement for all children, that it will then make them all easy to teach.)

We all know that there are no panaceas in education. We now have to translate that knowledge into practical terms. Not only is there no single program that works best with all children and no one type of teacher who reaches all children equally well; neither is there one school environment design that suits all children. But that does not mean that there are not any optimal conditions for different kinds of children and that these cannot be determined and provided within the context of a regular public school. It is, in fact, the only reasonable thing to do. It is not reasonable to keep doing what has been customary to date: meeting the needs of the average child, applauding the better than average child for his better than average achievement, and failing the others.

This brings to mind another one of society's current misinterpretations. We like to say that "children go to school to learn." This is incorrect. It is a distortion of what society had in mind when it started the institution of the school. Children go to school to be taught; we send our children there for that express purpose—*to be taught* to read, write, do arithmetic, spell, and so on. The extent to which they learn depends on how well they are taught—on their teachability and the instruction they receive. Children do not opt to go to school. The law mandates their attendance. How, then, can we justify the position that, once they are enrolled in school, the burden—the responsibility —for learning becomes theirs. Obviously, we cannot; yet we do.

What are the important factors in a school environment? I will list and discuss them separately, and try to identify which conditions suit the typical hard-to-teach child best.

Class Size

This is a most important concern. Throughout this book I have stressed the fact that the hard-to-teach child needs explicit, unambiguous instruction that is offered in limited portions and accompanied by more than the usual amount of drill and practice. This cannot be done in a classroom where twenty-five children congregate with one teacher. There is just not enough time in a school day for this teacher-student ratio to be effective. Children who can learn by themselves, with a minimum of direct instruction, will do all right under these circumstances, but not those who are hard to teach.

The hard-to-teach child should not have to share his teacher with more than six to eight other children, at least not during those portions of the day when the key subjects—reading and arithmetic—are being taught. Now, before the budget-minded among you throw this book down in disgust, saying that no school can afford such a small teacher-student ratio, let me offer a couple of counterbalancing suggestions. (I could call up the cliché that no school can afford *not* to do this, given the expense society assumes in looking after its educational failures—in welfare programs, jails, mental health services, and so forth, but I will not.)

First of all, some of the expense can be absorbed by assigning a counter-balancing, extra-large number of children—not hard-to-teach ones, to be sure —to another teacher. True, the children will have to be among the easy-to-teach, the program will have to be one that uses lots of interesting, self-instructional materials, and the teacher will have to be the type who can deal with such a program and the dynamics of a classroom where thirty-five or more easily-stimulated, active children are busy doing things that maintain their interest and add to their store of knowledge. But it is possible.

Another suggestion: Provide this special class-size arrangement for only sixty to ninety minutes per day—just for arithmetic and reading, say. This, of course, calls for special scheduling and regroupings, but it can be done.*

---

*Many schools are now providing a *Resource room* that fills this need. Ordinarily, a Resource room is staffed by a specially trained teacher and an aide. Children are assigned there for specific portions of the school day to receive special help instruction. Obviously, these rooms vary from school to school, but the concept is good and should be supported.

Class Homogeneity

This is the era of egalitarianism. The classroom is supposed to mirror society. It is supposed to house a mixture of all kinds of children, rich and poor, black and white, male and female, easy-to-teach and hard-to-teach, thereby providing conditions that will influence the children, making them more democratic and as a result reshaping the society of the future. (We adults are such hypocrites! We ask our children to do what we ourselves avoid.)

I have no quarrel with a class being made up of children from various socioeconomic levels, from different racial groups and different neighborhoods. But I do not agree with the indiscriminate mixing of easy-to-teach and hard-to-teach children. A teacher cannot do justice to all of her students if they vary widely in teachability. Regardless of her knowledge, temperament, and commitment, it just cannot be done. Some children will have to be ignored more than others. Guess who is most likely to be ignored? The hard-to-teach, obviously—and for good reasons. They need so much more time that it is not fair to the others. Hence even if they are fortunate enough to get the same number of minutes of direct instruction as the others, the hard-to-teach children will learn less—and their deficits will compound daily.

Heterogeneous classroom makeup is probably good for certain subjects. It is a fine thing for the hard-to-teach children to listen to their more teachable classmates respond in such classes as social studies and language arts, for example. They will actually learn something from this. But it is a total waste of time for the hard-to-teach child to listen to an easy-to-teach classmate read in a way that he can neither begin to approximate nor even figure out how his classmate does it. It demoralizes him; it does him no good at all.

Open Classroom Versus Traditional Classroom

In 1967 Joseph Featherstone wrote a series of articles in *The New Republic* about his observations in certain English elementary schools. The articles described how the children determined, more or less on their own, how they would spend their time during the school day. In effect they seemed to learn how to do arithmetic while engaging in pleasurable activities, like measuring and building things, keeping score of game events, and so on. They seemed to learn to read and spell in fortuitous, nondirected kinds of ways—reading what they could on their own, asking their teacher to help decode a word now and then, writing stories, and so on. According to the reports, each child worked at his own rate and level. The teacher did not teach, at least not in any traditional sense of the word. She simply asked pointed questions, answered questions, made suggestions, and in general functioned as an interested adult who was there to help.

The term *open classroom* was applied to such operations, and the idea captured the fancy of U.S. education. It was imported, translated into American "educationese," and put into operation. "Classrooms without walls" were built in many towns. These were approved by all segments of society. They appealed to the budget-minded because, lacking many interior walls, the structures were relatively less expensive to build. They appealed to the progressive parents because the programs sounded and looked as though they were fun: That was how schools should look—active, dynamic, children working independently and learning through self-inspired investigation and discovery. No oppressive teachers, no sitting quietly and listening to an authoritarian figure. Large spaces with children all over the place, conversing with each other. What a nice sight!

Many teachers, especially the older, experienced ones, were a bit skeptical and slow to get on the bandwagon. They were classified as old-fashioned, committed to archaic ideas. "Such nonsense; imagine wanting to lecture when children were obviously so capable of instructing themselves." Clearly, education had finally realized that "all children can learn; they simply needed the kind of stimulating environment that does not interfere with the children's natural intellectual curiosity and growth."

Books and articles were written on the open classroom. Educational writers praised it. England attained the position of instructional exemplar. Teacher-training programs were designed and put into operation.

What ultimately happened? Same old thing. Some children did very well in the open classroom. Why? Obviously—they were easy to teach. They thrived under conditions that allowed them to move at their own pace, to pursue their own interests, to devise their own structure, to set up their own instructional goals and achieve them.

How about the children with average teachability? They did all right, but not consistently so. Some of them really did gain from the experience; the inspiration was effective. Others floundered about, and one day someone took a look at them and said, "You know, they do not read that well. Maybe we had better give them some reading lessons." And if it was done, the problem usually disappeared.

And the hard-to-teach children? They were totally out of their element, utterly confused by the lack of structure. They wandered about, literally, often getting into trouble because they did not know the rules—no one had told them —nor did they know how to figure them out on their own, at least not without first creating some kind of crisis that necessitated it.

The hard-to-teach child needs precise, unambiguous, explicit instruction. He does not learn by exploration. He learns by remembering what his teacher tells him to remember, and he remembers it then only if his teacher tells it to him slowly and clearly, repeats it often enough, and shows him a system for retaining the information.

That does not mean that open-classroom concepts should be discarded. On the contrary, the open-classroom model is a wonderful thing for children who can learn adequately in such a setting. It is just not for the hard-to-teach child.

Structure

That brings us to the general topic of structure. I have used the term a few times already without bothering to define it. *Structure* means, literally, "something arranged in a definite pattern of organization." The open classroom model lacks structure—at least with respect to formal instruction.

Hard-to-teach children, as a rule of thumb, require more structure than their more teachable classmates. That does not mean that they need harsh, totalitarian conditions. Hardly. It means, in simple terms, that there has to be some predictability in their environment, that they have to be able to anticipate what they are expected to do and how they are expected to do it. This can apply to where coats and hats are to be stored in the classroom, to where on the paper they are to write their names, to how to go about getting permission to go to the bathroom, and so on. At a somewhat less concrete level it pertains also to how explicitly the systems that underlie reading and arithmetic are presented and how thoroughly the steps are covered in an instructional situation, as contrasted with teaching by example, where the child identifies the salient information on his own.

In other words, schools vary in the degree of structure, or organization, they provide. To the extent that structure is lacking, the hard-to-teach child will suffer. Provide order: Map out the child's work—what he is to do, when he is to do it and in what sequence, and how what he is doing today links up with what he did yesterday. Structure is based on landmarks—signals that the child can read to tell him "where" he is—figuratively as well as literally. Provide these landmarks and keep them consistent and reliable. If you do, the child will need them less as time goes by. He will learn to determine his own landmarks from existing information.

Graded Versus Nongraded

The term *nongraded* means that what the child is to accomplish is laid out in clear, behavioral language as a series of learning objectives. Hence, the only thing that is "reported" is which goals have been accomplished and which remain to be achieved. Qualitative differences in children's work are neutralized in such an approach. Children do not differ in *how well* they master the objectives, only in *when* they master them.

Nongraded, therefore, means an elimination of the traditional stratification of grade levels. Children are not identified as second-graders, for example. Instead, they are located somewhere in their arithmetic program, somewhere else in their reading program—all of this determined by the accomplishment of learning objectives rather than years spent in school and annual promotions in grade level.

It is not a bad idea. In essence, it is based on the notion that since children progress at different rates, we should design and provide instruction that accommodates those individual differences. Hence, even if one year after entering school, child A is much further ahead than child B, the long-term results will not be affected. All you have to do is give child B more time. He will get there, and once he does, both children will be equally educated.

It is a nice idea—in theory. In practice? Same old problem. Easy-to-teach children move along at a wonderfully rapid pace. In fact, many progress too rapidly, moving into levels of work that are, perhaps, not appropriate for them. The child with average teachability? He makes average progress, nothing different from what you would expect. And the hard-to-teach child? You guessed it. He plods along, working through lessons that fail to make the links between them adequately obvious, and he completes the year far behind his classmates. What has not been taken into consideration is the fact that although you can call a school nongraded, there is always a starting date and a termination date, and if the school comprises six grades, (or, to maintain the nongraded theme, if the child is expected to enter seventh grade once he leaves this school), then the terminal date usually comes along some five years and nine months after the starting date.

Thus the hard-to-teach child, even the one who stays with his lessons, looks up from his desk five years and nine months after he started and either discovers that his classmates are leaving him behind or, perhaps even worse, joins them despite his lack of accomplishment.

Homework Versus No Homework

This is a trivial concern when contrasted with the topics just discussed. But it is worth a little consideration. Is it appropriate to assign homework? You bet it is—but for a specific purpose. *Homework should be an activity designed to give the hard-to-teach child practice in what he can already do but not as easily as he should. It should not be used for teaching something new.*

So should homework be assigned? Sure, if the child needs additional practice at a task and there is insufficient time to accomplish this in school.

Summary

Schools are more than buildings containing classrooms. School means schedules, room assignments, teacher assignments, methods for evaluating student progress, and more. There was a time when the rules for designing a school environment were so fixed and accepted that all schools looked the same, no matter where you went. Then, with the end of World War II and the arrival of the era of boundless optimism that grew out of rapid technological advances, schools changed. They changed drastically—to the point where there did not appear to be any common rules; where a school administrator designed an environment that suited and redesigned it a year later if he felt like it and if something new came along that sounded interesting.

Now we are seeing a backlash. We have entered the "back to basics" period. Society is now trying to recover all those "good things" we once had, then threw out in our fit of optimism.

The truth of the matter, of course, is this: First, no single approach suits all children adequately. Second, the easy-to-teach child does well in any environment but thrives best in an environment that allows him to make some of the decisions himself, to provide at least some of the structure. Third, the hard-to-teach child needs structure. In effect, his improvement, if he makes any, can be charted in terms of his relative dependency on others to provide that structure. The more he progresses, the less he will need their help.

How does this translate operationally? Schools should be organized according to the students' teachability. They should provide self-directed learning environments for the easy-to-teach children, at least for part of their day. These children should be placed in the hands of good, knowledgeable, committed teachers who have the temperament to allow the children to do most of the teaching for themselves, teachers who will not mind the children milling about, talking to each other and to themselves, making progress at uneven rates, becoming distracted by an irrelevant topic for a while, asking more questions than one would necessarily welcome.

Moderately structured learning environments should be provided for children with average teachability, at least for part of the day.

And highly structured learning environments should be provided for the hard-to-teach children, again for part of the day.

Bring them all together, in various combinations, for instruction in those topics where a mixture is beneficial.

Can this be done? Sure, it can be done. But it requires some major conditions: a large enough student body to provide enough children with varying teachability; a competent faculty and a school administrator who accepts the fact that his chief concern is to make certain that the students learn, that is, are taught to the extent that they need to meet the requirements society has set for schools. All else—school buses, cafeterias, paper clips—matter only as they contribute to this process.

WHAT CAN PARENTS DO?

It is one thing for me to describe the kind of teacher your child needs and the kind of school environment that will benefit him. It is another matter—and no small accomplishment—to make it happen when what your child needs is not readily available in his school.

I have to confess that I have no simple, pat answer. There are too many variables involved here, too many differences among school districts in terms of size, money, available classrooms, and a host of other factors, to lay out a specific plan of action. I suppose that the best I can do is offer some general suggestions.

All public schools in this country are now mandated by federal law (U.S. Public Law 94-142) to provide children between the ages of three and twenty-one with whatever assistance they may need in order to achieve their educational potential. This, of course, opens up a remarkable number of debatable issues, such as: How do you determine a child's potential? How do you decide what he needs to achieve that potential? And so on.

But the fact remains that the mandate is there, school administrators know that it is there—although some are not that eager to advise parents of its existence—and the child's parents, therefore, have a right to insist that something be done.

As of the late 1970s states and communities within states vary in how they do that "something." Some states—Massachusetts, for one—are devoting large sums of money to fulfilling the obligations of the law. They are paying for such things as psychiatric consultations, eye and hearing examinations, psychological evaluations, and so on, in an attempt to identify the cause of children's learning difficulties. Children are being transported to private offices and clinics for treatments that are related to what was found in the evaluations. Special classes are being set up—often called resource rooms, where the child spends a portion of each day, though some are called L.D. classes, and the child spends full time there. In some cases private-school tuitions are being provided. This is not to imply that all of the above is having a beneficial effect —but it is being done.

Other states are doing virtually nothing different from what they did prior to the passage of the law. In effect they are pretending that the law does not exist, and chances are they will maintain this posture until compelled to do otherwise.

In practical terms this means that the parents of the kind of child we have been discussing here have the right to petition their child's school for aid. If that aid translates into a different kind of teacher, then so be it. If that aid means smaller classes, or even one-to-one tutoring for a portion of each day, then the request can legitimately be made.

Your first step should be to discuss the situation with the principal of your child's school. If you get satisfaction from this meeting—if your requests are fulfilled—then fine. If they are not, then work your way up through the administrative hierarchy of the school system until you finally do make contact with the person who will effect the changes your child needs.

In the event that you cannot find such a person in your child's school system, then what? Seek out community resources. Earlier in this book I mentioned the Association for Children with Learning Disabilities and provided the address of their national office (see page 65). Try first to locate a local ACLD chapter. If you succeed, you will be making contact with a number of parents who, like you, have children who are hard to teach and therefore need special help. They will be able to advise you on your specific situation far better than I can from this distance. If you cannot locate a local chapter of ACLD, then write to the national office and ask for guidance. You will receive a reply, and the information is likely to be helpful.

Finally—and do not take this lightly—prepare yourself for a long, frustrating struggle. But prepare yourself also to win that struggle if you do not waver. Remember, school decisions are made by persons who are on the public payroll. They are vulnerable to the influences of public opinion. They may appear to be unwavering, unassailable, protected by their office and their academic credentials. But be assured that beneath that veneer there are anxieties and, in truth, real concern over the children in their schools.

Do not hold back because of embarrassment or because you do not want to be thought of as a complainer, a nag, or a pest. The aphorism "the squeaky wheel gets the grease" is true: The parent who shows up often enough in the principal's office, the parent who makes it clear that he will not be satisfied until his child gets what he needs, is the parent who is likely to accomplish what he sets out to do. True, that parent may not be very well liked by the principal, but that is a small price to pay for a successful outcome to the kind of quest under discussion here.

A last resort—and one to be taken seriously by the parent of a hard-to-teach child—is to seek out a private tutor or, if necessary, an appropriate private school, a school that specializes in teaching such children. You may recall that I mentioned such a school in my preface: Pace School in Pittsburgh, Pennsylvania. When we started Pace, we did it because the community's public schools were not providing for such children. They are now, to some extent —some schools are doing better than others—but Pace continues to have a waiting list, because the problem has hardly been eliminated. There are still plenty of children who need more than what public education is offering. Expensive? Sure, but there are such things as scholarships and, in some states, help with tuition. Granted, there are too many hard-to-teach children to depend on the private schools to solve the problem; and there are too many parents who cannot meet the tuition payments. But private schools play another role in these cases.

If they do their job well, then they stand as models, showing that the job can be done if the conditions are right. And if they do this effectively, then ultimately public education must pick up the responsibility and provide similar services.

That has happened in many communities. It certainly happened in Pittsburgh, once Pace got started and demonstrated that it could provide what these children needed. Since that time many changes have occurred in the public schools of the Pittsburgh area, changes that serve the hard-to-teach child. Would they have occurred without the presence of a Pace School? Perhaps, but I am inclined to think that it would have taken longer and been less extensive. So if you cannot arrange for your child's needs in the public schools and you cannot find a tutor who can help him, then go to the private schools of your community and see what they have to offer. And at the same time continue to pressure the public schools to make these same (or better) conditions available.

The essential point is this: A hard-to-teach child can and will learn—if he is taught in the right way by the proper kind of teacher in the appropriate setting. Continue to believe that as you launch your campaign to find help for your child.

PART IV

Prevention

WHAT TO EXPECT FROM THE PRESCHOOL CHILD

Up to this point we have been primarily concerned with the child who is already failing in school. I have described tests that he can be given and discussed how to use the information derived from those tests to develop a plan of action—action designed to teach him the skills he needs to perform satisfactorily in school.

All this is useful, but it is far better to prevent the problem from ever occurring in the first place. That may be easier said than done, but there is little doubt that many learning problems can be prevented—and many others kept at a less severe level—if early action is taken. Said another way, there would be far fewer children with learning disabilities if, when they entered first grade, they were able to

1. Analyze relatively complex spatial patterns into their component parts and recognize the way those parts fit together—specifically, pass at least the first seven items of the TVAS
2. Analyze relatively complex speech patterns into their component parts and recognize the sequence of those parts—specifically pass at least the first three items of the TAAS
3. Print all the capital and lowercase letters from dictation
4. Count as many as ten objects accurately and record that amount by printing the appropriate numerals
5. Communicate orally in a way that is appropriate for six-year-olds.

The child who is able to display these five basic skills when he enters first grade is an extremely unlikely candidate for the label "learning disability." This does not imply that children who are unable to display all of these skills when they enter first grade will encounter learning problems. Many of them will do well in school, of course, just as most children did not contract polio even before there was a preventive vaccine. But if prevention is your goal, then why leave his school progress to chance? *Teach your child the five basic skills listed above before he starts first grade.*

How should you go about this? There are two routes. If you have no reason to think that your preschooler is a high-risk child—a child who shows signs of being a learning problem—you may approach the task of teaching him the five basic skills in a casual, unplanned way. This is the way most children are taught much of what they learn before they start their formal schooling. If, on the other hand, you have reason to believe that your child is "high-risk," then your efforts should be more organized and intentional. In either instance, however, you should make the effort to teach him those basic skills.

Although the high-risk child will display certain behavioral signs, there is no well-defined pattern. Some will display all the following characteristics, others will display only one or two. He may tend to be hyperactive, that is, unable to sit quietly for even short periods of time; distractible; generally awkward in both gross- and fine-motor actions (in walking and running as well as cutting, pasting, drawing, and manipulating an eating utensil). He may display poor speech and language development, that is, an inability to express himself verbally as well as most children his age; and his speech production skills may be less precise than is expected.

Many mothers have expressed it this way: "From the time he was an infant I knew something was wrong, but I could never put my finger on it, and no one else agreed with me. He seemed different from my other children, yet I knew he wasn't retarded or anything like that." In most cases the "something" that was wrong was a set of behavioral characteristics that are more typical of a younger child. This is not easy for a parent to evaluate effectively. In a way, there is nothing really wrong with the child. He just seems to be imma- ture; and even this is not completely consistent. Some days he seems fine; other days not so fine.

To add to the dilemma, he often appears to be quite bright, to know all he should know. On those occasions it is easy to say, "Oh, well, he'll grow out of it." And indeed he might. But the important concern is whether his develop- mental timetable will match the school's, whether he will grow out of it before he enters the world of symbolic representation—the first grade. If he does, then fine. If he does not, there will be trouble, trouble that will mount as the child encounters daily failures and frustrations in the classroom.

What should you do if your child shows signs of being high-risk? Insofar as you can, follow the testing plan that is described in the first portion of this book and reviewed in the following pages.

TESTS

Medical

Ask your family physician or pediatrician if some health factor could explain the high-risk signs you have noticed and also ask if the youngster is achieving his developmental milestones on schedule. It is fairly easy to get a reply to the first part of this question. He will be healthy or not, and if he is not, your physician will know what to do. Getting an assessment of his general development is not that easy in some places. Persist. If you cannot get it from your physician, call your county medical society or public health agency and find out if there is a clinic operating in your area that can answer your question.

Specifically you will want to know whether the child's large muscle skills and small muscle skills are emerging as expected. In addition you will want some opinion about his speech and language development, his social and emotional development, and his intellectual development. All of these can be evaluated, and all are important. If they are all emerging as expected, be grateful. If they are not, go into action. Ask for help from whoever did the assessment and, in addition, start to use the activities I will list in the pages that follow.

Vision and Hearing

Have his eyes examined. Do not settle for a visual screening by someone who is not an optometrist or ophthalmologist. Preschool children are very unreliable reporters, and screenings depend on the reliability of the patient. As I stressed earlier, you should find an eye doctor who will do more than assess the health of the child's eyes and the clarity of his eyesight. Both factors are important, of course, but they do not go far enough. Find someone who will assess visual function—how well the child uses his eyes, coordinates them, shifts and sustains focus. Both optometrists and ophthalmologists can do that *if they will take the time and trouble.* Impress upon the one you choose that you want him to take the time and trouble, and do not settle for less. If no visual problem is found, be grateful. If a problem is identified, follow the doctor's advice.

Then have his hearing tested. And if there is reason, have someone evaluate his speech and language development. Again, follow the professional's advice.

Perceptual Skills

Now, how about his perceptual skills? Who should assess these? The visual (TVAS) and auditory (TAAS) tests, described earlier, are not really designed to be used with prekindergarten children, and although I could suggest some other tests for this age group, I hesitate to do so. As already mentioned, very young children are notoriously unreliable test takers, particularly if the tests are administered by nonprofessionals. So if your child's visual or auditory perceptual skills are to be tested, and if he is younger than five, have a professional do it. Some optometrists and some psychologists test visual and auditory perceptual skills. So do some speech and hearing people. See if you can find someone competent in your community. If you can, good. If you cannot, then there is still something you can and should do. *Simply assume that the child's perceptual skills are not adequate when you design your plan of action.*

In other words, take nothing for granted—especially these crucial skills. If it turns out that you underestimated them, that his skills are adequate, then you caused no harm. It will soon become apparent what skills he has mastered. That is certainly more desirable than neglecting a deficit that ultimately will cause him to fail in school. In short, it is preferable to be overcautious than to ignore a significant problem. And do not delay. Act early.

STARTING SCHOOL

It is highly likely, in this era, that by the time a child is five years old, he will be enrolled in some kind of school. Many children start school at the age of three. You should choose your child's nursery school carefully, whether he is a high-risk or not. However, if he does show high-risk signs, you should be extra careful in your choice. Some nursery schools do not do well with distractible, inattentive children. They may be excellent schools, but not for him. He will taste failure there; he will lose much and gain nothing. Other nursery schools are just what the doctor ordered. Their staff will know how to handle the high-risk child, directing his limited attention in productive ways, teaching him skills when they can, and helping him to feel like an acceptable member of his group.

Another reason for the rush is that most children enter kindergarten at the age of five, and some—those whose birthdays fall in October, November, December, and in some places even January—at the age of four. The high-risk child should not enter a kindergarten that is part of a school system unless everyone (you, his teacher, the school principal) agrees *in advance* that he will not start first grade one year later unless he is really ready, no matter how smart or tall or eager he may be, and that he will not be treated as a failure in kindergarten. The high-risk child can profit mightily from proper preprimary experiences. School is a good place for him to be. But it should be a school where he will be able to learn—to acquire skills—and not a school where, once in, he is excluded and classified as a failure.

That is the reason for the rush. If you are to prevent problems, you will have to choose his school wisely, sending him there earlier if they offer what he needs, delaying his entry if they do not.

How do you assess a school?* That is a difficult question to answer. You visit it, you observe the class that your child would attend, you ask yourself, "Would *my* child do well here? Would this teacher be able to accept his periodic tendency to stop paying attention and start wandering about? Would

*For a more extensive discussion about what to look for in a school, see the section entitled "The Instructional Environment," pages 297–304.

they punish him, or merely refocus his attention?" And answer these questions *honestly*. Do not delude yourself into thinking that once the child enters this classroom, he will change, become a young scholar, and everyone will live happily ever after. It might indeed happen, but do not count on it. If you get the strong impression that the class you are observing is tightly controlled and strictly disciplined, watch out. If you get the impression that, in contrast, the class is a chaotic mass of little bodies bouncing around, once again watch out. What you want for your child is a class where order and rules prevail—but order and rules that are flexible, adaptive to the differences among the children; where children may interact freely but not disruptively and where they are praised for positive actions rather than punished for negative ones.

USING THE VISUAL, AUDITORY, AND GENERAL MOTOR PROGRAMS WITH PRESCHOOL CHILDREN

If the child's visual and auditory perceptual skills are not satisfactory, or if you are merely assuming that they are not, start using the visual, auditory, and general motor programs described in the earlier sections of this book. Do not concern yourself with placement tests. Just start the child with the easiest activities in each of the programs and work up to the more difficult ones as he shows progress. In other words, start him in the visual program with teaching pattern 1 and a 5-pin geoboard (see pages 76–82) in the auditory program with clapping in time to spoken words (see pages 94 and 96); and in the general motor program with activities designed to teach him how to balance, hop, skip, and use his hands, eyes, and speech production mechanisms more precisely (see pages 121–126).

In addition, teach him how to count aloud from 1 to 10 and how to count from one to ten objects and record that quantity with numerals. Teach him the letters of the alphabet. (See the suggested activities for reading and arithmetic, pages 144–158 and pages 232–238.) Set up a five-day-a-week schedule and stick to it.

But do more than that. Take advantage of the fact that he is not yet in school, where he is expected to learn to read, write, calculate, and spell. You can devote all your energy to teaching him basic skills rather than helping him with his homework. The pages that follow contain a variety of additional activities, appropriate for preschoolers and organized according to whether they are pertinent to visual, auditory, or general motor skills. They all have one characteristic in common: They are intended to make the child conscious of relevant details and the interrelationships of those details. In the section on visual perceptual skills, the details are embedded in various visual patterns. In the auditory perceptual skills section, the details are acoustical. And in the general motor skills portion, the details pertain to certain precise motor actions.

In most instances the categories are not clear-cut; many visual perceptual skills procedures also involve motor actions. So, too, do many of the auditory skills procedures. That is not important, and, in fact, if you think of a way to broaden a specific procedure—a visual task, for example, to also include an

315

auditory component—all the better. You are not, after all, managing a research study. You are teaching your child a variety of skills to aid him in sorting out and organizing information—information that, in one way or another, he will be expected to learn how to represent with codes, letters, and numerals—when he enters school. The more sensitive he is to these details (within reason, of course), the more readily he will grasp the concepts of the codes. The more readily he does this, the more capable he will be at extracting information from the codes. Hence the better learner he will be.

It might be worth mentioning that although these activities are designed for preschool children, they may also be used with older children if they appear to offer some reasonable challenge. The order in which they are listed does not imply levels of difficulty. They vary, and in fact, any activity may be made simpler by reducing the amount of detail involved, or more difficult by adding more details and demands.

One more point. How long should you use these activities, how much instruction should the child have? *He should receive regular instruction at least until he is able to display the five sets of basic skills listed at the beginning of this section.* When he can, you may stop teaching him if you and he wish. However, it will not harm him to go beyond that point, to acquire perceptual skills that are a little better than average so long as it is kept within reason.

So, unless teaching him creates an undesirable situation for either of you, continue to teach him beyond the very basic level. Obviously once he reaches this point, you may want to approach the task less formally and eliminate the schedule. That is all right. In fact, you will notice that your child will more and more *teach himself* as he engages in activities where he employs the basic skills you taught him, as he starts to use construction toys on his own, as he starts to use words with more facility, as he starts to see and hear details that he did not see or hear before.

ACTIVITIES THAT TEACH VISUAL PERCEPTUAL SKILLS TO PRESCHOOL CHILDREN

Sorting tasks. There is a vast array of materials that may be used for this activity. Whatever you use, have the child organize the materials according to a characteristic that you identify. Have him do the following:

    a. Sort buttons according to size. In every household there is usually a box full of buttons. Have the child sort these into containers, a specific size in a specific container.

    b. Sort buttons according to color.

    c. Sort buttons according to color *and* size. If you have enough buttons, this adds an extra dimension. Thus one container will hold all the black buttons of a certain size, for example, and another container all the white buttons of the same size. This is a good place to teach the concept that things can be the same one way, yet different another way. Proceed with care. This can be a confusing concept. Do not stress it. Simply point it out periodically. He will catch on in time.

d. Sort playing cards according to suit or numerical designation or both.

e. Sort screws, nails, nuts, bolts, washers, and other hardware items according to size.

f. Sort paint chips (cards showing various colors—these are usually obtainable from a paint store) according to color. Homemade chips can be made with crayons.

g. Sort food cans according to size or according to the pictures on the labels.

h. Sort samples of fabric according to texture; for example, all smooth fabrics in one pile, all rough fabrics in another.

i. Sort shapes. You will probably have to prepare this yourself, but it is quite easy. Cut paper into a variety of shapes—circles, squares, and triangles—and have the child sort these according to shape, size, color. Add more shapes when he appears to be ready for more complex tasks. (You may also have him cut out the shapes himself.)

j. Sort silverware according to size or function or both.

k. Sort books according to size or color of cover.

l. Sort strands of yarn according to color or length or both.

m. Sort photographs of people according to their sex, their family relationships, or their ages.

n. Sort cards showing capital letters. You may have to make these yourself, but it is easy to do. All you need is a pencil and some paper. Cut the paper (or have the child do it) into playing-card size and print a capital letter on each. Start off with only two or three different letters and add to the assortment as he shows competency. For example, "Put all the *A*'s in one pile, all the *B*'s in another."

o. Sort bottles according to weight. Purchase a number of medicine bottles from your local drug store and wrap adhesive tape around them so that the contents cannot be seen, or use empty tin cans or soft-drink bottles. Then pour sand (or salt or sugar or dried beans) into each container, so that even though they are equal in size, some are of one weight and others are either lighter or heavier.

This list could be extended, but I think you must have the idea by now. Any task is useful if it involves sorting objects that are similar in one way and vary in another—and if the child can figure it out.

Matching tasks. In all these activities you construct a pattern, and the child constructs one just like it, positioning his alongside yours. If he encounters difficulty matching your pattern, have him place his *on top* of yours rather than alongside. To add further interest and to foster better visual memory, play "Flash" with him. To do this, hide your pattern from the child's view with a sheet of cardboard. Tell him to get ready, then flash your pattern for a brief period (count to 10, or 5, or 1, or whatever works), then cover it again. The child is to match your pattern from memory. Start with simple patterns. Increase their complexity as he displays the ability to deal with them.

   a. Match playing cards. Line up one, two, or more playing cards and have the child match your pattern. (These need not be lined up; they can be arranged as a triangle, or what have you, so long as the child can manage the task.)

   b. Match silverware. Line up a spoon, a fork, and a knife, and have the child match your pattern.

   c. Match a button pattern.

   d. Match a color pattern, using crayons or other colored articles.

   e. Match a hardware pattern made up of screws, bolts, nuts, washers, and so on.

   f. Match letters. Construct your pattern with cards on which letters have been printed. Give similar cards to the child and have him match the pattern.

   g. Match shapes. Parquetry blocks are particularly useful here. You can purchase these in most toy and variety stores. They include three basic shapes (square, triangle, diamond). Arrange them in patterns and have the child match the patterns. Caution: Do not use complex patterns until the child shows that he can match simple ones.

   h. Match glassware (drinking glasses) of different shapes and sizes.

   i. Match pipe-cleaner patterns.

   j. Match toothpick patterns.

As you undoubtedly see by now, virtually any material can be used for this activity. Simply construct a pattern and have the child copy it. You can vary this by switching roles; have the child construct the pattern and you match it. He, of course, must then check your work for accuracy. Make an occasional error. He will enjoy finding them, and looking for them will sharpen his skills.

Organizing tasks. In these activities the child is given materials and asked to organize them according to some attribute. Show him how; give him a model to follow. Then, in time, withdraw your model and encourage him to figure it out for himself. For example, have him

   a. Organize buttons according to size. Give the child a number of buttons, one of each size. He is to arrange them in a row, from smallest to largest. If necessary, start out with only three buttons and add to the task as he grasps the concept.

   b. Organize playing cards according to their numerical designation.

That is, arrange them in a line from the ace to the ten.

c. Organize bolts, screws, washers, or other hardware items according to size, from smallest to largest.

d. Organize shoes according to size. For example, Dad's, Mom's, big sister's, baby's.

e. Organize shapes according to size—squares, circles, triangles, and others.

f. Organize colors according to hue, for example, from light blue to dark blue.

g. Organize pictures according to time sequence. Show the child three pictures that are sequentially related; for example, drawings from a comic strip that shows (1) the sunrise and a rooster crowing; (2) a child awakening; (3) a child playing. Then have him arrange them in a logical sequence. (Other examples: pictures of articles of clothing to be arranged in the order in which he puts them on when getting dressed or in the order in which he removes them when getting undressed; pictures of food items—appetizers, main course items, desserts—to be arranged according to the sequence in which they are customarily eaten.)

h. Organize wood blocks according to thickness, ranging from thin to thick, like a staircase.

i. Measure objects, rooms, or people, and organize them according to size. He can measure with a ruler, a length of rope, a footstep.

Again it is apparent that the number of activities involving the organizing of information is virtually unlimited. The general skill you are trying to foster here is the ability to order information.

Classification tasks. This is an extension of what has already been described. In these activities the child is shown a picture and asked to classify it. For example, have him

a. Classify food. Show him pictures cut out of magazines and have him classify them according to whether they are (1) good tasting or bad tasting; (2) breakfast food or dinner food; (3) eaten hot or cold; (4) appetizer, main course, or dessert; (5) eaten cooked or raw.

b. Classify household objects. Use pictures or real objects and have him classify them according to whether they are (1) hard to move or easy to move, that is, heavy or light; (2) for sitting on or lying on; (3) living-room pieces, bedroom pieces, or kitchen pieces; (4) constructed of metal, wood, or plastic; (5) rough or smooth in texture.

c. Classify clothing. Show him pictures and have him classify them according to whether they are (1) for boys or girls; (2) for winter or summer wear; (3) rough or smooth; (4) heavy or light; (5) worn above the waist or below the waist.

    d. Classify sports equipment. Show him pictures and have him classify them according to whether they are *(1)* used indoors or outdoors or both; *(2)* used in summer or winter; *(3)* heavyweight or lightweight; *(4)* thrown, kicked, or batted in some way (for example, a golf ball, a tennis ball, a football).

Find hidden shapes. Here the child is to learn the concept that large patterns contain collections of identifiable smaller patterns. For example, have him

    a. Find all the hidden circles. Show him pictures of automobiles, household objects, and other things, and have him find all of the hidden circles—for example, the *wheels* of an automobile; the *bottom* of a pot. You need not use pictures; real objects will do. Also, this may be extended to hidden squares, triangles, and so on.

    b. Find all the hidden numerals in a room—in calendars, clock dials, radio and television dials.

    c. Find all the hidden flowers in the house—in carpet and towel designs, hanging paintings, kitchenware.

    d. Find the hidden letters—on book covers, newspapers, mailboxes, street signs, billboards. (This procedure can be modified to focus the child on specific letters; for example, "Find all the *A*'s you can," or "Find the letters of your name."

Painting, drawing, and other graphic tasks. The purpose here is to give the child the opportunity to see and reproduce details—and have some fun doing it. This should range from coloring books and follow-the-dots, to weaving and finger painting. As I mentioned earlier, do not be afraid to use coloring books. I do not think it will limit his artistic development. Every creative artist worthy of the designation knows his craft and the potentials of his media. He knows these things as a result of disciplined training or disciplined self-instruction. Coloring books will not make your child into an artist, but neither will they prevent him from being one.

Block play and other construction activities. There are a great variety of construction toys on the market. They are all useful, so long as they do not impose unreasonable demands on the child. Start with simple ones, then progress to the more complex ones as he shows that he is able. You need not be limited to commercial toys. Popsicle or paste sticks and straws are all good construction materials that can be glued together. For that matter, so is construction paper, which may be cut into various shapes and assembled into a number of designs.

ACTIVITIES THAT TEACH AUDITORY PERCEPTUAL SKILLS TO PRESCHOOL CHILDREN

Matching tasks.

a. Fill a number of empty tin cans about halfway with various food articles—salt or sand, dried beans, and dried cereals. Cover each can with a foil lid so that the contents are not visible. Prepare at least two cans identically. The child is then to sort the cans according to the sounds they produce when shaken.

b. Tapping patterns. You tap a pattern with your hand on a table. The child is to match the pattern. Start with a simple tap-tap-tap and work into more complex patterns as the child shows progress.

c. Sound effects. You attempt to reproduce the sounds made by an airplane, a carpet sweeper, an automobile, a railroad train, a cat, a dog, a lion, and so forth. The child tries to copy you.

d. Musical tones. Fill three drinking glasses or soft-drink bottles with unequal amounts of water—one almost to its rim, the second about halfway, the third with very little. Each will emit a different tone when tapped with a wooden rod. You tap a tone pattern (high, low, middle); the child then attempts to reproduce your pattern. Start off with simple patterns and introduce more difficult ones as he shows that he can deal with them. (At first have him watch you. Then he is to listen only while looking in another direction.) This can be varied to include loud and quiet tones as well as long and short tones.

Classifying tasks.

a. Classify nonverbal sounds. Produce sounds for him (either taped sounds or ones that you imitate) and ask him to classify the sounds according to whether they are *(1)* animal or mechanical; *(2)* loud or quiet; *(3)* friendly animals or unfriendly ones.

b. Classify spoken words. Name objects and have him classify them according to whether they are *(1)* long words or short words— *astronaut* versus *cat; (2)* long sentences or short sentences.

Talking and listening. The most effective way to teach a child auditory perceptual skills is to foster his language development. Read to him. Talk to him. Teach him new words. When he engages in some of the visual tasks just described—sorting, say—teach him synonyms. Hence he should not only be sorting "big" and "little" objects but "huge" ones, "tremendous" ones, "tiny" ones, "long" ones, "wide" ones, and so forth. The more words he knows, the more likely it is that he will recognize that spoken words are constructed of spoken sounds. Encourage him to speak clearly as well as intelligently. Have him pronounce *all* of the sounds in words; including word endings. Help him avoid confusing the sequence of sounds in words *(pizzghetti* for *spaghetti).* Give him a chance to speak. Help him organize his thoughts but do not yield to the temptation of "helping" him by saying it for him. And inform his brothers and sisters that they, too, must give him a chance to speak for himself.

ACTIVITIES THAT TEACH GENERAL MOTOR SKILLS TO PRESCHOOL CHILDREN

In addition to the activities already described, the following are appropriate:

Imitation. This is, in effect, a matching task in which the child is asked to imitate a pose. Assume various postures and say to the child, "Do what I am doing," or, "Stand the way I am standing."
  a. Stand on one foot.
  b. Kneel on hands and knees.
  c. Show index finger on one hand.
  d. Place one hand on head, the other on chest.

Identify body parts. Ask the child to point to his eyes, ears, nose, mouth, shoulders, elbows, wrists, knees, hips, and toes. Then ask him to name those parts as you touch them.

Ask him to look surprised, shocked, frightened, sad, happy, tired. The child is to assume a pose that reflects the word.

Construct clay people showing their eyes, shoulders, arms, and various other major body parts.

Draw faces, showing eyes, ears, nose, lips, and other details.

Have him engage in some movement activity; then instruct him to "freeze" —stop all movement—in whatever position he may be when he hears (or sees) a signal such as a bell, a clap, the interruption of a musical record, or a light.

Walk with an object (book) balanced on his head.

Walk, or run, with a small object (a button, a wooden bead) cradled in a spoon held in his hand.

Sit or stand in various postures and sway to music without losing balance.

Stretch and reach. Child stands or sits in a designated position and attempts to reach and grasp objects located about him, without losing his balance.

Leaning tower. Child leans as far as possible in a designated direction (forward, backward, to the left, the right) without losing balance.

Speak with teeth clenched. Have him start off by saying his own name, the names of friends, relations, and so on. His goal is to speak clearly enough to be understood.

Lipreading. Have him move his lips in a way that enables others to read them. Can you recognize whose name he has articulated? What numeral he said, and so on? Then change roles.

Untie simple knots. Make certain that the knots have not been pulled too securely. Start with heavy string.

Tie simple knots. Start with heavy string or rope.

THE PRESCHOOL CHILD WHO IS NOT HIGH-RISK

What about the child who is not high-risk? That is a very good question and, in answering it, I will try to summarize my attitudes and ideas about manipulating children and their environments.

First of all, the simplest way to answer the question is to say, "Do nothing. Let natural circumstances govern the child's development. His day-to-day experiences will foster the acquisition of the basic skills he will need in school. He will be fine." That is not a bad answer. In most instances it is a correct one. Hundreds of thousands of children enter first grade without any special preschool preparation and learn to read, calculate, spell, and write without much difficulty. Would they have progressed faster and learned more if they had entered school with the basic skills well established? The truth is, we do not know. But it certainly is not unreasonable to argue that this indeed would have been the case. It is only logical to suggest that if the child arrives in first grade already familiar with the coding symbols—and the elements that are to be coded—he will learn better and faster.

"Well," the argument can proceed, "that is what his first-grade teacher is supposed to teach him, isn't it?" And that is correct. However, that first-grade teacher may have to deal with as many as thirty children, and they will differ. Some children will be better prepared—better learners. Some teachers prefer to teach this kind of child and do not work well with the opposite extreme.

Even if she does not particularly favor the one type of child, the teacher's time is limited. The principal of the school expects all the children to be at certain places in their various books by the end of the year, knowing full well that some will not be there. Those who are not are seen as slow; some are even labeled failures. Have they failed? No, the school failed them by not making certain that they had achieved the basic skills before imposing more complex and more abstract demands upon them. We do not try to build buildings without foundations, for we know they will topple. Yet we do try to do this in school, that is, teach elaborate skills to children who lack fundamental skills. They will surely topple. The architect who designs a building improperly and the builder who constructs it are seen as failures. In most schools it is the child who fails! Unjustifiable, but true!

324

Until schools become responsive to the individual differences of their students and are prepared to offer truly individualized education, I strongly recommend that parents teach their children the basic skills before they enter the first grade, even if they do not seem to be high-risk. Yes, the child may do very well without this extra effort, but even then, what is wrong with giving him a little bit of a head start?

And that brings me to the final section—some tempering remarks and perhaps even a warning that too much of a head start may not be such a good thing.

This book has focused on one aspect of a child's development—the cognitive; how to test and teach some of the skills that underlie a child's ability to code and ultimately to communicate abstract information with symbols. We all know, however, that children develop along more than a cognitive dimension; that they also grow and develop physically and emotionally. We know also that though we label and describe these three aspects of development separately—physical, cognitive, and emotional—they are inseparable. Changes in one will surely have effects on the other two.

The close ties between cognitive and physical development are apparent in this book. Consider how much stress I placed on the fact that the child's ability to analyze and organize visual and acoustical information will be enhanced if he also explores it physically with his hands and with his speech production mechanism.

What has not been acknowledged, and must be now, is the close relationship between these two aspects of development—physical and cognitive—and the third—emotional.

I make no pretense at extensive knowledge in this field, but one does not have to be a professional anything—except, perhaps, a human being—to recognize that unless a child's emotional development keeps pace with his physical and cognitive development, certain difficulties are likely to arise. In a sense these areas of development are like three pillars that support a structure. If they are all intact and equally and adequately developed, they form a sturdy base. Weaken or distort one, and the total supportive power of the three is affected. As the structure they bear becomes weightier, as demands on the pillars increase, the other two, initially intact, must assume some of the burden not carried by the third. As a result they too are weakened or distorted.

I do not want to belabor the illustration, but the point is important. Do not stimulate growth along one dimension of development at the expense of the other two. Thus, although I have just finished urging all parents to teach their children certain skills, I am at the same time urging them not to honor cognitive development to the extent that the child is placed in situations that he cannot cope with physically and emotionally.

We have all seen children who, for some reason or another, displayed an early facility with language or numbers or both. Their exceptional abilities earned them special attention and probably motivated them to practice and expand that ability even further. This is fine, unless it resulted in their being placed in a classroom with children who were older, more socially mature, more physically adept than they—albeit no "smarter."

Such situations impose stress on children, stress that may very well have negative effects on their total development. Life is more than doing well in school. The child is entitled to fulfill his developmental potential along all three dimensions—physical and emotional as well as cognitive.

The point, then, is simple. Yes, teach him the basic skills he will need to know. Yes, encourage him to be aware of details, to be able to sort them and organize them and classify them in a variety of ways. Yes, stimulate his interest in learning. But remember, he is a total child, not a walking brain, and provide him with the conditions he needs to fulfill all of his potentials. Do not stimulate one aspect of his development to the exclusion of the others, to the point where he finds himself in situations that are beyond him.

CONCLUSION

CHILDREN VARY in how well they do in school. Some are easy to teach; they do very well. Some are hard to teach; they do poorly. Some do well in certain subjects only and not so well in others. They vary for many reasons, one being their ability to learn under standard school conditions.

Schools serve the average learner best. The easy-to-teach child is served fairly well, especially if he is provided with interesting and instructive materials. The hard-to-teach child—whatever the cause of his problem—is served poorly. Group instruction imposes overwhelming demands on him. He quickly falls behind and remains there. And no one is upset, except the child himself and his parents. (The idea of rating children on a curve is firmly established; the term *average* requires that there be children both above and below that midrange level.) He becomes more and more accustomed to being excluded, not physically perhaps but certainly intellectually. In time he stops trying.

According to official records, he has failed. The major theme of this book has been that *he* did not fail. The schools failed; the system failed because it did not accommodate his needs.

Education has gone through phases. These tend to mirror society's goals for our children. We are now in an era when all parents want their children to achieve at least basic competency in reading and arithmetic, not necessarily in order to become scholars but to be able to read the newspaper, perform practical calculations, think for themselves.

Most of our children seem to be able to achieve these goals and more— but not our hard-to-teach youngsters. They continue to perplex us. Their failure to learn adequately is attributed to many causes—socioeconomic background, emotional problems, neurological deficits, and so on. The basic message of this book is that it is the school's job to *teach* all children, be they poor, emotionally upset, neurologically impaired, what have you. If a child is hard to teach—whatever the cause or causes—he can still learn. He simply needs more teaching.

This book is meant to serve as a source of aid for those children. I hope it serves its purpose.

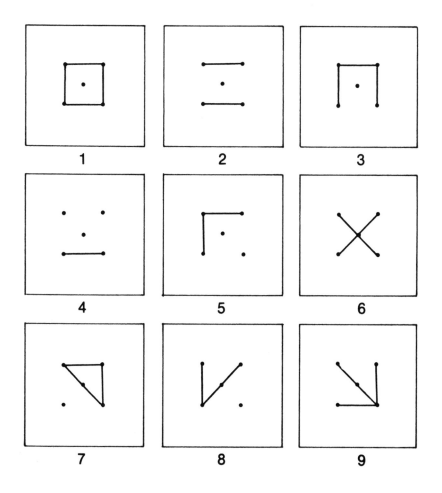

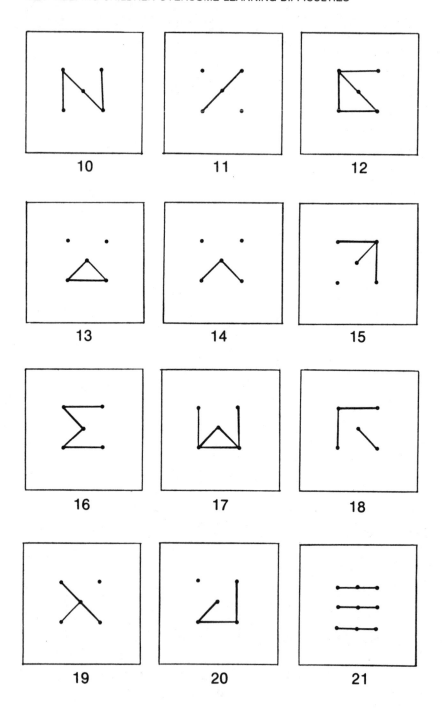

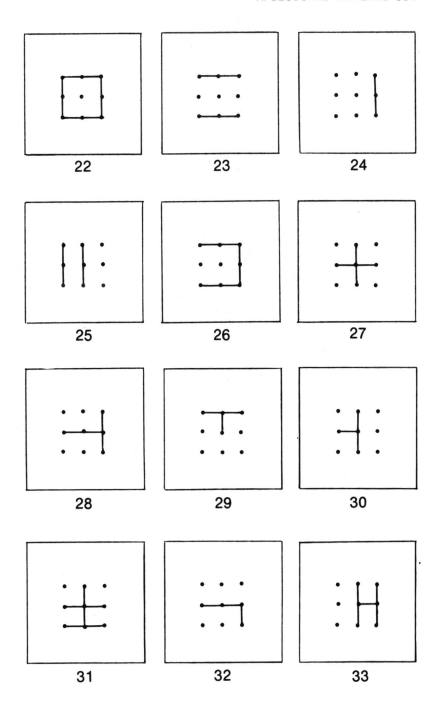

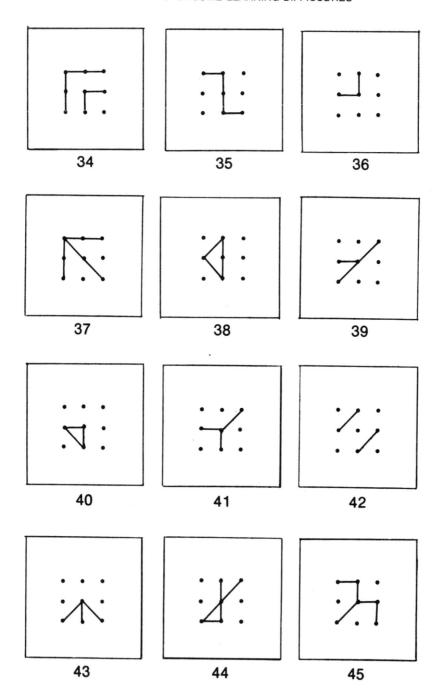

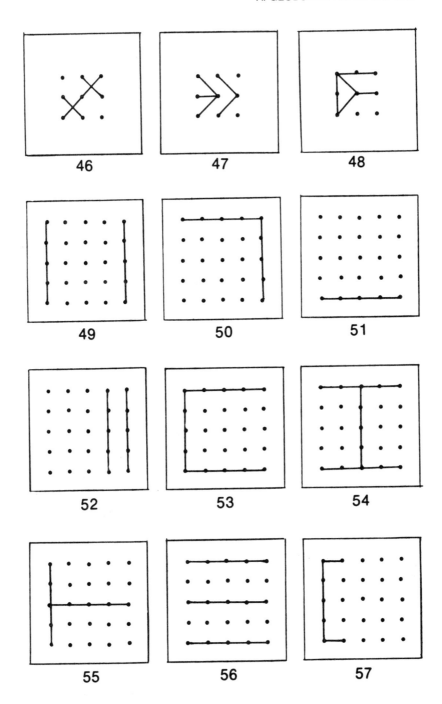

46

47

48

49

50

51

52

53

54

55

56

57

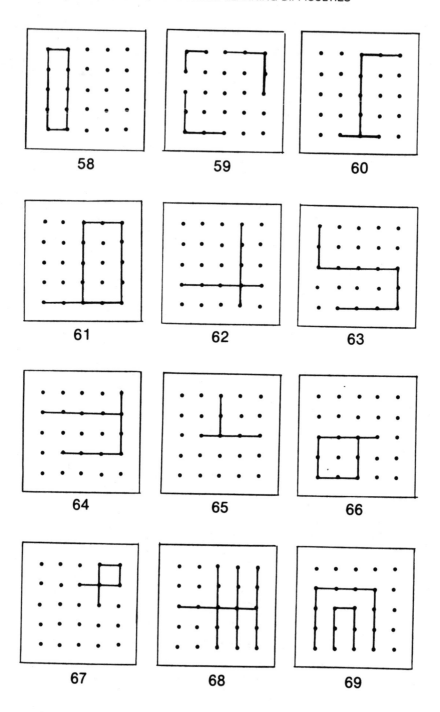

58

59

60

61

62

63

64

65

66

67

68

69

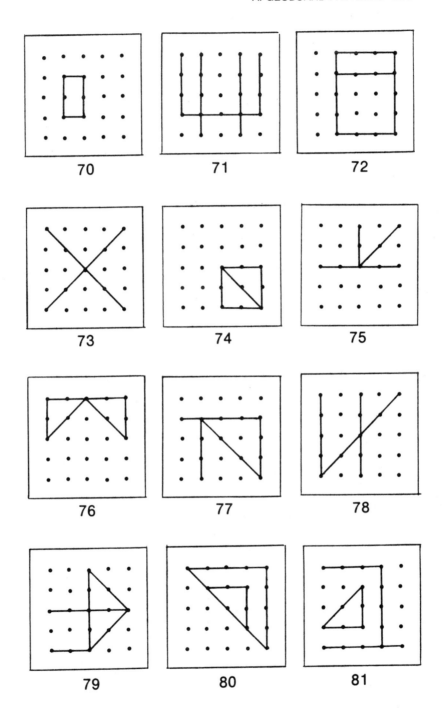

70   71   72

73   74   75

76   77   78

79   80   81

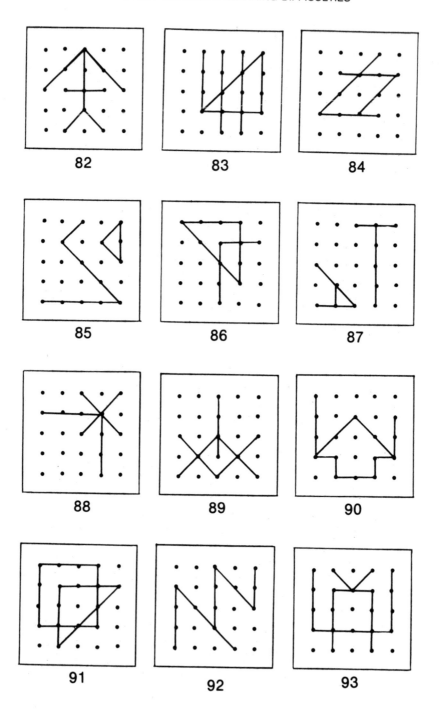

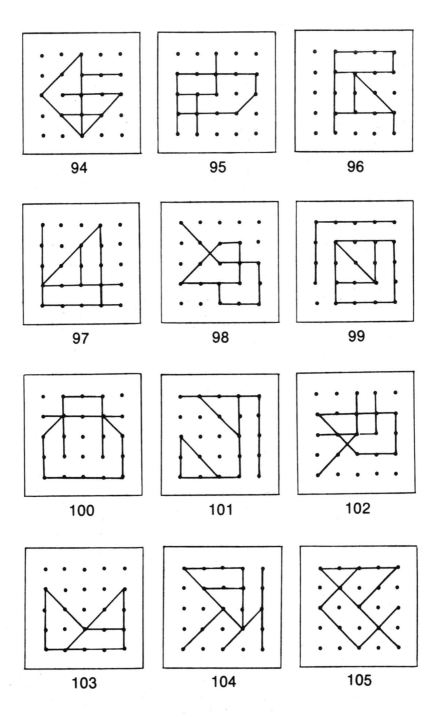

94 95 96

97 98 99

100 101 102

103 104 105

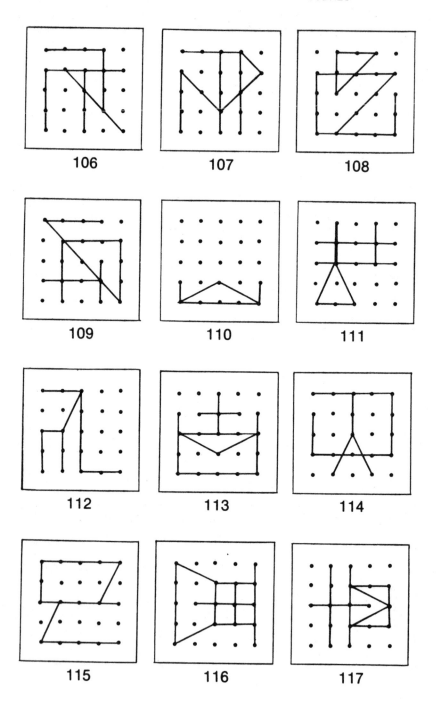

106

107

108

109

110

111

112

113

114

115

116

117

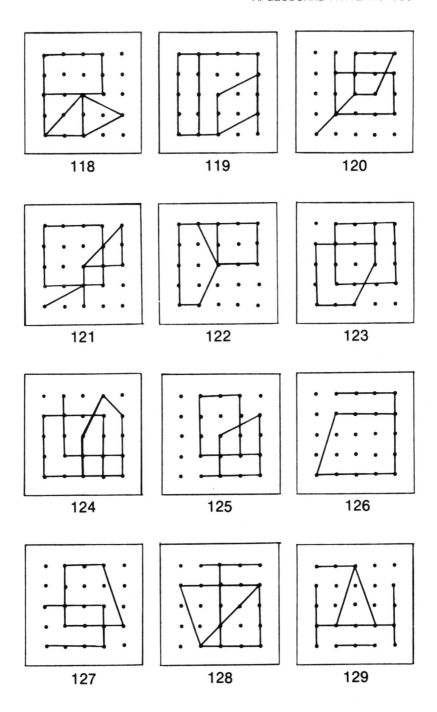

118

119

120

121

122

123

124

125

126

127

128

129

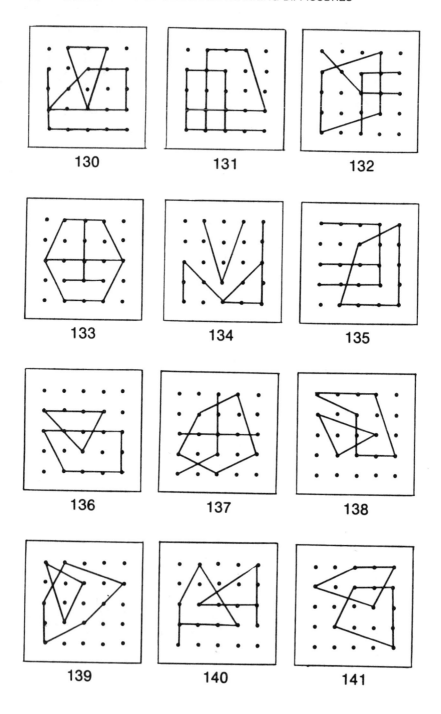

130

131

132

133

134

135

136

137

138

139

140

141

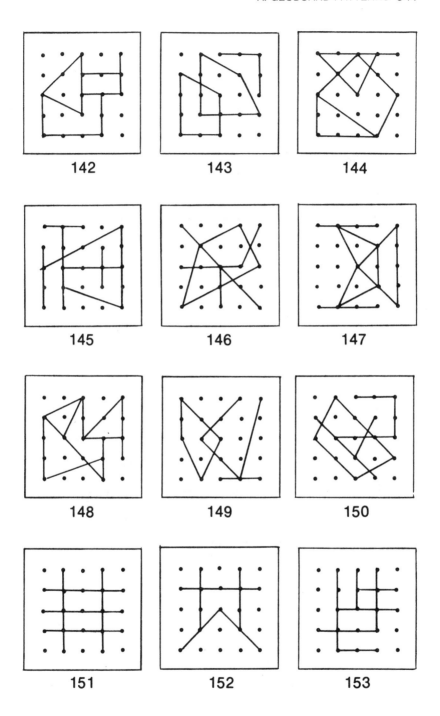

142

143

144

145

146

147

148

149

150

151

152

153

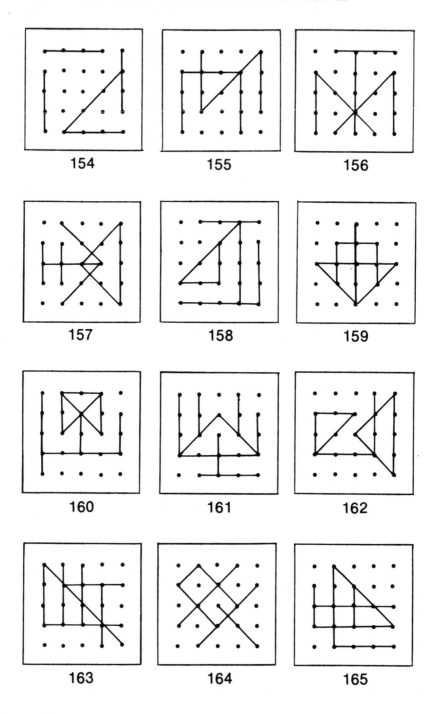

154

155

156

157

158

159

160

161

162

163

164

165

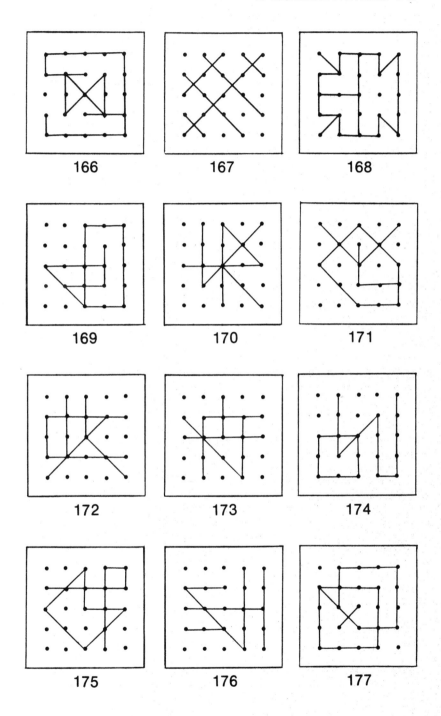

166   167   168

169   170   171

172   173   174

175   176   177

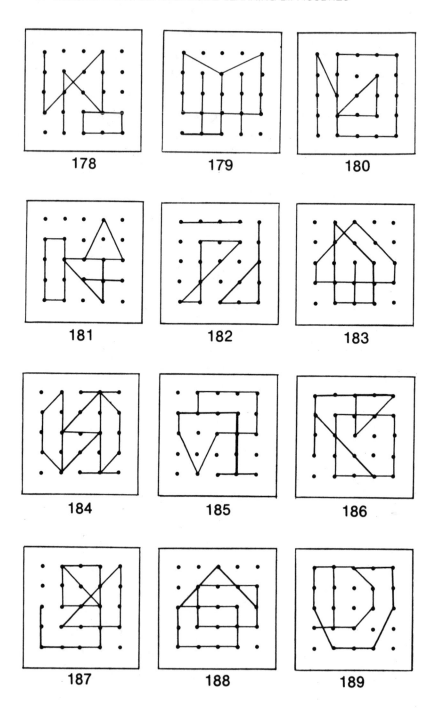

178

179

180

181

182

183

184

185

186

187

188

189

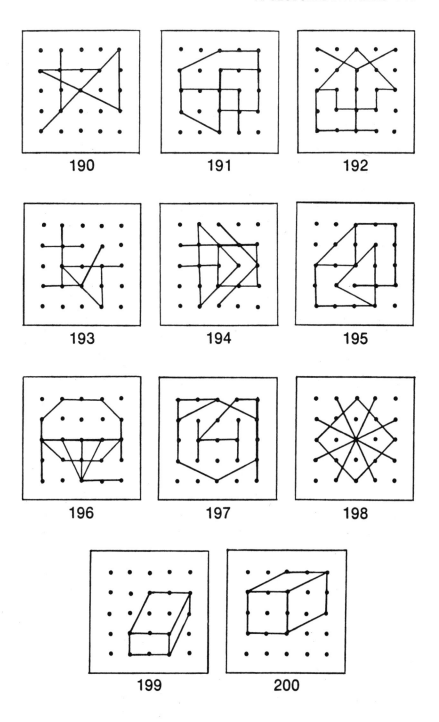

190

191

192

193

194

195

196

197

198

199

200

APPENDIX B:
PEGBOARD PATTERNS

The following are patterns for constructions that are described on pages 82–83.

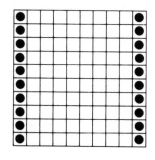

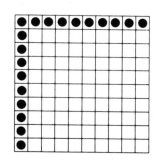

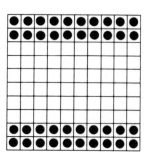

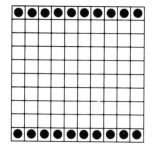

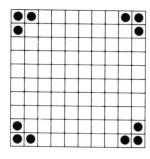

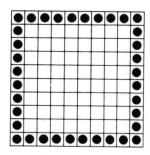

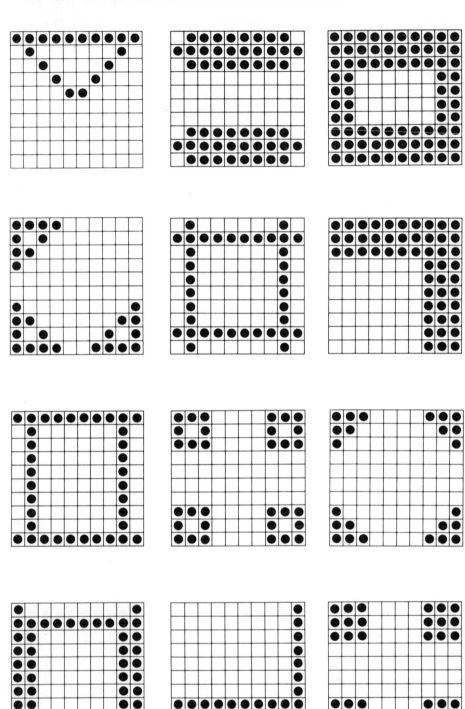

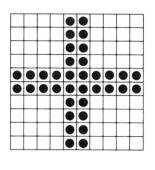
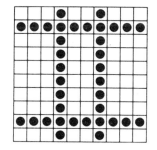
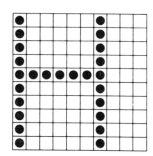

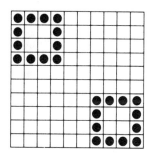
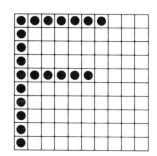
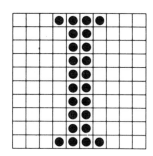

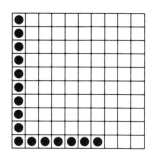
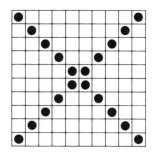
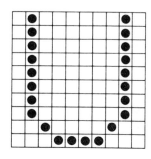

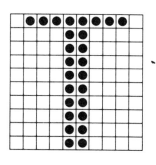
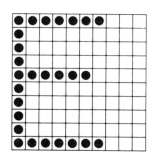

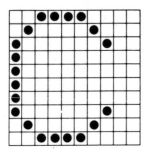
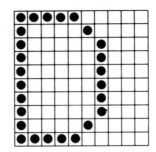
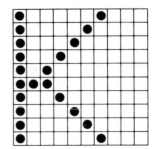

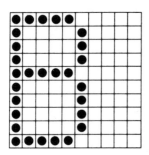
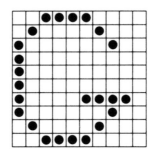
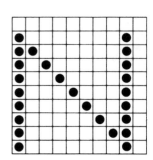

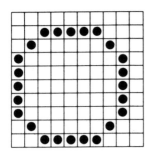
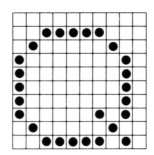
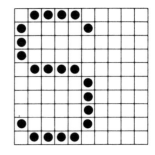

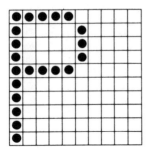
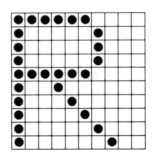
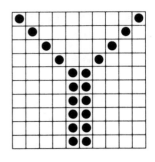

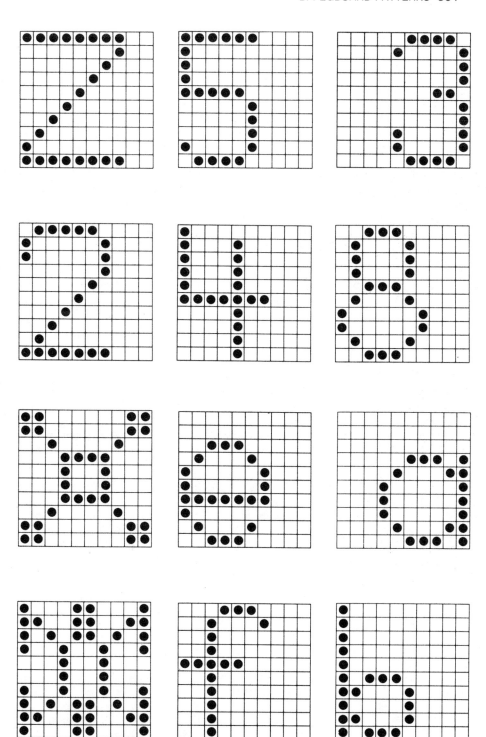

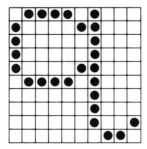
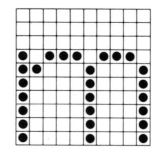
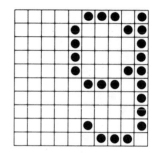

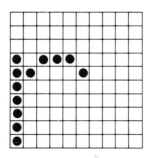
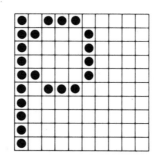
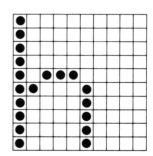

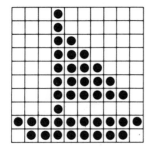
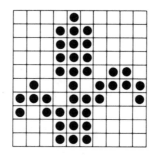
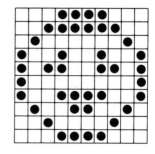

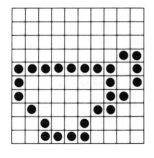
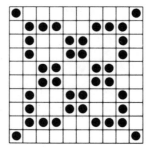
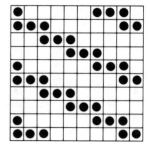

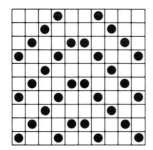 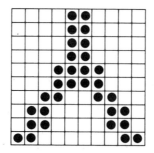

The following are parquetry patterns as described on page 83.

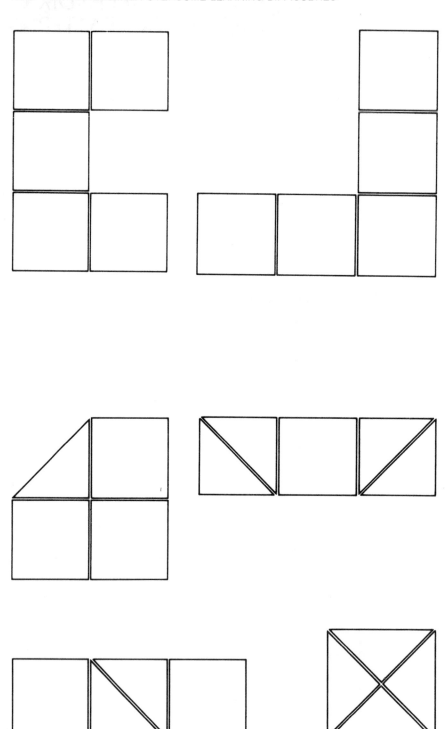

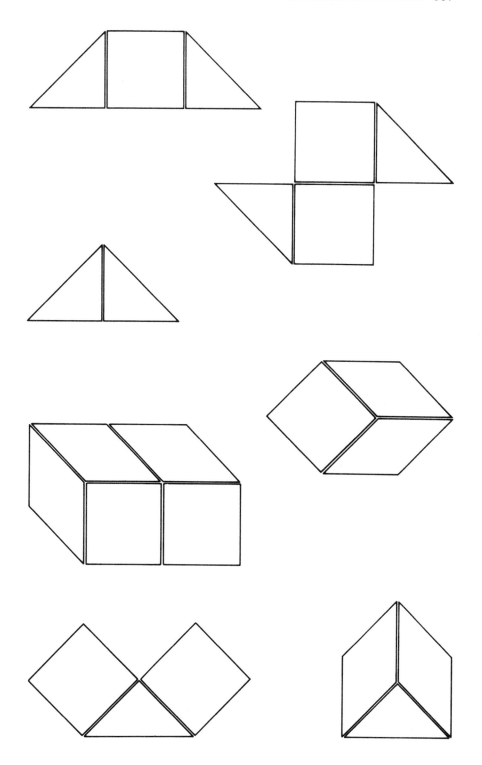

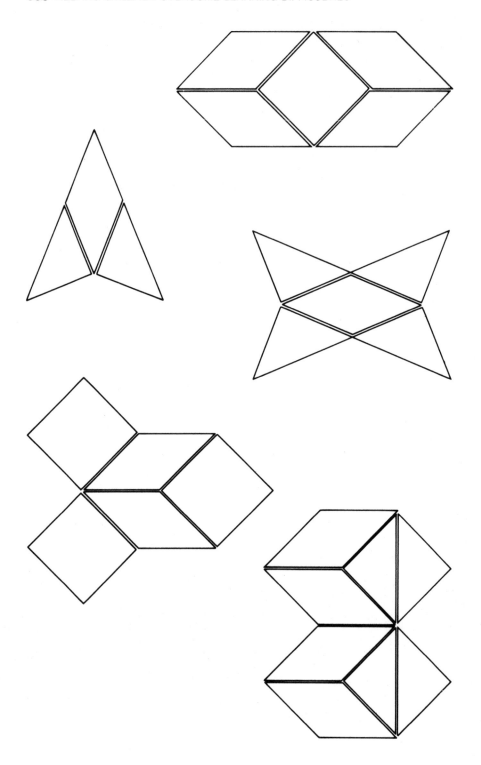

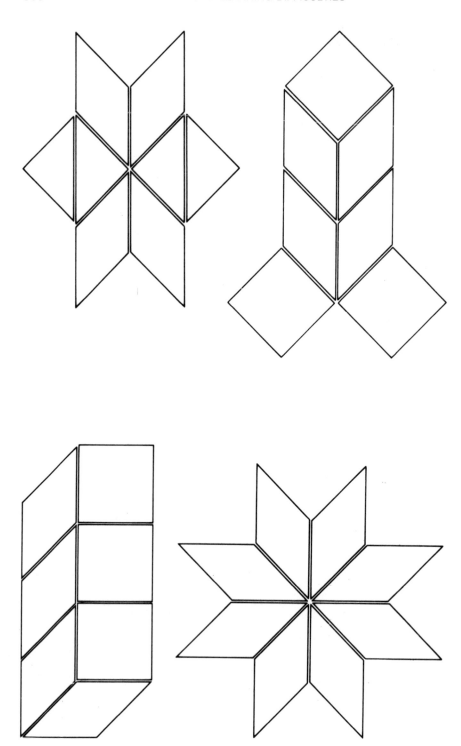

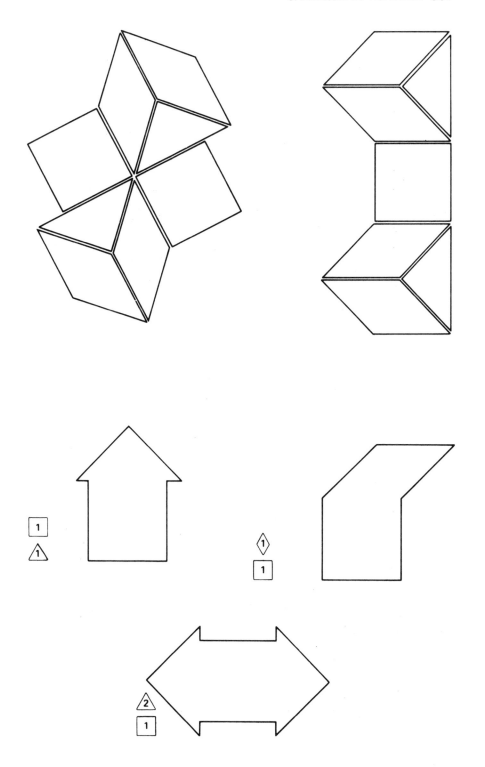

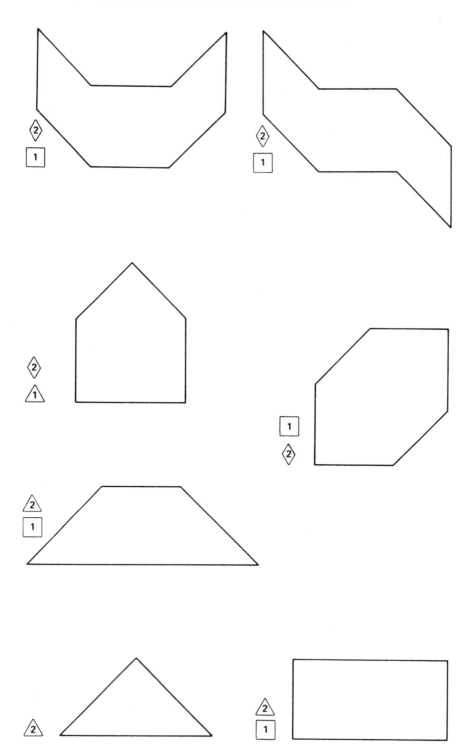

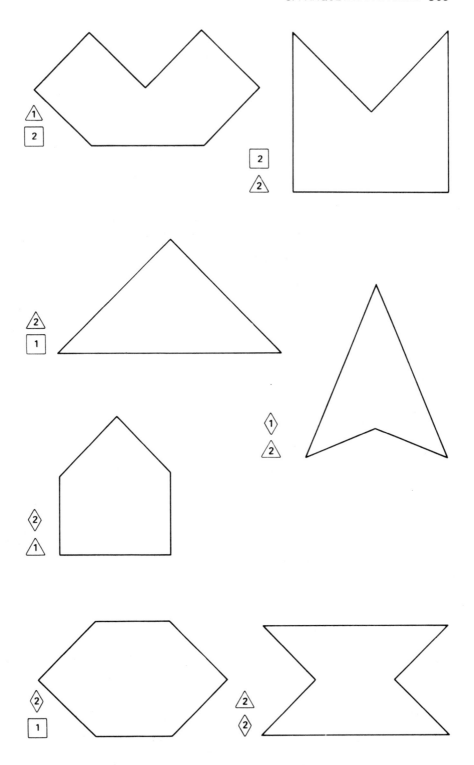

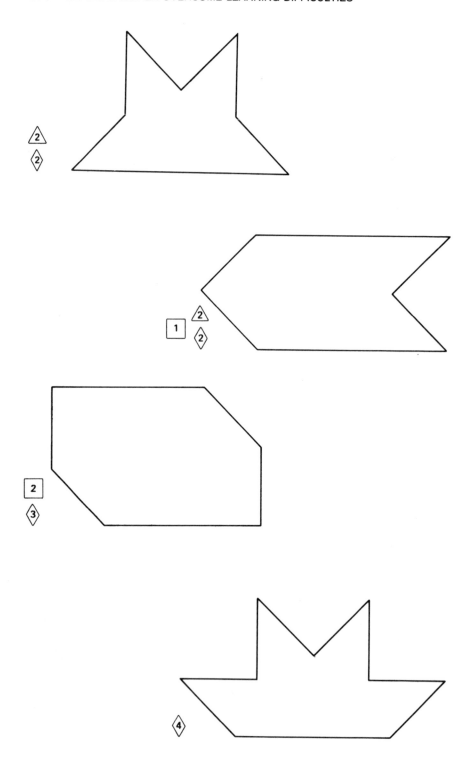

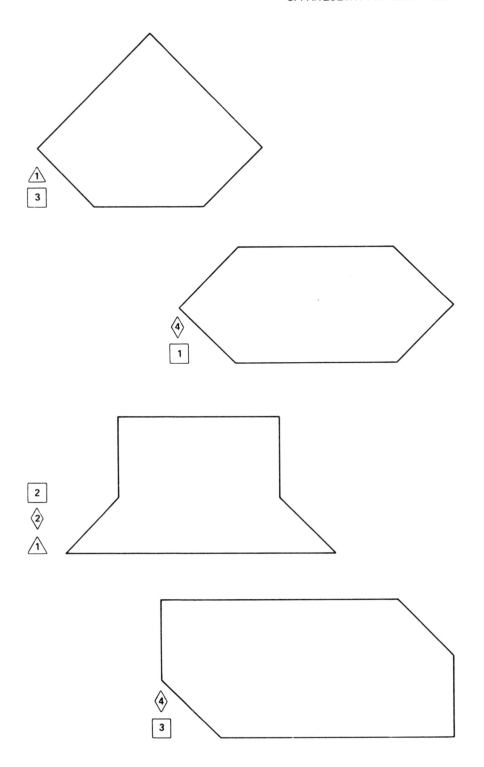

SELECTED BIBLIOGRAPHY

Baker, E. L. Beyond objectives: domain referenced tests for evaluation and instructional improvement. *Educational Technology,* 1974, **14**:6, 10–16.

Bateman, B. D. Educational implications of minimal brain dysfunction. In F. de la Cruz, B. Fox, & R. Roberts (Eds.), *Minimal Brain Dysfunction.* New York: Annals of the New York Academy of Sciences, 1973.

————. The efficacy of an auditory and a visual method of first grade reading instruction with auditory and visual learners. *College of Education Curriculum Bulletin,* 1967, **23**, 278, Eugene, Ore.: University of Oregon. 6–14. (a).

Beck, I. L., & Mitroff, D. D. *Rationale and Design of a Primary Grades Reading System For an Individualized Classroom.* Pittsburgh: Learning Research and Development Center, 1972. (LRDC Publication 1972/4)

Bender, L. A. *A Visual Motor Gestalt Test and Its Clinical Use.* New York: American Orthopsychiatric Association, 1938. (Research Monograph No. 3)

Bereiter, C., & Engelmann, S. *Teaching Disadvantaged Children in the Preschool.* Englewood Cliffs, N.J.: Prentice-Hall, 1966.

Birch, H. Dyslexia and maturation of visual function. In J. Money (Ed.), *Reading Disability. Progress and Research Needs in Dyslexia.* Baltimore: Johns Hopkins Press, 1962.

Bond, Guy L., Tinker, Miles A. *Reading Difficulties: Their Diagnosis and Correction.* Second Edition. New York: Appleton-Century-Crofts, Inc., 1967.

Bruce, D. J. The analysis of word sounds by young children. *British Journal of Educational Psychology,* 1964, **34**, 158–170.

Bruner, J. S. *Studies in Cognitive Growth.* New York: Wiley, 1967.

Chalfont, J.C., & Scheffelin, M. A. *Central Processing Dysfunctions in Children: A Review of the Research.* Washington, D. C.: U.S. Department of Health, Education, and Welfare, 1969. (NINDS Monograph No. 9)

367

Chall, Jeanne. *Learning to Read: The Great Debate.* New York: McGraw-Hill Book Company, Inc., 1967.

Clements, S. D. *Minimal Brain Dysfunction, Terminology and Identification.* Washington, D.C.: U.S. Department of Health, Education, and Welfare, 1966. (NINDB Monograph No. 3, Public Health Service Bulletin No. 1415)

————. *Minimal Brain Dysfunction in Children.* Washington, D.C.: U.S. Department of Health, Education, and Welfare, 1969. (N&SDCP Monograph, Public Health Service Bulletin No. 2015).

Coleman, B. "The Relationship Between Auditory and Visual Perceptual Skills and First Grade Reading Achievement Under An Initial Structural Linguistics Reading Approach." Unpublished doctoral dissertation, University of Pittsburgh, 1974.

Deutsch, M. The role of social class in language development and cognition. *American Journal of Orthopsychiatry,* 1965, **25**, 78–88.

Espenschade, A. S., & Eckert, H. M. *Motor Development.* Columbus, Ohio: Charles E. Merrill, Inc., 1967.

Fernald, Grace. *Remedial Techniques in the Basic School Subjects.* New York: The McGraw-Hill Book Co., 1956.

Frierson, E. C., & Barbe, B. B. *Educating Children With Learning Disabilities: Selected Readings.* New York: Appleton-Century-Crofts, 1967.

Frostig, M. *Frostig Program for the Development of Visual Perception.* Chicago: Follett Publishing Co., 1964.

Gagne, R. M. *The Conditions of Learning.* (Rev. ed.) New York: Holt, 1970.

————. Contributions of learning to human development. *Psychological Review,* 1968, **75**, 177–191.

———— & Rohwer, W. D. Instructional psychology. In P.H. Mussen & M. R. Rosenzweig (Eds.), *Annual Review of Psychology.* Vol. 20. Palo Alto, Ca: Annual Review, 1969, 381–418.

Gattegno, Caleb. *Words in Color.* Chicago: Encyclopedia Britannica Inc., 1964.

Gesell, A. *Infant Development.* New York: Harper & Brothers, 1952.

————, Ilg, F., & Bullis, G. *Vision: Its Development in Infant and Child.* New York: Paul B. Hoeber, Inc., 1949.

————, et al. *The First Five Years of Life: A Guide to the Study of the Preschool Child.* New York: Harper & Row, 1940.

Glaser, R. "Adaptive Education." Paper presented at the Conference on University Teaching and Learning, McGill University, Montreal, Canada, October 20–23, 1971.

————. Educational psychology and education. *American Psychologist,* 1973, **28**:7.

————. Individuals and learning: the new aptitudes. *Educational Researcher,* 1972. (Also, LRDC Publication 1972/13)

————, & Nitko, A. J. Measurement in learning and instruction. In R. L. Thorndike (Ed.), *Educational Measurement.* Washington, D.C.: American Council on Education, 1971, 601–622.

Haring, N.G., & Batemen, B. *Teaching the Learning Disabled Child.* Englewood Cliffs, N.J.: Prentice-Hall, 1977.

Held, R., & Hein, A. Movement-produced stimulation in the development of visually-guided behavior. *Journal of Comparative and Psychological Psychology,* 1963, **56,** 872–876.

Hively, W. Domain-referenced testing. *Educational Technology,* 1974, **14:**6, 5–10.

Howard, I. P., & Templeton, W. B. *Human Spatial Orientation.* New York: Wiley, 1966.

Ilg, F., & Ames, L. *School Readiness.* New York: Harper & Row, 1964.

Kaluger, G., & Kolson, C. *Reading and Learning Disabilities.* Columbus, Ohio: Charles E. Merrill, Inc., 1969.

Kephart, N. C. *The Slow Learner in the Classroom.* Columbus, Ohio: Charles E. Merrill, Inc., 1960.

Klein, S. D. *Psychological Testing of Children: A Consumer's Report.* Boston: The Exceptional Parent Press, 1977.

Laurendeau, M., & Pinard, A. *The Development of the Concept of Space in the Child.* New York: International University, 1970.

Lenneberg, E. H. *Biological Foundations of Language.* New York: Wiley, 1967.

Luria, A. R. *Higher Cortical Functions in Man.* New York: Basic Books, Inc., 1966.

Maccoby, E. E. Some speculations concerning the lag between perceiving and performing. *Child Development,* 1965, **36,** 367–378.

McCarthy, J. J., & McCarthy, J. F. *Learning Disabilities.* Boston: Allyn and Bacon, 1969.

McInnis, Philip. *McInnis/Hammondsport Plan.* New York: Walker Educational Book Corporation, 1977.

Miller, R. E. "The Effects of a Physical Education Program on Perceptual Development and Reading Readiness in Kindergarten Children." Unpublished doctoral dissertation, University of Pittsburgh, 1973.

Pace Perceptual Program. McKeesport, Pa.: Pace School, 1968. (Mimeographed report)

Phelps, Diana. A modified association method for use with learning disabled children. *Academic Therapy,* 1978, **14**(i), 35–48.

Piaget, J. *Psychology of Intelligence.* Paterson, N.J.: Littlefield, Adams & Co., 1960.

Resnick, L. B. *Design of an Early Learning Curriculum.* Pittsburgh: Learning Research and Development Center, 1967. (Working Paper 16)

————. Open education: some tasks for technology. *Educational Technology,*

1972, **12**(1), 70–76.

Rosner, J. Adapting primary grade reading instruction to individual differences in perceptual skills. *Reading World,* 1975, **14**(4), 293–307.

————. "Application of the IPI Model to a Perceptual Development Curriculum." In J. I. Arena (Ed.), *Meeting Total Needs of Learning-disabled Children: A Forward Look.* Proceedings of the Seventh Annual International Conference of the Association for Children with Learning Disabilities. San Rafael, California: Academic Therapy Publications, 1971, 95–107. (Also, LRDC Publication 1971/12)

————. Auditory analysis training with prereaders. *The Reading Teacher,* 1974, **27**(4), 379–384. (Also, LRDC Publication 1974/1).

————. Changes in first grade achievement and predictive validity of I.Q. scores, as a function of an adaptive instructional environment. *Educational Technology,* 1974, **14**(1), 32–36. (LRDC publication 1973/5). Originally presented at the annual meeting of the American Educational Research Assn., New Orleans, 1973.

————. "The Development and Validation of an Individualized Perceptual Skills Curriculum." Pittsburgh: Learning Research and Development Center, University of Pittsburgh, 1972. (Publication 1972/7)

————. Individualization of Instruction. In F. D. Connor, J. R. Wald, and M. J. Cohen (Eds.), *Professional Preparation for Educators of Crippled Children.* New York: Teachers College, Columbia University, 1970.

————. "Language Arts and Arithmetic Achievement, and Specifically Related Perceptual Skills." Paper presented at the annual meeting of the International Reading Association, Detroit, Mich., 1972. (Also, *American Educational Research Journal,* 1973, **10**(1), 59–68, and LRDC Publication 1973/2).

————. *The Perceptual Skills Curriculum.* New York: Walker Educational Book Corporation, 1973.

————. Testing for teaching in an adaptive educational environment. In W. Hively & M. C. Reynolds (Eds.), *Domain-Referenced Testing in Special Education.* Reston, Va.: Council for Exceptional Children, 1975.

————. Visual analysis training with preschool children, *American Optometric Assn. Journal,* 1974, **45**(5), 584–591.

————. Richman, V., & Scott, R. H. "The Identification of Children With Perceptual-Motor Dysfunction." Pittsburgh: Learning Research and Development Center, University of Pittsburgh, 1969. (Working Paper 47).

————, & Simon, D. The Auditory Analysis Test: an initial report." *Journal of Learning Disabilities,* 1971, **4**(7), 384–392. (Also, LRDC Publication 1971/3).

Simon, H. *The Sciences of the Artificial.* Cambridge: The MIT Press, 1969.

Slingerland, B. *Screening Test for Identifying Children With Specific Language Disabilities.* Cambridge, Mass.: Educators Publishing Service, 1962.

Starr, A. *The Rutgers Drawing Test.* New Brunswick, N.J.: Author, 1961.

Traub, Nina. *Recipe for Reading.* Second Edition. Cambridge, Mass.: Educators Publishing Service, Inc., 1975.

Wechsler, D. *The Wechsler Preschool and Primary Scale of Intelligence.* New York: The Psychological Corporation, 1967.

Weigers, R. M. "An Investigation of an Individualized Visual-Motor Curriculum on a Piagetian Test of Space Perception and the Visual-Motor Placement Test." Unpublished doctoral dissertation, University of Pittsburgh, 1973.

White, B. L. Experience and the development of motor mechanisms in infancy. In K. J. Connolly (Ed.), *Mechanisms of Motor Skill Development.* New York: Academic Press, 1970, 95–136.

Witkin, H. A., Dyk, R. B., Faterson, H. F., Goodenough, D. R., & Karp, S. A. *Psychological Differentiation.* New York: Wiley, 1962.

Zinchenko, V. P. Vicarious perceptual actions: a study of the motor components of recognition, immediate memory and thinking. In K. J. Connolly (Ed.), *Mechanisms of Motor Skill Development.* New York: Academic Press, 1970, 225–242.

INDEX